£30.00

D0303080

Sir Gawain and the Green Knight
and French Arthurian Romance

Sir Gawain and the Green Knight and French Arthurian Romance

AD PUTTER

CLARENDON PRESS · OXFORD
1995

Oxford University Press, Walton Street, Oxford OX2 6DP
Oxford New York
Athens Auckland Bangkok Bombay
Calcutta Cape Town Dar es Salaam Delhi
Florence Hong Kong Istanbul Karachi
Kuala Lumpur Madras Madrid Melbourne
Mexico City Nairobi Paris Singapore
Taipei Tokyo Toronto
and associated companies in
Berlin Ibadan

Oxford is a trade mark of Oxford University Press

Published in the United States
by Oxford University Press Inc., New York

© Ad Putter 1995

British Library Cataloguing in Publication Data
Data available

Library of Congress Cataloging in Publication Data
Putter Ad.
Sir Gawain and the Green Knight and French Arthurian romance / Ad Putter.
Includes bibliographical references (p).
1. Gawain and the Grene Knight. 2. Gawain (Legendary character)–
Romances—History and criticism. 3. Literature, Comparative–
English (Middle) and French (Old) 4. Literature, Comparative–
French (Old) and English (Middle) 5. French poetry—To 1500–
History and criticism. 6. Arthurian romances—History and criticism.
7. Romances, English—History and criticism.
8. Knights and knighthood in literature. 9. Chivalry in literature.
I. Title
PR2065.G31P88 1995 821'.1—dc20 94-30190

ISBN 0–19–818253–8

1 3 5 7 9 10 8 6 4 2

Typeset by Pure Tech Corporation, Pondicherry, India
Printed in Great Britain
on acid-free paper by
Bookcraft Ltd.
Midsomer Norton, Bath

TO MY PARENTS
Bets Dekker *and* Jan Putter

Acknowledgements

❧

THE TEXT of this book and its ideas owe much to the careful reading and competence of others. Richard Beadle, Tony Hasler, Peter Hurst, Erik Kooper, Helen Pandeli, James Simpson, Tony Spearing, Neil Wright, and Nicky Zeeman read parts of the book and I should like to thank them for their suggestions. I am also indebted to John Burrow and Christopher Page, who examined the Ph.D. dissertation on which this book is based, and whose comments have been of great value to me in revising the dissertation for publication. My thanks also go to the readers and editors of Oxford University Press, in particular to Andrea Hopkins, Andrew Lockett, and Dorothy McCarthy.

I wrote this book first as a research student and then as a Research Fellow at Cambridge, and I do not think I could have had a better working environment. I thank the Fellows of Jesus College for their kindness and generosity; my friends and family for listening and changing the subject; Clare Hall, the British Council, and the Jebb Fund for financial support; and the staff of the Cambridge University Library and the English Faculty Library for looking after me and their books so well.

I want finally to thank Jill Mann, who has given me the enormous benefit of her dedication, her learning, and her insight, ever since she agreed to supervise my postgraduate work. I am deeply grateful for her academic advice and personal support.

A.P.

Contents

List of Abbreviations

ઙ

AL	*Arthurian Literature*
BBSIA	*Bibliographical Bulletin of the International Arthurian Association*
CCM	*Cahiers de civilisation médiévale*
CCSL	Corpus Christianorum (Series Latina)
CFMA	Classiques français du moyen-âge
ChauR	*Chaucer Review*
Du Cange	Du Cange, *Glossarium mediae et infimae latinitatis*
EETS OS	Early English Text Society (original series)
EETS ES	Early English Text Society (extra series)
FMLS	*Forum for Modern Language Studies*
LCL	Loeb Classical Library
MAE	*Medium Aevum*
M&H	*Medievalia et Humanistica*
MED	*Middle English Dictionary*
MLQ	*Modern Language Quarterly*
MLR	*Modern Language Review*
MP	*Modern Philology*
MS	*Mediaeval Studies*
NLH	*New Literary History*
N&Q	*Notes and Queries*
NM	*Neuphilologische Mitteilungen*
PELL	*Papers in English Language and Linguistics*
PL	Patrologia Latina
PMLA	*Publications of the Modern Language Association of America*
RS	Rolls Series
SATF	Société des anciens textes français
SN	*Studia Neophilologica*
T-L	Tobler and Lommatzsch, *Altfranzösisches Wörterbuch*
TLF	Textes littéraires français

Note on References

꙰

REFERENCES TO *Sir Gawain and the Green Knight* are to the edition by J. R. R. Tolkien and E. V. Gordon, revised by Norman Davis (Oxford, 1967). I draw on a wide variety of primary and secondary texts, bibliographical details of which may be found in the footnotes and in the bibliography. The core of my comparative material consists of Arthurian literature in Latin and Old French. References to this corpus of Arthurian chronicles and romances are to the standard editions specified in the bibliography. Unless otherwise indicated, translations are my own. I have checked my translations of Chrétien de Troyes against D. D. R. Owen's complete translation of Chrétien's romances in *Chrétien de Troyes: Arthurian Romances* (London, 1978). Quotations from Chaucer and Langland are from *The Riverside Chaucer*, 3rd edition, ed. Larry D. Benson *et al.* (Boston, Mass., 1986), and from William Langland, *The Vision of Piers Plowman: A Complete Edition of the B-Text*, ed. A. V. C. Schmidt (London, 1978). For abbreviated references see the List of Abbreviations.

Introduction
Sir Gawain *and French Arthurian Romance*

ॐ

THE GREAT Ricardian poets bequeathed to modern criticism a
suspicion about the literary and moral seriousness of Arthurian
romance. We cannot be sure whether Chaucer knew the romances
of Chrétien de Troyes,[1] but the English adaptations of French
Arthurian romances which he certainly did read—*Sir Perceval of
Galles*, Thomas of Chestre's *Sir Launfal* and *Lybeaus Desconus*—
became the object of incisive parody in his *Tale of Sir Thopas*.
Chaucer may have known a version of the *Wedding of Sir Gawain
and Dame Ragnell*, a close analogue to his *Wife of Bath's Tale*, but
in his telling the Arthurian world is reduced to a self-consciously
fictitious setting: a time when fairy queens and their jolly company
might still be seen dancing in the meadows, and when an imaginary
England was 'fulfild of fayerye' (859). In this never-never land the
story unfolds, pointing the moral that true nobility lies not in
ancestry but in virtue. Chaucer may well have expected his audience
to take this moral to heart, but doing so depends precisely on not
taking the Arthurian setting seriously. Gower's *Tale of Sir Florent* in
the *Confessio Amantis*, an analogue to (or source of) Chaucer's
Wife of Bath's Tale, leaves no doubt about the weight of the moral,
which is why Gower cleansed all Arthurian traces from his story.
Some brief allusions apart, Gower ignored Arthur and his matter.[2]
For Langland, too, the Arthurian legend no longer had anything to

---

[1] A convincing case for Chaucer's familiarity with Chrétien has been made by
Derek S. Brewer, 'Chaucer and Chrétien and Arthurian Romance', in *Middle English
Studies in Honor of Rossell Hope Robbins*, ed. B. Rowland (London, 1974), 255–9.
It has since received support from Mary Hamel, '*The Franklin's Tale* and Chrétien de
Troyes', *ChauR* 17 (1983), 316–31. See also P. J. Frankis, 'Chaucer's "Vavasour"
and Chrétien de Troyes', *N&Q* 15 (1968), 46–7, and J. Pearcy, 'Chaucer's Franklin
and the Literary Vavasour', *ChauR* 8 (1973), 33–59.

[2] See Christopher Dean, 'Arthurian References in Non-Arthurian Literature', in his
*Arthur of England: English Attitudes to King Arthur and the Knights of the Round
Table in the Middle Ages and the Renaissance* (Toronto, 1987).

contribute to his searching analysis of contemporary life. By the late fourteenth century Arthurian literature must have appeared to him, as to Chaucer and Gower, outdated and old-fashioned.

It was not always so. In the twelfth century Arthurian romance was the most innovative artistic form, pioneered by Chrétien de Troyes, who could boast the patronage of the most powerful princes of his time: the Counts of Flanders and Champagne, and possibly King Henry II of England.[3] Two hundred years later, French Arthurian romances were still being read in bulk in England. A few English translations or adaptations of Chrétien's romances exist,[4] but these pale into insignificance in comparison with the large number of French Arthurian romances in verse and prose listed in the wills and inventories of the English royalty and nobility, or of clerics and wealthy merchants of the *Gawain*-poet's day.[5] Outside the world of literature, Chrétien's continuing popularity is apparent in his influence on English court-spectacles and misericords in parish churches.[6]

French Arthurian romance was quite simply the most popular form of literary entertainment for the higher strata of society.[7] But,

[3] Rita Lejeune, 'Rôle littéraire d'Aliénor d'Aquitaine et de sa famille', *Cultura Neolatina*, 14 (1954), 5–57. On the subject of Chrétien's links with England see also David J. Shirt, 'Chrétien de Troyes et une coutume anglaise', *Romania*, 94 (1973), 178–95, and Constance Bullock-Davies, 'Chrétien de Troyes and England', *AL* 1 (1981), 1–61.

[4] See Paul Steinbach, *Der Einfluss des Chrestien de Troyes auf die Altenglische Literatur*, published doctoral dissertation (Leipzig, 1886); *Ywain and Gawain*, ed. Albert B. Friedman and Norman T. Harrington, EETS OS 254 (London, 1964); David Fowler, 'Le Conte du Graal and Sir Perceval of Galles', *Comparative Literature Studies*, 13 (1975), 5–20; and Keith Busby, 'Sir Perceval of Galles, Le Conte du Graal, and La Continuation-Gauvain: The Methods of an English Adapter', *Études Anglaises*, 2 (1978), 198–202. Chrétien's work also seems to have been used by Thomas of Chestre and Malory: see M. Mills, 'The Huntsman and the Dwarf in *Erec* and *Libeaus Desconus*', *Romania*, 87 (1966), 33–58; and P. J. C. Field, 'Malory and Chrétien de Troyes', *Reading Medieval Studies*, 17 (1991), 19–30.

[5] For Arthurian literature in wills and inventories, see my 'Narrative Technique and Chivalric Ethos in Sir Gawain and the Green Knight and the Old French Roman Courtois', doctoral dissertation (University of Cambridge, 1992), 6–15.

[6] See Roger Sherman Loomis, 'Edward I, Arthurian Enthusiast', *Speculum*, 33 (1958), 242–55, and his 'Arthurian Influence on Sport and Spectacle', in *Arthurian Literature in the Middle Ages*, ed. Roger Sherman Loomis (Oxford, 1959), 553–9. On misericords inspired by Chrétien's *Yvain*, see Muriel Whitaker, *The Legends of King Arthur in Art* (Cambridge 1990), 97–8.

[7] John Scattergood, 'Literary Culture at the Court of Richard II', in *English Court Culture in the Later Middle Ages*, ed. V. J. Scattergood and J. W. Sherborne (London, 1983), 29–43, and Paul Strohm, 'The Social and Literary Scene in England', in *The Cambridge Chaucer Companion*, ed. Piero Boitani and Jill Mann (Cambridge, 1986), 1–18.

its amusement value apart, it seems marginal to the concerns of Chaucer, Langland, or Gower. As John Burrow and Anne Middleton have shown, their works are characterized by a lack of interest in fighting or in extraordinary feats of heroism. They focus instead on interpersonal relations and the ethical obligations and inner conflicts they impose on us. I leave this 'us' vague, because their 'public poetry' speaks not only for the interests of an élite audience, but for a much broader social spectrum: for clerics, noblemen, and merchants alike.[8]

If it was not for *Sir Gawain and the Green Knight*, Arthurian romance might indeed have seemed an unlikely vehicle for the concerns of the public poetry of the Ricardian era. Yet the *Gawain*-poet's sophistication and the subtlety of his moral vision are of a piece with those of his famous contemporaries. His romance consistently subordinates action to reflection, armed combat to psychological drama. It humanizes the hero, implicating him in an intricate plot that tests and strains his commitments to promises and to contracts he has entered into. What the plot requires of the hero is not prowess but honesty in social transactions. The *Gawain*-poet's romance is imbued with a conscientiousness concerning intersubjective relations, and with ethical assumptions that would have been relevant beyond the social circle of a small baronial household.

The social dimensions of *Sir Gawain* are manifest at other levels than that of the plot. They are inscribed in the idiosyncrasies of the *Gawain*-poet's style, marked, as Marie Borroff noted, by a tendency 'to see actions, whether major or minor, as reciprocal' and 'to see a given object or agent in relation to other objects or agents'.[9] They also account for his interest in courtliness and in etiquette, his elevation of this descriptive style as a technique for human interaction.

The *Gawain*-poet's interest in courtliness, his social awareness, his ethic of conscientious worldliness, and his broadening of the heroic experience, are clearly consonant with the outlook of his famous contemporaries. Moreover, like theirs, the *Gawain*-poet's breakthrough in the English vernacular was achieved through a profound engagement with inherited forms and styles. The problem for

---

[8] John A. Burrow, *Ricardian Poetry* (London, 1971), and Anne Middleton, 'The Idea of Public Poetry in the Reign of Richard II', *Speculum*, 53 (1978), 94–114.

[9] *Sir Gawain and the Green Knight: A Stylistic and Metrical Study* (New Haven, Conn., 1962), 121–3.

Gawain-criticism has been that, in the case of *Sir Gawain and the Green Knight*, these were the forms and styles of French Arthurian romance, which flourished two centuries earlier with the works of Chrétien de Troyes. And if this tradition seemed old-fashioned to Chaucer, Gower, or Langland, modern critics have found it equally difficult to reconcile the *Gawain*-poet's topicality with his reliance on courtly Arthurian romances. The readiness with which such labels as 'anti-romance' or 'meta-romance' are applied to *Gawain* is symptomatic of criticism that is caught between an awareness of the literary and moral self-consciousness of this romance, and the belief that it cannot accommodate these qualities without ceasing to be a romance proper.[10] Comparisons of *Gawain* with the French Arthurian romances that his contemporaries would have read serve in many critical accounts only as a basis for contrast with the *Gawain*-poet, against which his achievements supposedly stand in sharp relief. But might it not be possible that the courtly romances of Chrétien de Troyes and the writers who followed in his footsteps represented for the *Gawain*-poet not an obstacle he needed to overcome but a genre whose imaginative possibilities and whose ethos were compatible with the *Gawain*-poet's own assumptions and ambitions?

Existing source-studies are of limited use in settling this question. Many individual parallels and sources in Arthurian romance have been found,[11] but source-studies have tended to focus on similarities

[10] S. Bercovitch, 'Romance and Anti-Romance in *Sir Gawain and the Green Knight*', *Philological Quarterly*, 44 (1965), 30–7; S. S. Hussey, '*Sir Gawain and the Green Knight* and Romance Writing', *SN* 40 (1968), 161–74; and John Finlayson, 'The Expectations of Romance in *Sir Gawain and the Green Knight*', *Genre*, 12 (1979), 1–24.

[11] On *Gawain*'s links with the Vulgate Cycle, see Marjory Rigby, '*Sir Gawain and the Green Knight* and the Vulgate *Lancelot*', *MLR* 78 (1983), 257–66; Robert L. Kelly, 'Allusions to the Vulgate Cycle in *Sir Gawain and the Green Knight*', in *Literary and Historical Perspectives of the Middle Ages*, ed. D. W. Cummins *et al.* (Morgantown, W.Va., 1982), 183–99; and G. J. Smithers, 'What *Sir Gawain and the Green Knight* is About', *MAE* 32 (1963), 171–89. On *Gawain*'s links with the *Perlesvaus*, see W. A. Nitze, 'Is the Green Knight Story Really a Vegetation Myth?', *MP* 33 (1936), 351–66. For discussions of the sources in the *Chevalier à l'épée*, the *Mule sans frein*, and Chrétien de Troyes, see D. D. R. Owen, 'Parallel Readings with *Sir Gawain and the Green Knight*', in *Two Old French Gauvain Romances*, ed. D. D. R. Owen and R. C. Johnston (Edinburgh, 1972). More general studies are George L. Kittredge, *A Study of Sir Gawain and the Green Knight* (Cambridge, Mass., 1916); Larry D. Benson, *Art and Tradition in Sir Gawain and the Green Knight* (New York, 1965); and W. R. J. Barron, 'Chrétien de Troyes and the *Gawain*-Poet: Master and Pupil or Twin Temperaments?', in *The Legacy of Chrétien de Troyes*, ed. Norris J. Lacy, Douglas Kelly, and Keith Busby, 2 vols. (Amsterdam, 1988), ii. 255–84.

of plot, and most notably on analogues for the beheading game and the temptation scenes.[12] However, similarities of plot may establish no more than a remote relationship, in particular in the case of *Sir Gawain and the Green Knight*, whose story-line makes up so little of the romance. The *Gawain*-poet gives us descriptions, psychological and verbal deliberations, but relatively little action. When the romance is reduced to its bare plot, we end up, at most, with the 523 lines in which the poet of the ballad version of *Gawain* (*The Green Knight*) summarized his source. If we wish to discover what the *Gawain*-poet got out of French romance, we need a study that looks for broader connections—connections, for example, between the heroic ideal in *Gawain* and in earlier Arthurian romances, between their interest in polite manners, in peaceful interpersonal relations—and which considers the stock of literary motifs and conventions out of which courtly romancers constructed their fictional worlds. Reading *Gawain* alongside French Arthurian romance with these considerations in mind, as I shall do in this book, makes the many important continuities between the two visible.

There are many other types of chivalric romance besides French Arthurian romance which fall outside the scope of this study. I shall have little to say about the tradition of Anglo-Norman 'insular' romances, and their Middle English descendants, such as *Guy of Warwick, Bevis of Hamptoun,* or *Haveloc.*[13] *Sir Gawain and the Green Knight* is first of all an *Arthurian* romance, and in the numerous moments in *Gawain* when Arthurian characters are confronted with their reputation, the poet explicitly invites comparison with earlier Arthurian romances. Secondly, *Gawain* shares neither the ideological concerns nor the literary technique of Anglo-Norman or Middle English 'insular' romance. It takes no interest in the problems of land-ownership, inheritance, the perpetuation of the patrimony, or the preservation of feudal customs, which preoccupied the writers of 'insular' romance and the provincial baronial milieux in which they moved.[14] The questions raised by *Gawain* are

[12] Analogues to the plot-motifs of *Gawain* have been compiled by Elisabeth Brewer in *Sir Gawain and the Green Knight: Sources and Analogues* (1973, repr. Woodbridge, 1992).

[13] As Susan Crane has shown, Anglo-Norman chivalric romances and their English descendants form a coherent group. I borrow the term 'insular' from her study *Insular Romance: Politics, Faith, and Culture in Anglo-Norman and Middle-English Literature* (Berkeley, Calif., 1986).

[14] Ibid. 217–18.

more profound and more basic: Should one prefer honesty to death? Do unforeseen consequences nullify a contract one has entered into? Are the elevated ideals of chivalry in fact attainable by human beings? Like the best French Arthurian romances, which expose and explore the tensions between love and duty, conscience and worldly glory, obligation and self-interest, *Gawain* problematizes the moral laws we live by. Their Arthurian world is unrealistic only to the extent that it actualizes those unthinkable situations and dilemmas which life ordinarily spares us. Moreover, compared with *Gawain*, 'insular' romances lack sophistication, and, what is equally important, they lack a *sense* of their sophistication. To find a similar fondness for artfulness, for play with readers' expectations, for psychological probing, we do better to look not to popular or 'insular' romances, but to the Old French *roman courtois*.

The claim is not new. Critics have long recognized that *Gawain* is a romance in the 'French literary tradition',[15] even if they have made little progress in clarifying this vague observation. The aim of this study is to specify the characteristics that *Gawain* shares with this tradition: in what it says, how it says it, and what it asks of its audience. The corpus of Arthurian romances with which I shall compare *Gawain* is substantial. The romances of Chrétien de Troyes provide the main focus, but among romances in verse I also draw on the *Tristan* legends, the *First Continuation* of the *Conte du Graal*, Renaut de Beaujeu's *Bel Inconnu*, the *Chevalier à l'épée* and the *Mule sans frein*, probably composed in the twelfth century; the *Second Continuation* and the continuations by Manessier and Gerbert de Montreuil, Raoul de Houdenc's *La Vengeance Raguidel*, *L'Atre périlleux*, *Fergus*, *Yder*, and *Hunbaut*, all written in the first half of the thirteenth century; and Robert de Blois's *Beaudous* and Jehan's *Merveilles de Rigomer* from the second half of the thirteenth century. As authors who directly inspired, or were inspired by, the Arthurian *roman courtois*, Geoffrey of Monmouth, Wace, and the writers of the early prose romances, the *Didot-Perceval*, the *Perlesvaus*, and the Vulgate Cycle, will be included in the corpus.

I want to avoid treating this comparative material as a dull backcloth against which the brilliance of *Gawain* may appear all the more clearly. The world of the *Gawain*-poet's Arthurian romance is in many ways governed by the same conventions as that of his

---

[15] Morton Bloomfield, '*Sir Gawain and the Green Knight*: An Appraisal', in his *Essays and Explorations* (Cambridge, Mass., 1970), 131–57, at 142.

predecessors. As the following chapters will show, this is a world structured by the opposition between wilderness and civilization, between the forest and the castle. It is one in which knights exhibit a high degree of social awareness, and observe a complex etiquette of hospitality and polite conversation that bears a close resemblance to the advice given in the courtesy books of the period. Most importantly, the heroes and heroines who are its inhabitants are themselves avid readers of romance. Frequently romance conventions become issues of discussion and contention among the fictional characters. As the poets of Arthurian romance invoke familiar motifs and plot-lines to manipulate our expectations, so their characters use the conventions of romance to hide behind or mislead each other.

This awareness of romance conventions constitutes the poetic self-consciousness which critics of *Gawain* have so often praised. Unfortunately, this quality is still too often regarded as something that sets *Gawain* apart from earlier romances of its kind. Without wishing to belittle the *Gawain*-poet's achievements, I do not believe we should magnify them at the cost of casting romances such as those by Chrétien de Troyes as 'merely' conventional, at the cost of ignoring valuable analogues and sources for the very self-reflexiveness which characterizes *Gawain*. If we want to find Arthurian romances about romance, we will find *Gawain* is only one among a line of courtly romances.

Nor is the *Gawain*-poet alone in adapting Arthurian matter for the concerns of his own day and age. It may be possible to see the ethos of his work, marked by a sensitivity to social decorum and ethical responsibility, as the culmination of a historical development in which earlier Arthurian romances participated. As Aldo Scaglione puts it in his study *Knights at Court*: '*Sir Gawain* clearly marks the high point of the civilizing process.'[16] The civilizing process, the gradual transformation of the independent feudal warrior into the well-mannered courtier, has already proved its conceptual usefulness in the field of history,[17] but critics are only just beginning to chart the important role which the clerical poets of Arthurian romance, from Chrétien de Troyes to the *Gawain*-poet, may have played in promoting this process.

[16] Aldo Scaglione, *Knights at Court: Courtliness, Chivalry, and Courtesy from Ottonian Germany to the Italian Renaissance* (Berkeley, Calif., 1991), 137.
[17] Norbert Elias, *The Civilizing Process*, trans. E. Jephcott, 2 vols. (New York, 1982).

The emphasis on *courtoisie* is perhaps the clearest indication of the civilizing impulse which permeates the *roman courtois* and *Gawain*. But the concern with the cultivation of a new kind of sensibility also informs their descriptions and the plot of their romances as a whole. It informs the heroic ideal which Chrétien, his continuators, and the *Gawain*-poet put forward, namely, the ideal of the 'courtly knight' who combines chivalry with clerical restraint, discipline, and scruples. Throughout the chapters which examine the conventions of Arthurian romance, we will see the ubiquitous presence of a civilizing impulse aimed at enhancing the knight's sensitivity to social decorum and ethical responsibilities. As I shall show, this didactic strain is intimately related both to historical events such as the growth of courts, cities, or bureaucracies, and to literary events such as the emergence of the courtesy book, and the rediscovery of classical moral philosophy. The thread which runs through all discussions of individual motifs and conventions is the way courtly romancers explore the value of courtliness, the supervision of self, and of outward forms and appearances, the way they seek to perpetuate this mastery, and their insights into the special problems that studied behaviour entails. A final chapter on the social function of Arthurian romances will pick up this thread and address the question of why courtly romances place such a high premium on *courtoisie* and the many values it comprises: good manners, an adherence to an elaborate etiquette of hospitality and polite speech, a respect for contracts, self-restraint, and self-awareness. What group was responsible for the dissemination of these values, which groups would benefit from it? Rather than supporting the notion that courtly romance was merely a chapter in the history of escapist fiction or of idealistic aspirations, the answers to these questions will suggest the topicality of its engagement with history.

This book thus has two aims: on the one hand to trace the literary influences that lie behind *Sir Gawain and the Green Knight*, and on the other hand to understand the tradition to which it belongs historically. Combining the study of sources and analogues with that of historical contexts has its notorious difficulties, particularly because the two can offer different explanations for similarities in form or content in the works of two poets. The first may account for these in terms of literary influence or direct borrowing; the second in terms of a convergence of the poets' personalities, their social background, or their ideological aims and constraints. Either might be right. But, more often than not, we need both explanations, one complementing the other—which is why I have attempted to balance the two approaches in the discussion below.

1 The Landscape of Courtly Romance

෯

Introduction

I WANT to begin my exploration of the civilizing impulse in *Sir Gawain and the Green Knight* by considering the opposite of civilization, the world outside the castle. The descriptions of the hostile winter weather and the awe-inspiring landscape through which Gawain travels have been universally praised for their artistry. Unlike most romances, which invoke a setting only in vague and general terms by selecting some of the standard locales such as the 'forest aventureuse' or the 'bele lande' to suit the particular adventure they are describing,[1] the *Gawain*-poet has an eye for the detail that can create an illusion of reality. The geographical precision in *Gawain* has sent many critics to the map of medieval England to reconstruct Gawain's itinerary and, less successfully, to identify a castle which may have served the *Gawain*-poet as a model for Castle Hautdesert.[2] With the same precision, the *Gawain*-poet evokes the bitter cold and the forbidding wilderness which Gawain encounters along the way.

There is, however, a danger in calling the *Gawain*-poet's setting 'realistic' or 'naturalistic', if we understand by this that the descriptions correspond to concrete reality, to what an actual winter day in fourteenth-century England may have been like.[3] For the descriptive

[1] See Marie-Luce Chênerie, *Le Chevalier errant dans les romans arthuriens en vers des XIIe et XIIIe siècles* (Geneva, 1986), 208–10.
[2] For reconstructions of Gawain's itinerary see John McNeal Dodgson, 'Sir Gawain's Arrival in Wirral', *Early English and Norse Studies Presented to Hugh Smith*, ed. Arthur Browne and Peter Foote (London, 1963), 19–25; P. L. Heyworth, 'Sir Gawain's Crossing of Dee', *MAE* 41 (1972), 124–7; Alfred L. Kellogg, 'The Localisation of the Green Chapel in *Sir Gawain and the Green Knight*', in his *Chaucer, Langland, Arthur: Essays in Middle English Literature* (New Brunswick, NJ, 1972), 6–10; and M. W. Thompson, 'The Green Knight's Castle', in *Studies in Medieval History Presented to Allen Brown*, ed. C. Harper-Bill *et al.* (Woodbridge, 1989), 317–25.
[3] This is the view propounded by Francis Berry, 'Sir Gawayne and the Grene Knight', in *The Age of Chaucer*, ed. Boris Ford, Pelican Guide to English Literature (Harmondsworth, 1954), 148–58, at 148.

and geographical details are not simply mimetic: they are determined both by the internal logic of the narrative itself, and by a long
literary tradition of representations of nature, with which the
Gawain-poet was familiar.

So far, criticism has focused on precedents in the rhetorical tradition. As Derek Pearsall has shown, the *Gawain*-poet's account of
the passing of the four seasons (500–33) suggests his acquaintance
with rhetorical handbooks such as Matthew of Vendôme's *Ars
Versificatoria*, which recommends this theme as an elegant variation
on the *descriptio temporis* topos.[4] That two poets with a schooling
in rhetoric could produce very similar results in improvising on the
theme of the changing seasons may be seen from the work of
Henryson. We have no reason to believe Henryson knew *Gawain*,
but his account of the passing seasons in the *Preaching of the
Swallow* (1678–1712) shows some remarkable correspondences to
Gawain:

> Syne wynter wan, quhen austerne Eolus,
> God off the wynd, with blastis boreall,
> The grene garment off somer glorious
> Hes all to-rent and reuin in pecis small.
> Than flouris fair faidit with froist man fall,
> And birdis blyith changeis thair noitis sweit
> In styll murning, neir slane with snaw and sleit.
> (*Preaching of the Swallow*, 1692–8)[5]

Compare these lines with the following from *Gawain*:

> Wroþe wynde of þe welkyn wrastelez with þe sunne,
> Þe leuez lancen fro þe lynde and lyȝten on þe grounde,
> And al grayes þe gres þat grene watz ere . . .   (525–7)
>
> Ner slayn wyth þe slete he sleped in his yrnes . . .   (729)
>
> Þe hasel and þe haȝþorne were harled al samen
> . . . .
> With mony bryddez vnblyþe vpon bare twyges,
> Þat pitosly þer piped for pyne of þe colde.   (744–7)

It is not just the verbal phrases or the descriptive details which
correspond. Both poets achieve a similar contrastive effect. They

[4] 'Rhetorical *Descriptio* in *Sir Gawain and the Green Knight*', MLR 50 (1955), 129–34.
For Matthew of Vendôme's advice see the *Ars Versificatoria, Les Arts poétiques du XIIe et
du XIIIe siècle*, ed. E. Faral (1924, repr. Paris, 1958), 106–93, at 146.
[5] *The Poems of Robert Henryson*, ed. Denton Fox (Oxford, 1981).

make us feel the pain of winter by cruelly transplanting the flora and fauna that made summer glorious to an inhospitable landscape and climate where they pine away in misery. The birds whose songs had heralded the spring now pipe piteously in the cold, the green grass and the leaves shrivel and die, the hazel and the hawthorn, traditionally associated with springtime, are now 'harled al samen' as winter takes its toll.

Neither in *Gawain* nor the *Preaching of the Swallow* are these descriptions merely set-pieces, easily detachable from the themes of the works as a whole. In both, the ineluctable mutability of nature reminds, or should remind, the animals and knights of the necessity to face up to the fate which their own lives have in store. As summer turns into winter, Gawain's carefree happiness must give way to anxiety when the 'wynter wage' reminds him of his obligations:

> Til Meʒelmas mone
> Watz cumen wyth wynter wage;
> Þen þenkkez Gawan ful sone
> Of his anious uyage. (532–5)

Rather than being realistic, the evocation of the arrival of winter functions in this passage as an objective correlative to the fluctuations of Gawain's mind; a technique that is again entirely in accordance with medieval rhetorical theory.[6]

The *Gawain*-poet uses this technique even at the cost of strict verisimilitude. On route to Castle Hautdesert, the natural forces are as bleak as Gawain's thoughts, but when he spots a castle that can shelter him, the scenery changes abruptly. As Gawain cheers up, the landscape suddenly becomes suffused with light:

> As hit schemered and schon þurʒ the shyre okez . . . (772)

> Chalkwhyt chymnees þer ches he innoʒe
> Vpon bastel rouez, þat blenked ful quyte . . . (798–9)

One glimpse of the castle, and the surroundings promptly lose their threatening aspect. Instead, the descriptions of the landscape take on a positively friendly tone. With Gawain apparently safe in the castle, the mornings become crisp and clear:

---

[6] Pearsall, 'Rhetorical *Descriptio*', 132–3. Cf. Manfred Markus, *Moderne Erzählperspektive in den Werken des Gawain-Autors* (Regensburg, 1971), 88–91, 106–11.

Ferly fayre watz þe folde, for þe forst clenged;
In rede rudede vpon rak rises þe sunne,
And ful clere costez the clowdes of þe welkyn. (1694–6)

The Lady of the Castle, as if sensing the power of nature's suggestion, draws Gawain's attention to the charming weather to dispel
the gloom of her guest, who is destined to meet the Green Knight on
the next day:

> 'A! mon, how may þou slepe,
> Þis morning is so clere?'
> He watz in drowping depe,
> Bot þenne he con hir here. (1746–9)

But the pleasant face of nature vanishes as quickly as it has come. In
the early hours of Gawain's day of doom a storm breaks out
(2000–8), which in its turbulence matches Gawain's own disquiet.

In organizing the various descriptions of nature around Gawain's
frame of mind, the *Gawain*-poet subordinates nature to his artistic
design rather than vice versa. But the *Gawain*-poet did not draw on
rhetorical traditions alone. It is primarily a grounding in romance-
writing which influences his vision of the landscape. Gawain's route
through England, which must have been familiar to the *Gawain*-
poet's audience—this was the route which Richard II took on his
expedition to Ireland[7]—becomes in the poet's hands an unfamiliar
wilderness where dragons, giants, and other enemies of mankind
lurk in hope of victims. In stories where errant knights ride out to
confront the unknown, this defamiliarization of a well-charted
territory produces just what romance calls for: a realm of adventure.
The romancer of the *Perlesvaus*, whose knights return to the same
site with such unstinting frequency that every inch of it has been
fully explored, resolved the difficulty by imagining a landscape
which continually changes its appearance and its stock of available
aventure. When Gawain and Lancelot retrace their steps to the
Waste City, they find the surroundings altered beyond recognition:

Misire Gavains e Lanceloz, qui les forés quiderent conoistre, troverent la
terre si muee et si diverse qu'il ne savoient o il erent enbatu. Josephes nos
tesmoigne que les samblanches des isles se muoient por les diverses aventures qui par le plaisir de Dieu i avenoient, e si ne plot mie as chevaliers tant

---

[7] Michael J. Bennett, 'Courtly Literature and North-West England in the Later
Middle Ages', in *Court and Poet*, ed. G. S. Burgess (Liverpool, 1981), 69–78, at 76.

la queste des aventures se il nes trovasent diverses, car quant il avoient entré
en .i. forest e en une isle o il avoient trové aucunne aventure, se il revenoient
autre foiz si troveroient il recés e chasteaus e aventures d'autre maniere . . .
(*Perlesvaus*, p. 282)

Sir Gawain and Lancelot, who thought they knew the forests, found the
country changed and altered to such an extent that they did not know where
they had ended up. Josephus testifies that the appearance of the isles
changed for the sake of the various adventures that took place there, as God
desired. And knights would not have liked their quest for adventures much
if they were not varied. Therefore, if they returned on another occasion to
a forest or an island where they had found adventure before, they found
very different fortifications and castles and adventures . . .

The author of the *Perlesvaus* can only supply the need for unfamiliar lands by turning the well-beaten paths into an ever-changing
stage-set which he manipulates at will. Tongue in cheek, Chrétien
de Troyes transforms his landscapes in similar ways. The forest
of Broceliande, which had been carefully but fruitlessly scru-
tinized by Wace for any evidence of magic,[8] becomes in *Yvain* a
mysterious and marvellous forest, ideal for knights in search of
adventures.

The landscape in *Gawain*, like that of the *Perlesvaus* or *Yvain*, is
a symbolic one. To be sure, his itinerary may be mapped without
much difficulty:

> Now ridez þis renk þurȝ þe ryalme of Logres,
> Sir Gauan, on Godez halue, þaȝ hym no gomen þoȝt.
> · · · · · · · · · · ·
> Til þat he neȝed ful neghe into þe Norþe Walez.
> Alle þe iles of Anglesay on lyft half he haldez,
> And farez ouer þe fordez by þe forlondez,
> Ouer at þe Holy Hede, til he hade eft bonk
> In þe wyldrenesse of Wyrale . . .   (691–701)

But the geographical precision does not transform the nature of the
wild forest. For Gawain the lands remain 'contrayez straunge'
(713). The point emerges clearly when we compare the passage from
Gawain with one from *Yder* which rivals *Gawain*'s geographical
precision. Arthur and his fellow knights have expressed their wish
to seek adventures to a lady who is well informed about the places

---

[8] In his *Roman de Rou*, Wace tells how he had explored the forest of Broceliande
to verify rumours of supernatural occurrences: 'Merueilles quis, mes ne trouai . . .'
(6417); ed. A. J. Holden, 3 vols. (Paris, 1970–3).

where adventures are in supply. She mentions a beautiful knife, guarded by two cruel giants:

> Li reis demande ou ço poet estre.
> 'C'est pres,' dist ele, 'Wircercestre
> Dedens la forest de Malverne
> Qui siet sor la val de Saverne.'
> 'Sire Gagains,' dist li reis, 'sire,
> Ço est en Gloccestresire.'
> 'La vos savrai jo bien mener,'
> Dist Keis, 'si joen m'en voil pener'.   (*Yder*, 5359–65)

The king asks where this may be. 'It is near Worcester', she says, 'in the forest of Malvern, which lies in the Severn valley.' 'Sir Gawain,' says the king, 'sir, that is in Gloucestershire.' 'I can lead you there without any difficulty,' says Kay, 'should I wish to apply myself to it.'

After Arthur demonstrates his topographical knowledge, Kay, to whom the region of Gloucestershire is apparently quite familiar, offers to lead the way. With the help of this excellent guide the band of knights eventually find the two well-known local hazards. Whether the *Yder*-poet was conscious of it or not,[9] the mixture of geographical detail and supernatural giants is patently absurd. The romance concept of the 'chevalier errant', who searches and finds adventures haphazardly, makes way for the map-reader.

Despite the similarities between *Gawain* and *Yder*, there is one significant difference. For all the geographical detail, Gawain remains a knight errant. He rides without a fixed goal, without knowing where the Green Chapel is situated. Like the heroes of courtly romance he rides off and journeys at hazard, in the knowledge that, if he is worthy and endures, the Green Chapel will find *him*. The sense of purpose and familiarity conveyed by the geographical detail exists only for the reader, not for the hero. We look at Gawain as we would look at a fly crawling on a map of England.

The setting of *Gawain* may thus legitimately be compared with that of other romances. In the following section I shall look in particular at the role which the forest plays in *Gawain* and the *roman courtois*, first as a threatening wilderness which all adventurous knights must confront, and most importantly as an embodiment

---

[9] If, as Beate Schmolke-Hasselmann has suggested, *Yder* is a *roman à clef*, with King John as the depraved Arthur, the geographical name-dropping may well serve its topical purpose. See her 'King Arthur as Villain in the Thirteenth-Century Romance *Yder*', *Reading Medieval Studies*, 6 (1980), 31–43.

of everything which the court is not: as the court's diametrical opposite.

The Wild Forest

While Gawain's itinerary may have been known to his contemporaries, the wilderness, and obviously its supernatural inhabitants, are the products of romance rather than reality. In 1250 the last surviving wild forest, the Forest of Dean, disappeared to make way for what forests were in late medieval England—carefully surveyed, managed, and circumscribed woodlands, whose profitable reservoirs of timber, minerals, and venison had been brought under strict control and supervision.[10] The romances of Chrétien de Troyes, the pioneer of the motif of the 'gaste forest',[11] were likewise written at a time when actual wild forests were quickly disappearing. From a historical angle, if not a literary one, the twelfth century witnesses the most dramatic progress in the clearing of forests.[12] The Counts of Champagne, the county where Chrétien presumably composed his romances, were quick to see the economic advantages that could accrue from selling licences to those wishing to turn wasteland into fields fit for cultivation.[13] As the poet of *Partenopeu de Blois* (c.1180) realized, wild forests had largely become a thing of the past. He imagined France under King Clovis as a wild country, in implicit contrast to the civilized countryside of his own day and age:

> Dont n'i avoit castiaus ne tors,
> Viles, cités, dongons, ne bors,
> Ains manoient tote la gent,
> Ça deus, ça trois, esparsement.
> Li plus de France estoit gastine,
> De bois plaine et de savesine ... (347–52)[14]

[10] Oliver Rackham, *Trees and Woodland in the British Landscape* (London, 1976, repr. 1981), 64–5, and Charles R. Young, *The Royal Forests of Medieval England* (Leicester, 1979), 58.
[11] Manfred Gsteiger, *Die Landschaftschilderungen in den Romanen Chrestiens de Troyes* (Berne, 1958), 26.
[12] See M. M. Postan, *The Agrarian Life of the Middle Ages*, Cambridge Economic History of Europe (Cambridge, 1966), 70–4, and Georges Duby, *Guerriers et paysans* (Paris, 1973), 225–36.
[13] Georges Duby, *L'Économie rurale et la vie des campagnes dans l'occident médiévale* (Paris, 1962), 154–6, 196.
[14] Ed. Joseph Gildea, 2 vols. (Villanova, Penn., 1967), vol. i.

There were no castles then, no towers, no villages, cities, keeps, or fortified towns. But people lived scattered throughout the country; here two, there three. Most of France was wasteland, full of forests and wildness.

Paradoxically, then, Chrétien introduced the literary motif of the Wild Forest just when the countryside itself was changing from a 'region . . . of relative wilderness and sparse settlement to one of increasingly populous villages and towns'.[15]

In examining the role of the wilderness in the romances of Chrétien and the *Gawain*-poet we must therefore turn first to the imaginary world of their romances.[16] As one of the first interpreters of the romances of Chrétien, Hartmann von Aue succinctly summarizes the sense of horror which the forest instils in the Arthurian knights who are trapped in it. Describing Erec's impatience to leave the Arthurian assembly, he uses the following simile:

> der tugenthafte man,
> zewâre er gedâhte von dan,
> wol alsô balde,
> als er in einem walde
> waere âne obedach,
> eine âne allen gemach,
> dâ den unvalschen degen
> beide wint unde regen
> harte sêre muote. (7242–50)[17]

This noble knight was as eager to leave soon as if he were alone in the forest without shelter or any comforts and exposed to wind and rain.[18]

In *Sir Gawain and the Green Knight*, the hero is no less anxious about this hostile environment. Even before he sets out he dreads the 'anious viage' (600). Depending on whether we date *Sir Gawain* before or after Chaucer's *Tale of Melibee*, this is the first or second recorded use of the word 'anious' in the English language. But for a

---

[15] Theodore Evergates, *Feudal Society in the Baillage of Troyes under the Counts of Champagne, 1152–1284* (Baltimore, 1975), 8.

[16] For the role of the forest in courtly romances in general see Marianne Stauffer, *Der Wald: Zur Darstellung und Deutung der Natur im Mittelalter* (Berne, 1959); Chênerie, *Le Chevalier*, 147–60; Laurent Ajam, 'La Forêt dans l'œuvre de Chrétien de Troyes', *Europe* (Oct. 1982), 120–5; Rosemary Morris, 'Time and Place in French Arthurian Verse Romances', *French Studies*, 42 (1988), 257–77; and especially the recent and comprehensive study by Corinne Saunders, *The Forest of Medieval Romance* (Woodbridge, 1993).

[17] Hartmann von Aue, *Erec*, ed. Albert Leitzmann (Tübingen, 1985).

[18] Trans. J. W. Thomas (Lincoln, Nebr., 1982), 113.

writer familiar with Old French romance the word would naturally have come to mind. This is the adjective which the courtly romances favour in describing the annoyance which the journey through the alien regions causes. To the Perceval of the *Second Continuation*, the road to the Fisher King's castle appears 'espinouse et anniose' (28246), and in Chrétien's *Yvain*, too, the journeys through the impenetrable forests bring 'enui' or 'grant ennui' (*Yvain*, 182, 4837). As a final example, take *Hunbaut*, whose author expresses his whole-hearted sympathy with his hero's exasperated response to the forest:

> S'est bien raissons qu'il li anuit,
> Quant el bos l'a souspris la nuit,
> U il n'a maison ne herberge.   (*Hunbaut*, 1869–71)

He is annoyed for good reason, because he is trapped at night in the forest, where there is neither a house nor a hostel.

What does the forest mean to these Arthurian characters for it to evoke such revulsion? To some extent, it is the sheer physicality of the forest which the heroes dread. The thick growth of the romance forest denies the knights any easy passage. Gawain rides in

> a forest ful dep, þat ferly watz wylde,
> Hiȝe hillez on vche a halue, and holtwodez vnder,
> Of hore okez ful hoge a hundreth togeder;
> Þe hasel and þe haȝþorne were harled al samen . . .   (741–4)

Like the forest in *Gawain*, the wildernesses in the romances of Chrétien are characterized by their huge dimensions which engulf the questing knights. In *Gawain* the forest is 'ful dep', while Chrétien variously portrays it as 'haute' (*Erec*, 3916), or 'parfonde' (*Yvain*, 3338). As in *Gawain*, the forests are overgrown so densely that any progress is virtually impossible. In *Yvain*, Calogrenant enters

> une forest espesse.
> Molt i ot voie felenesse,
> de ronces et d'espines plainne.   (*Yvain*, 179–81)

a dense forest. The track was terrible, full of briars and thorns.

Remote from civilization, the forest seems to stretch out endlessly, without ever offering the knight any clues about where he is or where he should be heading. In the *Second Continuation* (24549–52), Perceval wanders in the forest for three days without finding

lodging. Here, Gawain spends his miserable evenings in the open air—'mo nyghtes þen innoȝe' (730)—in regions totally alien to him:

> Þe knyȝt tok gates straunge
> In mony a bonk vnbene . . .   (709–10)

As in Old French romance, the hero rides out without knowing where: 'ne set ou, mes en aventure' (*Erec*, 2763), and ends up, like Gawain in the *First Continuation*, in unknown territories:

> Si dirai un poi de Gavain
> Qui par un bois chevalce a plain.
> . . . .
> Mais il ne set ou n'en quel terre
> L'avoit aventure amené
> . . . .
> ne set a cui acointier
> se puist por demander sa voie.
> . . . .
> Uns jor de quarentaine
> Ert, n'il ne sot terre ne plaine;
> S'en a tel doel qu'a poi n'enrage.
> (*First Continuation*, I. 1194–1229)

Now I will speak for a while about Gawain, who rides straight through a forest . . . But he does not know where adventure has led him . . . and does not know to whom he can turn to ask for directions . . . One day he is without food, knowing neither country nor plain. It grieves him so much that he almost goes mad.

As Gawain discovers, little assistance can be expected from human beings. He encounters no one of whom he can ask the way.[19] Fergus is more fortunate in finding people who can point out the way:

> Chevauchant vint dalés la coste
> D'une forest qui molt ert grande;
> Mais il enquiert molt et demande
> A cels que il voit trespasser
> La voie par u puist aler.
> . . . .

---

[19] The motif of asking for directions frequently occurs in the context of the quest. Cf. the *Second Continuation*: 'Toute lou jor antier chevaucha. | Onques chevalier n'ancontra, | Ne meschine ne damoiselle, | A qui il apreïst novelle . . .' ('He rode all day long, but never met a knight, a squire, or a damsel, from whom he could get information': 28247–50).

> Ases trove qui li ensaigne.
> Fergus s'en entre en une plaigne
> Bien grant qui est entre deus mons.
> Lés tertres et lés vaus parfons
> A tant chevauchié que il voit
> Une montaigne qui paroit
> Qui jusqu'as nues avenoit
> Et qui tot le ciel sostenoit . . .   (*Fergus*, 2046–60)

He comes riding along the edge of a great forest, continually asking passers-by about the way he should take . . . He finds many who help him. Fergus enters a wide plain between two mountains. Along hills and deep valleys he rides, until he sees a mountain appear which seemed to reach up towards the clouds and support the entire sky.

Like Fergus, Gawain frequently questions passers-by about the whereabouts of the Green Chapel, although he does so with no success:

> And ay he frayned, as he ferde, at frekez þat he met,
> If þay hade herde any karp of a kynȝt grene,
> In any grounde þeraboute, of þe grene chapel;
> And al nykked hym wyth nay . . .   (703–6)

Some other similarities between the representations of the landscape of *Gawain* and *Fergus* may be noted. In Fitt IV, which contains yet another quest through the wilderness, Gawain, like Fergus, rides along the edge of a forest through hills and valleys, 'Schowuez in bi a schore at a schaȝe syde, | Ridez þurȝ þe roȝe bonk ryȝt to þe dale' (2161–2). Here, surrounded on both sides by mountains—'hyghe bonkkez and brent vpon boþe halue' (2165)—he has, like Fergus, a vision of the mountain tops which seem to reach out to the clouds above. Compare the remarkable image in *Fergus* with that of the *Gawain*-poet:

> il voit
> Une montaigne qui paroit,
> Qui jusqu'as nues avenoit
> Et qui tot le ciel sostenoit . . .

he sees a mountain appear which seemed to reach up towards the clouds and support the entire sky.

> Þe skwez of þe scowtes skayned hym þoȝt.   (2167)

Rather than plain descriptions of the setting, we have here an evocation of its effect on the knights who see it, a representation not

so much of the landscape as of the way it is experienced by the heroes.

Far from any forms of organized settlement, the wilderness in courtly romance is also a place of lawlessness, chaos, and gratuitous violence. In Chrétien's forest, Erec, for example, has to battle it out with robbers who reside in the forests, ready to attack unsuspecting travellers:

> uns chevalier del bois issi,
> qui de roberie vivoit . . .   (*Erec*, 2792–3)

A knight emerged from the forest, who made his living by robbery.

In the forest also dwell the two giants who mutilate innocent travellers (*Erec*, 4316–17). As the author of *Hunbaut* puts it, the forest is a 'terre gaste':

> Car cascuns taut et reube et hape
> Si com en terre sans justice,
> Que nus ne destraint ne justice,
> Ne ne fait raisson ne droiture.   (*Hunbaut*, 304–7)

For everyone here robs and steals, as in a land without justice. No one controls or keeps the law, and no one does what is reasonable and right.

In the 'terre sans justice' neither reason nor law commands respect, and the hero is under constant danger of attack from anarchical elements.[20] Wild animals make the forest even more threatening, and anyone who values his or her life must always be on guard. Chrétien's Enide (*Erec*, 3093–6), or Perceval in the *Second Continuation*, spends the night watching out for ubiquitous peril:

> Percevaux sur l'erbe se jut,
> Mais onques n'i manja ne but,
> Car il n'ot quoi, ce poise lui.
> Et ce li torne a grant annui
> Que des iauz n'osa someillier,
> Por ce qu'il garda son destrier.
> La nuit a toute ainsint veillie . . .
> (*Second Continuation*, 22263–9)

Perceval lies on the grass, without drinking or eating a thing, since there is nothing for him, and that grieves him. And it greatly annoys him that he

---

[20] Cf. *Perlesvaus*, p. 165: 'Sire, fet Lanceloz, que fetes vos de ces armes?—Sire, fet il, ceste forest est molt soutaigne, et si est loing de gent . . . Quant robeor et male gent nos viennent assailir, si nos desfendon' ('Sir, what do you need these weapons for?—Sir, he says, this forest is isolated and far removed from any people . . . When robbers and wicked men come to attack us, we defend ourselves').

dare not sleep because of the beasts, and must keep watch over his horse.
Thus he stays awake, all night long . . .

Gawain, too, must deliver himself from pursuing giants, from foes
'foule and felle', and ferocious beasts (718–23).

If not, strictly speaking, wild beasts or outlaws, the inhabitants of
the wilderness are typically pagans or atheists. The relation between the wilderness and spiritual barrenness has firm roots in
medieval thought. In several glosses on Psalm 30, *silva* is associated
with those who have not seen the light of God.[21] Thus Alan of Lille
writes that the fire of the Holy Ghost set alight the forest of the
world, to wit, the minds of the 'silvestres et rudes'.[22] Pope Honorius
III talks of the conversion of Baltic pagans as a 'vast desert land . . .
watered by the showers of divine grace and cultivated by the
ploughshare of holy preaching'.[23] In the English vernacular, William
Langland links uncultivated land with paganism:

> 'Hethen' is to mene after heeth and untiled erthe—
> As in wilde wildernesse wexeth wilde beestes,
> Rude and unresonable, rennynge withouten keperes.
> (*Piers Plowman*, XV. 457–9)

In romance, too, this association surfaces. In the forest of *Gawain*
wanders the 'wodwo', the Wild Man 'devoid—perhaps incapable—
of any knowledge of God'.[24] Here Chrétien's Perceval becomes
oblivious to time and to his religious duties. The remote realm of
Galloway, Gawain is warned, is 'rough and full of cruelty, and the
people there are perverse' ('mout dure et mout est felenesse, | et s'i
est la genz mout perversse': *Perceval*, 6363–4). The romance of
Fergus expands Chrétien's lines and describes the inhabitants of this
backward country as follows:

> Mais cil des païs sont molt niche;
> Que ja n'enterront en mostier;
> Pas ne leur calt de Diu proier,
> Tant sont niches et bestïaus.   (*Fergus*, 196–9)

---

[21] The conversions by the apostles are described in Lombard's glosses on the
Psalms as the fire of the Holy Ghost setting fire to the *silva mundi*, the non-believers:
Commentarium in psalmos, PL 191, col. 313. The image occurs also in St Augus-
tine's glosses on Psalm 30 in his *Enarrationes in psalmos*, CCSL 38, 219.

[22] *Distinctiones dictionum theologicalium*, PL 210, col. 944.

[23] Quoted by Robert Bartlett, *The Making of Europe: Conquest, Colonization and
Cultural Change 950–1350* (London, 1993), 153.

[24] R. Bernheimer, *Wild Men in the Middle Ages* (Cambridge, Mass., 1952), 11–12.

But people in this country are very stupid, since they never go to church.
They do not care about praying to God: that is how foolish and bestial they
are.

The *Gawain*-poet depicts the locals of the 'wyldrenesse of Wyrale'
in a similar way:

> wonde þer bot lyte
> Þat auþer God oþer gome wyth goud hert louied. (701–2)

Any association with these barbarians is best avoided.

The feeling which therefore impresses itself on errant knights is
one of intense loneliness. In the absence of like-minded companions,
the questing knight rides, like Gawain, 'fer floten fro his frendez'
(714), 'Oft leudlez alone' (693). In the world of reversals that is the
forest, Gawain the great 'luf-talker' ends up with only his horse as a
companion and only God to talk to:

> Hade he no fere bot his fole bi frythez and dounez,
> Ne no gome bot God bi gate wyth to karp . . .   (695–6)

To convey this sense of solitude, the Old French romances will refer
to the forest as 'soltive' or 'soutainne' (*Perceval*, 75, 1701, 6979).
The unnaturalness of solitude for a knight is voiced in Calogrenant's
story of his misfortunes in the forest where he wandered 'seus come
païsanz' (*Yvain*, 174). Solitude may be an inevitable part of a quest
for adventure, but the ideal of courtliness, dependent as it is on a
display of good manners, and hence a discerning audience, will not
strike root in the wilderness.[25]

The knight's solitude influences in its turn his behaviour, which
deviates completely from the elated and extroverted interaction
which accompanies life at court. In the forest, the bravest of knights
give full vent to their vexations. Take, for example, Perceval in
Manessier's *Continuation*:

> Onques nul home n'ancontra;
> De la lande an un bois entra,

---

[25] The negative valorization of solitude seems to be typical of pro-court writings.
Cf. *De regimine principium* by Aegidius Romanus (*c.*1243–1316), who puts the
coarseness and vulgarity of peasants down to their solitary way of life; Klaus
Schreiner, ' "Hof" (*curia*) und "höfische Lebensführung" (*vita curialis*) als Heraus-
forderung an die Christliche Theologie und Frömmigkeit', in *Höfische Literatur,
Hofgesellschaft, Höfische Lebensformen um 1200*, ed. Gert Kaiser and Jan-Dirk
Müller (Düsseldorf, 1986), 67–138, at 137.

> Lou cief baissié, ala pansant.
>
> . . . .
>
> Desoz un chesne s'est asis,
> Iriez et mornes et pansis;
> A soi meïsmes prist a dire,
> Correciez et maz et plains d'ire . . .
>   (37863–5, 37891–4)

He never encountered anyone. Leaving the fields he entered a forest, and he went along with bent head, deep in thought. He sat down under an oak tree, angry, sad, and thoughtful, and began to talk to himself, irritated, tired, and full of anger.

In the forests heroes are thrown back on themselves, and meditate on their follies. Chrétien's lines in *Perceval*:

> Et Percevax el santier antre,
> qui sopire del cuer del vantre
> por ce que mesfez se savoit
> vers Dieu et si s'an repantoit.
> Plorant s'an vet vers le boschage . . .   (*Perceval*, 6121–5)

And Perceval enters the path, sighing from his heart because he knows he has sinned against God, and repents. Weeping he rides towards the forest.

and the lines from the forest scene in *Gawain*, 'He rode in his prayere, | And cryed for his mysdede' (759–60), are succinct expressions of the same narrative motif.[26]

We have come to the function of the forest which is most typical of the *roman courtois*. What becomes visible in the representations of the forest and the knight's dejected response to it is the extent to which the forest functions as the reprehensible counterpart of the court, and the *joie* which the courtly milieu demands. Removed from the comforts and consolation of a peer group of courtiers whose lives are organized around ceremonies of hospitality or feasts, the errant knight is immersed in a savage environment that is indifferent, even antithetical, to the cultural refinement for which he stands.

This is why the courtly romancer resorts so often to negative statements when describing the hero's stay in the forest:

[26] For similarities between Gawain and Chrétien's Perceval in these scenes of contrition in the forest see Alain Renoir, '*Gawain* and *Parzival*', SN 31 (1958), 155–8. Renoir sees even closer parallels between *Gawain* and Wolfram von Eschenbach's *Parzival*. We have, however, no evidence of any influence of Middle High German texts on fourteenth-century English literature.

> An la foreste jut toute nuit,
> N'i ot *ne* feste *ne* deduit,
> *Ne* que boivre *ne* que mangier . . .
>
> (*Second Continuation*, 26107–9; italics mine)

He spent all night in the forest, having neither good cheer, nor pleasure, no drink, and no food . . .

The forest is thus defined by what it is not, in terms of the luxury and festivities which, unlike the court, it cannot offer its guests. It is the zero-point of courtliness, the zero-point of hospitality. Thus the court makes its presence felt even in descriptions of the forest, as the norm from which the forest departs.

This is why forest scenes in courtly romance so often rely on the same motifs as scenes set at court, used this time in a negative modulation. Food, cutlery, wine, or napkins: all enter into descriptions of the forests where their absence or inadequacy is carefully detailed. Living in the forest on the verge of madness, Yvain still maintains some culinary refinement when he is reduced to a diet that consists solely of the uncooked meat of wild animals:

> Mes del mangier *ne* fu deduiz
> qu'il *n*'i ot pein *ne* vin *ne* sel,
> *ne* nape, *ne* coutel, *ne* el . . .   (*Yvain*, 3462–4)

But he took no delight in the food, as there was no bread, no wine, no salt, no table-cloth, no knife, or anything else . . .

Once more, life at court functions as an implied norm to which the forest compares badly. Chrétien's probable source for this passage, Beroul's version of the lovers' afflictions in the Forest of Morholt in the common version of *Tristan et Yseult*,[27] relies on the antithesis between court and forest as well. Like Yvain, the lovers have to make do with the yields of the hunt. With bitter sarcasm, Beroul comments on their plight:

> Molt avoient a faire queu!
> Il *n*'avoient *ne* lait *ne* sel
> A cele foiz a lor ostel . . .

. . . . . .

[27] For a short discussion of the different representations of the forest in the separate versions see Stauffer, *Der Wald*, 55–72. It has long been known that it is the common version represented by Beroul and Eilhart, rather than the branch of the *Tristan* legend represented by Thomas D'Angleterre and Gottfried von Strassburg, with which Chrétien was familiar. See E. Hoepffner, 'Chrétien de Troyes et Thomas D'Angleterre', *Romania*, 55 (1929), 1–16.

Seignors, eisi font longuement
En la forest parfondement,
Longuement sont en cel desert.
(Beroul's *Tristan*, 1296–1306)

They had much to cook with! They had neither milk nor salt in their hostel ... Lords, thus they survive for a long time in the deep forest, and for a long time they live in this wasteland.

What is the Forest of Morholt, from Beroul's point of view, but a kitchen without the necessary utensils and provisions, an inhospitable 'ostel'?

The hero of *Sir Gawain* is as fastidious as Yvain or Beroul. Food there is, but none to Gawain's liking:

Þer he fonde noȝt hym byfore þe fare þat he lyked. (694)

To argue that Gawain or Chrétien's Yvain might be asking too much under the circumstances would be to miss the point both poets are making. Both Yvain and Gawain find themselves displaced in an environment which fails to provide the essentials of civilized life: cutlery, spices, napkins, in short, the utensils which might make it possible for them to transform raw meat or food into *haute cuisine*, to transform nature into culture. Yvain and Gawain's particular palates are in effect an indication of their courtesy, and an indication of their ability to uphold certain standards no matter how 'villainous' the circumstances.

The setting of the forest, we may conclude, appears in Arthurian romance as neither a realistic nor a neutral décor. For the knight's quest from one court to another, it had already in Chrétien's earliest romances become the standard setting, well suited to connect the various hospitality episodes. As the space in between the centres of civilization where knights usually take their lodging, the representations of the forest in courtly romance succeed in providing the marked contrast needed to differentiate the structural unit of the quest from other units such as the feast or hospitality. But, despite their accentuation, the descriptions of the forest remain remarkably consonant with the concern for *courtoisie* which typifies romances such as *Gawain* or *Yvain*. The court may well provide the ideal *locus* where courtly values can be explored, but in the accounts of the forest a concern for standards of refinement can continue to be a preoccupation of the narrative, precisely because it is cast as the inverted mirror image of the court or castle. The result is a setting capable of providing contrast without fragmenting the outlook which these romances offer on their fictive world. Thus, both knight and romancer survive the forest without succumbing to its dangers. As Gawain and, with more difficulty, Yvain manage ultimately to maintain their identity in an environment which isolates and alienates them from their roots, the poets uphold in these episodes their own evaluative standards by privileging the court as the norm from which the forest and all it embodies deviate.

From Forest to Castle

In order to see how the literary device of the setting functions in accomplishing the shift from the quest in the forest to a return to civilization, let us look at the transition in *Gawain* and some of its possible sources and analogues. Riding through a cold and wet forest, the desperate Gawain calls on heaven for succour:

> I beseche þe, lorde,
> And Mary, þat is myldest moder so dere,
> Of sum herber þer heȝly I myȝt here masse,
> Ande þy matynez to-morne, mekely I ask,
> And þerto prestly I pray my pater and aue
> and crede.'　　　　　　　　　(753–8)

> Nade he sayned hymself, segge bot þrye,
> Er he watz war in þe wod of a won in a mote,
> Abof a launde, on a lawe, loken under boȝez
> Of mony borelych bole aboute bi þe diches:
> A castel þe comlokest þat euer knyȝt aȝte,
> Pyched on a prayere, a park al aboute,
> With a pyked palays, pyned ful þik,
> Þat vmbeteȝe mony tre mo þen two myle.　　(763–70)

> Þe bryge watz breme vpbrayde,
> Þe ȝatez wer stoken faste,
> Þe wallez were wel arayed,
> Hit dut no wyndez blaste.　　(781–4)

The efficacious prayer, the sudden changes in the landscape, and the vision of the castle: these are the three motifs with which the reader of Chrétien and his continuators may be familiar. To see the similarities in the way the *Gawain*-poet and the Old French romancers handled these motifs let us look first of all at the Maiden Quest in

Chrétien's *Yvain*. Like Gawain, the maiden, who has taken it upon herself to find the Knight with the Lion, traverses the forest in customary solitude with considerable difficulty:

> Si li enuia molt la nuiz,
> et de ce dobla li enuiz
> qu'il plovoit a si grant desroi,
> con Damedex avoit de coi,
> e fu el bois molt au parfont.
> Et la nuiz, et li bois li font
> grant enui, et plus li enuie
> que la nuiz, ne li bois, la pluie.
> Et li chemins estoit si max
> que sovant estoit ses chevax
> jusque pres des cengles en tai;
> si pooit estre an grant esmai
> pucele au bois, et sanz conduit,
> par male tans, et par noire nuit,
> si noire qu'ele ne veoit
> le cheval sor qu'ele seoit.
> Et por ce reclamoit adés
> Deu avant, et sa mere aprés,
> et puis toz sainz et totes saintes;
> et dist la nuit orisons maintes
> que Dex a ostel la menast
> et fors de ce bois la gitast.
> Si crïa tant que ele oï
> un cor dont molt se resjoï
> qu'ele cuide qu'ele truisse
> ostel, mes que venir i puisse;
> si s'est vers la voiz adreciee
> tant qu'ele antre en une chauciee.
>
> . . . .
>
> Einsi par aventure asane
> au chastel . . .   (*Yvain*, 4831–73)

The night alarmed her, and what made things worse was that it rained as hard as God could make it. And the forest was deep, and while the night and the forest worried her, the rain was even worse. And the path was so muddy that her horse was often sunk in the mud up to its girth. A maiden might well be upset in a forest, alone, in bad weather, and in such darkness that she could not see the horse she was sitting on. That is why she called first on God, then on his mother, and next on all the saints, and often said her prayers that night, so that God might lead her to a hostel, and out of the woods. Thus she cried, until she heard the sound of a horn which raised her spirits, since she thought she had found lodging, if only she could get to it. She went in the direction of the noise, until she came to a road . . . Thus by chance she comes to the castle.

Gawain's transition from forest to castle corresponds with this passage from *Yvain* in many respects. Both characters find themselves in dire circumstances, wading 'þurgh mony misy and myre' (749). What grieves them above all is the weather. Gawain may have to fight many foes, but, as the *Gawain*-poet says, this is nothing in comparison with the weather:

> For werre wrathed hym not so much þat wynter nas wors,
> When þe colde cler water fro þe cloudez schadde . . .   (726–7)

The maiden in *Yvain* has a similar assessment of her predicament. A night in the forest may be troublesome, but in a scale of comparison, the weather tops all that:

> Et la nuiz, et li bois li font
> grant enui, et plus li enuie
> que la nuiz, ne li bois, la pluie.

If the night and the forest worried her, the rain was still worse.

As hyperbolic as the description of the weather are the descriptions of their religious fervour. Both call on Mary and God for help. Both devoutly say their prayers in the hope that God will come to their rescue. And indeed he does. Gawain crosses himself, sees a castle, and 'full chauncely' chooses the road that leads him to it. The maiden, too, is immersed in prayer when she hears the sound of a horn, and she makes her way to the paved track which 'par aventure' brings her into safety. But as the *Gawain*-poet and Chrétien suggest, behind the apparent fortuitousness with which they stumble upon their shelters, divine intervention is at work:

> *Si* cria *tant qu*'ele oï
> un cor dont molt se resjoï . . .

Thus she cried, until she heard the sound of a horn which raised her spirit . . .

> *Nade* he sayned hymself, segge, *bot* þrye,
> *Er* he watz war in þe wod of a won . . .

By linking the prayers and the subsequent revelations syntactically—'Si . . . tant que' and 'Nade . . . bot . . . er'—the poets can suggest a causative link without dissociating themselves entirely from their characters' perspectives, from which divine intervention and chance cannot readily be distinguished.

Another analogue to the motif of the efficacious sign of the cross or prayer may be found in the *First Continuation* of Chrétien's *Perceval*. Trapped in the forest at night, a violent storm threatens Gawain's very life:

> Cele nuis fu noire et oscure,
> Car il tona molt longuement
> Et plus et fist un si grant vent
> Que li arbre parmi fendoient.
> Foldres espessement chaoient,
> Et si durement espartoit
> Que merveille est que ne moroit
> Mesire Gavains li gentieus.
> Mais tant vos di que en toz lius
> Le salvoit sa grans loiautez
> Et sa grans debonairetez.
> E cele nuit demainement
> Le gari cil Diex qui ne ment,
> Iche sachiez bien vraiement.
> (*First Continuation*, I. 13004–17)

That night it was dark and gloomy, and it thundered for a long time, and there was such a strong wind that trees were split in two. Lightning struck everywhere and with such force that it was a miracle that the noble Sir Gawain did not die. But I will have you know that wherever he went his loyalty and humility saved him. And that night he was saved by God, who never lies.

In *Gawain*, too, the narrator assures us that only Gawain's upright nature saved him from an otherwise certain death. Compare lines 13010–16 with the *Gawain*-poet's assertion that:

> Nade he ben duȝty and dryȝe, and Dryȝtyn had serued,
> Douteles he hade ben ded and dreped ful ofte.   (724–5)

Morever, as is the case in *Gawain*, the sign of the cross puts a swift end to the hero's tortures:

> Si se saigne . . .
> Et li mals tans s'acoisa lors
> Et la grans pluie remest tote,
> Que plus ne venta ne plus goute,
> Ains devint la nuis clere et pure;
> Si s'en torne grant aleüre.
> (*First Continuation*, I. 13055–60)

So he crossed himself . . . and the storm abated, and the rain stopped completely, so that there was no more wind or rain. The night became crisp and clear, and he pressed on at great speed.

When Gawain crosses himself, the storm miraculously abates, though for the French hero a hostel is still far from the horizon. In this respect, the *Didot-Perceval* offers a closer analogue to *Gawain*. In the middle of a dense forest, Perceval's prayer for a lodging is answered when a castle reveals itself to his eyes:

Et Percevaus quant il fu departis del chevalier cevauca toute jor que onques aventure ne trova, et aproisma li vespres et il proia nostre Segnor que il li envoiast ostel u il se peüst herbergier, car il en avoit un mauvais eü la nuit devant. Et lors garda par devant lui, si vit aparoir parmi l'espesse de le forest le pumel d'une tor qui molt estoit biau et gros. (*Didot-Perceval*, pp. 165–6)

And after Perceval had left, he rode all day without finding an adventure. Evening approached, and he prayed our Lord to send him a hostel where he could spend the night, because he had only had bad lodging the night before. And then he looked ahead, and in the midst of the dense forest the top of a beautiful and big tower loomed up.

In both romances a prayer for lodgings is rewarded when the heroes glimpse amidst the 'espesse de la forest' or 'thurȝ the shyre okes' the castle they had been hoping for.

From this moment, the bleak wilderness seems to undergo a metamorphosis. In the proximity of the castle, the forest, once wild, has been domesticated to suit the tastes of Hautdesert's inhabitants. The impenetrable track becomes a 'chef gate', the wilderness makes way for 'a lande', a 'prayere' and a 'park al aboute'. Around Castle Hautdesert, the forces of nature no longer have free play. Even the blasting winds must acknowledge defeat in the face of this superior power. Castle Hautdesert 'dut no wyndez blaste'. This is the first similarity to note between Gawain's arrival at Castle Hautdesert and Perceval's vision of Gornemant de Gohort's castle in the *Conte du Graal*:

> Et li vaslez sanz nul arest
> s'an va poignant par la forest
> tant que es terres plainnes vint
> sor une riviere qui tint
> de lé plus d'une arbalestee,
> si s'estoit tote l'eve antree

et retrete an son grant conduit.
Vers la grant riviere qui bruit
S'en va tote une praerie,
mes an l'eve n'antra il mie,
qu'il la vit mout parfonde et noire
et asez plus corrant que Loire.
Si s'an va tot selonc la rive
lez une grant roche naïve,
et de l'autre part l'eve estoit
si que l'eve au pié li batoit.
Sor cele roche, an un pandant
qui vers mer aloit descendant,
ot un chastel mout riche et fort.
Si com l'eve aloit au regort,
torna li vaslez a senestre
et vit les torz del chastel nestre,
qu'avis li fu qu'eles nessoient
et que fors del chastel issoient.
En mi le chastel, an estant,
ot une tor et fort et grant;
une barbacane mout fort
avoit tornee vers le gort
qui a la mer se conbatoit,
et la mers au pié li batoit.
A .iiii. parties del mur,
don li quarrel estoient dur,
avoit .iiii. basses torneles,
qui mout estoient forz et beles.
Li chastiax fu mout bien seanz
et bien aeisiez par dedanz.
Devant le chastelet reont
ot sur l'eve drecié un pont
de pierre et d'areinne et de chauz.
Li ponz estoit et forz et hauz,
a batailles estoit antor,
qu'anmi le pont ot une tor
et devant, un pont torneïz,
qui estoit fez et establiz
a ce que sa droiture aporte:
le jor ert ponz, et la nuit porte.
Li vaslez vers le pont chemine.   (*Perceval*, 1301–47)

The youth rides through the forest without stopping, until he came to a
plain by a river that was wider than the shot of a crossbow and whose

waters were channelled and restricted to their proper conduit. He rides through a meadow, towards the roaring river, but did not wade through it, seeing it was dark and deep, and more swift-flowing than the Loire. He follows the bank past a huge rock on the other side of the river whose waters beat against its foot. On this rock, on a slope that ran down towards the sea, stood a castle rich and strong. Where the water debouched into a bay, the youth turned left and he saw the towers of the castle loom up, so that it seemed to him that they were growing and emerging from the castle. Rising from within the castle was a strong and big tower. A strong barbican faced the bay, which waged war against the sea, while the sea beat against its foot. At the four corners of the wall, made of tough bricks, were four low turrets, strong and beautiful. Around them, the castle was comfortably and safely situated. Before the round gatehouse was a bridge of stone, sand, and lime. The bridge was strong and high, and was entirely fortified. In the middle of the bridge was a tower and in front of it a drawbridge, fittingly designed and used as a bridge during the day and as a gate at night. The youth rides towards the bridge.

As Castle Hautdesert puts a decisive mark on its surroundings, the presence of a castle in *Perceval* announces itself in advance through changes in the landscape. Perceval emerges out of the forest and enters 'es terres plainnes', a rough synonym for the 'lande' which Gawain sees from a distance, and which leads Calogrenant out of the forest in *Yvain*.

> De la foreste, en une lande
> entrai, et vi une bretesche . . .   (*Yvain*, 188–9)

From the forest, I entered a plain and saw a castle . . .

Before reaching the 'praerie', Perceval sees a river which rushes along violently but which is symbolically channelled and restricted to its proper bed. If Bertilac's castle successfully fends off the attack of the natural elements, Gornemant's castle does so at least equally well. The river, whose waves break against the rocks on which the castle is built, fights a fruitless battle against the barbican:

> une barbacane mout fort
> avoit tornee vers le gort
> qui a la mer se conbatoit,
> et la mers au pié li batoit.

A strong barbican faced the bay, which waged war against the sea, while the sea beat against its foot.

In both *Gawain* and *Perceval* the castles stand as shields against the
onslaughts of nature, as civilizing forces from which the wilderness
seems to recoil to make way for 'terres plaines', a 'lande', a 'praerie'
or a 'prayere', and a 'park', the familiar signposts to civilization in
the romances of Chrétien.[28]

The most significant parallel between the *Gawain*-poet and Chrétien lies in their use of a subjective viewpoint and their emphasis on
aesthetic detail. Let us look again at Gawain's first glimpses of the
castle, and the detailed description of the castle which follows:

> Nade he sayned hymself, segge, bot þrye,
> Er he watz war in þe wod of a won in a mote,
> Abof a launde, on a lawe, loken under boȝez
> Of mony borelych bole aboute bi þe diches:
> A castel þe comlokest þat ever knyȝt aȝte,
> Pyched on a prayere, a park al aboute,
> With a pyked palays, pyned ful þik,
> Þat vmbeteȝe mony tre mo þen two myle.
> Þat holde on þat on syde þe haþel auysed,
> As it schemered and schon þurȝ þe schyre okez;
>
>   .   .   .   .
>
> Þe burne bode on blonk, þat on bonk houed
> Of þe depe double dich þat drof to þe place;
> Þe walle wod in þe water wonderly depe,
> Ande eft a ful huge heȝt hit haled vpon lofte,
> Of harde hewen ston vp to þe tablez,
> Enbaned vnder þe abataylment in þe best lawe;
> And syþen garytez ful gaye gered bitwene,
> Wyth mony luflych loupe þat louked ful clene:
> A better barbican þat burne blusched vpon neuer.
> And innermore he behelde þat halle ful hyȝe,
> Towres telded bytwene, trochet ful þik,
> Fayre fylyolez þat fyȝed, and ferlyly long,
> With coruon coprounes craftyly sleȝe.
> Chalkwhyt chymnees þer ches he innoȝe,
> Vpon bastel rouez, þat blenked ful quyte;
> So mony pynakle payntet watz poudred ayquere,
> Among þe castel carnelez clambred so þik,
> Þat pared out of papure purely hit semed.   (763–802)

---

[28] This representation of the castle as a force which puts the marks of civilization
on the surrounding landscape is by no means fantastic. It was with a view to
cultivating wastelands that the Counts of Champagne had castles constructed in
forested lands. See Gabriel Fournier, *Le Château dans la France médiévale: Essai de
sociologie monumentale* (Paris, 1978), 188–91.

This passage has often been analysed, and although some of the architectural terms are still not understood, it is evident that many details correspond to the latest fashion of the day. The originality of the description lies precisely in the *Gawain*-poet's use of detail to convey the strength and, above all, the beauty of the building. Another notable feature is the poet's masterful use of a subjective point of view to suggest how the castle appears to Gawain, to his eyes and his mind.

Larry Benson has suggested that the *Gawain*-poet's use of a subjective viewpoint may be located in the context of the medieval dream visions, rather than of romance:

> A romance always takes place in some remote past, and its narrator is always a clerk, depending on some written authority, recounting, ostensibly unchanged, the ancient story 'as the book tells.' The dream or vision on the other hand is always . . . a personal experience related by a narrator who, he asserts, saw everything with his own eyes.[29]

What Benson overlooks, however, is that the personal and dramatic point of view is in fact one of the most notable innovations which Chrétien introduced into Old French romance.[30] Furthermore, although the story of romance may be set in a pseudo-mythical past, courtly romancers consistently sought to adapt this past to the sensibilities and life-styles of their audience. There is a similar flaw in R. W. Ackerman's suggestion that the descriptions of castles in *Gawain* or Chrétien's romances are characterized by a visionary quality and a timelessness which Ackerman believes derive ultimately from a tradition of apocalyptic dream visions.[31]

Before discussing the alleged 'timelessness' of these castles, let us turn first to the question of the subjective viewpoint. Both Chrétien and the *Gawain*-poet describe the castles of Gornemant and Bertilac consistently from the knight's point of view, a technique which, at their respective periods, was as much a novelty in Old French romance as in Middle English romance. As Manfred Gsteiger notes apropos of Perceval's vision of Gornemant's castle: 'New in this

---

[29] Larry D. Benson, *Art and Tradition in Sir Gawain and the Green Knight* (New York, 1965), 180–1.

[30] For the innovative use of the subjective viewpoint in the *roman courtois* see Robert W. Hanning's chapter on mimesis in *The Individual in Twelfth-Century Romance* (New Haven, Conn., 1974), 139–70.

[31] 'Castle Hautdesert in *Sir Gawain and the Green Knight*', in *Mélanges Jean Frappier*, 2 vols. (Geneva, 1970), i. 1–7.

depiction is the altered perspective. The world is no longer seen from an infallible and objective point of view . . . but from the individual perspective of the protagonist . . . An individual way of seeing has emerged.'[32] This new technique in *Perceval* and *Gawain* appears not only from the verbs which describe the act of seeing— 'auysed', 'behelde', 'ches' in *Gawain* and 'vit' and 'avis li fu' in *Perceval*—but also from the kinds of details which they make available. What we register is made dependent on the relative position of the protagonists whose movements we follow. Compare the *Gawain*-poet's 'þat holde *on þat on syde* þe haþel auysed' with Chrétien's 'torna li vaslez *a senestre* | et vit les torz del chastel nestre'. The sequence of architectural features suggests the heroes' changing perspectives, which in its turn imparts the illusion of movement.[33] Both Gawain and Perceval see the castle first from a distance, where they cannot yet make out any specific details but only the natural surroundings in which the castle is set: 'Abof a launde, on a lawe' and Chrétien's 'Sor cele roche en un pendant'. Only as both knights approach does the castle grow, and only when they are close enough are the heroes allowed to look 'innermore', 'enmi le chastel', to see the keep rising above the outer walls.

That there is a magic about these descriptions is undeniable, but the magic lies not in the castles but in the eyes of their beholders. To the approaching Perceval, the towers seem to grow out of the walls, and to Gawain, overwhelmed by joy and by the majesty of the castle, it seems 'pared out of papure', too good to be true. The description of the castle and the light which suffuses it are a perfect correlative to Gawain's exuberance which swiftly replaces his gloom in the forest.

Chrétien de Troyes similarly portrays Perceval's changing states of mind in his account of his arrival at the Grail Castle. Perceval has been given directions to the castle by a fisherman, and he impatiently curses his assistance when the castle does not immediately reveal itself:

---

[32] 'Neuartig ist an dieser Schilderung der veränderte Gesichtspunkt: Die Welt wird nicht mehr unter einem schlechthin gültigen, objektiven Aspekt gesehen . . . sondern unter dem individuellen Gesichtspunkt einer handelnden Person . . . eine individuellere Anschauungsweise beginnt sich durchzusetzen' (Gsteiger, *Landschaftsschilderungen*, 13).

[33] On Chrétien's use of a dramatic point of view in this passage, see Peter Haidu's important observations in *Aesthetic Distance in Chrétien de Troyes: Irony and Comedy in Cligés and Perceval* (Geneva, 1968), 148. For the *Gawain*-poet's use of this technique, see Markus, *Moderne Erzählperspektive*.

> 'Peschierres, qui ce me deïs,
> trop grant desleauté feïs
> se tu me deïs por mal.'   (*Perceval*, 3041–3)

'You fisherman, who said this to me, committed an act of disloyalty if you told me a lie.'

Hardly has Perceval spoken these words when the castle appears. Perceval quickly revises his opinion about the fisherman:

> Lors vit devant lui an un val
> le chief d'une tor qui parut.
> L'an ne trovast jusqu'a Barut
> si bele ne si bien asise.
> Quarree fu, de pierre bise,
> si avoit torneles antor.
>
> . . . . . .
>
> Li vaslez cele part avale,
> Et dit que bien l'a avoié
> cil qui la l'avoit anvoié.   (*Perceval*, 3044–54)

Then he sees the top of a tower appear in a valley before him. From here to Beirut one would not be able to find a castle that was more beautiful or better situated. It was square, built of grey stone, and was flanked by smaller towers ... The youth turns this way, saying that the man who directed him towards it had done well.

Like Chrétien, the *Gawain*-poet is an expert in suggesting his characters' fluctuating moods. The most obvious example is Gawain's sense of relief after he has been to confession:

> Vche mon had daynté þare
> Of hym, and sayde, 'Iwysse,
> Þus myry he watz neuer are,
> Syn he com hider, er þis.'   (1889–2)

I quote this passage not only to illustrate the flawless psychological pictures which the *Gawain*-poet, like Chrétien, can sketch, but also to underline that the subjective pressures which influence their heroes' perceptions and judgements can invite questions about their accuracy.

As Gawain's relief after his confession turns out to have been premature, the sense of security with which both Chrétien's Perceval and Gawain enter into the hospitality episodes of the Grail Castle and Hautdesert proves misconceived. Indeed, it is precisely their belief that they have briefly left the hardships of their quests behind which adds to the difficulties they will face in their hostels. As familiar as the Grail Castle and Hautdesert may seem to Perceval and Gawain, reminiscent as they are of Gornemant's fortress or of Arthur's court, which they have just left behind, they are inhabited by strangers, and surrounded by an ambivalence which characterizes hospitality at large. As we will see in the following chapter, hospitality, too, has its pitfalls, which are all the more treacherous for not being readily apparent. Gawain and Perceval's joy at returning to civilization blinds them to its ambivalence. Gawain enjoys a prolonged stay at Hautdesert while ignorant of the fact that the adventures lie not in the wilderness around the Green Chapel but within the walls that shelter him. To Perceval, the Grail Castle is simply another castle like Gornemant's, and he does not realize that the most critical adventure of his chivalric career will take place here. The same childlike response which Perceval shows when he swings from condemnation to approval of the fisherman is to manifest itself again when he follows to the letter Gornemant's advice not to speak too much, and fails to ask the question which would have delivered the Fisher King from his misery. The personal and dramatic perspective through which we see the world of *Gawain* and Chrétien's romances allows, in other words, for the possibility of a blind spot, to which later developments in their romances will alert the heroes.

To call the castles of Bertilac, Gornemant, or the Grail King 'otherworldly' is to miss the narrative technique of a personalized point of view with which Chrétien and the *Gawain*-poet were working. If we are to call them visionary, it is because they are objects of Perceval's or Gawain's vision, rather than phantoms of fairy. Another fact that the accounts of the castles in Chrétien's *Perceval* and *Gawain* as supernatural apparitions overlook is their striking modernity.

Gornemant's castle is fully abreast of the latest developments in castle construction. One of these was the appearance of the central keep: 'The appearance and spread of the castle with keep, characterized by the presence of a high and strong tower within . . . represents an essential stage in the history of the medieval castle.'[34] It was only in the thirteenth century that this new type of castle

[34] 'L'apparition et la diffusion du château à donjon, caractérisé par la présence d'une haute et puissante tour à l'intérieur . . . représentent une étape essentielle dans l'histoire du château médiéval' (Fournier, *Le Château*, 65).

became the rule, but Gornemant de Gohort is already a proud
owner of one:

> En mi le chastel, an estant,
> ot une tor et fort et grant . . .

Rising from within the castle was a strong and big tower.

Gornemant has a battlemented stone bridge and a central tower
from which a drawbridge is suspended. Why does Chrétien show
such interest in this bridge? The answer lies again in the latest
architectural fashion. 'In no other direction', Léon Gautier wrote
on the subject of the gateway, 'did the architects of the Middle
Ages bring their art to such perfection. It is a far cry from the
cumbersome donjon of wood perched on the mound; here, from
the threshold of their only door beyond the moat, there was nothing but the rickety bridge, the *pons ligneus*, which was more like a
mill ladder than a bridge . . .'.[35] In comparison with this kind of
bridge, Gornemant's gateway must have been progress epitomized.
In the context of the most revolutionary change in castle construction, the replacement of wood by stone,[36] Chrétien's assurances that
Gornemant's castle is made of 'quarrel dure' and his bridge 'de
pierre et d'areinne et de chauz' would have served to suggest the
richness and modernity of the castle. By the late twelfth century
masonry had become a defensive necessity which only a few could
afford:

The profound transformations in military architecture from the end of the
twelfth century entailed a considerable rise in the price of construction and
maintenance of new castles: only the well-off lords could follow the trend
and adapt their castles to the tastes of the day, while the non-modernized
castles of the less affluent lost their military importance.[37]

Yet while the trends of the day may have been hard to follow for the
lesser nobility, Gornemant's castle is equipped not simply with
the bare defensive requirements, but even with 'tornelles . . . forz

[35] Léon Gautier, *Chivalry*, ed. Jacques Levron, trans. D. C. Dunning (London,
1965), 190.

[36] Fournier, *Le Château*, 80–6.

[37] 'En effet, les profondes transformations de l'architecture militaire à partir de la
fin du XIIe siècle augmentèrent considérablement le prix de revient de la construction
et de l'entretien des nouveaux châteaux: seuls les châtelains suffisamment riches
purent suivre le mouvement et mettre au goût du jour leurs châteaux, tandis que ceux
des seigneurs moins riches, non modernisés, perdirent de leur importance militaire'
(ibid. 148).

et beles' which flank his keep, another innovation seen first in the twelfth century, and designed for pure ostentation rather than for any military purpose: 'From the twelfth century, the keep was sometimes flanked by towers and turrets. These flanking devices were designed with great imagination, without much regard to necessity.'[38] The same features recur in Chrétien's description of the Grail Castle. This castle, too, is built of stone, equipped with a keep, a drawbridge, and decorative towers.

The *Gawain*-poet tries to bring out the modernity and tastefulness of Bertilac's castle as well. A few details still correspond to the basic design of Gornemant's castle. Both are built on a slope, 'on a lawe' or 'en un pendant'; towering above the outer walls is the keep, built with 'harde hewen ston' or 'quarrel dur'. Both are fitted with barbicans and drawbridges. But, like Chrétien, the *Gawain*-poet is describing the latest fashion, and the details he selects are therefore very different.

The art of masonry, still new in Chrétien's days, had by the *Gawain*-poet's day culminated in a taste for ornamental turrets and pinnacles, abundantly present on the roof of Castle Hautdesert:

> And syþen garytez ful gaye gered bitwene,
> Wyth mony luflych loupe þat louked ful clene . . .
>
> . . . .
>
> Towres telded bytwene, trochet ful þik,
> Fayre fylyolez þat fy3ed, and ferlyly long,
> With coruon coprounes craftyly sle3e.

The delicate masonry, the battlemented towers complete with parapets and pinnacles, reflect contemporary fashions in architecture, indeed, royal tastes.[39] The 'chalkwyt chymnees' which Gawain spots on the roof also correspond to a contemporary development: the increasing taste for domesticity and comfort. In the reign of Edward III chimneys began to replace draughty open windows, which in turn paved the way for the larger open fireplace, in front of which Gawain 'achaufed hym chefly' (883).[40] Even the 'park al aboute'

---

[38] 'A partir du XIIe siècle, il [le donjon] fut parfois flanqué de tours et de tournelles . . . Ces quelques organes de flanquement . . . étaient dessinés avec une grande fantaisie, sans grand souci des nécessités . . .' (Fournier, *Le Château*, 84).

[39] See Nicola Coldstream, 'Art and Architecture in the Late Middle Ages', in *The Later Middle Ages*, ed. Stephen Medcalf (London, 1981), 172–224, at 190.

[40] Ibid. 201. See also John Burke, *Life in the Castle of Medieval England* (London, 1978), 104.

may reflect the increasing trend of emparking woodlands among landlords of the fourteenth century.[41]

Surely the view that the castles in *Perceval* or *Gawain* have an 'aura of the otherworld'[42] is hard to maintain in the light of the recent architectural finesse which these romances portray at such length.

Imaginary Landscapes and the Civilizing Process

Perhaps the most profound polarity to emerge from the analysis of the landscape in Chrétien and *Gawain* is that of the castle and the forest, the court and the wilderness, valorized as beautiful versus bleak, refined versus uncouth. This kind of polarity was not new to the Middle Ages. The dichotomy between centres of civilization, embodied by towns, and the barbarism of the countryside had been a fixture of classical thought. But, as Jacques Le Goff has noted, 'this opposition is not found again in the medieval west, or rather it appeared only in part, when the urban renaissance which began in the twelfth century was accompanied by literary and legal revivals'.[43] The opposition between city and countryside, of which the opposition between castle and forest is a variant,[44] is thus firmly rooted in economic and social developments.

If, in the course of this urban expansion, the city gradually regained its status as the centre of cultural innovation, it also entailed a stigmatization of the forest as the obstacle in its way:

Any progress in medieval western Europe meant clearings, struggle and victory over brushwood and bushes, or, if it was necessary and if tools and

[41] R. E. Glasscock, 'England *circa* 1334', in *A New Historical Geography of England*, ed. H. C. Darby (Cambridge, 1973), 136–85, at 167.

[42] Ackerman, 'Castle Hautdesert', 6–7. Roger Sherman Loomis has a line similar to Ackerman's on Gornemant's castle: *Arthurian Tradition and Chrétien de Troyes* (New York, 1961), 362.

[43] 'The Town as an Agent of Civilisation', in *The Middle Ages*, ed. Carlo M. Cipolla, Fontana Economic History of Europe (London, 1972), 71–106, at 71.

[44] Ibid. 75: 'It should be noted that . . . compared with the insecurity of open country and forest, the castle offered a place of safety of the same kind as the towns. Several of the texts quoted elsewhere associate castle and town . . .'. This was not just so in the twelfth century. In his *Decameron*, Boccaccio refers to castles as 'little cities': 'le castella, che simili erano nella loro picolezza alla città', ed. C. Segre (1966, repr. Milan, 1984), 36. As Le Goff rightly points out, the opposition between city and countryside resurfaces in the Middle Ages as an opposition between 'that which is built and cultivated versus the desert'. See Le Goff, 'The Wilderness in the Medieval West', in *The Medieval Imagination*, trans. A. Goldhammer (Chicago, 1988), 47–59, at 58.

skills permitted, over standing trees, the virgin forest, the 'gaste forêt' of Perceval or Dante's 'selva oscura'.[45]

Inspired by an idea of progress similar to that described by Le Goff, Gerald of Wales expresses his low opinions of the forest and its inhabitants as follows in his *Topographia Hibernica*:

Est autem gens haec gens silvestris, gens inhospita, gens ex bestiis solum et bestialiter vivens; gens a primo pastoralis vitae vivendi modo non recedens. Cum enim a silvis ad agros, ab agris ad villas, civiumque convictus, humani generis ordo processerit, gens haec, agriculturae labores aspernans, et civiles gazas parum affectans, civiumque jura multum detrectans, in silvis et pascuis vitam quam hactenus assueverat nec desuescere novit nec descire. (*Topographia*, III. x)[46]

This is after all a savage nation, an inhospitable people, who live only on beasts and live like them; it is a people who have not progressed much from a primitive life-style. Whereas human civilization has developed from forests to fields, from fields to villages, and from villages to communities of citizens, this people, who scorn agricultural labour, who care little for the riches of commerce, who set no store by the laws of citizenship, hold fast to their former life in woods and meadows, wishing neither to abandon nor to disown it.

The motif of the Wild Forest which appears for the first time in the late twelfth-century *roman courtois*,[47] and Gerald of Wales's redeployment of the Ciceronian account of the advancement of culture from forest to fields to human settlements,[48] are thus intimately bound up with the clearings of the forest and the revival of 'civium convictus' to which the twelfth century gave such an impetus.

Yet, whatever hurdles the forest put in the way of progress, its representation as an enemy of civilization reveals more about the development of a sensibility than about urban renaissance. Already in Gerald of Wales's *Topographia*, the forest represents as much a wilderness of the mind as a geographically locatable place. This is how he describes the Irish, who still have not moved on from their primitive sylvan existence:

[45] Jacques Le Goff, *Medieval Civilisation*, trans. Julia Barrow (Oxford, 1988), 131.
[46] *Giraldus Cambrensis, Opera*, 8 vols., RS (London, 1861–91), vol. v: *Topographia Hibernica*, ed. James F. Dimmock (1867), 151.
[47] Ernst Robert Curtius, *European Literature and the Latin Middle Ages*, trans. Willard R. Trask (New York, 1953), 201.
[48] Cf. Cicero, *De Inventione*, ed. T. E. Page, LCL (London, 1959), I. ii. 2, and *De Oratore*, ed. E. H. Warmington, LCL (London, 1967), I. viii. 33.

Gens igitur haec gens barbara, et vere barbara. Quia non tantum barbaro vestium ritu, verum etiam comis et barbis luxuriantibus, juxta modernas novitates, incultissima; et omnes eorum mores barbarissimi sunt. Sed cum a convictu mores formentur, quoniam a communi terrarum orbe in his extremitatibus, tanquam in orbe quodam altero, sunt tam remoti, et a modestis et morigeratis populis tam segregati, solam nimirum barbariem in qua et nati et nutrituti sapiunt et assuescunt, et tanquam alteram naturam amplectuntur. (*Topographia*, III. x)

This people is barbarous, truly barbarous. For not only do they dress like barbarians, but they let their hair and beards grow wild. Their habits are, judging by modern standards, very coarse. But because manners develop in communities, and since, in these marginal regions, they are so remote from the ordinary world of men—living as it were in a world of their own—and since they are segregated from modest and well-behaved people, they only know and recognize the barbarism in which they were born and bred, and embrace it as their second nature.

As Gerald's deprecatory comments on the Irish make clear, living in forests implies for him barbarity; their habitat on the fringes of communities implies they are cut off from proper behaviour, from the latest fashion in clothing or manners, from order and respect for laws. Gerald's forest, like the Wild Forest of courtly romance, resounds with pejorative moral connotations of brutality and foulness.

Other writers of the period did much to foster these associations. The word *silva* and its derivatives are continually used to describe ignorance or uncouthness. Thus Orderic Vitalis, who in the twelfth century coined the new word *sylvaticus*, used the word to mean '*agrestis, incultus, aspero ingenio*' ('wild, uncultured, and of rude wit').[49] Alan of Lille mentions '*silvestres et rudes*' in the same breath.[50] Dante stretches the connotations of *silva* still further when he warns his audience in the *De vulgari eloquentia* to avoid coarse words ('*verba . . . silvestra propter austeritatem*'), recommending rather the use of a courtly Italian, which may 'root out the thorny bushes from the Italian wood' ('*extirpat sentosos frutices de ytalia silva*').[51] Another medieval writer to exploit the metaphorical resonances of *silva* was Bernardus Silvestris—himself

---

[49] Cf. Du Cange, s.v. 'sylvaticus'.
[50] *Distinctiones*, PL 210, col. 944.
[51] Dante Alighieri, *De vulgari eloquentia*, ed. Vincenzo Mengaldo (Padua, 1967), I. xviii and II. vii.

nicknamed 'Bernardin li Sauvages'[52]—who glossed *silva* as '*obumbratio, ignorantia*' ('dimness, ignorance').[53] In his adaptation of Plato's creation myth in the *Timaeus*, which tells of the transformation of initially formless and chaotic matter into an orderly universe, Bernard Silvestris' description of this primal matter, which through Chalcidius' commentary on the *Timaeus* had become known as *silva*, resounds with connotations of bestiality and uncouthness.[54] To answer Nature's plea that 'the universe be more beautifully wrought', Silva's savageness, lawlessness, and coarseness must be reformed. Noys promises to 'refine away the greater part of her coarseness', to temper her 'rude, undisciplined, and recalcitrant materials', and to transform her 'rough, and as it were, uncivilized strain . . . to co-operation'. Along with the reform of Silva's uncouthness, her anarchical internal warfare disappears: 'Thus the contentious and discordant multitude of warring factions, as though laying aside their arms, entered into a condition of peaceful unity.'[55]

A direct connection between Bernard's *Cosmographia* and the representations of the forest in writers such as Gerald of Wales or the courtly romancers has never been proved, although the similarity between the Wild Forest and Bernard's *silva* has kindled critical discussion.[56] But even without positing a direct connection, it is possible to see in these various works a coherent mentality in which the forest figures as an imagined space of brutality and

[52] In Henri D'Andeli's *Bataille des vii ars*, ed. L. J. Paetow (Berkeley, Calif., 1914), l. 328. Etymologically, 'silva' and 'sauvage' are indeed related; on the significance of the etymology of 'silva' see Roland Bechmann, *Trees and Man: The Forest in the Middle Ages* (New York, 1990), 283.

[53] *The Commentary on the First Six Books of the Aeneid of Vergil Commonly Attributed to Bernardus Silvestris*, ed. Julian Ward Jones and Elizabeth Francis Jones (Lincoln, Nebr., 1977), 94.

[54] For Bernard's new departures in his representation of *silva* see Brian Stock, *Myth and Science in the Twelfth Century: A Study of Bernardus Silvestris* (Princeton, NJ, 1972), 63–137.

[55] Bernardus Silvestris, *Cosmographia*, trans. Winthrop Wetherbee (New York, 1973), 67–73. For the Latin, see Peter Dronke's edition of the *Cosmographia* (Leiden, 1978), 96, 99–101.

[56] See Leo Pollman, *Chrétien de Troyes und der Conte du Graal* (Tübingen, 1965), 83–99, and Pierre Gallais, *Perceval et l'initiation* (Paris, 1972), 22–3. For discussions of the influence of Bernard's thought on the vernacular poets in general see Peter Dronke's edition of the *Cosmographia*, 12–15; Peter Dronke and Jill Mann, 'Chaucer and the Medieval Latin Poets', in *Geoffrey Chaucer*, ed. D. S. Brewer (London, 1974), 154–83, at 154–72; and Winthrop Wetherbee, *Platonism and Poetry in the Twelfth Century* (Princeton, NJ, 1972).

coarseness that must be conquered or transcended for a 'more beautifully wrought world' to appear.[57]

Precisely as an imagined space, the Wild Forest survives long after it posed any real threat to the progress of civilization. Even in Chrétien's days the Counts of Champagne, always quick to see opportunities for economic exploitation, had established their rule over uncultivated areas by leasing wastelands to farmers, or by building castles in the forests and marches of their principality to stimulate agrarian activity. In their flight from the world, Cistercians founded new monasteries in wastelands, and from these pockets of civilization set out to tame the wilderness and to extirpate pagan beliefs, two projects which were firmly linked in the medieval mind.[58] Yet while assarts were gradually clearing the wildernesses, their importance in Chrétien's *œuvre* was only to increase. Nor did this end with Chrétien. As we have seen, the motif of the 'gaste forest' was alive and well in the works of his continuators. In late medieval England, where the countryside no longer differed substantially from the way it is now,[59] the forest continued to be thought of as 'perilous, beyond law, antithetical to human values'.[60] Take, for example, John Trevisa's translation of the encyclopedia *De proprietatibus rerum*:

In woode is place of deceipte . . . There place is of hydynge and of lurkynge, for ofte in wodes þeues beþ yhudde and oftere in here awaytes and deceytes passynge men comeþ and beþ yspoyled and yrobbed and ofte yslawe. Also for many and dyuerse weyes and vncerteyn straunge men ofte erreþ and goth oute of þe weye, and takeþ vncerteyn weye and þe weye þat is vnknowe tofore þe weye þat is yknowe, and comeþ ofte to place þere þeues liggeþ in awayte and nouȝt wiþoute perille . . .[61]

[57] Bernard's anthropocentric descriptions of *silva* would support this view. As Stock writes, 'Bernard uses the same language—*cultus, rudis, silvestris,* and *asperitas*—to describe the unrefined state of matter as did Macrobius to portray the uncultivated state of man before the arrival of civilization': *Myth and Science*, 81. See on this point also Saunders, *The Forest*, 22–4. Bernard's creation myth is in other words as much a myth of progress as Gerald of Wales's *Topographia*.

[58] Bechmann, *Trees and Man*, 287.

[59] Rackham, *Trees and Woodland*, 49, and Duby, *L'Économie rurale*, 153.

[60] V. A. Kolve, *Chaucer and the Imagery of Narrative: The First Five Canterbury Tales* (London, 1984), 111. Kolve's discussion of the *Knight's Tale* has many relevant comments about the polarity between castle and forest. On this subject see also Paul Piehler's *The Visionary Landscape: A Study in Medieval Allegory* (London, 1971), 73–6, 111–17; Wilhelm Ganzemüller, *Das Naturgefühl im Mittelalter* (Leipzig, 1914); and Derek Pearsall and Elizabeth Salter, *Landscapes and Seasons of the Medieval World* (London, 1973).

[61] Bartholomaeus Anglicus, *On the Properties of Things*, trans. John Trevisa, ed. M. C. Seymour *et al.*, 2 vols. (Oxford, 1975), ii. 1040–1.

And so deserte is vntiliede and ful of þornes and pricchinge busshes, place of crepyng wormes and venymouse bestes and of wylde bestes, and it is þe home of flemyd men and of þeues . . . londe of wastynge and grysenesse, londe of mysgoynge and of errynge.[62]

Thus Trevisa translated the misgivings of the thirteenth-century Franciscan Bartholomaeus Anglicus, whose bias may well reflect his Order's vested interests in the town or the city which it had preferred to the countryside as a base for its activities.[63] At any rate, the forest or the desert of his encyclopedia continues to be imagined in terms of the 'gaste forest' as invented by twelfth-century romance.

It is this imagined wilderness that the mythical figure of the Wild Man inhabits. It is no coincidence that this fiction of savageness and bestiality exerted such a fascination on medieval writers from the twelfth century onwards.[64] For, as a representation of crudeness and barbarity, this creature who lived in the forest is inextricably bound up with the myth of progress from forest to fields and settlements which writers such as Gerald of Wales revived. The route which Yvain follows as he flees from his fellow men to live 'com hom forsenez et salvage' (2830)—a route which takes him from 'paveillons' (2805) to 'chans' (2809) to enclosed woodland, 'parc' (2817), to the 'bois' (2826)—is in fact an inversion of Gerald's trajectory of civilization. The fiction of this primitive being outlasted the twelfth century as well. According to Froissart's chronicles, King Charles VI of France, who did so much to establish the Parisian court as the centre of fashion and elegance,[65] owed his periodic insanity to an encounter with a Wild Man during a foray through the forest.[66] In the *Gawain*-poet's work, too, the figure lives on, not only in the 'wodwos' who attack Gawain in the wilderness of Wirral but also

[62] Ibid. 721.

[63] On the friars' economic dependence on an urban environment, see R. W. Southern, *Western Society and the Church in the Middle Ages* (Harmondsworth, 1970), 273–7. Bartholomaeus Anglicus himself wrote and taught in Paris.

[64] Bernheimer, *Wild Men*, 21. A related and contemporary development is the interest in monsters, who, from the twelfth century onwards, invade the margins of manuscripts or the woodwork of cathedrals. In the words of Jean-Claude Schmitt, 'Image d'une apparente inversion de l'ordre de la nature et de la culture, qui est au centre de la réflexion philosophique, morale, et esthétique du clercs, le monstre devient à cette épôque plus utile que jamais, car la transgression sert à l'affirmation de la norme': *La Raison des gestes dans l'Occident médiévale* (Paris, 1990), 186.

[65] Gervase Mathew, *The Court of Richard II* (London, 1968), 7–9.

[66] The episode has been analysed by Penelope Doob, *Nebuchadnezzar's Children: Conventions of Madness in the Middle Ages* (New Haven, Conn., 1974), 45–6.

in the story of Nebuchadnezzar in *Cleanness*, who, as a punishment for his presumption, is banished from the easy living of the court and condemned to a life of bestiality in the wild:

> his solace he leues,
> And carfully is outkast to contre vnknawen,
> Fer into a fyr fryth þere frekes neuer comen.
> His hert heldet vnhole, he hoped non oþer
> Bot a best þat he be . . .
>
> (*Cleanness*, 1678–82)[67]

Surely the processes of urban renaissance can do little to explain the lasting popularity of the 'fyr fryth' or the Wild Man. It may be more promising to look for answers to the cultivation of politeness, courtliness, refinement, and civilized forms of behaviour. To develop such concepts, and to ensure they remain meaningful, one cannot but at the same time imagine their contraries. As Jean de Meun put it:

> Ainsinc va des contreres choses,
> les unes sunt des autres gloses;
> et qui l'une an veust defenir,
> de l'autre li doit souvenir,
> ou ja, par nule antancion,
> n'i metra diffinicion . . .
>
> (*Roman de la Rose*, 21543–8)[68]

Thus it goes with opposites, the one is the gloss of the other; and he who wants to define one must remember the other, or he will never define it, whatever he tries.

In promulgating ideas of civilization and good manners, the Forest and the Wild Man provide the opposites essential in creating and stabilizing these ideas. As a 'souvenir de l'autre' they appeared and continued to be called to mind.

Hence the prominence of the motif of the 'gaste forest' in the romances of Chrétien and *Gawain*. As we will see in the following chapter on hospitality, the cultivation of proper behaviour is absolutely central to their romances. Their commitment to ideals of *courtoisie*, the high standards of refinement and delicacy imperative at court, inevitably entails a similar emphasis on coarseness and a

---

[67] *Cleanness*, ed. J. J. Anderson (Manchester, 1977).
[68] Guillaume de Lorris and Jean de Meun, *Le Roman de la Rose*, ed. F. Lecoy, 3 vols. (Paris, 1976–82), vol. iii.

locus to which it is intrinsic. For what is courtliness or civilization but the invention of boorishness and wild places, the superimposition of a landscape of the mind on that of matter?

Admittedly, the forest is at times seen differently in their romances. In the hunting scenes in *Gawain* it appears as a source of vitality, a place where natural forces can be confronted in their most elementary form, in contrast to the oblique cut and thrust that typifies *courtoisie* in, for example, the temptation scenes. The forest evokes in these scenes not repulsion but sheer elation. Here Bertilac hunts the boar 'for blys abloy' (1174). Chrétien represents the forest as hunting-ground with similar exhilaration. As Manfred Gsteiger summarizes: 'What is emphasized in the forest as hunting-ground is not its danger but its positive and life-giving qualities.'[69] The same sense of liberation which the hunt in the forest inspires comes across in Richard Fitz Nigel's description of the benefits of forests in the *Dialogue of the Exchequer*, written around the same time as Chrétien's romances:

In forestis enim penetralia regum sunt et eorum maxime delicie. Ad has enim uenandi causa, curis quandoque depositis, accedunt ut modica quiete recreentur. Illic, seriis simul et innatis curie tumultibus omissis, in naturalis libertatis gratiam paulisper respirant . . .[70]

In the forests are the sanctuaries of kings and their great delights. Here they go hunting, and having set their worries aside, they come here to get some rest. Here, unburdened by the hectic life at court, they can catch their breath in the freedom of nature . . .

Yet the forest as hunting-ground appears in these instances, no less than the 'gaste forest', as an imagined landscape, structured by the same binary opposition between castle and forest, court and wilderness, tilted this time in favour of the forest as a place which offers a release from the 'tumultibus' of the court.

Moreover, there is an important historical distinction between the forest as hunting-ground and the wild forest which may help to account for its different valorization in literature. The forest in

[69] '[Als Jagdgrund] ist nicht ein gefahrdrohender Aspekt in den Vordergrund gerückt, sondern ein positiver, vital-lebensspendender' (Gsteiger, *Landschaftschilderungen*, 21). Gsteiger's observations hold true for courtly romances in general. Cf. the similar findings of Uwe Ruberg, *Raum und Zeit im Prosa-Lancelot* (Munich, 1965), 58–62, or Ulrich von Zatzikhoven's *Lanzelet*, which combines repugnant descriptions of forests (713–17) with idyllic evocations of the forest as a hunting-ground (3988–95).
[70] *Dialogus de Scaccario*, ed. and trans. Charles Johnson (London, 1950), 60.

which Bertilac and his retainers hunt is presumably the 'park' observed by Gawain, a stretch of woodland enclosed by landlords for the purpose of hunting.[71] In this sense, too, we meet the word in Chrétien's *Yvain* where Yvain robs a stunned hunter of his bow and arrows in a 'parc' (2817) on his way to the forest proper where he lives like an animal, in temporary derangement. From a historical perspective, these enclosed woodlands may best be seen as forests jealously guarded against cultivation in order to safeguard a preserve for the exclusive and therefore immensely prestigious re-creation of the hunt. Rather than wild forests, these were forests whose wildness was carefully preserved from the tides of progress which were sweeping later medieval Europe; these forests had been deliberately kept 'gaste'.[72] As Chrétien and the *Gawain*-poet were still vividly imagining the Wild Forest when it was disappearing or had disappeared, the nobility of France and England in their way preserved the 'gaste forest', a 'souvenir de l'autre', a memory of the Wild Forest in a rapidly changing countryside. Their forests, en-closed or marked off from the surrounding landscape by strict boundary lines,[73] offered no less than a ritualized encounter with the brute forces of nature. The exhilaration with which Chrétien and the *Gawain*-poet express this encounter comes closer to acknow-ledging the fecundity of the Forest as an indispensable construct and realm of experience on which civilization feeds and depends for meaning and self-definition.

The same need drives the knight to confront the forest in his quest. For while civilization may be based on the repression of wildness, it cannot be fully removed. Civilizations, as Mary Douglas writes, are like gardens: 'if all the weeds are removed, the soil is impoverished. Somehow the gardener must preserve fertility by returning what he

[71] A brief elucidation of the meaning of the word 'park' in the Middle Ages is provided by W. G. Hoskins, *The Making of the English Landscape* (Harmonds-worth, 1955), 93.

[72] Forest laws, as implemented by the Counts of Champagne and the English kings and nobility, prohibited the clearing of any part of the forest for timber or agricul-tural exploitation. Enforcing a monopoly over the hunt and the grounds required for it, forest laws put a check on the conversion of woodland into arable land. See Charles Petit-Dutaillis, 'The Forest', trans. W. T. Waugh, in *Studies and Notes Supplementary to Stubbs's Constitutional History*, 3 vols. (Manchester, 1914), i. 147–251, and Young, *Royal Forests*, 117–22. On the conflicting interests of economic exploitation on the one hand and the preservation of hunting-grounds on the other, with particular reference to the Counts of Champagne, see Duby, *L'Économie rurale*, 154.

[73] Rackham, *Trees and Woodland*, 49, 68.

has taken out.'[74] And so the knight, whether in the hunt or on adventure, must ride out into the forest, bearing the castle into the wilderness, and bringing back something of the wilderness to the castle.[75]

Apart from the hunting scenes, however, the forest appears in the courtly romances as the reprehensible counterpart of court and castle. And as we see the landscape through the eyes of the poets of these romances, we cannot fail to detect the vantage point they look out from. Their abhorrence of the forest, and the uncouthness which characterizes it, reveal much about the sense of their own place, which is unmistakably that of the city or the court, the vanguard of civilization and high culture.

Their descriptions of castles communicate precisely their self-assertion as cultivators of refinement. In their descriptive design, each detail evokes the power, richness, but, above all, the taste of its owner. Risen above the plane of mere defensive necessity, the castles in Chrétien and the *Gawain*-poet are demonstrations of elegance at its most modern. When Guivret points out King Evrain's splendid castle to Erec, he explains that Evrain built the magnificent front not for defensive reasons but because of its aesthetic appeal:

> fermer ne le fist il mie
> por ce qu'il dotast nules genz,
> mes li chastiax an est plus genz . . . (*Erec*, 5360–2)

He did not fortify it out of fear for anyone, but because it would make the castle more handsome.

This is the destiny of Castle Hautdesert, Evrain's Brandigant, or Gornemant's castle: to be designed and to be beheld by connoisseurs of architecture rather than by warmongering knights. The aestheticization of the defensive rampart represents yet another victory of civilization over bare existence and a celebration of the possibilities of culture.

---

[74] *Purity and Danger: An Analysis of the Concepts of Pollution and Taboo* (1966, repr. London, 1989), 163.

[75] I owe this point to A. C. Spearing's paper 'Public and Private Spaces in *Sir Gawain and the Green Knight*', read at the International Congress on Medieval Studies, Kalamazoo, Mich., 1993.

2 The Convention of Hospitality

Introduction

I HAVE suggested in my previous chapter that the representation of the landscape shows Chrétien and the *Gawain*-poet's marked interest in the cultivation of refinement. If one concept encapsulates this preoccupation in their Arthurian romances as a whole, it is the notion of *courtoisie*. The concept is notoriously difficult to define, but, as Henri Dupin observed in his study of the meaning of courtesy, the art of hosting strangers and acting a fitting part as a guest was a crucial accomplishment of the *chevalier courtois*.[1] As Philippe de Navarre wrote in his early thirteenth-century *Quatre Ages de l'homme*, the young knight:

doit estre cortois et larges, *et accoilir biau la gent*, et faire cortoisement a plaisir selonc son pooir as privez et as estranges. (*Quatre Ages*, p. 38)[2]

should be courtly and liberal, and receive people well, and be as nice and courteous as possible to friends and strangers.

It is not surprising, then, that courtly romances dwell on hospitality scenes at such length, for they offer a fine opportunity for analysing the art of 'accoilir biau la gent'. In the first section of this chapter I shall compare the hospitality scenes in *Gawain* with those of Old French Arthurian romances, and show that both represent a

[1] *La Courtoisie au Moyen Age* (Paris, 1931), 27–8. See also Joachim Bumke's seminal study *Höfische Kultur: Literatur und Gesellschaft im hohen Mittelalter*, 2 vols. (Munich, 1986), ii. 425–30.

[2] Philippe de Navarre, *Les Quatre Ages de l'homme*, ed. M. de Fréville, SATF (Paris, 1888). Cf. the definition of courtesy in *L'Enseignement* (457–60) by the twelfth-century Provençal poet Garin le Brun: 'Cortesia es en guarnir | e en gent accuilir; | cortesia es d'onrar | e es en gen parlar . . .' ('Courtliness consists of taking care of people and receiving them. Courtliness lies in honouring and talking to people . . .'). '*L'Enseignement* de Garin le Brun', ed. Carl Appel, *Revue des langues romanes*, 33 (1889), 403–22. Andreas Capellanus, too, mentions hospitality as an essential social grace. The courtly lover should readily provide hospitality to strangers: 'Hospitalem se cunctis debet praestare libenter.' *De Amore*, ed. P. G. Walsh (London, 1982), 84.

remarkably similar protocol of hospitality, which, as we shall see, is intimately connected with the etiquette prescribed by the courtesy books of the period.

In the careful observance of an etiquette of hospitality, the court is diametrically opposed to the forest. The forest, as we have seen, appears in courtly romance as a zero-point of hospitality, a place of savageness, disorder, and uncouthness. As Gerald of Wales writes in his *Topographia*, a 'gens silvestris' is at the same time a 'gens inhospita', characterized by coarseness and, so it follows, by a lack of respect for the rules of hospitality.[3] Unlike the ferocious forest-dwellers, the guests and hosts of courtly romance display a consummate feel for the finer points of behaviour. Both the *Gawain* poet, and Chrétien and his continuators, valued this cultural mastery of instinct highly, and actively promoted it in their romances.

It may appear that the ceremonials which regulate the interaction between guest and host make the host's court a safer abode than the 'gaste forest'. Certainly the courtly knights themselves breathe with a sense of security when they emerge from the forest and can make their renewed acquaintance with the rituals of courtly society. But this sense of security can be false. For one thing, situations in which strangers take hospitality from strangers have always been permeated with ambiguity and potential conflict, and all advanced cultures have found it necessary to subject the stages of hospitality to an elaborate protocol in order to minimize the risk of collision.[4] The etiquette of hospitality in courtly romance, too, attempts to regulate the movements of guest and host, and the very fact that this regulation is deemed necessary should alert us to their underlying danger.

There is a second reason why hospitality scenes are surrounded by uncertainty. Behaviour based on codified etiquette can be consciously acted and dissembled. Guest and host may follow the rules of hospitality but who is to tell what feelings or what intentions the studied observance of etiquette hides? As court-criticism never tires of observing, the glaring dangers of the forest may in fact be

---

[3] Gerald of Wales, *Topographia*, 151. Wildness and inhospitableness are thus virtual synonyms. Cf. the opening line of Petrarch's sonnet 176: 'Per mezz'i boschi inospiti et selvaggi' ('Amidst the inhospitable and savage forests'); *Petrarch's Lyric Poems*, ed. Robert M. Durling (Cambridge, Mass., 1976).

[4] Felicity Heal, *Hospitality in Early Modern Europe* (Oxford, 1990), 6–9.

preferable to the potentially deceptive surfaces of courtly interaction.[5] In the forest you at least recognize an enemy when you see one. In the final two sections of this chapter I shall look at the dangers of hospitality for the Arthurian knights, and at the way Chrétien and the *Gawain*-poet, in particular, exploit the dramatic potential of hospitality. Far from being a marginal incident, motivated by the law of nature that knights on quests need places to stay, hospitality becomes in their romances an adventure in its own right, one which determines the outcome of their quests in the narrative developments to come.

The Etiquette of Hospitality

In his article '*Sir Gawain and the Green Knight* and the Expectations of Romance',[6] John Finlayson has noted the affinity between the hospitality episode in *Gawain* and those in the Old French *roman courtois*. Indeed, the *Gawain*-poet himself seems to indicate his indebtedness to French models when he refers to the elaborately polite behaviour at Castle Hautdesert as 'frenkish fare' (1116). Nevertheless, no source study has systematically explored the relationship between hospitality in *Gawain* and Old French romance. Because of the one-sided concern of previous source studies with the plot of the English romance, it is easy to see why the *Gawain*-poet's handling of the convention of hospitality has been largely ignored. Lengthy as the descriptions of Gawain's reception are, they contribute little to the plot-line. A beheading game or an exchange of winnings have caught the eye, but the details of a knight entering a castle, being made welcome, dining, and leaving again have been considered too insignificant to merit any careful attention.

This lack of interest in hospitality, however misguided in the study of courtly romances, seems to have been largely shared by the writers of Middle English romances. The author of *Sir Perceval of Galles*, who adapted Chrétien's *Perceval* and the *First Continuation*,

[5] See, for example, Geoffrey of Monmouth's *Vita Merlini*, ll. 542–7, ed. E. Faral, *La Légende arthurienne: Études et documents*, 3 vols. (1929, repr. Paris, 1969), vol. iii, and Sir Francis Bryant, *Dispraise of the Life of a Courtier* (London, 1548), cap. 4.
[6] *Genre*, 12 (1979), 1–24. The similarities have also been noted by Hanneke Wirtjes, 'Bertilak de Hautdesert and the Literary Vavasour', *English Studies*, 64 (1984), 291–301.

wasted no time on long descriptions of Perceval's stay with a hospitable host. The hero and the host arrive at the castle and take their seats at the dinner table without needless ceremony:

> Þe blythere wexe þe knyghte.
> By his haulle þaire gates felle,
> And ȝerne he prayed Percyvell,
> Þat he solde þer with hym duelle
> And be þer all þat nyghte.
> Full wele he couthe a geste calle;
> He broghte þe childe in to þe haulle,
> So faire he spake hym with-alle
> Þat he es doun lyghte;
> His stede es in stable sett
> And hym-selfe to þe haulle fett,
> And þan with-owtten any lett
> To þe mette þay þam dighte.   (936–48)[7]

Like the heroes who hasten to table, the romancer perfunctorily rushes through the hospitality scene 'with-owtten any lett'. The difference between this passage and Gawain's reception at Castle Hautdesert is conspicuous. In leisurely fashion the *Gawain*-poet develops his descriptions of hospitality, elaborating on its various motifs without worrying about the most succinct or economical way of advancing the story. The decorous exterior is precisely what captures the *Gawain*-poet's imagination. There is in his work a correlation between the lavishness of Gawain's reception and the *Gawain*-poet's own rhetorical amplification, a correlation which critics have long noted to be characteristic of the *roman courtois*.[8] The ceremoniousness and sumptuousness displayed by characters in the courtly romance call for a corresponding extravagance on the part of the romancer. Long descriptions of meals and rich attire in the romances of *Gawain* and Chrétien de Troyes are a case in point. If, as Geoffrey de Vinsauf recommends, literary motifs and devices should be as rich and varied as courses of a banquet,[9] then these

---

[7] Ed. J. Campion and F. Holthausen, Alt- und Mittelenglische Texte 5 (Heidelberg, 1913).

[8] Paul Zumthor, 'Le Roman courtois: Essai de définition', *Études littéraires*, 4 (1971), 75–90. This correlation in *Gawain* has been noted by Derek Pearsall, 'Rhetorical *Descriptio* in *Sir Gawain and the Green Knight*', MLR 50 (1955), 129–34.

[9] Geoffrey de Vinsauf, *Poetria Nova*, ed. and trans. Ernest Gallo, *The Poetria Nova and its Sources in Early Rhetorical Doctrine* (The Hague, 1971), ll. 265–71 and 562–4.

romancers give us no less of a treat than the one their fictional hosts provide for their guests.[10] But, apart from stylistic parallels, the *Gawain*-poet overlaps with the techniques of the *roman courtois* in content. The similarities between the conventions of hospitality within which both work may be borne out by focusing on individual motifs of hospitality, which represent a single action, and which in combination describe the progression of the knight from arrival to departure.[11]

In *Gawain*, the hero calls the porter, and is kindly offered hospitality on his request.

> He calde, and sone þer com
> A porter pure plesaunt,
> On þe wal his ernd he nome,
> And haylsed þe knyȝt erraunt.
>
> 'Gode sir,' quoþ Gawan, 'woldez þou go myn ernde
> To þe heȝ lorde of þis hous, herber to crave?'
> 'Ȝe, Peter,' quoþ þe porter, 'and purely I trowee
> Þat ȝe be, wyȝe, welcum to won quyle yow lykez.'   (807–14)

The questing maiden in *Yvain*, who, as we have seen in the previous chapter, emerges from the forest and enters on the road to her lodgings with similar good fortune, likewise addresses the porter who greets her and offers her hospitality:

> Tantost con la gueite la voit,
> si la salüe et puis descent
> et la clef de la porte prent

[10] In contrast, when describing an attire or a meal which is poor or mediocre, Chrétien often cuts his descriptions abruptly short: 'Del hernois a parler ne fet, | car la grande povretez ne let . . .' (*Erec*, 735–6), or 'S'il fu bien serviz au soper | De ce ne quier je ja parler' (*Lancelot*, 2071–2).

[11] I have profited greatly from Matilda Tomaryn Bruckner's thorough discussion of the convention of hospitality and its motifs: *Narrative Invention in Twelfth-Century French Romance: The Convention of Hospitality (1160–1200)* (Lexington, Ky., 1980). A similarly rich treatment of the theme is given by Marie-Luce Chênerie, *Le Chevalier errant dans les romans arthuriens en vers des XIIe et XIIIe siècles* (Geneva, 1986), 503–91, and Hugo Oschinsky, *Der Ritter unterwegs und die Pflege der Gastfreundschaft*, published dissertation (Halle, 1900). See also the section on hospitality in E. H. Ruck's *An Index of Themes and Motifs in Twelfth-Century French Arthurian Poetry* (Cambridge, 1991), 49–51; J. Mandel's 'Proper Behaviour in Chrétien's *Charrete*: The Guest–Host Relationship', *French Review*, 48 (1974–5), 683–9; Charles Foulon, 'Les Quatre Repas de Perceval', in *Mélanges J. Wathelet-Willems* (Liège, 1978), 147–87; and K. Halasz, *Structures narratives chez Chrétien de Troyes* (Debrecen, 1980), 64–78.

si li oevre et dit: 'Bien veigniez,
pucele, qui que vos soiez.
Anquenuit avroiz boen hostel.'
—'Je ne demant enuit mes el,'
fet la pucele . . .   (*Yvain*, 4878–85)

As soon as the porter sees her, he greets her, then descends, brings the key to the gate, opens it and says: 'Welcome, maiden, whoever you may be. This night you will be well lodged.' 'That is all I ask for tonight,' the maiden replies . . .

Greetings, requests, and offers of hospitality are exchanged between the questing damsel, Gawain, and the porters. Before long, Gawain finds himself surrounded by helpful servants who run out to meet him, and kneel down to honour him:

Þen ȝede the wyȝe ȝerne and com aȝayn swyþe,
And folke frely hym wyth, to fonge þe knyȝt.
Þay let doun þe grete draȝt and derely out ȝeden,
And kneled doun on her knes vpon þe colde erþe
To welcum þis ilk wyȝ as worþy hom þoȝt . . .   (815–9)

Compare this with Yvain's reception. In his case, too, the inhabitants of the castle lower the drawbridge so that they can rush out to meet their guest with honour:

La plus droite voie s'en va
mes sire Yvains vers le recet;
et vaslet saillent jusqu'a set,
qui li ont un pont avalé,
si li sont a l'encontre alé.   (*Yvain*, 3778–83)

Sir Yvain takes the straightest way to the castle; and as many as seven servants jump up. Having lowered the bridge, they come to meet him.

In Chrétien's *Perceval*, too, a multitude of servants throng around to assist their guest Gawain:

Atant vindrent vaslet a flotes,
et tuit mout bien vestu de cotes,
si se metent tuit a genolz . . .   (*Perceval*, 7631–3)

Promptly numerous servants come, all well-dressed, and they all kneel down . . .

Like the 'folk' of Castle Hautdesert, they kneel down to receive him worthily. When the English Gawain next enters and dismounts, his hosts are quick to take care of his horse, and to disarm him:

Þay ȝolden hym þe brode ȝate, ȝarked vp wyde,
And he hem raysed rekenly, and rod ouer þe brygge.
Sere seggez hym sesed by sadel, quel he lyȝt,
And syþen stabeled his stede stif men innoȝe.
Knyȝtez and swyerez comen doun þenne
For to bryng þis buurne wyth blys into halle;
Quen he hef vp his helme, þer hiȝed innoghe
For to hent hit at his honde, þe hende to seruen . . .   (820–7)

Again the *Gawain*-poet uses four standard motifs of hospitality: 'enter', 'dismount', 'take care of horse', and 'disarm'. Compare the procedure with the following passages from Chrétien's *Perceval*:

Par sor le pont s'an est alez,
et vaslet corent contre lui,
quatre, sel desarment li dui,
et li tierz son cheval an moinne,
si li done fuerre et avoinne.   (*Perceval*, 3058–62)

He proceeds to the bridge, and four servants run towards him; two disarm him, a third leads away his horse, and gives it hay and oats.

Vers un palés covert d'atoise
l'ont li .iiii. sergent mené
et descendu et desarmé.   (*Perceval*, 1772–4)

The four servants lead him towards a slated hall, and they helped him dismount and disarm.

After these preliminaries, the guest can be made comfortable. Sir Gawain is placed before the fireplace on a chair decked out with soft cushions, and he is given a mantle better suited to life indoors:

A cheyer before þe chemné, þer charcole brenned,
Watz grayþed for Sir Gawan grayþely with cloþez,
Whyssynes vpon queldepoyntes þat koynt wer boþe;
And þenne a meré mantyle watz on þat mon cast
Of a broun bleeaunt, enbrauded ful ryche
And fayre furred wythinne with fellez of þe best,
Alle of ermyn in erde, his hode of þe same;
And he sete in þat settel semlych ryche,
And achaufed hym chefly, and þenne his cher mended.   (875–83)

Much has been made of Gawain's change of clothes. It has been argued that the replacement of armour by a mantle suggests a moral laxity on the part of Gawain, but the opposite is true. The change of outfit is part of the protocol of hospitality, and to keep one's armour on amounts to a breach of etiquette which implies that the guest is hostile or suspicious about his hosts.[12] Like Gawain, the heroes of Chrétien are clothed in a mantle after they have been disarmed:

> A vestir desor sa chemise
> li a baillié un nuef sorcot,
> et un mantel sanz harigot,
> veir d'escarlate, au col li met . . . (*Yvain*, 5420-3)

She gave him a fine surcoat to wear over his shirt, and she put around his shoulders a mantle without holes, trimmed with fur.

And, like Gawain, Chrétien's heroes are seated in a comfortable place which their hosts have prepared for them. Thus, Erec, too, finds the seats in front of the fire fitted out with cushions:

> La dame an ert devant alee
> qui la meison ot atornee;
> coutes porpointes et tapiz,
> ot estanduz par sor les liz
> ou il se sont asis tuit troi:
> Erec la pucele ot lez soi
> et li sires de l'autre part.
> Li feus molt clers devant ax art. (*Erec*, 477-84)

The lady had gone ahead to make the house ready; she had spread embroidered quilts and coverlets on the beds, where all three of them sat down. Erec sat beside the maiden and, on his other side, beside the lord. The fire was burning brightly before them.

While the guest relaxes, the meal is prepared, the table is set with all the essentials, including the bowls of water for washing hands:

> Sone watz telded vp a tabil on trestez ful fayre,
> Clad wyth a clene cloþe that cler quyt schewed,
> Sanap, and salure, and syluerin sponez.
> Þe wyȝe wesche at his wylle, and went to his mete.
> Seggez hym serued semly innoȝe . . .   (884-8)

Compare the table arrangements sketched by Chrétien:

> Par l'uis qu'il ont trové overt
> antrent anz, et voient covert
> un dois d'un tablier grant et lé;
> et sus estoient aporté
> li mes, et les chandoiles mises

---

[12] See. *Perlesvaus*, p. 203.

es chandeliers totes esprises,
et li henap d'argent doré,
et dui pot, l'uns plains de moré
et li autres de fort vin blanc.
Delez le dois, au chief d'un banc,
troverent deus bacins toz plains
d'eve chaude a laver lor mains.   (*Lancelot*, 983–94)

They entered through the door, which they found open, and saw the table covered with a big and wide table-cloth, on which their meal had been placed, and burning candles set in holders, and silver-gilt goblets, and two pots, one full of mulberry wine and the other full of strong white wine. Beside the table, at the end of a bench, they found two basins full of warm water so that they could wash their hands.

When the hands have been washed, the heroes of courtly romance can finally start to eat. Only after a detailed discussion of the polite rituals of hospitality do Chrétien and the *Gawain*-poet get around to the dinner, a stage at which the author of *Sir Perceval* has already arrived after a couple of lines.

The attention devoted to etiquette persists. After a day spent in the lap of luxury, Gawain tells Bertilac he has to leave, but Bertilac courteously insists that his guest should stay:

Þe lorde fast can hym payne
To holde lenger þe kny3t;
To hym answarez Gawayn
Bi non way þat he my3t.   (1042–5)

Compare this with Arthur's polite but fruitless insistence in *Erec*:

Ancor de remenoir l'enortent
li rois et tuit li chevalier;
mes proiere n'i a mestier,
que por rien ne volt demorer. (*Erec*, 4258–61)

Yet again the king and all the knights ask him to stay, but the pleading is to no avail, because there is nothing that can make him stay.

When Bertilac informs Gawain that the Green Chapel is nearby, his attempts to keep Gawain at Hautdesert pay off. When he himself cannot be around to look after his guest, he delegates his duties to someone else, so that all his needs can be met:

3e schal lenge in your lofte, and ly3e in your ese
To-morn quyle þe messequyle, and to mete wende

When ȝe wyl, wyth my wyf, þat wyth yow schall sitte
And comfort yow with company, til I to cort torne . . . (1096–9)

In Chrétien's *Perceval*, the host likewise excuses himself when the
hunt prevents him from attending to his guest, but he assures
Gawain that he will have delightful company until his return:

> Bien est hui mes tans et reisons
> de herbergier, s'il ne vos poise.
> J'ai une seror mout cortoise,
> qui de vos grant joie fera.
>
> .   .   .   .   .   .
>
> Tel solaz et tel conpaignie
> li face, se ne li poist mie,
> tant que nos soions revenu.   (*Perceval*, 5656–75)

It is now the right time and occasion to take lodging, if you do not mind. I
have a very courtly sister, who will receive you joyously . . . She will make
him comfortable, and keep him such company as will not displease him,
until we have returned.

In the morning the religious duties are piously observed:

> And he ryches hym to ryse, and rapes hym sone,
> Clepes to his chamberlayn, choses his wede,
> Boȝez forth, quen he watz boun, blyþely to masse . . . (1309–11)

> Au main . . .
>
> .   .   .   .   .
>
> se leva mout isnelemant
> mes sire Yvains et sa pucele;
> s'oïrent a une chapele
> messe . . .   (*Yvain*, 5442–9)

In the morning . . . Yvain and the maiden get up quickly to hear mass in a
chapel . . .

Then, before setting off, the guests remind their hosts of their plans
and the arrangements for their departure on the following day, and
politely ask their permission to leave:

> Þenne loȝly his leue at þe lorde fyrst
> Fochchez þis fre mon, and fayre he hym þonkkes:
> 'Of such a selly soiorne as I haf hade here,
> Your honour at þis hyȝe fest, the hyȝe kyng yow ȝelde!
> I ȝef yow me for on of yourez, if yowreself lykez,
> For I mot nedes, as ȝe wot, meue to-morne,

And ȝe me take sum tolke to teche, as ȝe hyȝt,
Þe gate to þe grene chapel . . .'   (1960–7)

> Erec li dist au congié prandre
> 'Sire, je ne puis plus atandre
> que je ne m'an aille an ma terre;
> feites apareillier et querre
> que j'aie tot mon estovoir:
> je voldrai par matin movoir,
> tantost com il iert ajorné.   (*Erec*, 5217–23)

Erec says to him as he takes his leave, 'Sir, I can no longer delay my return home. Have my things made ready and prepared. I want to leave this morning, at the early dawn.'

These passages clearly demonstrate that the *Gawain*-poet was familiar with the way the Old French *roman courtois* describes hospitality. I am not suggesting that the *Gawain*-poet was slavishly following Chrétien. The motifs of hospitality—request and offer hospitality, go forward to meet, kneel down, dismount, disarm, take care of horse, keep company, set table, wash hands, ask to stay, ask leave—are, after all, only commonplace in many courtly romances.[13] Rather than supporting claims of borrowing, originality, and imitation, the motifs belong to a conventional repertoire from which poets could draw, without necessarily having a particular passage in an earlier romance in mind. But what the juxtaposition of passages from *Gawain* and Chrétien does show is that the *Gawain*-poet had mastered this repertoire of motifs, and was familiar with the expressive means with which Chrétien verbalized the motifs in the surface structure of his romances.

Why is it that, unlike the popular romancer, the *Gawain*-poet, or Chrétien, devotes so much time to describing the code of hospitality? Undoubtedly, part of the answer lies in the social milieu for which their romances were produced. Both poets appear to have written for an aristocratic household where the art of 'biau acoillir' counted, as we have seen, as one of the accomplishments in which the courtier should excel. We know little about the audience of popular romances, but the reluctance of the poet of *Sir Perceval* to pursue the refined intricacies of hospitality would seem to support W. R. J. Barron's conclusions about the milieu in which popular romance was produced:

[13] Cf. Bruckner, *Convention of Hospitality*, 192–5.

The general character of English romance makes clear that its primary audience was not aristocratic . . . The range of regional dialects represented in the corpus and its readiness to acknowledge chivalric values without being preoccupied by the inherent contradictions of courtly codes suggest a provincial audience of less than the highest rank.[14]

For this milieu the elaborate rituals of hospitality and courtesy may have been of less interest than for the audience of the *roman courtois*. Sir Perceval is a popular hero, 'to be judged by the values proper for a knight in combat, martial prowess, loyalty, and magnanimity, and not by the more graceful and subtle values which are best displayed in a world intent upon civilizing itself'.[15]

But the difference between popular and courtly romances cannot simply be ascribed to two divergent textual communities, one 'intent upon civilizing itself' and another intent only on being amused.[16] For whatever the actual textual communities, there is a sense in which a romance *creates* a kind of audience for itself. As V. A. Kolve puts it, 'The author even controls, to some degree, the social milieu in which the work is read or heard for he invites the audience to think of themselves in certain ways, to *become* a certain kind of audience' (my italics).[17] In the absence of any firm evidence for different social milieux for courtly romance and popular romance— the hypothesized audience is usually itself derived from internal evidence[18]—it is at any rate clear that there is a distinction between the ideal audience which courtly and popular romancers respectively envisage. Whether or not the interest in etiquette reflects the tastes of a community 'intent upon civilizing itself' we do not know for sure. What we can say with certainty is that the romances of Chrétien and the *Gawain*-poet invite their audience to model themselves on such a community.

[14] W. R. J. Barron, *English Medieval Romance* (London, 1985), 233.
[15] Arlyn Diamond, 'Sir Gawain and the Green Knight: An Alliterative Romance', *Philological Quarterly*, 55 (1976), 10–29, at 12.
[16] As Derek Pearsall has shown, English popular romances may have had a wide social range of audiences: 'Middle English Romance and its Audiences', in *Historical and Editorial Studies in Medieval and Early Modern English for Johan Gerritsen*, ed. Hanneke Wirtjes and Hans Jansen (Groningen, 1985), 37–47.
[17] V. A. Kolve, *Chaucer and the Imagery of Narrative: The First Five Canterbury Tales* (London, 1984), n. on 74.
[18] But see Karl Brunner's 'Middle English Metrical Romances and their Audience', in *Studies in Medieval Literature in Honor of Professor Albert Croll Baugh*, ed. M. Leach (Philadelphia, 1961), 219–27, and John J. Thompson's, *Robert Thornton and the London Thornton Manuscript* (Woodbridge, 1987), which draw some tentative conclusions about audience on the basis of manuscript evidence.

These remarks are not without consequence for the way we read their romances as a whole. All too often, they have been viewed as flattering representations of the nobility for whom they were written.[19] In actual fact, their romances contain a strong didactic impulse. They do not just eulogize or reflect the courtly way of life: they teach it. This didactic impulse is implicit, for example, in the way Chrétien and the *Gawain*-poet and the characters of their romances praise gestures of hospitality as proper or courteous. Here is how Chrétien describes the moment in which Gawain is offered a mantle by his hostess's servant after he has been disarmed:

> Lors s'est la pucele avant trete,
> cele qui premiers fu venue,
> et mon seignor Gauvain salue
> et dit: 'Ma dame vos anvoie
> a vestir, ainz qu'ele vos voie,
> ceste robe, que ele cuide,
> com cel qui n'est pas vuide
> de corteisie ne de san,
> que grant travail et grant ahan
> et grant enui eü avez.'
> . . . .
> Et mes sire Gauvains respont
> come li plus cortois del mont:
> 'Ma dame la reïne saut
> cil sire an cui nul bien ne faut,
> et vos come la bien parlanz
> et la cortoise et l'avenanz!
> Mout est, ce cuit, la dame sage,
> quant si cortois sont si message.' (*Perceval*, 7699–7724)

Then the first maiden came forward and greeted Sir Gawain and said: 'Before she sees you, my lady sends you this robe to wear, because, being full of courtesy and sense, she thinks you have endured much hardship and much trouble.' . . . And Gawain, the most courteous man in the world, replies: 'May the Lord who lacks no goodness save my lady the queen, and you too for your nice words, your courtesy and charm. I think the lady must be wise when her messengers are so courtly.'

First the 'pucele' extols the courtesy of the Lady's kind offer of a mantle. Then Gawain expresses his gratitude, for which the narrator commends him as 'li plus cortois del mont'. And what does Gawain do but praise the girl for praising the Lady for her praiseworthy act? The *Gawain*-poet, too, singles out courteous gestures of hospitality for admiration. Bertilac's retainers ride out to meet their host 'rekenly' (821), Gawain greets everyone 'ful hendly' (828), while Bertilac makes ready to meet his guest 'wyth menske' (834). On leaving he thanks the host 'fayre' (1962), for the courteous way in which he has been made welcome. By praising the careful attention guest and host pay to polite behaviour, and by having their heroes congratulate each other for subscribing to the protocol of hospitality, the *Gawain*-poet and Chrétien actively recommend the refined gestures to their audience. Like courtesy books, they build up a sense of what is done and what is not done.

The courtly romances thus have much in common with courtesy books. Indeed, Jonathan Nicholls has argued that the *Gawain*-poet was greatly indebted to this overtly didactic material in his representations of hospitality.[20] But it is not just *Gawain* which covers a similar ground as the books of courtesy. From the very beginning, Arthurian romance gives advice similar to that found in courtesy books, and manifests in its detailed descriptions of feasts, meals, and polite conversation, a shared interest in etiquette. Paris, BN MS f. fr. 24301, the most accurate and complete manuscript of Robert of Blois's Arthurian romance *Beaudous*, illustrates the close links between the two. Beaudous asks his mother for permission to go to Arthur's court where his father, Gawain, will be crowned and married to the maiden of Wales. Before she sends him off, Beaudous's mother instructs him in the customs of Arthur's household. After a few pieces of advice the romance proper breaks off in the manuscript.[21] Along with other works by Robert, two courtesy books, *L'Enseignement des Princes* and the *Chastoiement des Dames*, follow. Only after these didactic works does the romance plot continue. The linkage of courtesy books and romance, obviously inspired by Chrétien's *Perceval*, in which Perceval's mother imparts useful advice to her son, goes further. For despite the

[20] *The Matter of Courtesy: Medieval Courtesy Books and the Gawain-Poet* (Woodbridge, 1985).
[21] Roberta L. Krueger has recently argued for the probable authenticity of the organization of Robert of Blois's works in the Paris manuscript: 'Constructing Sexual Identity in the High Middle Ages: The Didactic Poetry of Robert de Blois', *Paragraph*, 13 (1990), 105–31.

separation of the Arthurian story and the didactic works which are neatly embedded within it, there is a continual interplay between the two genres.[22] *L'Enseignement* uses King Arthur as a shining example of noble conduct, and his foundation of the Round Table as an illustration of the achievements which 'grant sens' makes possible. The story in its turn not only proceeds to translate this advice into action, but at times halts to repeat the lesson which it dramatizes. This, for example, is what happens when Beaudous returns a horse to its owner, whom he has just defeated:

> Et quant li rois tenir le vist
> Merveille s'en por quoi le fist
> Si dist: 'chevaliers, par ta foi,
> Di moi la veritei por quoi
> Tu venis mon estrier tenir.'
> 'Sire', fait il, 'bien doit servir
> Par tot li plu haut li plus bas;
> Roi estes et je nel sui pas.'
> 'Mout estes', dist li rois, 'garnis
> De grant proesce, et bien apris!' (*Beaudous*, 3230–9)[23]

And when the king saw him bringing it, he was surprised by it, and said: 'Knight, by your faith, tell me in truth why you have come to bring my horse.' 'Sir', he replied, 'it is fitting that the lowly should serve the high in all ways; you are a king and I am not.' The king said, 'You are blessed with great virtue, and are well brought up!'

Beaudous clearly shows that even in Arthurian romances much earlier than *Gawain* there is a large common ground between romance and courtesy books.

Whether romance influenced the courtesy book or vice versa remains an open question. Both are roughly contemporaneous developments. The *Disciplina Clericalis* by Petrus Alfonsus, cleric and physician at the court of Henry I of England, has two sections on table etiquette and on the skills of conversation, which stand at the very beginning of programmes of education aimed at social

---

[22] For other examples of this interplay between the overtly didactic material of the courtesy book and romance, see Philippe de Navarre's *Quatre Ages de l'homme*, 23–4, which draws on an episode of the Vulgate Cycle—in which Pharien chastises his nephew Lambègues for rudely interrupting the conversation in order to make the point that one should always let wiser or more distinguished people speak first.

[23] Ed. Jacob Ulrich, *Robert de Blois: Sämtliche Werke*, 3 vols. (Berlin, 1889–95), vol. i.

success.[24] But some decades earlier the enigmatic *Ruodlieb*, often looked upon as the first courtly romance, already exudes the spirit of courtly refinement, combining a pleasant story with pieces of practical advice that are later to be found in courtesy books.[25] Two Latin courtesy books, the *Facetus moribus et vita* and the *Facetus cum nihil utilius*, date, like Chrétien's romances, from the twelfth century.[26] In the 1170s the *Facetus moribus et vita* is referred to by a German cleric, while another mention of a *Facetus*, probably the *Facetus cum nihil utilius*, occurs in 1192 in a work by Utigio, archbishop of Ferrara.[27] The *Facetus* material becomes so popular—partly by virtue of its being a school-text—that translations in the vernacular, first in French and Dutch, begin to appear in the thirteenth century.[28] Versions of the *Facetus* would certainly have been available to courtly romancers like Chrétien. English translations of the *Facetus* take off only in the late fourteenth century, a development likewise contemporaneous with *Gawain*'s date of composition. However, it is just as likely that courtly romancers arrived at their presentations of polite interaction independently of courtesy books, or even that they influenced *Facetus* literature. On the basis of a work like *Beaudous* it may be safest to describe the relation between the two in terms of interaction rather than unilateral influence, or as one of common ground. Since both courtly romances and courtesy books were for the most part composed by court-clerics, writing for (and creating) a milieu where good manners and

[24] Petrus Alfonsus, *Disciplina Clericalis*, ed. A. Hilka and W. Söderhjelm (Helsinki, 1911), 8, 37–8. One century later the topics of *De Modo Cenandi* and *De Silentio*, briefly discussed by Petrus Alfonsus, had caused enough anxiety as to require full-length treatises.

[25] Peter Dronke, '*Ruodlieb*: Les Premières Traces du roman courtois', CCM 12 (1969), 365–82, and H. Zeydel's introduction to his edition: *Ruodlieb: The Earliest Courtly Novel* (Chapel Hill, NC, 1959), 16–18.

[26] To avoid confusion between the two I shall refer to the *Facetus moribus et vita* only by its full title. I accept Dronke's estimated date for the work: Peter Dronke, 'Pseudo-Ovid, *Facetus*, and the Arts of Love', *Mittellateinisches Jahrbuch*, 11 (1976), 126–31.

[27] See F. Brentano, *Relationship of the Latin Facetus Literature to the Medieval English Courtesy Poems*, Bulletin of the University of Kansas, Humanistic Studies, 52 (Lawrence, Kan., 1936). This study contains a useful survey of the historical development of the genre. For a history of the genre see also Servus Gieben, 'Robert Grosseteste and Medieval Courtesy-Books', *Vivarium*, 5 (1967), 47–74; Diane Bornstein, *Mirrors of Courtesy* (Hamden, Conn., 1975), 63–84; and Nicholls, *The Matter of Courtesy*, 1–74.

[28] Jozef Morawski (ed.), *Le Facet en français* (Poznan, 1923), p. xx. A medieval Dutch version of the *Facetus* is most easily available in a modern Dutch translation by Theo Meder in his *Hoofsheid is een ernstig spel* (Amsterdam, 1988).

self-restraint were indispensable, the explanation for the similarities between the two genres is probably as much social as philological.[29]

One of the common interests of courtesy books and Arthurian romance is the topic of hospitality. So important was the subject that, when the *Facetus* material grew in the thirteenth century, courtesy books almost exclusively concerned with the proper behaviour of guest and host started circulating independently.[30] The earliest courtly romances frequently contain injunctions likewise found in courtesy books. Let me give a few examples from some courtly romances before turning to the question of how courtesy rules shape the romances of Chrétien and the *Gawain*-poet.[31] *Urbanus Magnus* advises the guest to send an advance messenger so that the hosts have more time to prepare:

> Visere cum cupias caros, fidosque sodales,
> Nuntius aduentum precedens nuntiet illis.
> (*Urbanus Magnus*, 1445–6)[32]

When you wish to visit friends and faithful companions, let a messenger go ahead to announce your arrival.

When, in the *Chevalier à l'épée*, Gawain and his host are on their way to the host's castle, the host himself speeds ahead to ensure all is ready for his guest's arrival. He explains the principle to Gawain:

> 'Sire,' fet il, 'entendez ça:
> Toz jor est costume et usage,
> S'uns chevaliers cortois et sage
> En moinne un autre aveques lui,
> Que il envoie devant lui
> Fere son ostel atorner . . .'
> (*Chevalier à l'épée*, 134–9)

'Sir,' he says, 'listen to this: it is always the rule and the custom that if a courtly and wise knight brings another knight home with him he should send someone ahead to prepare his lodging . . .'

---

[29] See the final chapter for a discussion of the social position of the courtly romancers and the composers of the courtesy books.

[30] Thirteenth-century tracts such as the *Phagifacetus* and the *De modo cenandi* deal as much with the wider issue of the proper behaviour of guests and hosts as with table manners: Brentano, *Latin Facetus Literature*, 26.

[31] The following examination of *Facetus* material draws on courtesy books in Latin, Anglo-Norman and French, and English, from the late twelfth to the fifteenth century. Since courtesy books form a notably coherent genre this eclecticism seems to me justified, and may do justice to the enormous quantity in which these works were copied and translated.

[32] Daniel of Beccles, *Urbanus Magnus*, ed. J. Gilbart Smyly (Dublin, 1939).

Courtesy books stipulate that the guest should obey the host and should value the happy atmosphere more than the meal itself:

> Ton hoste en sa meson
> Contredire n'est pas reason . . . (*Petit traitise*, 163–4)[33]

It is not done to contradict your host in his house . . .

> And when þe borde is thynne I as of seruyse
> Nought replenesshed with grete diuersite
> Of mete & drink good chere may then suffise.
>
> . . . .
>
> The poet saith I hou that a poure borde
> Men may enriche I with cheerful wil & worde.
> (*Caxton's Book of Curtesye*, 253–9)[34]

When we turn to courtly romances we find the same injunctions. Without being concerned about the number of courses, Yder thoroughly enjoys his meal:

> E mult vint a Yder a gré,
> Kar la bele chiere li plout
> Sor tuz les autres mes qu'il out . . . (*Yder*, 659–61)

And Yder was contented, for the happy atmosphere pleased him more than the courses of the meal . . .

In Ulrich van Zatzikhoven's *Lanzelet*, a translation of a lost Anglo-Norman original, Lanzelet echoes the rule that the guest should not disagree with the host:

> ich waen es noch ein site sî
> das man den wirter nâch giht. (*Lanzelet*, 6332–3)[35]

I fancy it is still the custom that one agrees with the host.[36]

Similar parallels can be found in the romances of Chrétien and the *Gawain*-poet. The *Urbanus Magnus* gives the following advice to the host:

> Clericus aut miles ad te si uenerit hospes,
> Occurrens properes illi mellire salutes.
> Si tibi sit carus, amplexus, oscula prestes . . .
> (*Urbanus Magnus*, 2343–5)

[33] Ed. Rosamund H. Parsons, 'Anglo-Norman Books of Courtesy and Nurture', *PMLA* 44 (1929), 383–455.
[34] Ed. F. J. Furnivall, EETS ES 3 (London, 1868).
[35] Ulrich von Zatzikhoven, *Lanzelet*, ed. K. A. Hahn (1845, repr. Berlin, 1965).
[36] Trans. K. G. Webster and revised by R. S. Loomis (New York, 1951).

If a cleric or a knight comes to you as a guest, run towards him and hasten to greet him sweetly. If he is dear to you, embrace and kiss him . . .

When Chrétien's Erec visits the poor vavasour, Enide's father, his host puts this advice into practice:

> Li vavasors contre lui cort;
> einz qu'Erec li eüst dit mot,
> Li vavasors salüé l'ot:
> 'Biax sire, fet il, bien vaigniez.
> Se o moi herbergier daigniez,
> vez l'ostel aparellié ci.'
> Erec respont: 'Vostre merci.'   (*Erec*, 384–90)

The vavasour runs towards him. Before Erec could say a word the vavasour had greeted him. 'Dear sir', he says, 'welcome. If you would do me the honour of staying with me, see here your lodging all set.' Erec replies: 'Thank you.'

Bertilac in *Sir Gawain* likewise hastens to meet his guest and greets him while Gawain politely thanks the host for his offer. The passage closely resembles Erec's reception:

> Þenne þe lorde of þe lede loutez fro his chambre
> For to mete wyth menske þe mon on þe flor;
> He sayde, 'ȝe are welcum to welde as yow lykez
> Þat here is; al is yowre awen, to haue at yowre wylle
>   and welde.'
>   'Graunt mercy,' quoþ Gawayn,
>   Þer Kryst hit yow forȝelde.'   (833–9)

When Erec and Gawain return to a household which they know very well, Arthur's court, we find the embraces and the kisses which *Urbanus Magnus* recommends. In *Erec*, the arrival of Erec and Enide is announced by Gawain:

> 'Sire, fet il, or vos covient
> joie feire, vos et ma dame,
> que ci vient Erec et sa fame.'
>   .   .   .   .   .   .
> Li rois les acole et salue,
> Et la reine dolcemant
> les beise et acole ausimant;
> n'i a nul qui joi n'en face.   (*Erec*, 4172–87)

'Sir', he says, 'let you and my lady be happy, for here come Erec and his wife.' The king embraces and greets them, and the queen kisses them sweetly and embraces them too. There is no one who is not happy about it.

Erec's reception by the king, the queen, and their subjects, in descending order of importance, provides a close parallel to the effusion lavished on Gawain when he returns to Arthur's court:

> Þer wakned wele in þat wone when wyst þe grete
> Þat gode Gawayn watz commen; gayn hit hym þoȝt.
> Þe kyng kyssez þe knyȝt, and þe whene alce,
> And syþen mony syker knyȝt þat soȝt hym to haylce . . . (2490–3)

Not only do the welcoming gestures correspond, but the order of the hero's welcoming committee is in both passages the same: first the king, then the queen 'ausimant' or 'alce', and finally the peer-group.

Courtesy books also stipulate that the host should help his guests mount or dismount:

> Ascendens si uir fuerit dignus famulatu,
> Ascendentis equum uel descendentis ab illo,
> Strigilis instantis manibus teneatur utrisque.
> (*Urbanus Magnus*, 1351–3)[37]

If a man worthy of service should be getting on his horse, promptly hold the stirrup with both hands while he gets on or off his horse.

When Yder and his *amie* arrive at Arthur's court in *Erec*, the courteous Gawain helps the damsel descend (1173–4). Enide's father is also ready to hold the stirrup on Erec's horse (393–6), while, in *Yvain*, Arthur shows such grounding in etiquette that he pre-empts this move when visiting Laudine's court. In a public performance of modesty he quickly dismounts before Laudine has the chance to take hold of the horse's stirrup:

> Ne peut estre qu'a toz respondre
> li rois, qui vers lui voit venir
> la dame a son estrié tenir.
> Et ce ne vost il pas atendre,
> Einz se haste molt de descendre . . . (*Yvain*, 2374–8)

The king cannot respond to all. He sees the lady come towards him to hold his stirrup. But he does not want to wait for that, but quickly descends.

---

[37] Compare Gawain's disparagement of his host's courtesy in the *Perlesvaus*, where no one offers him a hand while he dismounts: 'Par foi, fait Missire Gavains, il ne sont pas bien ensoigniés car encor ne m'ont il pas aresnié' ('By my faith, says Sir Gawain, they are not well brought up, for they still have not taken my stirrup': p. 122).

Bertilac's retainers are just as eager as Laudine to help their guest dismount and to take the horse off his hands:

> Sere seggez hym sesed by sadel, quel he lyȝt,
> And syþen stabeled his stede stif men innoȝe. (822–3)

More parallels between courtesy books and the romances of Chrétien and the *Gawain*-poet will be drawn later in this chapter, but the above examples suffice to illustrate the extensive etiquette to which courtesy books and romances subject guests and hosts.

By following this etiquette, the heroes of *Gawain* and Chrétien's romances can display their intimate knowledge of civilized life and its ways, their *savoir-faire*. In their dramatizations of rules of courtesy, the romances reveal a pedagogic project similar to the *Facetus* material. Delightful as their stories are, they contain a subtle didactic element. As Chrétien de Troyes writes, his purpose is to produce finely wrought but also instructive romances:

> Por ce dist Crestien de Troies
> que reisons est que totevoies
> doit chascuns panser et antandre
> a bien dire et a bien apandre. (*Erec*, 9–12)

Thus Chrétien says that it is proper that everyone should give thought and effort to speaking well and to teaching well.

And as the moralistic literature of the later medieval period indicates, among the instruction which clerics in the employment of secular princes should provide is the art of playing the appropriate roles as guest or host:

Li maitre as filz de riche homme se doivent mout traveillier d'apanre a eus cortoisie et biau parler, et honorer la gent, *et cortoisement recoillir*, et eux faire apanre les estoires et les livres des autors . . . (*Quatre Ages*, p. 13)

The teachers of the sons of rich men should do their best to teach them courtesy and the art of speaking well, and how to honour people and receive them politely, and they should teach them the stories and books of the great authors.

In the context of this programme of instruction which the 'maitre' was meant to provide, the *Gawain*-poet and Chrétien, effectively combining 'estoires' with the finer points of 'cortoisement recoillir', must have acquitted themselves of their tasks successfully.

The Motif of Joy: Etiquette and Deception

In the social rituals of hospitality, one motif—the motif of joy—
plays a crucial role in *Gawain* and the courtly romance.[38] Cheerfulness is an essential ingredient in scenes of hospitality, or in scenes at
court in general. Since these social occasions provide the setting for
most of the narrative in *Gawain*, its sounds of joy and laughter,
which have long been recognized as one of its most characteristic
features,[39] will not come as a surprise.

Some lines from *Sir Thopas*, Chaucer's parody of the English
chivalric romances of his day, will indicate the conventionality of
revelry at social occasions:

> His myrie men comanded he
> To make hym both game and glee,
>   For nedes moste he fighte
> With a geaunt with hevedes three,
> For paramour and jolitee
>   Of oon that shoon ful brighte.   (*Sir Thopas*, 839–44)

These lines also suggest the problems this convention presents to
poets aiming at a more lifelike representation of the feelings and
emotions of the characters they created. The convention imposes
limits on the variety of emotions that can be explored. Sir Thopas is
about to fight a three-headed giant, a point at which, in a verisimilar
representation of character, one might expect feelings of inquietude.
But the emotive words in this stanza from *Sir Thopas*—'myrie',
'game and glee', 'jolitee'—evoke the customary joyfulness, even
though there seems little to be joyful about. The presence of the
motif of joy is here one of the many non-functional conventions
which in *Sir Thopas* become the butt of parody.

How did Chrétien and the *Gawain*-poet's renditions of feasts and
hospitality episodes avoid the meaninglessness which Chaucer
parodied in the passage from *Sir Thopas*? For an answer let us look
at Yvain's reception by Gawain's relatives. Yvain has found lodging
with this noble family, who, to his surprise, vacillate between joy
and grief:

---

[38] The importance of the motif in chivalric literature as a whole has been observed
by S. Bayrav, 'Le Thème de la joie dans la littérature chevaleresque', *Dialogues*, 3
(1953), 3–19.
[39] Cf. Edward T. Jones, 'The Sound of Laughter in *Sir Gawain and the Green
Knight*', MS 31 (1969), 343–5, and Martin Stevens, 'Laughter and Game in
Sir Gawain and the Green Knight', *Speculum*, 47 (1972), 65–78.

Li font joie et formant s'an painnent;
a grant joie a l'ostel l'en mainnent.
et tant grant joie li ont feite.
Une dolors, qui les desheite,
lor refet la joie oblïer;
si recomancent a crïer
et plorent, et si s'esgratinent.
Ensi molt longuement ne finent
de joie feire et de plorer:
joie por lor oste enorer
font, sanz ce que talant n'en aient ...   (*Yvain*, 3809–19)

They create joy and try hard to do so, leading him to the castle with great joy and giving him a jubilant welcome. But grief, which pains them, makes them forget their joy, and they begin to cry again, and to weep, and to tear at their faces. For a long time they alternate between joyfulness and wailing: they make cheer to honour their host, but their heart is not in it.

Yvain is taken aback by this unorthodox reception and asks his host the cause for their grief. The host reveals that the giant Harpin de la Montagne will kill his four sons unless he hands him his daughter:

Et por ce n'est mie mervoille,
biax sire chiers, se nos plorons;
mes por vos tant con nos poons
nos resforçons a la foiee
de feire contenance liee;
que fos est, qui prodome atret
entor lui, s'enor ne li fet ...   (*Yvain*, 3872–8)

So do not be surprised if we weep, dear sir; but for your sake we attempt at the same time to look happy; because he who receives a gentleman is foolish if he does not honour him.

This episode from *Yvain* is important for an understanding of the nature of joy, both in Chrétien and *Gawain*. Joy is in this passage not a romantic 'spontaneous overflow of powerful feelings', or, as Chrétien puts it, a reflection of 'talant'. As the phrases that refer to its expressions suggest, it is a quality that can be acted ('resforcée') to cover up an inner turmoil. Yvain's host in fact indicates that such deceit is honourable. Joy is part and parcel of the honour due to the guest. It is an obligatory sentiment on social occasions, and to abstain from manifesting it is, in the words of Yvain's host, 'fos'.[40] Once again, Chrétien's heroes dramatize a rule of hospitality which also appears in courtesy books. The twelfth-century *Facetus cum nihil utilius* stipulates that:

> Hospitibus laetum debes ostendere vultum;
> vultus enim laetus dandi duplicat tibi cultum.   (*Facetus*, 79)[41]

You should show your guests a happy face; a happy face will redound to your honour.

In the event that a guest or a host is not joyful, courtesy books recommend the strategy which Yvain's hosts try to follow:

> Si uario fuerit tua mens hamata dolore,
> Sit facies leta, mentiri gaudia discat.
> (*Urbanus Magnus*, 857–8)

If your mind should be upset by some grief, let your appearance be joyful. Learn to lie with joy.

The sad man who is courteous must on certain occasions attempt to appear happy.[42]

In the opening scene of Arthur's court at Camelot in *Gawain* joy is still spontaneous:

> Bot Arthure wolde not ete til al were serued,
> He watz so joly of his joyfnes, and sumquat childgered:
> His lif liked hym ly3t . . .   (85–7)

The joy of Arthur and his household is here as natural as that of a child, whose life is as yet untroubled by matters of grave importance. The association of Arthur's court with youth underlines the appropriateness and harmlessness of their carefree behaviour. Critics reading moral disapproval into the poet's description of Arthur must do so by ignoring the *Gawain*-poet's pun in the word

[40] That this rule also pertains at Arthur's court is most succinctly expressed by Gawain in the *First Continuation* of Chrétien's *Perceval*, who rebukes Arthur for being pensive: 'Il n'est ne bel ne avenant | Qu'aiez ire ne mautalent | Dont vos doiés estre pensis, | Voiant tans haus barons de pris | Com entor vos poëz veoir | Molt vos devroit plaire et seoir | Lor solas et lor compaignie' ('It is not good and proper that anger or a bad mood should make you pensive, when there are so many important and noble barons around you. You should cherish their joy and their company': 1. 8913–20).
[41] Ed. Carl Schroeder, *Der deutsche Facetus* (Berlin, 1911).
[42] In *Bliocadran*, a prologue which in some manuscripts precedes Chrétien's *Perceval*, the rule appears as well: 'Mais tout adés ne doit on mie | Duel demener, car c'est folie; | Ains doit on faindre c'on soit lié . . .' ('But after a while one should no longer be sad, for that is foolish. Instead one should feign joy': 31–3); ed. L. D. Wolfgang (Tübingen, 1976).

'joyfnes' (meaning both 'youth' and 'jollity'). The word may derive from another Old French romance, *Le Roman de la Rose*, with which the *Gawain*-poet was certainly familiar:

> Aprés se tint, mon esciant
> Joinece, au vis cler e riant
> qui n'avoit pas encor passez,
> si com je cuit, -xii- anz d'assez.
> Niceite fu, e si ne pensoit
> nul mal ne nul engin qui soit
> mes mout ert envoisie e gaie . . .
> (*Roman de la Rose*, 1259–65)

I think I saw Youth next, his face fresh and cheerful. It seemed to me that he was under twelve years of age. He was a bit childish, but there was no wickedness or treachery in his thoughts; he was elated and happy . . .

Like Arthur, 'Joinece' is described as a bit childish (compare the *Gawain*-poet's 'childgered'), but, as Guillaume de Lorris hastens to add, he intends no harm. The word-play of 'Joinece', in which being joyful and young are inextricably bound up, was lost in Chaucer's translation of the *Roman de la Rose*, which uses the word 'Youthe'.[43] But *Gawain* has a similar pun in 'joyfnes'—the earliest and possibly only occurrence of the word in the English language—which can only suggest the innocence and appropriateness of joy to people 'in their first age'.[44]

However, the appearance of the Green Knight soon makes the natural and effortless expression of joy impossible. With the court frightened and dismayed, joy survives only as an emotion that is 'made'. Here, for example, are Arthur and Gawain, laughing nervously, and keeping up the pretence they are not impressed by the beheading they have just seen:

> Þe kyng and Gawen þare
> At þat grene þay laȝe and grenne,
> Ȝet breued watz hit ful bare
> A meruayl among þo menne.

---

[43] *The Romaunt of the Rose and Le Roman de la Rose: A Parallel-Text Edition*, ed. R. Sutherland (Oxford, 1967).

[44] *A philosophre* (*c*.1475) has 'innesse', which is perhaps derived from the French 'ionece'; MED s.v. 'junesse'. For the associations between youth and jollity see Philippe de Navarre's *Quatre Ages*: 'Jones doit bien estre joliz et mener joieuse vie . . .' ('The young should be jolly and lead a joyful life': p. 38). Cf. John A. Burrow's *The Ages of Man* (Oxford, 1986), 174.

> Þa3 Arþer þe hende kyng at hert hade wonder,
> He let no semblaunt be sene, bot seyde ful hy3e
> To þe comlych quene, wyth cortays speche,
> 'Dere dame, to-day demay yow neuer;
> Wel bycommes such craft vpon Cristmasse . . .'   (463–71)

No matter what personal misgivings, the show must go on; if social occasions are to be conducted properly, joy must be expressed, even when it is not felt 'at herte'. And so, in this passage from *Sir Gawain*, Arthur and Gawain display joy, as if the gruesome beheading they have just witnessed had indeed been no more than a fitting Christmas spectacle.

The conventionality of joy at social occasions, as the passages from Chrétien and *Gawain* have demonstrated, does not rule out a lifelike representation of the characters' emotions. Joy, the obligatory narrative ingredient of *Sir Thopas*, has become in the romances of Chrétien and *Gawain* a rule of behaviour of which the heroes themselves are conscious. As a result Chrétien and the *Gawain*-poet have set up a potential dichotomy between the face of joy and the actuality of feeling. The motif of joy has become psychologically meaningful: joy can express or repress, and thus suggest a wide range of human emotions.

In the hospitality sequence in *Sir Gawain* the potential discrepancy between manifestations of joy and 'talant' is further explored:

> Þenne watz spyed and spured vpon spare wyse
> Bi preué poyntez of þat prynce, put to hymseluen,
> Þat he beknew cortaysly of þe court þat he were,
> Þat aþel Arthure þe hende haldez hym one,
> Þat is þe ryche ryal kyng of þe Rounde Table;
> And hit watz Wawen hymself þat in þat won syttez,
> Comen to þat Krystmasse, as case hym þen lymped.
> When þe lorde hade lerned þat he þe leude hade,
> Loude la3ed he þerat, so lef hit him þo3t,
> And alle þe men in þat mote maden muche joye . . .   (901–10)

One will notice in this passage that joy is 'made', and subsequent phrases describing manifestations of joy—for example, 'made gret chere', (1259), 'made merþe' (982), 'made blyþe' (1398), 'blyþe semblaunt' (1273)—likewise suggest that the expression of joy can involve a conscious effort and thus the possibility of deceit.

There might be a temptation to read the joy that Bertilac and his attendants create as the 'loud merriment of a practical joker' who has just caught his prospective victim,[45] or as a treacherous joy that is meant to lure Gawain into a false sense of security. Without reading retrospectively, such an interpretation may seem, as J. A. Burrow argues, unwarranted: 'So, in the absence of any articulated sinister meaning, one finds oneself thinking simply of a genial host rejoicing at the prospect of a distinguished and interesting guest.'[46] There is, before the moment of revelation in Fitt IV, little reason to assume that Bertilac and his household are playing tricks on Gawain. That the joy they create will therefore come across as innocuous is brought out forcefully if we compare this passage with Yvain's welcome at the town of Pesme Aventure. Yvain receives hospitality from a host who will later spring a deadly combat on him:

> Se ne sai ge s'il le deçoivent,
> mes a grant joie le reçoivent,
> et font sanblant que molt lor pleise,
> qu'il soit herbergiez a grant eise.   (Yvain, 5401–4)

I do not know whether they are deceiving him, but they receive him with great joy, and show great concern that he should be comfortably lodged.

Chrétien's seemingly naïve claim that he does not know whether Yvain is being deceived can only mean that he *is* being deceived. Otherwise the authorial intrusion into the narrative would be irrelevant. The phrase 'font sanblant', like similar phrases Chrétien uses to describe behaviour: 'feire contenance', 'feire chere', has a pejorative connotative meaning of deceit, which is here exploited to suggest the illusory nature of Yvain's friendly welcome. The joy that is here created is treacherous: it is not 'resforcée' to honour the host, but it is meant to lure an unwitting victim of the evil custom the host has established. The motives behind the joy are as perverted as those behind the care they give to Yvain's horse:

> Cui chaut! Que bien les establerent
> cil qui l'un an cuident avoir . . .   (Yvain, 5348–9)

What does it matter! Those who stable the horses think they already own them . . .

If the *Gawain*-poet used this passage, in which the apparently friendly host becomes, in structural terms, the guest's 'opponent', he

---

[45] R. H. Bowers, '*Gawain and the Green Knight* as Entertainment', *MLQ* 24 (1963), 333–41, at 339.
[46] *A Reading of Sir Gawain and the Green Knight* (London, 1965), 59.

made a significant change. Nowhere in the hospitality sequence in *Gawain* does it become clear that the joy of Bertilac and his household is perverted, or is anything other than a point of etiquette. For the displays of joy which ensue when the knight discloses his name in *Gawain* are another of the many rules of hospitality. There is a similar outburst of joy when Erec reveals his identity.

> 'Filz sui d'un riche roi puissant:
> mes peres li rois Lac a non,
> Erec m'apelent li Breton;
> de la cort le roi Artus sui,
> bien ai esté trois anz a lui.'
>
> . . . . . .
>
> —Ha! biax sire, est ce veritez?
> Erec, li filz Lac, estes vos?
> —Ce sui mon, fet il, a estros.'
> Li ostes molt s'an esjoï
> Et dist: 'Bien avomes oï
> de vos parler an cest païs.
> Or vos aim assez plus et pris,
> car molt estes preuz et hardiz . . .'
> Grant joie font tuit par leanz:
> li peres an ert molt joianz,
> et la mere plore de joie,
> et la pucele ert tote coie,
> mes molt estoit joianz et liee.   (*Erec*, 650–85)

'I am the son of a rich and mighty king: my father is called Lac, and the Britons call me Erec. I belong to Arthur's court, and have been with him for three years.' . . . 'Really, dear sir, is that the truth?' 'That is my name', he says. The host is delighted and says: 'We have heard so much about you in this country. Now I love and esteem you the more, since you are strong and brave . . .' Kindly all make good cheer: the father is very happy, and the mother weeps for joy, and the maiden does not say a word . . . but she is glad and happy.

There are many reasons why the *Gawain*-poet may have chosen to withhold from the reader the privileged perspective which Chrétien allows the reader in *Yvain*. It keeps the reader in suspense, and keeps the same surprise as awaits Gawain in store for us. The limited perspective which we share with Gawain is also more sympathetic both to Gawain and to Bertilac. If Gawain has been lured into a false sense of security, so has the reader. And whereas Bertilac's displays of joy might have been interpreted in an unfavourable light if we had known that Bertilac, like Yvain's host, is here deceiving his guest, he will now appear simply as a 'genial host'.

This is not to say that the joy that Bertilac and his retainers show is as genuine and straightforward as Burrow seems to imply. The joy that Bertilac displays is not necessarily quite as deeply felt. Face and feeling in *Gawain*, and in the romances of Chrétien, are not always identical. We have seen this at Arthur's court after the beheading of the Green Knight, and it can be seen again in the appearance of Gawain's friends on the day of his departure—'Mony joylez for þat jentyle japes þer maden' (542)—or in the hospitality sequence where joy seems to involve a conscious effort and can be 'made' on command: 'Þe lorde luflych aloft lepes ful ofte, | Mynned merthe to be made vpon mony sythes' (981–2).[47] The display of joy may not have clearly articulated sinister overtones, but one cannot dispense with overtones altogether in fixing the meaning of the phrases 'made joy', 'made gret cher', or 'blyþe semblaunt'. They imply a potential difference between the joyful face and actual feelings, and carry overtones of play-acting.

There is of course more acting in the hospitality episode of *Sir Gawain* than that which goes into producing joy. In the bedroom scenes in particular there are suggestions that the Lady of the Castle is acting her role as Gawain's would-be lover. From the first visit of the Lady onwards the *Gawain*-poet plays with the double meaning of the word 'lete':[48]

> Ful lufly con ho lete,
> Wyth lyppez smal laȝande. (1206–7)

'Lete' can mean no more than 'to behave'. It can also mean 'to pretend'.[49] It is indeed the second meaning that is confirmed when the Green Knight reveals that the Lady has been acting under his own direction. A similar verbal ambiguity occurs in Gawain's words to the Lady during her final visit:

> I am derely to yow biholde
> Bicause of your sembelaunt. (1842–3)

---

[47] Cf. *Erec et Enide*: 'trestuit de joie feire tancent' ('everyone strives to make joy': 1994).

[48] I owe this point to a series of lectures on *Gawain* given by Jill Mann for the English Faculty, University of Cambridge, 1988.

[49] *MED* s.v. 'leten' 16, 17b.

Gawain politely thanks the Lady for her 'sembelaunt', her kindly demeanour. Had he been aware that it is also her 'sembelaunt' in its extended meaning, her deceptive behaviour,[50] that is to cost him the nick of the axe, he would have realized the dramatic irony embedded in his words.

Whether we are meant to see the joy that Bertilac and his household create as 'false semblaunce', and, like the Lady's advances, as part of the role-play the Green Knight turns out to have staged, is a question that will certainly occur to the reader who took or takes up *Gawain* for the second time.[51] Since, in contrast to Yvain's reception at Pesme Aventure, deception is never made explicit, we may decide to read the display of joy as the production of smiles for a photograph, as the playing of a part which is agreed to be fitting under the circumstances, although that part differs from inner realities. However, the line that separates 'arranged behaviour' from treachery is often thin; so thin that the difference between the two may disappear behind the inauthenticity which the two have in common.

The passage from *Yvain* will help me to make the point. Yvain may be alone in being unable to detect the host's role as trickster behind his guise of host, but would not the reader, too, have been deceived if Chrétien had not chosen to intervene for our benefit? *Gawain* raises a similar interpretative problem: Is the joy and laughter that is 'made' in the hospitality scene simply a matter of politeness, or is it part of a devious play Bertilac is directing? Both are possible, and at different points in the process of reading we rule out one possibility and are satisfied with the other. Once we find out Gawain has been framed, the rituals of hospitality take on an entirely different aspect. What the *Gawain*-poet reveals is just how difficult it is to distinguish politeness from trickery. As in Yvain's reception at Pesme Aventure, a disturbing ambivalence surrounds Bertilac's gestures of hospitality. They may—or may not—hide a deceptive design. And, surely, neither Chrétien nor the *Gawain*-poet would have composed a romance which reveals a hidden agenda beneath the polished appearances of their knights' reception if the opacity of the ceremonials of hospitality was of no concern to them.

---

[50] *MED* s.v. 'semblaunce' 1b.

[51] It has in the past been too readily assumed that *Gawain* was recited in public rather than read in private. The many illuminations, and the careful organization of the text by means of *capitula* in the manuscript, would have been of no benefit to listeners, and they suggest that the contemporary audience included readers.

This ambivalence also occupied other writers of the period. In the *Chevalier à l'épée*, Gawain is invited by a stranger to spend the night in his castle. As he approaches the castle, the passers-by prematurely lament his death for they have not seen any knight return alive from the hostel.[52] All those who have contradicted the host have met a gruesome death. Yet, despite these warnings, first from the bystanders, then from the host's daughter, who reveals that the bedroom where she and Gawain will sleep is a death-trap, the host shows no public signs of malevolence. Everything about the reception conforms to the prescribed etiquette. He comes to meet Gawain, makes much joy at his arrival, and ensures that he is disarmed and his horse stabled:

> Encontre lui est acouru
> Li sires, qui fait grant sanblant
> Qu'il soit de son venir joiant.
> Les armes reçut un vaslet,
> Uns autre prist lou Gringalet,
> Li tierz les esperons li oste.
> (*Chevalier à l'épée*, 222–7)

The lord ran to meet him, looking as if he were happy about his arrival. A servant takes his arms, another takes Gringalet, and a third takes off his spurs.

Meanwhile a meal is prepared, the table is set, and the hands are washed (344–54). The host insists on cheerfulness and Gawain, knowing full well that he cannot afford to disobey, does his best to comply:

> 'Sire, car fetes bele chiere,'
> Fet il a monsaignor Gauvain.
>   .   .   .   .   .   .
> 'Sire, sachiez de verité'
> Fet Gauvains, 'que je suis haitié.'
> (*Chevalier à l'épée*, 446–53)

'Sir, be happy,' he says to Sir Gawain . . . 'Sir, know this for sure,' says Gawain, 'I am elated.'

If the cheer which the host makes hides his thirst for blood, Gawain's 'bele chiere', too, disguises his knowledge of the host's

---

[52] The correspondences between *Gawain* and this episode have been examined in detail by D. D. R. Owen, 'Parallel Readings with *Sir Gawain and the Green Knight*', in *Two Old French Gauvain Romances*, ed. D. D. R. Owen and R. C. Johnston (Edinburgh, 1972), 159–208, at 183–5.

real intentions. Etiquette is minutely observed, even when Gawain and the maiden are dispatched to the room where so many knights have died:

> Amedui l'en ont mercïé
> Et font sanblant que mout lor plese.
> (*Chevalier à l'épée*, 464–5)

The two thank him, and act as if it pleases them greatly.

The entire ritual of hospitality is a charade, a show of appearances which allows both guest and host to hide what they know or think. And how could one look behind these masks of *noblesse oblige*? Even Gawain finds it difficult to believe that the host who has received him so fittingly and courteously harbours him a grudge. When the daughter warns him, he tells her he sees no reason why she should disparage her father:

> Il m'amena en sa meson,
> Si m'i a fet mout bel sanblant;
> Ne ja des ici en avant,
> Quant il m'a fet anor et bien,
> Ne doteré de nule rien . . .
> (*Chevalier à l'épée*, 408–12)

He has led me to his house, and has made me good cheer. He has honoured me and welcomed me, and I have no reason to be suspicious.

Like Yvain's adventure at Pesme Aventure and Bertilac's stage-play at Hautdesert, the polite faces and gestures which hospitality requires form a perfect and impenetrable front for a test or a deadly custom.

Take as a final example Lancelot's tragic adventure in the *Perlesvaus*. Unbeknown to him, Lancelot is on route to a castle which is the hide-out of five robber knights. Intending to lure him to their castle, the robbers send a lady to meet Lancelot. She politely offers him hospitality:

Ele est venue sor la voie si conme Lanceloz dut passer . . . Tantost conme Lanceloz la choisi si descendi de son cheval et li vint encontre. Lanceloz la salue, et ele fet molt grant joie par samblant. 'Sire, fet ele, tornez cel centier . . . si trouverez un recet qui mi ancessor firent por herbegier les chevaliers qui trespasseroient par ceste forest.' (*Perlesvaus*, p. 202)

She came to the road where Lancelot was due to pass . . . As soon as Lancelot saw her he got off his horse and went to meet her. Lancelot greets her, and she appears very happy. 'Sir', she says, 'turn on to this path . . . and you will find a castle made by my ancestors as a lodging-place for knights who traverse this forest.'

On arrival his horse is swiftly stabled, and a dwarf diligently attends to his needs:

Li nains prist le cheval Lancelot si s'establa. Il vint amont en la sale et s'abandona molt de lui servir. (*Perlesvaus*, p. 203)

The dwarf took Lancelot's horse and stabled it. He came into the hall, and was at pains to serve him.

Sensing something is wrong—dwarfs are usually bad omens in Arthurian literature—Lancelot will not disarm. His armour is light, he claims, polite enough not to share his misgivings with his hosts. Having been shown to his room, he falls asleep and wakes up to discover his sword has been stolen. Unarmed, Lancelot is an easy prey for the robbers, who imprison him in their castle. Abandoning their act as gracious hosts, they are quick to take advantage of Lancelot's vulnerability.

In all these hospitality episodes, the romancers reflect on the dichotomy that can exist between polite gestures and underlying intentions. The ease with which the theme generates surprising narrative developments may account for its popularity in romances of the later Middle Ages.[53] But the codification of an etiquette of hospitality in the courtesy books which start circulating around the twelfth century may well have increased interest in the theme.[54] Like other forms of codification, courtesy books objectify practices, creating a distance between the actor and his actions, between what he is and what he does.[55] Readers of etiquette tend to exchange spontaneous behaviour for self-conscious performances. And, expert readers that the characters of courtly romances are, they deal, to

[53] For another example see *Claris et Laris*, ll. 20755–64, in which Gawain is warned of a seemingly conscientious host, who observes the protocol of hospitality until his guests are asleep, when he murders them. It may be noted that the theme of the treacherous host becomes popular in other genres around the twelfth century, most notably in satire. See Ronald Pepin, *Literature of Satire in the Twelfth Century: A Neglected Medieval Genre* (Lampeter, 1988), 68–9.

[54] I disagree here with Felicity Heal's statement that the 'idea of a "law of hospitality", that is a clearly formulated series of conventions that dictated behaviour towards outsiders, is a late arrival in the writing of the early modern period': *Hospitality*, 4. *Facetus* material and courtly romances already contain and perpetuate conventional rules of hospitality.

[55] Pierre Bourdieu, 'Codification', in his *In Other Words: Essays Towards a Reflexive Sociology*, trans. Matthew Adamson (Cambridge, 1990), 76–86, at 78.

some extent, in insincerity. The gestures of hospitality they rehearse are frequently carefully calculated, and sometimes deceptive. Of the loss of perspicacity which the codification of an etiquette of hospitality entails, these romances seem acutely aware.

The Challenge and the Danger of Hospitality

The codification of a protocol of hospitality might also alert us to the dangers to which hospitality exposes both guest and host. As Pierre Bourdieu writes:

> One can formulate the general rule that the more dangerous the situation is, the more the practice tends to be codified. The degree of codification varies in proportion with the degree of risk . . . The more a situation is pregnant with violence, the more people will have to respect the conventions, the more behaviour freely vested in the improvisations of the habitus will give way to behaviour expressly determined by a methodically instituted, even codified, ritual.[56]

The many rules of hospitality which regulate the interaction between guest and host and aim to lead it into safe waters are thus always an acknowledgement of the risks which hospitality involves. Guest and host in the romances of Chrétien are typically strangers to each other, and at any stage during the ritual of hospitality either of them can transform into an enemy.[57] The Latin word *hospes*, meaning both 'guest and host' and 'stranger', a word derived through **hosti-pes* from the word *hostis* (enemy), suggests the age-old uncertainties and the dramatic potential inherent in the guest–host relationship.[58] The host can always be hostile. As the *Chevalier à l'épée* puts it in a proverb probably borrowed from the *Facetus cum nihil utilius*:

---

[56] Bourdieu, 'Codification', 78.
[57] Hospitality rules cannot put an end to the danger but can only try to contain it. Julian Pitt-Rivers puts it succinctly: 'The law of hospitality is founded upon ambivalence. It imposes order . . . makes the unknown knowable, and replaces conflict by reciprocal honour. It does not eliminate the conflict altogether, but places it in abeyance and prohibits its expression.' 'The Law of Hospitality', in his *The Fate of Shechem* (Cambridge, 1977), 94–112, at 104.
[58] Chênerie, *Le Chevalier*, 505–6, and Tony Tanner, *Adultery in the Novel: Contract and Transgression* (Baltimore, 1979), 24–7. Tanner's book traces this dramatic potential inherent in hospitality sequences throughout Western literature, from Homer to *Wuthering Heights*.

> Li vilains dist en reprovier,
> Si lou dïent encor plusor,
> Q'au vespre loe l'en lo jor,
> Quant l'en voit que bele est la fin,
> Si fet l'en son hoste au matin;
> Et Dieus, si con je lo desir
> Vos en doint a joie partir,
> De vostre oste sanz mautalant.
> (*Chevalier à l'épée*, 416–23)[59]

There is a common saying, still in use today, that you should praise the day only in the evening when you see it has turned out well. And you should thank your host in the morning. And God, as I wish, will let you leave in joy from your host, without ill will.

Do not thank your host prematurely, for you never know what he will turn out to be. Only in the morning when you depart will you know whether he has done you harm or not, whether you will leave with 'joie' or with 'mautalant'. The host takes a similar risk with a guest. The Provençal Arthurian romance *Jaufré* reveals the uncertainties which the host must accept:

> No sap om qui-s va ni qui-s ve,
> Ni can fa mal ni can fa be,
> Per que fa ades bon servir
> A om estrains, qui-l ve venir,
> O d'aculir, o de parlar,
> O de sun aver a donar.   (*Jaufré*, 5815–20)[60]

One does not know who will come and who will go, whether he will do you harm or do you good. That is why it is always wise to be helpful to a stranger when you see one arrive, to take him in, to talk to him, and to share your goods with him.

As Bourdieu suggests, it is the host's awareness of the risks involved which prompts an adherence to polite forms of behaviour. These risks become most obvious in the dramatic consequences triggered off when a guest deliberately deviates from the rules of hospitality that seek to transform him into a benign presence. As Tony Tanner has written: 'both guest and host had to observe the rules [of hospitality] meticulously, of course: any deviation could instantly revive the possibility of some kind of disruption of the previous

---

[59] *Facetus*, 78: 'Noctem mane, diem cubiturus vespere laudes, | hospitibus tuis, dum discedis, dato laudes' ('Praise the night in the morning, and the day before you go to sleep in the evening, and give thanks to your hosts when you leave').

[60] *Jaufré*, ed. and trans. R. Lavaud and R. Nelli in *Les Troubadours* (Paris, 1960).

order, or some terrible retribution or vengeance to be visited on the transgressor—or both.'[61] The romances of Chrétien exploit this dramatic potential to the full. Though many of the prescribed rules of hospitality are specific to the culture of the period, the consequences of not respecting them are those described by Tony Tanner: a provocation to private or open warfare:

> La ou Kex seoit au mangier,
> a tant ez vos un chevalier
> qui vint a cort molt acesmez,
> de totes ses armes armez.
> Li chevaliers a tel conroi
> s'ant vint jusque devant le roi
> la ou antre ses barons sist;
> nel salua pas, einz li dist:
> 'Rois Artus, j'ai en ma prison
> de ta terre et de ta meison
> chevaliers, dames et puceles . . .'   (*Lancelot*, 43–53)

Just as Kay had sat down for dinner, in came a knight armed to the teeth. Thus arrayed, he rides right up to the king, who was seated among his barons. He did not greet anyone, but said: 'King Arthur, I have in my prison knights, ladies, and damsels of your court . . .'

In this passage from Chrétien's *Lancelot*, Meleagant delivers his challenge to Arthur's court. He addresses Arthur with the irreverent pronoun, a form of address the Green Knight will use as well,[62] and when Kay proposes to take up the challenge a clash between Meleagant and the knights of King Arthur is inescapable.

Meleagant's challenge is, however, not merely verbal: he refuses to obey the rules of hospitality by riding up straight to King Arthur's seat on his horse, without dismounting, without greeting, and without maintaining a respectful distance from the host:

> Si fueris missus, prudenter praemeditare,
> et manibus iunctis nolito nimis prope stare.   (*Facetus*, 141)

Should you be sent on a mission, prepare carefully, keep your hands together, and do not stand too close to people.

Chrétien's *Perceval*, still ignorant of etiquette, rides up to Arthur's seat on his horse as well, and he gets so close that on turning around he sends his hat flying on to the dais:

---

[61] Tanner, *Adultery*, 25–6.
[62] The Green Knight repeatedly addresses Arthur as 'þou' (258–9, and 272–3). See Burrow, *A Reading*, 17.

Tantost del retorner s'atorne,
le chief de son chaceor torne,
mes si pres del roi l'ot mené
a guise d'ome mal sené
que devant lui, sanz nul fable,
li abati desor la table
del chief un chapel de bonet.   (*Perceval*, 929–35)

Suddenly he prepares to go away, and he turns his horse's head. But in his foolish way he had led it so close to the king that, without a lie, he knocked his hat off his head on to the table in front of him.

But while Perceval's rudeness is due to ignorance, Meleagant's movements are calculated. He withdraws from the system of courtly exchanges and communicates in his actions what he will later state in words: that he has come as an enemy, not as a guest.

Meleagant, who shows his disrespect for the rules of hospitality and for King Arthur's court who practise them, bears many resemblances to the Green Knight in Fitt I:

Þis haþel heldez hym in and þe halle entres,
Driuande to þe heȝe dece, dut he no woþe,
Haylsed he neuer one, bot heȝe he ouer loked.
Þe fyrst word þat he warp, 'Where is', he sayd,
'Þe gouernour of this gyng? . . .'

Þenn Arþour bifore þe hiȝ dece þat auenture byholdez,
And rekenly hym reuerenced, for rad was he neuer,
And sayde, 'Wyȝe, welcum iwys to þis place,
Þe hede of þis ostel Arthour I hat;
Liȝt luflych adoun and lenge, I þe praye,
And quat-so þy wylle is we schal wyt after.'
'Nay, as help me,' quoþ þe haþel, 'he þat on hyȝe syttes,
To wone any quyle in þis won, hit watz not myn ernde;
Bot for þe los of þe, lede, is lyft vp so hyȝe,
And þy burȝ and þy burnes best ar holden

·   ·   ·   ·   ·   ·   ·   ·   ·   ·   ·

And here is kydde cortaysye, as I haf herd carp,
And þat hatz wayned me hider, iwyis, at þis tyme.
Ȝe may be seker bi þis braunch þat I bere here
Þat I passe as in pes, and no plyȝt seche

·   ·   ·   ·   ·   ·   ·   ·   ·   ·   ·

Bot for I wolde no were, my wedez ar softer.
Bot if þou be so bold as alle burnez tellen,
Þou wyl grant me godly þe gomen þat I ask
      bi ryȝt.'

> Arthour con onsware,
> And sayd, 'Sir cortays kny3t,
> If þou craue batayl bare,
> Here faylez þou not to fy3t.'   (221–78)

Like Meleagant, the Green Knight rides up to the high table on his horse, without prior notification, without dismounting, without greeting anyone, and with a threatening axe in his hands. And, like Chrétien's Perceval, the Green Knight refuses to dismount, even when Arthur asks him to. Compare the exchange of words between the king and the Green Knight with Arthur's words to Perceval, on which they are possibly modelled:

> 'Wy3e, welcum iwys to þis place.
> . . . .
> Li3t luflych adoun and lenge, I þe praye,
> And quat-so þy wylle is we schal wyt after.'
> 'Nay, as help me,' quoþ þe haþel, 'he þat on hy3e syttes,
> To wone any quyle in þis won, hit watz not myn ernde . . .'   (252–7)

> Amis, fet li rois, descendez . . .
> et vostre volanté fera.
> . . . .
> —Ja, par mon chief, n'i descendrai,
> mes fetes tost, si m'an irai.   (*Perceval*, 977–88)

'Friend,' says the king, 'get off your horse . . . and what you wish will be done.' 'By my head, I will never get off. Do what I asked you quickly, and I will be off.'

For hospitality and its rituals neither hero has any time.

In contrast to the courteous heroes of Chrétien and the *Gawain*-poet, both challengers flout the rules of hospitality that seek to convert the stranger/enemy into the guest. Courtesy books specify the guest's obligation not to take the host by surprise, to disarm, to dismount, and to greet those he approaches:

> Hostia tectum
> Non caput intranti tibi sit, nec sit latus ense
> Accinctum, nec eques intres, nisi sis rogitatus.
> (*Urbanus Magnus*, 1448–50)

Do not enter the door with your head covered, do not have a sword girded by your side, do not go in on your horse, unless you are asked to.

> Ad quamcumque domum perrexeris, ante screato
> quam subeas, nullaque loquens et ad ostia stato.   (*Facetus*, 126)[63]

---

[63] Cf. *Urbanus Magnus*, 1360–4: 'Ingrediens uacuas edes errans alienas | Ocius exclames inquirens quis sit in ede . . . | . . . non sis rudis intrusor thalamorum' ('Be-

When you arrive at a house, make some noise before you go in, and wait at the door in silence.

> Cui das occursum, sibi dulcia verba loquaris
> dicque frequenter ave; sic non virtute pravaris. (*Facetus*, 149)

If you meet someone, speak kind words to him, and often greet him. That way your virtue will not be lessened.

The Green Knight's refusal of Arthur's offer of hospitality under-lines his unwillingness to be taken in by Arthur's household because of an assumed superiority most succinctly expressed by the phrase 'he3e he ouer loked'.[64]

There is thus a calculated element of *desmesure* in the Green Knight's actions. And, as in the *roman courtois*, this *desmesure* finds a correlative in the challenger's enormous height.[65] Compare the descriptions of the Green Knight's size with those of the abusive Mabonograin or the messenger who enters Arthur's court in the romance of *Rigomer*:

> Þer hales in at þe halle dor an aghlich mayster,
> On þe most on þe molde on mesure hyghe;
> Fro þe swyre to þe swange so sware and so þik,
> And his lyndes and his lymes so longe and so grete,
> Half etayn in erde I hope þat he were,
> Bot mon most I algate mynn hym to bene,
> And þat þe myriest in his muckel that my3t ride . . . (136–42)

> Þe stif mon hym bifore stod vpon hy3t,
> Herre þen ani in þe hous by þe hede and more. (332–3)

> A tant ez vos un chevalier
>
> . . . .
>
> qui estoit granz a merevoilles,
> et, s'il ne fust granz a enui
> soz ciel n'eüst plus bel de lui,
> mes il estoit un pié plus granz,
> a tesmoing de totes les genz,
> que chevalier que l'an seüst. (*Erec*, 5847–55)

fore entering an open building, call out quickly to enquire who is in the room . . . do not be a rude intruder of rooms').

[64] The *Book of Demeanor* warns against these haughty glances: 'Let not thy browes be backward drawn, | it is a sign of pride. | Escalt them not, it shewes a hart | most arrogant beside' (29–31); ed. F. J. Furnivall, in *The Book of Nurture &c.*, EETS os 32 (London, 1868).

[65] For the association of height and *desmesure*, see Halasz, *Structures narratives*, 14.

Along comes a knight . . . who is exceptionally tall, and if it was not for the
fact that he was too tall, no knight under the heavens would have been more
handsome than he. But, as everyone could see, he was a foot taller than any
knight they knew.

> Tant vint avant que mels le virent,
> Tant l'esgarderent qu'il coisirent
> Que çou uns chevaliers estoit,
> Qui sour .i. grant cheval seoit.
> Il meïsmes estoit si grans
> Qu'il dïent que c'ert .i. gaians,
> 'Et bien sachiés,' font il, 'sans faile,
> Qu'il vient querre joste u bataille.'
> Quant esgarderent son sanblant,
> Il nel tinrent mie a gaiant,
> Ains virent qu'il ert chevaliers
> Hardis et corajous et fiers.
> Mais onques n'orent veü
> Si grant chevalier comm'il fu.   (*Rigomer*, 6743–56)

He came nearer so that they could see him better, and they looked so hard
that they could see it was a knight seated on a huge horse. He himself was
so big that they said he was a giant. 'I am positive', each said, 'that he has
come to seek a joust or battle.' When they could see his face, they no longer
took him for a giant, but they saw he was a brave, courageous, and fierce
knight. But they had never seen a knight as big as he was.

The striking similarities between these descriptions in *Gawain* and
Rigomer, particularly apparent in the hesitation about whether the
challenger is a giant or a man, and hence, whether he comes to do
battle or whether he comes in peace, may be coincidental, but it
seems likely that the *Gawain*-poet knew of the conventional associations between inordinate height and arrogance.[66]

The Green Knight's *desmesure* is later expressed in words when
the Green Knight has recourse to another conventional motif
Chrétien applies to the hostile opponents of his Arthurian knights.
His boast of superiority—'If I were hasped in armes on heȝe stede, |
Here is no mon me to mach, for myȝtez so wayke' (281–2)—harks
back to the descriptions of the arrogant opponents of Erec and
Yvain:

[66] Note also the description of the giants in the *Polychronicon*, whose 'gretnesse of
herte answereþ and accordeþ to þe hugenesse of body'; quoted in Andrea Hopkins,
The Sinful Knights: A Study of Middle English Penitential Romance (Oxford, 1990),
166.

> Chevaliers estoit forz et buens;
> mes de ce fist que fos li cuens
> qu'il n'ot que l'escu et la lance:
> an sa vertu ot tel fiance
> qu'armer ne se volt autrement. (*Erec*, 3581–5)

He was a strong and competent knight; but foolishly the man only had a shield and a lance with him; he had such faith in his prowess that he did not want it any other way.

> Le jaiant a trové desclos,
> qui an sa force se fioit,
> tant que armer ne se voloit. (*Yvain*, 4202–4)

He found the giant unprotected: he had such faith in his own strength that he did not want to arm himself.

Such a pose of arrogance, a conventional pose for the hostile challenger,[67] leaves no doubt about the Green Knight's personal view of the 'los' and the 'curtaysie' of Arthur's court of which he speaks, and which he is careful to attribute to hearsay: 'is lyft vp so hyȝe', 'best ar holden', 'as I haf herde carp', 'as alle burnes tellen'. This praise by fame is not simply flattery. It is the Green Knight's way of stirring Arthur into action; it invites him to become what he is renowned to be. As Arthur in *Cligés* cannot but accept the service of Cligés when he praises Arthur's greatness—'se de vos ne mant | renomee qui vos renome' ('if your reputation does not belie you': 336–7)—so he must here grant the Green Knight his request if he is to live up to his fame. As Bruckner writes, 'praise by fame = challenge'.[68]

The Green Knight tops Meleagant's discourteous display with two details at which the author of the courtesy book *Facetus cum nihil utilius* would have cringed. This is how he acts when he has delivered his message to Arthur's court:

> Þe renk on his rouncé hym ruched in his sadel,
> And runischly his rede yȝen he reled aboute,
> Bende his bresed broȝes, blycande grene,
> Wayued his berde for to wayte quo-so wolde ryse. (303–6)

Conversely, the *Facetus* recommends the following behaviour to the messenger:

[67] See, for another example, *Jaufré*, ll. 5957–63.
[68] Bruckner, *Convention of Hospitality*, 54.

Dum steteris coram dominis, haec quinque tenebis:
iunge manus, compone pedes, caput erige, visu
non dispergaris, sine iussu pauca loquaris.   (*Facetus*, 181)

When you are in the presence of a lord, remember these five things: join your hands, put your feet together, keep your head straight, do not let your eyes wander around, and do not talk too much unless you have been asked to.

Instead of a firm gaze and a steady and controlled posture, the Green Knight communicates with violent and unrestrained body-talk. Like Perceval's impetuous movements at Arthur's court (929–35), or the bizarre posture of a challenger in *Lancelot*, who comes riding in with one foot in the stirrup and the other resting on his horse's neck (*Lancelot*, 2572–5), wild gestures signify rudeness and are likely to cause affront.[69] Despite his offer of peace, the Green Knight's performance aims to provoke, and does provoke. Arthur's indirect declaration of war understandably follows from the provocations of the Green Knight, who will not be 'taken in', either by Arthur's court, or by the repute attributed to it.

We may define the challenge as an attempt at hospitality, frustrated from the very start by a guest who flouts the rules of hospitality and thus states that he has come as an enemy, not as a guest, thus precipitating a series of perilous adventures. The hospitality episodes may confront the guest, too, with a *hospes* turned *hostis*. In the adventure of Pesme Aventure, the apparently friendly host inconveniences Yvain with an evil custom to which all his guests must submit in return for the hospitality they have received, a condition of which they are kept ignorant until the very last. Under the guise of 'helper', Yvain's host, like Bertilac, turns out to be, in structural terms, his 'opponent'. Lancelot, too, is tricked into a mortal combat when, convinced that he and his hostess are alone, he must suddenly defend her from a number of knights who appear to be ravishing her, only to discover that they are merely members of her own household 'acting' on her orders. Like Gawain, Lancelot is here the victim of a play designed by the host to test his mettle.

Another similarity between the hospitality episodes in *Gawain*, *Lancelot*, and *Yvain* is the threats posed by a hostess whose sense of hospitality slides across into amorous concerns. Gawain is put into

---

[69] On the pejorative connotations of agitated movements of the body see also Jean-Claude Schmitt, *La Raison des gestes dans l'Occident médiévale* (Paris, 1990), 29.

a predicament by an amorous hostess whose advances he must fend off. Lancelot is in a similar quandary when his hostess stipulates that he must pay for his hospitality by sleeping with her. Yvain's host, after springing a mortal combat on him, offers him the hand—likewise unsought—of his daughter. These examples demonstrate the frequency with which hospitality spills over into a combat or into an adventure of love. These developments are not always unwelcome. Erec and Perceval, for example, meet their lady-loves while being entertained as guests. As guests, Erec and Perceval also willingly agree to do combat in order to rid their hosts of evil oppressors.

Hospitality in Chrétien thus determines the development of the narrative, characteristically by generating adventures of love or combat, sought or unsought. There are in fact only two hospitality episodes in the romances of Chrétien that have no function in the development of the narrative.[70] These are the sections in which Calogrenant and Yvain, who only repeats Calogrenant's experience, are offered hospitality before their adventure of the supernatural spring. They contribute nothing to what follows, and they stand out as Chrétien's only hospitality sequences that can be deleted without interrupting the continuity of the story.

Calogrenant's hospitality gets off to a promising start. He takes his lodging with a noble vavasour and is entertained by his beautiful and intelligent daughter:

> La la trovai si afeitiee,
> si bien parlant, si anseigniee,
> de tel solaz et de tel estre,
> que molt m'i delitoit a estre,
> ne ja mes por nul estovoir
> ne m'an queïsse removoir;
> mes tant me fist, la nuit, de guerre,
> li vavasors, qu'il me vint querre,
> qant de soper fu tans et ore . . .   (*Yvain*, 239–47)

I found her so charming, so well-spoken and so well-mannered, such delightful company and so beautiful that her presence delighted me and I

---

[70] The same cannot always be said of other Arthurian romances. For structurally irrelevant hospitality scenes see, for example, the *Didot-Perceval*, pp. 184–6, or *Rigomer*, which contains one superfluous hospitality scene after another. This also holds true for the longer burlesque romances, such as the *Vengeance Raguidel* and *L'Atre périlleux*, which abound in irrelevant hospitality scenes. Given their humorous portrayals of Gawain's aimless wanderings which substitute for the missions he forgets, the structural superfluity of these scenes is probably deliberate.

would not have left the place for anything in the world. But the vavasour thwarted me when he came to fetch me for supper.

But the next morning Calogrenant departs without the damsel and without a ticket to adventure. Fortunately he meets the Giant Herdsman, who directs him to the miraculous spring, where he is defeated by an unknown knight in combat. Calogrenant returns to the noble vavasour, and then sets off to Arthur's court, where, years later, he musters the courage to narrate his adventures. Unlike Chrétien, who uses hospitality as a springboard to love or prowess, Calogrenant tells a story in which hospitality is uneventful and conjoined with neither. Unable to produce a *conjointure*, Calogrenant is, as Eugene Vance aptly puts it, a 'bad poet'.[71]

But the bad poet is certainly not Chrétien, who is quite deliberately playing with his audience's expectations that the hospitality offered to Calogrenant will affect future events. The expectation arises in particular from a corresponding passage from *Erec et Enide*, a romance which *Yvain* deliberately mirrors in many ways.[72] The first hospitality sequence in *Erec* offers close parallels to the first in *Yvain*. Erec is offered hospitality by a vavasour and is looked after by his beautiful and wise daughter Enide. He leaves the vavasour to fight with Yder over the possession of the sparrowhawk, after which he returns to the vavasour for one more night.

The difference between the two hospitality sequences in *Yvain* and in *Erec* is that in the latter the expected links between hospitality,

---

[71] From *Topic to Tale: Logic and Narrativity in the Middle Ages* (Minneapolis, 1987), 9.

[72] After Yvain and Laudine's wedding, for example, Gawain persuades Yvain to leave his wife by warning him of the dangers of a secluded life in marriage. The insiders among Chrétien's audience would surely have had *Erec*'s episode of *recreantise* in mind. As critics have long noted, among other works which constitute *Yvain*'s frame of reference is also Chrétien's *Lancelot*. Chrétien refers to Gawain's search for Guinevere in the *Lancelot* to explain why Gawain is not available to come to the aid of his relatives (*Yvain*, 3295 ff.). Of course, these allusions to *Erec* or *Lancelot* may have been lost on many members of Chrétien's audience, who would have been perfectly capable of following the story without appreciating its intertextual subtleties. Though there is some evidence for readership, most laymen were illiterate and heard romances recited in public. I fully agree with Bumke, *Höfische Kultur*, 700–7, 721–9, that, given these circumstances, we must be careful not to overestimate the critical acuity of Chrétien's audience. Nevertheless, Chrétien frequently winks to the informed reader or listener, who, however rare in reality, clearly constitutes his ideal audience, the audience he projects in his romances, and to whom the actual audience is asked to conform. As I have emphasized earlier, the art of courtly romance lies not simply in reflecting refinement or sophistication but in calling it forth.

love, and combat are all met. Erec falls in love with Enide, and is encouraged by his well-wishing host to undertake the combat of the sparrowhawk. Similar expectations operate in the passage in which Calogrenant takes lodging. Seated with the host's beautiful daughter in an enclosed garden, the standard *locus amoenus* for amorous developments, Calogrenant also conceives an immediate fancy for her.[73] But his plans with the beautiful maiden are thwarted by the host, who announces dinnertime. Moreover, although the vavasour knows that Calogrenant is a knight in search of adventure (see 258), he proves less co-operative than Erec's host. Curiously enough, he fails to inform his guest of the nearby adventure, though, as we learn later (570–76), he knew of the adventure of the boiling spring all along.

Modelled on this episode from *Erec*, Calogrenant's hospitality raises promising possibilities, but the suggestions of chivalric or amorous developments are left dangling. In comparison with Erec's adventure, Calogrenant is to find his own extremely uneventful and his own summary says it all: 'Einsi alai, einsi reving' ('Thus I came, and thus I returned': 577). The game Chrétien here plays with his audience is one in which expectations of structural links between hospitality and love or combat are consistently defeated. In its marginality to the subsequent narrative this hospitality episode is the deliberate exception that proves the rule.

A marginal structural link, or so the *Gawain*-poet leads us to believe, also holds between the hospitality episode in *Gawain* and the combat to which Gawain must passively submit. The organic function of hospitality in determining the development of the narrative seems to rest solely on a guide obtained from the host, and a girdle given by the hostess. With these Gawain and the reader set forth, confident that the trials and tribulations of hospitality constituted only marginal incidents. Like the hospitality Calogrenant has received, they seem to have sunk into an irrevocable past without leaving ripples that might upset the present. But in *Gawain* the status of hospitality as a marginal incident is not sustained. More fundamentally than Chrétien, the *Gawain*-poet is to assert the vital link of hospitality with combat, and more

[73] The expectations raised by the enclosed garden in this episode are discussed in more detail by Peter Haidu, 'Romance: Idealistic Genre or Historical Text?', in *The Craft of Fiction: Essays in Medieval Poetics*, ed. Leigh A. Arrathoon (Rochester, Mich., 1984), 1–47, at 22–3.

fundamentally than Chrétien too, he is to show the danger of hospitality.

For, at the Green Chapel, Gawain finds himself, without knowing it, an actor in an allegory of the hospitality scenes, 'a narrative which obviously and continuously refers to another simultaneous structure of events or ideas, whether historical events, moral or philosophical ideas, or natural phenomena'.[74] In his passive combat Gawain is reliving the 'historical events' of his adventure of hospitality. The simultaneity of past and present may be illustrated by Gawain's vision of the Chapel, which recalls his earlier vision of Castle Hautdesert:

> þenne he houed, and wythhylde his hors at þat tyde,
> And ofte chaunged his cher þe chapel to seche:
> He seȝ non suche in no syde, and selly hym þoȝt
> Saue, a lyttel on a launde, a lawe as hit were;
> A balȝ berȝ bi a bonke þe brymme bysyde . . .   (2168–72)

Like Castle Hautdesert, the Green Chapel is emphatically seen from Gawain's point of view. Moreover, the lines correspond closely to those used of Gawain on his journey to Castle Hautdesert in Fitt II: 'His cher ful oft con chaunge | Þat chapel er he myȝt sene' (711–12), and 'Þe burne bode on blonk, þat on bonk houed' (785). If we then compare Gawain's first impressions of the Green Chapel, 'a lyttel on a launde, a lawe as hit were', with his first impressions of Castle Hautdesert, 'abof a launde, on a lawe' (765), the correlation between the Castle and the Chapel becomes apparent.

Once Gawain has detected the Chapel, these reverberations of his earlier adventure persist. The Green Knight's polite welcoming words: 'Ywisse þou art welcom, wyȝe, to my place' (2246), recall Gawain's earlier welcome at the Castle. His remark that he and Gawain are alone—'And we ar in þis valay verayly oure one . . .' (2245)—echoes the Lady's words on having trapped Gawain in the bedroom: 'And now ȝe ar here, iwysse, and we bot oure one . . .' (1230). When the Green Knight questions Gawain's bravery—'Þou art not Gawain', quoþ þe gome, 'þat is so goud halden' (2270)—the reader will recall how the Lady had questioned his identity—'Bot þat ȝe be Gawen, hit gotz in mynde . . . So god as Gawayn gaynly is halden' (1293–7).

---

[74] Northrop Frye, 'Allegory', in *Encyclopedia of Poetry and Poetics*, ed. A. Preminger (Princeton, NJ, 1965), 12–15.

If Gawain has thus far been blind to the larger significance of his experiences at the Green Chapel, the Green Knight will enlighten him. The three strokes, as he reveals, mirror the three temptations and exchanges and their outcomes. In the first two Gawain has kept his word and so escapes scot-free. The third, in which he accepts and wrongly keeps the girdle, is reflected by the third stroke, with which the Green Knight deals Gawain a nick in the neck. The Green Knight interprets his strokes allegorically; he insists that they have a significance beyond themselves, that they unite past and present. So, we may note, does the *Gawain*-poet when he fuses the harm done to Bertilac—'I halde hit hardily hole, þe harm that I hade' (2390)— and the physical harm inflicted on Gawain, which heals as quickly as Bertilac's: 'þe hurt watz hole þat he hade hent in his nek' (2484).

Thus, while relating Gawain's experiences at the Green Chapel, the *Gawain*-poet retells the hospitality episode in a narrative that double-exposes the Castle and the Chapel, Gawain's grim opponent and the Lady, his test of his reputation for bravery and her test of his reputation as a lover, the three strokes of the axe and the three temptations and exchanges, and the nick of the axe with the harm done to Bertilac. By shifting the courtly *plaisanterie* of hospitality to another plane of meaning, that of a sinister combat, the *Gawain*-poet gives the reader a powerful and poetic vision of the actual danger the adventure of hospitality has constituted all along. The danger of the Castle has been that of the Chapel, the 'enmy kene' (2406) has, as the Green Knight reveals, been the Lady, her test of his dalliance has ultimately been a test of his bravery in a matter of life and death, dangerous like the strokes of an axe. The hospitality scene, which we thought we had left behind, returns with a vengeance. As I have suggested, the *Gawain*-poet recalls and reinterprets it in an allegory, the mode which, in Joel Fineman's words, 'makes up for the distance, or heals the gap, between the present and the disappearing past, which without interpretation, would be otherwise irretrievable and foreclosed'.[75]

A final parallel between the literary methods of the *Gawain*-poet and those of Chrétien may here be drawn. As a recent interpreter of *Erec et Enide* has argued, Erec also finds himself, without realizing

---

[75] 'The Structure of Allegorical Desire', in *Allegory and Representation*, ed. Stephen J. Greenblatt (Baltimore, 1981), 26–60, at 29.

it, an actor in an allegory.[76] In the adventure of the Joy of the Court he liberates Mabonograin from the secluded world of love into the community, and thus re-enacts the way in which he, in this romance, has liberated himself from isolation into the public world. The scene of recognition which takes place after the combat, when Mabonograin and his *amie* turn out to be old acquaintances of Erec and Enide, plays on the implication that Erec has been fighting his former self.[77] As Erec says, Mabonograin should be able to recognize him: 'You should know me well' ('Dons me doit tu conuistre bien . . .': *Erec*, 5594). As the allegory of Gawain's combat has retold and reinterpreted the hospitality scenes, so 'in the heightened term of medieval allegory, the Joie de la Cort retells the "san", the moral, of Erec's quest'.[78]

What can we conclude from the comparison of the conventions of hospitality in *Gawain* and the courtly romances in Old French? For one thing, it has become clear that the *Gawain*-poet was familiar with the repertoire of hospitality-motifs as they occur in various modulations in the *roman courtois*. That the expression of these motifs was a matter of great importance in *Gawain* and the romances of Chrétien de Troyes, in contrast to a popular romance such as *Sir Perceval of Galles*, testifies not simply to a difference in social milieu but also to the didactic aspirations of Chrétien and the *Gawain*-poet. Like courtesy books, their courtly romances formalize an etiquette which regulates the behaviour of guest and host, an etiquette which their heroes put into action and which their romances seek to hand on to their audience. We have already

[76] Marguerite S. Murphy, 'The Allegory of "Joie" in Chrétien's *Erec et Enide*', in *Allegory, Myth, and Symbol*, ed. Morton W. Bloomfield (Cambridge, Mass., 1981), 109–28.

[77] As Eugene Vance has pointed out, the implication that Erec's combat is an allegory of Erec has had to fight with himself is developed in Hartmann von Aue's *Erec*, in which the hero himself expounds this reading of the significance of the adventure of the Joy of the Court. See Vance's 'Le Combat érotique chez Chrétien de Troyes', *Poétique*, 12 (1972), 544–71, at 568–9. The significance of the fact that Erec and Mabonograin and their wives are related, and are old acquaintances, has been pointed out by B. N. Sargent, ' "L'Autre" chez Chrétien de Troyes', *CCM* 10 (1967), 199–205. Metaphors of kinship frequently express similarities of character in medieval literature. Note, for example, the exclamation of the destitute hero of the Middle English romance *Sir Amadace*, who recognizes himself in the person of a merchant whose liberality proved fatal: 'He myghte full wele be of my kynne' | For ryght so have I wroghte' (209–10); ed. M. Mills, *Six Middle English Romances*, Everyman Library (London, 1973).

[78] Murphy, 'Allegory of "Joie" ', 110.

detected this civilizing impulse in the previous chapter on the land-scape of courtly romance, and the following chapters will document this impulse further.

To the assumption that representations of conventions of hos-pitality are of no literary interest, both poets give the lie. Precisely because they are conventional, the minute observations of the polite protocol are potentially deceptive appearances. Their fictional char-acters have absorbed the injunctions of courtesy books with a self-consciousness unmatched by the heroes of popular romance, and, like no other romancers, Chrétien and the *Gawain*-poet explore the discrepancies between faces and feelings that go hand in hand with the codification of an etiquette of hospitality to which the courtesy books were giving a start. And alongside the discrep-ancy between faces and feelings which etiquette encourages, there appears the possibility of deceit, a theme that appears with great frequency in the romances of Chrétien, his continuators, and *Ga-wain*.

Moreover, in their romances as a whole, hospitality has a vital structural function. Their hospitality episodes confront the Arthur-ian knight with the perennial dangers of hosts, or, as in the chal-lenge, guests, who become dangerous enemies, or hostesses who offer their love solicited or unsolicited. I could not think of a more powerful exposé of the hazards and the treacherous undercurrents of the polite gestures of hospitality than the *Gawain*-poet's retelling of Gawain's stay at Castle Hautdesert as an allegory of decapitation.

3 The Temptation Scenes

֍

Introduction

THE ROMANCE of *Perlesvaus,* or *Le Haut Livre du Graal,* was
written in the first half of the thirteenth century, perhaps in England
or at least by a writer with some knowledge of its geography and its
recent historical events.[1] The work recounts the adventures of Perceval, Lancelot, and Gawain, who has undertaken the quest for the
sword of Saint John. The relation between the *Perlesvaus* and *Sir
Gawain and the Green Knight* has already been a matter of considerable speculation.[2] Like *Gawain,* the prose romance contains a
beheading game. After chopping off the head of a suicidal knight,
Lancelot returns to the Waste City one year later for a return blow.
When his opponent raises his axe he sees that Lancelot flinches, and
impugns his bravery. While he prepares himself for a second attempt, two damsels who have observed the scene from afar beg
Lancelot's enemy to spare his life. He does so because, since Lancelot has kept his promise to return, the Waste City has been restored
to prosperity.

   The presence of a beheading game alone is of course hardly a basis
for claiming the *Perlesvaus* as a source for *Gawain.* Among works
in French, the *First Continuation* of Chrétien's *Perceval,* the *Mule
sans frein,* and *Hunbaut* likewise depict beheading games. But there
is another, more revealing analogue to *Gawain* in the *Perlesvaus,*

---

   [1] Thomas E. Kelly, *Le Haut Livre du Graal: A Structural Study* (Geneva, 1974),
18. *Perlesvaus*'s link with England is borne out by its manuscript tradition. The
Oxford Manuscript in the Bodleian (Hatton 82) was probably copied in England,
and was definitely circulating in England from the early fourteenth century onwards.
It was known to the English author of *Fouke FitzWarin* and to Malory, as noted by
R. H. Wilson, 'Malory and the *Perlesvaus*', MP 30 (1932), 13–21, and P. J. C. Field,
'Malory and the *Perlesvaus*', MAE 62 (1993), 259–69. The *Gawain*-poet could
therefore have had first-hand knowledge of the work.
   [2] See W. A. Nitze, 'Is the Green Knight Story Really a Vegetation Myth?', MP 33
(1936), 351–66.

which is less well known.[3] The romance describes an attempted seduction which bears some intriguing resemblances to the temptation scenes in *Gawain*. On his quest, Gawain meets two knights who offer him hospitality. As he sits down for supper in a pavilion two ladies enter:

Que que Messire Gavains menjoit, atant ez vos. ii. damoiseles qui viennent en la tente e le saluent molt hautement; et il leur respont au plus bele qu'il sot . . . 'Sire, fet l'ainznee, comment est vostre nons?—Damoisele, g'é non Gavains.—Sire, fet ele, tant vos amons nos mielz . . . E qant il fu cochiez eles s'asieent devant lui, e ont le clerge alumé, e s'apoient desus la coche, e li presentent molt leur service. E Messire Gavains ne leur respont autre chose que granz merciz, car il ne pense fors a dormir e a reposer. 'Par Dieu, fet l'une a l'autre, se ce fust cil Gavains qui niés est le roi Artu, il parlast a nos autrement, e trovissions en lui plus de deduit que est en cestui; mes cist est un Gavains contrefez . . .' Atant ez vos le naim o vient. 'Biax amis, font les damoiseles, garde nos cest chevalier qu'il ne s'enfuie. Ainsi va il d'ostel en ostel par truandise; si se fet apeler Messire Gavains, mes il no sanble pas, car se ce fust il, e nos volssissions veillier .iii. nuiz, s'en veillast il quatre . . .' Messire Gavains ot bien ce que les damoiseles dient, e ne leur respont neent . . . (*Perlesvaus*, pp. 95–6)

While Sir Gawain was eating, two damsels entered the pavilion and greeted him emphatically; and he answered them as best as he could . . . 'Sir,' said the eldest, 'what is your name?' 'Maiden, my name is Gawain.' 'Sir,' she said, 'then we love you all the more . . .' And when Gawain had gone to bed, they seated themselves before him, lit the candle and, leaning on his bed, they fervently presented their services. And Sir Gawain only said, 'Thank you very much', for he thought only of sleeping and resting. 'By God,' one said to the other, 'if this were indeed Gawain, Arthur's nephew, he would have talked to us differently, and we would have found more fun in him than in this one. This Gawain is counterfeit . . .' Then the dwarf joined them. 'Dear friend,' say the damsels, 'make sure this knight does not run away. This deceiver goes from hostel to hostel calling himself Sir Gawain, but he does not resemble him, for if it was him and we would have wanted to stay awake for three nights, he would have added a fourth . . .' Sir Gawain heard all too well what the damsels were saying, but did not say a word.

The next day Gawain must do battle with a knight who can only be killed by piercing his Achilles' heel. When Gawain defeats the knight, the ladies decide that he must indeed be the genuine article. For the second time they offer their services:

[3] Only Larry D. Benson, *Art and Tradition in Sir Gawain and the Green Knight* (New York, 1965), 221–2, notes the analogue.

Sire, font eles, encore vos offrons nos nostre service, car nos savons bien que vos estes li buens chevaliers. Recevez a amie la quele que vos volez.—Granz merciz, damoiseles, fet Messire Gavains. Vostre amor ne refus ge pas, e a Dieu vos commant. (*Perlesvaus*, p. 99)

'Sir,' they say, 'again we offer you our services, for we know well that you are the good knight. Take as your friend whomever you fancy.' 'Many thanks, damsels,' says Sir Gawain. 'I shall not refuse your love, and I commend you to God.'

With these words Gawain rides off, leaving the ladies to bewail their lost opportunity.

Gawain's adventure from the fifth branch of the *Perlesvaus* has admittedly nothing of the ingenuity with which the Lady and Gawain combat each other in *Sir Gawain and the Green Knight*. But if the *Perlesvaus* differs from *Gawain*'s temptation scenes in this respect, the thirteenth-century romance may nevertheless elucidate some of the strategies to which the Lady, Gawain, and the *Gawain*-poet resort. Like the Lady in *Gawain*, the two 'damoiseles' know Gawain's literary reputation as a ladies' man very well.[4] Having offered their 'service', a euphemism for their sexual favours, their astonishment when Gawain instead retires to sleep is great. So great that they are, or pretend to be, convinced that this Gawain must be an impostor, for the real Gawain would have known better what to do with two damsels. He would have wished to 'keep vigil' even longer than they themselves. There is no indication in the text that they address their complaint directly to Gawain. But Gawain over-hears, and the ladies no doubt mean him to overhear. For it is with words that they tempt him. They reason and argue but their over-tures never depart from the field of language. In fact the temptations in *Perlesvaus* and in *Gawain* take the similar form of an invitation to become the 'Sir Gawain' about whom their seductresses have obviously heard so much. Why this form should be effective, and whence the ladies derive Gawain's reputation as a womanizer, will be the subject of my first section.

The adventure from *Le Haut Livre du Graal* resembles the temp-tation scenes from *Gawain* in another respect. Gawain's dilemma in the *Perlesvaus* and *Gawain* is not simply one of whether to give in or to resist. Like Gawain in the *Perlesvaus*, Gawain has to refuse politely. In the second section I will show that, like the French

---

[4] On this aspect of the *Perlesvaus* see Thomas E. Kelly, 'Love in the *Perlesvaus*: Sinful Passion or Redemptive Force?', *Romanic Review*, 66 (1975), 1–12.

Gawain, our hero finds a way of circumventing the dilemma he faces by using the saving ambiguity inherent in 'luf-talk'. Its potential to be a facet of gallantry, and nothing more, means it is always open to misunderstanding, or the pretence of misunderstanding. This is what Gawain in the *Perlesvaus* exploits when he responds to the offer of 'service', or the offer of an 'amie', which may mean no more than 'friend', with the polite reply that he is honoured to accept their love. But when he next commends the two ladies to God, it becomes clear that his reply has been no more than an urbane figure of speech, precisely the way in which he pretends to have taken the ladies' words. In the second section I want to show how Gawain in the English romance turns the ambiguity of love-talk to his advantage.

Unlike his counterpart in the *Perlesvaus*, however, Gawain does not leave the Lady of the Castle empty-handed, but with a green girdle which, as the Lady of the Castle assures him, will save his life. While refusing to merge with the 'Gawain' of earlier works, the fantasy of ladies of romance whose love-gifts protect knights on their quests proves irresistible for Gawain. And, like Gawain, the reader, too, momentarily shares the illusion of being in a narrative where magic talismans might work. Of course, all Arthurian romances ask us to believe in their enchanted worlds, but the spell is not usually broken until the romance is finished and we return to reality. The *Gawain*-poet, however, breaks his spell much earlier, when, at the Green Chapel, he reveals to us and Gawain that the green girdle was, after all, only a matter of make-believe. Chrétien de Troyes plays similar games with his audience and heroes, and I want to explore in a final section how both poets confront us in the course of their romances with our suspension of disbelief.

Narrative Fashioning

As the *Gawain*-poet makes abundantly clear, Gawain is beset by temptations which are to a large extent of a verbal nature.[5] Wherever the *Gawain*-poet talks of the Lady's attack or Gawain's resist-

[5] The point is lucidly made by Thomas L. Wright in an analysis of the temptation scenes: 'Luf-Talking in *Sir Gawain and the Green Knight*', in *Approaches to Teaching Sir Gawain and the Green Knight*, ed. M. Y. Miller and J. Chance (New York, 1986), 77–86.

ance, he refers in fact to the thrust and parry of the words with which the Lady seduces and Gawain rebuffs her, as if to bring home the force which words exert on lives. Indeed, the words used to describe seduction in *Gawain* are almost indistinguishable from, or used synonymously with, words that describe acts of speech. In the following line, for example, 'tempting' (fonden) and 'questioning' (fraynen) are practically interchangeable:

> Þus hym frayned þat fre and fondet hym ofte,
> For to haf wonnen hym to woȝe, what-so scho thoȝt ellez . . .
>
> (1549–50)

The temptation lurks, so it seems, in the very act of 'frayning'. Let us look at one such question which the Lady puts to Gawain to see why such a verbal temptation should be effective.

> 'I woled wyt at yow, wyȝe,' þat worþy þer sayde,
> 'And yow wrathed not þerwyth, what were þe skylle
> Þat so ȝong and so ȝepe as ȝe at þis tyme,
> So cortayse, so knyȝtyly, as ȝe ar knowen oute—
> And of alle cheualry to chose, þe chef þyng alosed
> Is þe lel layk of luf, þe lettrure of armes;
> For to telle of þis teuelyng of þis trwe knyȝtez,
> Hit is þe tytelet token and tyxt of her werkkez,
> How ledes for her lele luf hor lyuez han auntered,
> Endured for her drury dulful stoundez,
> And after wenged with her walour and voyded her care,
> And broȝt blysse into boure with bountees hor awen—
> And ȝe ar knyȝt comlokest kyd of your elde,
> Your worde and your worchip walkez ayquere,
> And I haf seten by yourself here sere twyes,
> ȝet herde I neuer of your hed helde no wordez
> Þat euer longed to luf, lasse ne more.'   (1508–24)

At first sight, the Lady's question, posed during her second bedroom visit, suffers from a lack of organization. Just as the Lady broaches the topic of Gawain's reputation for courtesy and chivalry, her sentence seems to founder. She proceeds to give her reading of chivalric romance and picks up the loose end only at line 1520. Her lecture on medieval romance, however, is both accurate and pertinent to her project. Chrétien's romances, Thomas's or Beroul's *Tristan* are some of the many 'werkkez' the Lady could quote in support of the 'chivalry topos' she expounds. This topos, formulated for the first time in Arthurian literature in Geoffrey of

Monmouth's *Historia Regum Britanniae*, sought to resolve the incompatibility between the warrior and the lover by showing how love inspires excellent deeds. Chrétien puts the effect of love on the knight's bravery concisely when he describes Lancelot as 'the knight made noble and strong by love, and courageous in all things' ('cil cui Amors fet riche | et puissant, et hardi par tot . . .': *Lancelot*, 630–1). It follows, so the Lady reasons, that there can be no 'trwe kny3tes' who do not at the same time benefit from the spur of 'lele luf'.

The topos is a powerful weapon against unwilling men: witness the use that ladies in medieval romance make of it. In the *Lanzelet*, the host's daughter tries to seduce her guests with lines such as:

> jâ solten helde ziere,
> die durch diu lant alsus varnt
> unt sich mit hübscheit bewarnt,
> etwaz reden von den wîben
> und die zît hin vertrîben
> mit sprechenne den besten wol. (*Lanzelet*, 908–13)

Why, fine knights who travel abroad this way and take pains to behave courteously should converse somewhat about women and while away the time in most pleasant conversation.

> daz ist wâr,
> er gewan nie manlîchen muot,
> der nicht toerlîche tuot,
> etswenne durch diu wîp. (*Lanzelet*, 1016–19)

The truth is that nobody ever achieved real manhood who did not at some time or other act indiscreetly for the sake of a woman.[6]

Note also the scathing remarks of the young widow, when her object of desire, Petit Jehan de Saintré, confesses to not having a lady-friend:

Ha! failli gentil homme, et dictes vous que n'en avez nulle? A ce cop cognois je bien que jamais ne vauldrez riens. Eu! failli cuer que vous estes, d'ou sont venues les grans vaillances, les grans emprises et les chevalereux faiz de Lancelot, de Gauvain, de Tristan, de Guron le courtois, et des autres preux de la Table Ronde . . . sinon par le service d'amours acquerir et eulz entretenir an la grace de leurs tres desirees dames! (*Jehan de Saintré*, pp. 6–7)

Ha! feeble young man, and you tell me that you have none? Then I know immediately that you will never be worthy. Alas! you coward, whence came the bravery, the magnanimity, and the chivalrous deeds of Lancelot, of

---

[6] Trans. K. G. Webster, *Lanzelet* (New York, 1951), 39.

Gawain, of Tristan, of Guiron the courteous, and of the other heroes of the Round Table . . . if not from the love-service they rendered to acquire and maintain themselves in the grace of their dearly beloved ladies!

The Lady of the Castle, too, applies the rhetorical weapon of the 'chivalry topos' unremittingly to her guest. Like the heroes of her 'werkkez' Gawain has excellence: *ergo*, he must have a lover. The Lady, then, does not simply offer her love; she claims on the basis of her reading that to accept her is only proper. When Gawain does not speak a word 'þat . . . longed to luf', she concludes he must be 'lewed', not simply in the sense of 'uncouth', which is how most modern editions gloss it, but also in the original sense of 'illiterate', that is to say, unable to read the 'werkkez' which the Lady adduces as sure proof that Gawain's behaviour goes against the letter.

Gawain has very good reasons besides modesty to decline the Lady's offer to 'take þe toruayle to myself to trwluf expoun, | And towche þe temes of tyxt and talez of armez' (1540–1). Not only has the Lady mastered the art of story-telling herself, as Gawain remarks, but the 'tyxt and talez' she wishes to hear would only underline the fact that the heroes of old acted differently. Gawain deviates from the 'lettrure' by failing to provide the happy ending of romances when knights bring 'blysse into boure'.

The Lady's tactical use of romance paradigms has an interesting analogue in Renaut de Beaujeu's startling conclusion to his romance of the *Bel Inconnu* (*c*.1185–90). The romance relates the adventures of Guinglain, a young knight in search of his identity. Unbeknown to him, he is Gawain's son, and in various adventures he discovers and proves himself worthy of his name and his ancestry. The Bel Inconnu first liberates the Fairy Maiden with the White Hands, and he is instantly struck by her great beauty. Unfortunately, he is bound by a promise to liberate the castle of the Blonde Esmeree and is thus forced to leave her. He successfully puts an end to the spells and enchantments which had transformed the Blonde Esmeree into a serpent. Esmeree presses her claims for Guinglain's hand but, still enamoured of the Fairy Maiden, Guinglain abandons her. Esmeree, however, remains intent on marrying her hero and with Arthur's help a tournament is announced in the hope of luring him away from his true love. When Guinglain turns up at the tournament, Esmeree exerts her influence on him, and Gawain's son is pressurized into a marriage with Esmeree which Arthur's court has been busily preparing. At this moment, when it seems that Guinglain will forever be joined to the lady of his second choice, the narrator suddenly stops and concludes his romance by addressing the lady whose love has inspired him to compose it:

> Ci faut li roumans et define.
> Bele, vers cui mes cuers s'acline,
> Renals de Biauju molt vos prie
> Por Diu que ne l'obliés mie.
> De cuer vos veut tos jors amer,
> Ce ne li poés vos veer.
> Quant vos plaira, dira avant,
> U il se taira ore a tant.
> Mais por un biau sanblant mostrer
> Vos feroit Guinglain retrover
> S'amie, que il a perdue,
> Qu'entre ses bras le tenroit nue.
> Se de çou li faites delai,
> Si ert Guinglains en tel esmai
> Que ja mais n'avera s'amie.
> D'autre vengeance n'a il mie,
> Mais por la soie grant grevance
> Ert sor Guinglain ceste vengance,
> Que ja mais jor n'en parlerai
> Tant que le bel sanblant avrai.
> EXPLICIT DEL BEL DESCONEÜ
> (*Bel Inconnu*, 6247–66)

Here the end is missing, and the romance comes to a halt. Sweetheart, to whom my heart inclines, Renaut de Beaujeu begs you for God's sake not to forget him. He wants to love you sincerely forever, and you cannot deny him this. When it pleases you, he will continue, if not, he will forever be silent. But for a wink he will make Guinglain find his lost lady-love again, so that he may hold her naked in his arms. If you delay, Guinglain will have the misfortune of never seeing his love again. He has no other vengeance but to take out his anger on Guinglain, and I will not continue until I have your wink. This is the end of the 'Bel Inconnu'.

This is one of the most shameless pieces of emotional blackmail in medieval literature.[7] If Renaut's Lady wants a happy ending, she

---

[7] The point of its conclusion seems to have been lost on much criticism of the romance. Thus Laurence de Looze argues that the open ending of the work shows the author's conviction that 'writing, like loving, demands freedom, and that endings and genres cannot be forced upon the reader'. That the open ending is the narrator's trump card in a manipulation of an unwilling lover, and thus aims at restricting freedom, is overlooked: 'Generic Clash, Reader Response, and the Poetics of the Non-Ending in *Le Bel Inconnu*', in *Courtly Literature: Culture and Context*, ed.

must first give her admirer her 'bel sanblant'. If she does not, Renaut threatens, the 'grevance' he suffers will be avenged on his fictional character. The possible gratification of the desires of Guinglain and the Fairy depends on the Lady's willingness to gratify the desires of the poet. The tale thus awaits an ending which only Renaut's addressee can provide. The romance of Guinglain and the Fairy, so Renaut implies, is really about himself and his lady. They will reap the misery or the joy of their fictional characters.

As the Lady of the Castle banks on Gawain's desire to bring his story in line with the chivalric romances about the 'blysse' of knights and their lovers, so Renaut de Beaujeu manipulates the Lady's desire to bring the aborted poem to a satisfactory conclusion. The romance paradigm, culminating in the knight's 'blysse' with a lady whom he may hold 'entre ses bras . . . nue', is used in both these cases as a magnetic force to whose pull Gawain and Renaut's lady are urged to yield. Renaut and the Lady of the Castle tell romances not in order to amuse their listeners, but in the hope that they will root their own wishes in them, in the hope that their listeners make the love that torments the fictional heroes and heroines their own. In the relationship between the tale-teller and the listener the romance insinuates itself as a mediator of desire.[8]

The lure of the Lady of the Castle's 'tyxt' and 'talez' is, like that of Renaut's romance, mimetic. She projects in her words a lover of ladies to whom a long tradition of chivalric romance has given its seal of approval, so that Gawain may model himself on the ideal these romances have constructed.[9] Herein lies the temptation of the

K. Busby and E. Kooper (Amsterdam, 1990), 113–23, at 115. The editor of *Le Bel Inconnu* called the work 'banal dans son fond' (p. x), while Keith Busby in the *Arthurian Encyclopedia*, ed. Norris J. Lacy (Cambridge, 1986) claims the French romance is 'brought to a satisfactory conclusion'. Busby may here be confusing the work with the English adaptation by Thomas of Chestre, in which the Fairy Maiden becomes a malevolent enchantress from whom Guinglain narrowly escapes. Thomas of Chestre, who provided the happy ending missing in his French source, thus succumbed to the desire for a satisfactory closure on which the narrator relies. See Jeri S. Guthrie, 'The *JE(U)* in *Le Bel Inconnu*', *Romanic Review*, 75 (1984), 147–61, for an illuminating discussion of Renaut de Beaujeu's ending.

[8] I draw here on René Girard's model of mimetic desire. Rather than assuming that there is a direct line from desiring subject to object of desire, Girard argues that desire is triangular. There is always a third party whose desire or imagined desire for the same object makes that object alluring. See his *Mensonge romantique et vérité romanesque* (Paris, 1961).

[9] Geraldine Heng, 'A Woman Wants: The Lady, *Gawain*, and the Forms of Seduction', *Yale Journal of Criticism*, 5 (1992), 101–35.

Lady's narrative fashioning. It holds out to Gawain the possibility of satisfying the need for recognition, the human desire to find oneself confirmed in the language of the other, in the act of identifying with the heroes of romantic invention.[10] Prominent among these ideals is the 'Gawain' of late twelfth- and thirteenth-century romance. It is necessary here to look briefly at his reputation in these romances.[11] I will do so with specific reference to two episodes from the continuations of Chrétien's *Perceval* which seem to have influenced the *Gawain*-poet directly.

I take my first episode from the *First Continuation* of Chrétien's *Perceval*. When Arthur lays siege to Brun de Branlant's castle, Gawain, injured though he is, rides out on a beautiful day to divert himself. He chances on a pavilion where he finds an attractive damsel all on her own. When Gawain greets her she replies:

[10] Two notorious victims of precisely this temptation are Dante's Paolo and Francesca who, on reading about Lancelot and Guinevere's affair in the Vulgate *Lancelot*, give each other their first kiss and become involved in a passionate relationship whose consequences they now suffer in Hell. As René Girard writes: 'The written word exercises a veritable fascination . . . it is a mirror in which they gaze, discovering in themselves the semblances of their brilliant models': 'From the *Divine Comedy* to the Sociology of the Novel', in *Sociology of Literature and Drama*, ed. Elisabeth and Tom Burns (Harmondsworth, 1973), 101–8, at 102.

[11] Much work has been done on the character of Gawain in medieval literature. The broadest studies are Keith Busby's *Gauvain in Old French Literature* (Amsterdam, 1980); Bartlett J. Whiting, 'Gawain: His Reputation, His Courtesy, and His Appearance in Chaucer's *Squire's Tale*', MS 9 (1947), 189–244; and Per Nykrog, 'Trajectory of the Hero: Gauvain, Paragon of Chivalry 1130–1230', in *Medieval Narrative: A Symposium*, ed. H. Bekker-Nielsen et al. (Odense, 1979), 82–93. Martin B. Shichtman has written on Gawain's appearance in Wace and Laȝamon; 'Gawain in Wace and Laȝamon: A Case of Metahistorical Evolution', in *Medieval Texts and Contemporary Readers*, ed. Laurie A. Finke and Martin B. Shichtman (Ithaca, NY, 1987), 103–19. For studies of the character of Gawain in the romances of Chrétien in particular see William A. Nitze, 'Gauvain in the Romances of Chrétien de Troyes', *MP* 50 (1952–3), 219–25, and Douglas Kelly, 'Gawain and *Fin Amors* in the poems of Chrétien de Troyes', *Studies in Philology*, 67 (1970), 453–60. On the role of Gawain in thirteenth-century prose and verse romances see Fanni Bogdanow, 'The Character of Gawain in the Thirteenth-Century Prose Romances', *MAE* 27 (1958), 154–61; and Beate Schmolke-Hasselmann, 'Eine Idealfigur in Zwiespalt: Ritter oder Liebhaber', in her book *Der Arthurische Versroman von Chrestien bis Froissart* (Tübingen, 1980). Three recent studies of Gawain in English romances are Heinz Bergner's 'Gawein und seine literarischen Realisationen in der englischen Literatur des Spätmittelalters', in *Artusrittertum im späten Mittelalter: Ethos und Ideologie*, ed. Friedrich Wolfzettel (Giessen, 1984), 3–15; Alfred Schopf, 'Die Gestalt Gawains bei Chrétien, Wolfram von Eschenbach, und in *Sir Gawain and the Green Knight*', in *Spätmittelalterliche Artusliteratur*, ed. Karl Heinz Göller (Paderborn, 1984), 85–104; and Philip C. Boardman, 'Middle English Arthurian Romance: The Repetition and Reputation of Gawain', in *The Vitality of the Arthurian Legend*, ed. M. Pors (Odense, 1988), 71–90.

'Et cil qui fist et soir et main
Salt et gart monseignor Gavain
Et vos aprés, et beneïe.'
(*First Continuation*, I. 2629–31)

'And may he who made morning and evening save, guard, and bless Sir Gawain, and then you.'

Asked why she greets both 'Gavain' and himself, she replies that ever since she first heard about Gawain she has loved him for his excellent qualities:

Qu'en lui a plus sens et larguece,
De cortoisie et de proëce,
Qu'il nait en chevalier vivant.   (I. 2649–51)

Because he has in him more wisdom and liberality, more courtesy and prowess, than any living knight.

Despite Gawain's assurances that he is in fact this 'Gavain', she refuses to believe him at first. When he insists, she asks him to wait while she checks his appearance with an embroidered image of her idol. The lady quickly returns when she has verified her guest's claims:

A lui s'en vient et si l'embrache,
Baise lui oex et boche et face
Plus de vint fois en un randon.
'Amis, fait ele, en abandon
Vos met mon cors et vos presant.
Vostre serai tot mon vivant.'
. . . .
D'amor, de jeu, de cortoisie
Ont puis ensamble tant parlé
Et bonement ris et jüé,
Tant qu'a perdu non de pucele,
S'a non amie et damoisele.   (I. 2699–716)

She comes up to him and embraces him, kisses his eyes, mouth, and face more than twenty times in a go. 'Friend,' she says, 'I surrender and present to you my body. I will be yours while I live.' . . . Of love, of fun, and of courtesy they talked, and they laughed and played together, until she had lost the name of 'maiden', and had become lover and lady.

The passage is the first in French romance in which a lady falls in love with the idea of Gawain rather than the man himself. She shows no interest in her guest before she positively identifies him as Gawain. Later romancers borrowed the motif of the woman who has fallen in love with Gawain before ever having seen him. That is why it becomes essential for these ladies to be able to identify him should he be passing by. The lady in the *First Continuation* has an embroidered portrait of her idol, the heroines of later romances use a lifelike statue, or an engraving in a ring. Other ladies hire a servant who is conversant with all the faces of the Arthurian knights, or rely on the expertise of local inhabitants to spot the hero and to report his whereabouts.[12] Like Bertilac's wife, the 'pucelle' of the *First Continuation* has a preconceived notion of Gawain and both refuse to believe they are dealing with him when he fails to meet their expectations. Compare 'J'ai non Gavains'—'Gavains, fait ele; | Pas ne le croi' (2661–2), with the Lady of the Castle's 'Bot þat ȝe be Gawan, hit gotz in mynde' (1293). In both cases the ladies take the initiative and embrace their guests; in *Gawain* 'Ho commes nerre with þat, and cachez hym in armez, | Loutez luflych adoun and þe leude kyssez . . .' (1305–6), and in the *Continuation* 'A lui s'en vient et si l'embrache, | Baise lui . . .'. Even more striking are the correspondences in the way the ladies offer their favours to their guests. Compare lines 2702–4 from the *Continuation* above with the Lady of the Castle's words:

> 'Ȝe ar welcum to my cors,
> Yowre awen won to wale,
> Me behouez of fyne force
> Your seruaunt be, and schale.' (1237–40)

Both ladies offer their 'cors' and promise they will always 'your seruaunt be' or 'vostre serai'.

La Pucelle de Lis is of course genuinely attracted to her guest and is not merely pretending. For a temptation scene in which a lady feigns interest we may turn to the little-read *Fourth Continuation* by Gerbert de Montreuil, composed in the early thirteenth century. As Gawain wanders about on his horse 'le Gringalet', he is offered hospitality in the castle of a beautiful lady. Immediately, he offers her his services. The Lady, who is in fact out to revenge her brother's death on any knight who happens to pass by, and ideally on Gawain, the alleged murderer, feigns a passionate interest in her guest. The temptation scene corresponds very closely to

[12] These medieval equivalents of the 'wanted' photograph and the bounty hunter are used in *Hunbaut*, the Non-Cyclic *Lancelot*, *L'Atre périlleux*, and the *Perlesvaus* respectively.

Gawain, as these passages, juxtaposed with extracts from *Gawain*, will show.

> Malement estera sozpris
> Me sire Gavains cele fois,
> Se Dieus ne li aïue et fois.
> (*Fourth Continuation*, 12418–20)

This time Sir Gawain will be in trouble, unless God comes to his aid.

> Gret perile bitwene hem stod,
> Nif Maré of hir kny3t mynne. (1768–9)

> 'Certes, por vostre chevalier
> Me poez d'ore e avant prendre.'
> E cele por lui plus esprendre
> Et eschaufer de musardie;
> 'Sire, ne lairai ne vous die,
> Onques nul jor ne m'entremis
> D'amours. Je ne sai qu'est amis,
> Ne je nel quier nul jor savoir,
> N'en mois n'a pas tant de savoir,
> Ke chevalier amer seüsse . . .'
> (*Fourth Continuation*, 12430–9)

'Certainly, you may from now on consider me your knight.' And to rouse him even more, and egg him on to foolishness, she said: 'I should tell you that I have never had anything to do with love before. I do not know what a boyfriend is, and never wished to know, ignorant as I am about how to love a knight.'

> my souerayn I holde yow,
> And yowre kny3t I becom . . . (1278–9)

> And 3e, þat ar so cortays and coynt of your hetes,
> Oghe to a 3onke þynk 3ern to schewe
> And teche sum tokenez of trweluf craftes.
>   .   .   .   .   .   .
> I com hider sengel, and sitte
> To lerne at yow sum game;
> Dos, techez me of your wytte,
> Whil my lorde is fro hame.   (1525–34)

> Et neporquant, se je deüsse
> A nul homme doner m'amor,
> Vous l'avriiez tot sanz demour
> Tant vous voi bel et avenant . . .
> (*Fourth Continuation*, 1240–3)

But nevertheless, if I had to give my love to any man, you would have it
without demur, since you are so handsome and nice.

> 'And I schulde chepen and chose to cheue me a lorde,
> For þe costes þat I haf knowen vpon þe, knyȝt, here,
> Of bewté and debonerté and blyþe semblaunt,
> And þat I haf er herkkened and halde hit here trwee,
> Þer schulde no freke vpon folde bifore yow be chosen.' (1271–5)

> Le regarde por mieus esprendre
> En sozpirant, puis li a dit:
> 'Sire, ore ostez sans contredit
> Vos armes, tanz est de souper;
> N'i arez compaignon ne per
> Fors moi et deus cousins germains
> Que chi veez; ne plus ne mains,
> N'ai de maisnie, ce sachiez.'
> (*Fourth Continuation*, 12468–75)

She looks at him to excite him further, and sighing, she says: 'Sir, take off
your arms, without protest. It is time for supper; there will be no other
companion apart from me and my two cousins, who you see here. You
should know that they are the only people in my household.'

> And now ȝe ar here, iwysse, and we are bot oure one;
> My lorde and his ledez ar on lenþe faren,
> Oþer burnez in her bedde, and my burdez als ... (1230–2)

Gawain's adventure from Gerbert de Montreuil's romance reads
almost like a handbook of seduction. In order to excite her guest the
Lady pretends to be a novice in the art of love, pretends that if she
had to make a choice Gawain would be her favourite, and emphasizes that he can expect to be left undisturbed. The Lady's
tactics, which, as the passages from *Gawain* show, the Lady of the
Castle seems to have studied closely, prove a great success. But just
as Gawain approaches to join the Lady in bed, he remembers to
cross himself, and then finds the knife which she has hidden under
her bed. Now Gawain hides it from the Lady and works his will:

> Weille ou non, sosfrir li estuet
> Le ju de mon seignor Gavain.
> (*Fourth Continuation*, 12638–9)

Like it or not, she has to submit to Sir Gawain's game.

But the *First* and *Fourth Continuation* are not simply implicated
as sources which influenced the *Gawain*-poet. They influence the

poet's fictional characters in turn. The Lady uses them to prove that her representations of Gawain as a womanizer must be correct. Gerbert de Montreuil's episode, and Gawain's later account of his adventure with the Pucelle de Lis in the *First Continuation* in which he confesses to having raped her,[13] can be used, for example, to suggest to her guest that he could—or rather, is expected to—take her by force:

> 3e ar stif innoghe to constrayne wyth strenkþe, 3if yow lykez. (1496)

She invokes a literary tradition of a Gawain renowned for his love-affairs to show Gawain that he is unfaithful to the 'lettrure of armes'.

Her narrative fashioning is not, I think, innocuous.[14] It poses a threat to Gawain, based on the fact that it is ultimately language which realizes notions of identity in reality. Misrepresented in the language of the Lady, who speaks with the powerful backing of a long-standing literary tradition, Gawain faces the loss of his identity:

> 'Bot þat 3e be Gawan, hit gotz in mynde.' (1293)

> 'Sir, 3if 3e be Wawen, wonder me þynkkez . . .' (1481)

The possibility of regaining his name, his identity, by identifying with the 'Gawain' constructed by the Lady and the literature of the past is the bait which the temptations hold out to him.

The effects of the Lady's strategy leave their marks on Gawain's responses. Note, for example, Gawain's response to her observations that he cannot be the real Gawain because he lacks the amorous leanings of the romance-hero:

---

[13] Gawain's confession of rape does not match the adventure as the poet has narrated it earlier. For an attempt to resolve this contradiction see Jean Frappier, 'Le Personnage de Gauvain dans la *Première Continuation* du *Conte du Graal*', *Romance Philology*, 11 (1957), 331–44. Frappier's ingenious argument that Gawain confesses rape in order to exonerate the maiden has been called into question by Pierre Gallais, 'Gauvain et la Pucelle de Lis', in *Mélanges offerts à Maurice Delbouille*, 2 vols. (Gembloux, 1964), ii. 207–29.

[14] Communicative acts, as Ross Chambers and Stephen Greenblatt have emphasized, have the power to produce new situations, to change the relationship between speaker and listener. Their interpretation of narratives not simply in their contexts, but also with an eye to the new contexts they seek to produce, is of particular relevance to *Gawain*, where seduction and story-telling go hand in hand. See Ross Chambers, *Story and Situation: Narrative Seduction and the Power of Fiction* (Minneapolis, 1984), and Stephen J. Greenblatt, 'The Improvisation of Power', in *Literature and Society: Selected Papers from the English Institute: 1978*, ed. Edward W. Said (Baltimore, 1980), 57–99, reprinted in Greenblatt's *Renaissance Self-Fashioning* (Chicago, 1984), 222–54. I borrow the term 'narrative fashioning' from Greenblatt's essay.

'Querfore?' quoþ þe freke, and freschly he askez,
Ferde lest he hade fayled in fourme of his castes;
Bot þe burde hym blessed, and 'Bi þis skyl' sayde:
'So god as Gawayn gaynly is halden,
And cortaysye is closed so clene in hymseluen,
Couth not lyȝtly haf lenged so long wyth a lady,
Bot he had craued a cosse, bi his courtaysye,
Bi sum towch of summe tryfle at sum talez ende.'
Þen quoþ Wowen: 'Iwysse, worþe as yow lykez;
I schal kysse at your comaundement, as a knyȝt fallez,
And fire, lest he displese yow, so plede hit no more.'

(1294–1304)

Again the Lady confronts Gawain with his reputation in the verse romances as 'the wooer of almost any available girl'.[15] The image of his fictional *alter ego* does not leave Gawain entirely cold. He asks the Lady eagerly, 'freschly', what her observed distinction between 'Gawayn' and himself might be. Moreover, he does grant her a 'cosse', for which the Lady's 'Gawayn' is renowned, and one wonders whether Gawain would have done so if it were not for the Lady's reminiscences about the 'Gawayn' everyone admires.

It is no coincidence that just at the moment when Gawain complies with her request for a kiss, when Gawain's self and his model overlap, the words of Gawain's concession conflate the grammatical person 'I' with which we represent ourselves, and the 'he' by which we are signified in the discourse of others. Instead of saying: 'I will grant you a kiss lest I displease you', Gawain's answer registers a striking shift to the third person: 'I will grant you a kiss, lest *he* displease you.' At the point where Gawain and his image in the Lady's words merge, he inscribes himself into the Lady's narrative where he figures as a 'he', and abandons the 'I' which realizes his identity as a separate individual. The Lady's bait, the appealing possibility of adequate representation in the discourse of the other, thus entails a relinquishment of personal autonomy.

I do not wish to suggest that Gawain's curious change from 'I' to 'he' is a Freudian slip uttered under pressure. For one thing, Gawain is in fact highly alert to the need to insist on the incompatibility of himself and the Lady's 'Gawayn'. His protest: '*I* be not now *he* þat ye of speken' (1242) focuses precisely on the difference between 'I' and 'he'. Certainly, this defence shows an acute awareness that it is at the space which separates the two that the Lady takes aim.

[15] Whiting, 'Gawain', 232.

Moreover, Gawain's peculiar handling of personal pronouns does not spring from involuntary confusion. On the contrary, the point of Gawain's answer is that he *announces* his self-cancellation as he is about to kiss her. He will kiss her 'at her commaundement', not because the idea has come from within, but merely to do 'as a knyʒt fallez'. 'I will conform myself to your image of me so as to please you' is what Gawain seems to be saying here. The confusion between himself and his model is deliberate and purely symbolic, serving not to abolish the difference between the two but to keep it in place. For, as Gawain implies, the Lady will embrace not himself but her own image of the knight. When the lady believes she has moulded her interlocutor in the exact likeness of the Gawain of her romances by exacting a kiss, Gawain declares himself momentarily non-existent in order to evade the fixative symmetry of himself and the romantic model in which the Lady attempts to capture him. If the Lady's temptations fail they do so not because her narrative seduction can do no harm but because Gawain senses the strategies employed against him.

Before turning to Gawain's use of tact as a subtle weapon of defence, it should be made clear that *Gawain* is far from being the only romance to acknowledge the power of fictions to shape or manipulate the present. I have used Renaut de Beaujeu's startling conclusion to *Le Bel Inconnu* as an illustration of this power at work. For another example we may turn to Chrétien's *Cligés*. When the three wise men from Salerno have come to pay their last respects to Fenice, who has faked death, they suddenly recall a famous story of a *morte fausse*:

> Lors lor sovint de Salemon,
> Que sa fame tant le haï
> Que come morte le trahi.   (*Cligés*, 5802–4)

Then he remembers the story about Solomon, whom his wife hated so much that she betrayed him by playing dead.

Having called to mind the legend of Solomon and his wife who feigned death, the three would-be Magi begin to entertain the possibility that the legend may well have inspired Fenice. When they fail to bring her back to life they apply torture in the vain hope that this will prove right their suspicion that Fenice is actually following the well-known script of the story of Solomon's wife.[16] In *Cligés*,

---

[16] This episode from *Cligés* has been suggestively analysed by Robert W. Hanning, ' "I Shal Finde It in a Maner Glose": Versions of Textual Harassment in Medieval

too, literary works, be it the legend of Solomon or the *Tristan* legend, have the power to ensnare Chrétien's characters. In the final lines of *Cligés*, Chrétien shows an awareness that this power inheres even in his own narrative:

> Einz puis n'i ot empereor
> N'eüst de sa fame peor
> Qu'ele nel deüst decevoir,
> Se il oï ramantevoir
> Comant Fenice Alis deçut.
>
> . . . .
>
> Por ce einsi com an prison
> Est gardee an Constantinoble . . . (*Cligés*, 6645–53)

After this any emperor who heard tell of how Fenice deceived Alis was afraid that his wife might deceive him too . . . That is why the empress is kept locked in prison in Constantinople . . .

Once again, the telling of a story, the history of Fenice's deception, has a remarkable effect on reality. Constructed as potential Fenices, all empresses remain jealously guarded lest another Cligés should come along. The story of *Cligés*, 'l'uevre Crestïen', captivates its audience in the most literal sense of the word. Like the Lady of the Castle, the characters in *Cligés* fashion themselves and others according to the powerful models provided by a literary tradition, a tradition which, so Chrétien seems to imply, includes his own romance.

Gawain's Discretion

The hero of the Anglo-Norman romance of *Yder* is, like Gawain, accosted by his host's wife. The poet of *Yder* describes the ensuing scene as follows.

> Quanques il puet se treit ariere
> Mes ele se treit tot dis soentre.
> Yder la feirt del pié al ventre
> Si qu'el chei ariere enverse
> E qu'el en devint tot perse.

Literature', in *Medieval Texts and Contemporary Readers*, ed. Laurie A. Finke and Martin B. Shichtman (Ithaca, NY, 1987), 27–51. It should be noted that Hanning's proposed reading of the three physicians as 'exegetes who all but annihilate the poetic value of a text' (39) overlooks the troublesome fact that their interpretation of Fenice as a 'morte fausse' is essentially correct.

> Jo nel sai pas de ço reprendre
> Kar il ne se poeit defendre.   (*Yder*, 374–80)

Whenever he can he draws back, but she immediately advances. Yder kicks her with his foot in the stomach, so that she falls over backwards and turns blue all over. I do not think I can reproach him for it, because it was the only way of defending himself.

That this episode should rank as one of the *Gawain*-poet's possible sources does not strike me as self-evident.[17] To be sure, a superficial similarity between *Yder* and the temptation scenes in *Gawain* exists. The host's wife attempts to seduce the hero. But this is about as far as the similarities go. The poet of *Yder* excels at slapstick effects. The lack of dialogue is made up for by the physical exuberance of the two combatants, the one backing off, the other instantly drawing closer, in the end discomfited only by violence. Lest we make heavy weather of Yder's behaviour, the poet wittily pleads self-defence. The *Gawain*-poet, too, speaks of defensive movements: 'The freke ferde with defence, and feted ful fayre' (1282), but as the Lady confronts Gawain almost entirely on the plane of language, so, too, Gawain must defend himself with words. Yder has a means of repulsing the lady which never seems feasible to Gawain, who faces the more arduous task of discouraging the Lady without causing offence.

Gawain does so with patience and subtlety. Even when, in the third temptation scene, Gawain's resistance has reached a low point, he manages to remain polite:

> With luf-laȝyng a lyt he layd hym bysyde
> Alle þe spechez of specialté þat sprange of her mouthe.   (1777–8)

Instead of Yder's shove, Gawain first gives a gently dismissive smile, and next utters a not-today-thank-you. Here, in miniature, we see the difference between *Yder* and *Gawain*. In the former, the hero and the temptress act without restraint or control. Their movements seem somehow always in excess of what is either necessary or natural. Yder does not just push the lady, he kicks her in the belly. The Lady does not just fall, she topples over backwards and changes colour. In *Gawain*, however, appearances and words are minutely

---

[17] Both this scene from *Yder* and Lancelot's seduction in the Vulgate *Lancelot*, included in E. Brewer's *Sir Gawain and the Green Knight: Sources and Analogues*, bear only a vague resemblance to the temptation scenes in *Gawain*, certainly in comparison with the seduction of Gawain in Gerbert de Montreuil's *Continuation*.

controlled. No pause or laugh seems unwilled. In a scene where the closing of a door can be an invitation, and Gawain's little 'luf-lagh' a rejection, all is understated rather than hyperbolic.

Despite the delicacy of Gawain's refusal, critical consensus has seen in the *Gawain*-poet's report of his dilemma a sign of Gawain's weakness:

> For þat prynces of pris depresed hym so þikke,
> Nurned hym so neȝe þe þred, þat nede hym bihoued
> Oþer lach þer hir luf, oþer lodly refuse.
> He cared for his cortaysye, lest craþayn he were,
> And more for his meschef ȝif he schulde make synne,
> And be traytor to þat tolke þat þat telde aȝt. (1770–5)

It is not immediately obvious why the *Gawain*-poet feels that Gawain's rejection of the Lady's advances should compromise his 'cortaysye'. The assumption is usually that the poet reports the dilemma only as Gawain himself perceives it. On this account, it becomes possible to argue, as A. C. Spearing does,[18] that Gawain has already succumbed to the Lady's definition of 'cortaysye' in, for example, line 1300, 'Bot he had craued a cosse, bi his courtaysye . . .', where courtesy refers, in Dame Ragnell's blunt words, to 'cortesy in bed'.[19] Having accepted this definition, Gawain now feels he must betray the value of courtesy for which the Lady supposes him to stand. The word 'cortaysye' in this passage must, in this view, be read as if in inverted commas. This interpretation involves, however, a significant simplification of the problem that here concerns Gawain, a simplification which has been a tendency of most discussions of the temptation scenes.[20] Courtesy versus sin is glossed as an internal conflict between the two options of sleeping with the Lady

[18] 'Sir Gawain and the Green Knight', in his *Criticism and Medieval Poetry* (London, 1962, 2nd edn. London, 1972), 28–50, at 39–40.

[19] *Wedding of Sir Gawain*, l. 639. The use of the word by Dame Ragnell shows up the inadequacies in Tony Hunt's argument in 'Irony and Ambiguity in *Sir Gawain and the Green Knight*', FMLS 12 (1976), 1–16, which sees in the temptation scenes a conflict between the Lady's 'continental', understanding of the word 'courtesy' and Gawain's 'English' notion of 'courtesy', in which, as Hunt mistakenly claims, amorous implications were absent. The conflict as I see it turns on an opposition between courtesy as politeness and courtesy as a first stage of courtship. The tension between these two conceptions is the topic of a medieval debate which cuts across national boundaries. See the illustrative material in D. W. Robertson, 'Courtly Love and Courtesy', in his *A Preface to Chaucer* (Princeton, NJ, 1962), 448–63.

[20] But see Benson's perspicacious reading of Gawain's predicament in *Art and Tradition*, 46.

or turning her down. When all is said and done, Gawain and Yder are envisaged as being in the same situation. Yet what bothers Gawain here is the thought that he, too, may have to resort to an unsubtle rejection *à la* Yder. For, as the passage makes clear, Gawain does not equate a refusal with a breach of courtesy. It is the possibility of refusing her 'lodly', of refusing her in a way that might cause offence, which brings on the concern for 'cortaysye'. The face Gawain is trying to save, in other words, is not his own, but the Lady's. He feels he can at this juncture no longer counter her temptations without hurting her. To understand why, we need to examine how Gawain had managed to do so earlier.

When the Lady first enters Gawain's bedroom, Gawain carefully lifts up the curtain to see what is going on, and decides on the following plan:

> Hit watz þe ladi, loflyest to beholde,
> Þat droȝ þe dor after hir ful dernly and stylle,
> And boȝed towarde þe bed; and þe burne schamed,
> And layde hym doun lystyly and let as he slepte;
> And ho stepped stilly and stel to his bedde,
> Kest vp þe cortyn and creped withinne,
> And set hir ful softly on þe bed-syde,
> And lenged þere selly longe to loke quen he wakened.'
> Þe lede lay lurked a ful longe quyle,
> Compast in his concience to quat þat cace myȝt
> Meue oþer amount—to meruayle hym þoȝt,
> Bot ȝet he sayde in hymself: 'More semly hit were
> To aspye wyth my spelle in space quat ho wolde.'
> Þen he wakenede, and wroth, and to hir warde torned,
> And vnlouked his yȝe-lyddez and let as hym wondered,
> And sayned hym, as bi his saȝe þe sauer to worthe,
>   with hande.   (1187–1203)

The *Gawain*-poet endows his character with a psychological depth which is the more remarkable for the shortness of the scene. Gawain's response to the awkward situation he finds himself in when a strange woman sneaks into his room is brilliantly conceived. The reason for the Lady's intrusion into Gawain's bedroom is as yet obscure. She may have other motives than her interest in her guest. Gawain simply cannot tell as yet. Even if she is here for a different reason than love, however, she might think Gawain is construing her motives as such. Imagine the embarrassment to which this what-

must-he-be-thinking situation could give rise. Gawain therefore deliberately decides he has not seen a thing. But when the Lady settles
on his bed for a 'ful longe quyle' it becomes impossible to ignore her.
Again Gawain is careful to avoid embarrassment. To stop 'letting', to
admit, in other words, that he has been aware of her presence all
along, would be an acknowledgement of the fact that he has indeed
used tact; an admission that the situation is indeed embarrassing. If,
on the other hand, Gawain does not show surprise he might seem to
suggest that to wake up with his host's wife on the bed is nothing out
of the ordinary for him. Gawain therefore crosses and stretches
himself elaborately, and while acting 'as him wondered', the pretence
of surprise will invite her to make her intentions clear.

The scene is rich in situational humour, and shows Gawain's
extraordinary awareness of the intricate realities of social interaction. This awareness, which, as Erving Goffman has noted,[21] involves the inhibition of all acts and statements that might cause
embarrassment, has been claimed to be a unique feature of English
Arthurian romance.[22] Exceptional it indeed is, but a comparison
with a scene from *Yvain* will show that Chrétien de Troyes was
equally capable of representing and poking gentle fun at the social
game of keeping up appearances.

The episode I refer to is one in which two damsels and their lady
happen upon a naked man in the middle of the forest. To the
maiden's astonishment, the man turns out to be Yvain. She decides,
however, not to wake him up:

> Molt s'an seigne, et si s'an mervoille;
> cele ne le bote, n'esvoille . . .   (*Yvain*, 2909–10)

She frequently crosses herself in amazement; but she does not touch or wake
him . . .

Fortunately her lady has a box of ointment received from Morgan
la Fee which can cure any form of madness. She gives it to the
damsel on the condition that it must not be applied too lavishly, but
the maiden gets so carried away in massaging the naked Yvain that
she has soon finished the content of the box:

[21] Erving Goffman's *The Presentation of Self in Everyday Life* (Harmondsworth,
1959, repr. 1975) is an illuminating attempt to analyse social interaction from the
point of view of conscious role-playing. His discussion of tact (222–30) has proved
particularly useful in the following discussion.
[22] Morton Donner, 'Tact as a Criterion of Reality in *Sir Gawain and the Green
Knight*', *PELL* 1 (1965), 306–15.

S'il en eüst cinc setiers,
s'eüst ele autel fet, ce cuit. (3005–6)
And the same would have happened if she had had five gallons, I think.

She fanatically rubs his body with this ointment, leaves a suit of clothes, and hides behind a tree while Yvain gets dressed:

Derriers un grant chasne s'areste
tant que cil ot dormi assez,
qui fu gariz et respassez,
et rot son san et son mimoire.
Mes nuz se voit com un yvoire;
s'a grant honte; et plus grant eüst
se il s'aventure seüst.
. . . .
et de sa char que il voit nue
est trespansez et esbaïz
et dit que morz est et traïz,
s'einsi l'a trové ne veü
. . . .
Or ne vialt mes plus arester
la dameisele, ainz est montee,
et par delez lui est passee,
si con s'ele ne l'i seüst.
. . . .
Et la dameisele autresi
vet regardant environ li
con s'ele ne sache qu'il a.
Esbaïe, vet ça et la
que droit vers lui ne vialt aler.
Et cil comance a rapeler:
'Dameseile, de ça, de ça!'
Et la dameseile adreça
vers lui son palefroi anblant.
Cuidier li fist par ce sanblant
qu'ele de lui rien ne seüst,
n'onques la veü ne l'eüst,
et san et corteisie fist . . .   (*Yvain*, 3012–59)

She hides behind a great oak until he had slept enough, and woke up better and cured, in possession of his senses and his memory. But he sees that he is naked like ivory, and is greatly embarrassed, though he would have been even more embarrassed if he had known what had happened . . . His naked body causes him alarm and shame, and he says he is dead and betrayed if he is found or seen like this . . . Now the damsel waits no more, but gets on

her palfrey and rides in his direction, as if she did not know that he was
there . . . Looking bewildered, she goes now here and now there, since she
did not want to go straight at him. And he calls out: 'Damsel, here, here!'
And the damsel turned her ambling palfrey towards him, making him
believe that she did not know anything about him and had not seen a thing.
She acted cleverly and courteously . . .

Like Gawain, this 'dameseile' has mastered the art of pretending.
The potential *gêne* for both parties is great. Yvain is stark naked,
but to be seen naked, or to be observed watching someone naked,
would be much worse, as both Yvain's monologue and the Lady's
actions suggest. How can the damsel give Yvain the opportunity to
extricate himself from his compromising position? She strikes on the
same solution as Gawain. She pretends not to have seen, and hides
behind the tree until Yvain is presentable. Even when Yvain has
dressed she must tread carefully. Her act goes much further than a
momentary look in the other direction. Like Gawain, the damsel
realizes that to be seen to have purposefully 'not seen' something
would only draw attention to the fact that something potentially
embarrassing has taken place. She therefore does not make for
Yvain directly, but purports only to be riding by as if wholly
ignorant of his presence. She thus convinces Yvain that he has seen
her first, and to complete her performance she pretends at first not
to hear him as he calls out for help. The witty episode in Chrétien
need not necessarily have influenced the *Gawain*-poet. But we find
such a display of tact only rarely in medieval literature.[23] Where we
do find it, it is never as developed or minutely observed. In his *De
Nugis Curialium*, for example, Walter Map praises Henry II for his
courtesy when, on seeing a monk's private parts exposed, 'Rex, ut
omnis facecie thesaurus, dissimulans uultum auertit, et tacuit.' ('The
king, like the treasury of all courtliness, turned his face and was
silent'.)[24] If this is courtliness, then how much more praise do
Gawain and the damsel in *Yvain* deserve!

In addition to *Yvain*, the *Gawain*-poet seems to have made use of
Chrétien's *Lancelot*. In one episode, which I have discussed elsewhere, Lancelot receives hospitality from a Lady who has engineered

[23] As B. N. Sargent has shown, there is certainly no medieval writer before Chrétien
whose fictional characters have as much social sensitivity. See her 'Old and New in the
Character-Drawing of Chrétien de Troyes', in *Innovation in Medieval Literature:
Essays for Alan Markman*, ed. D. Radcliff-Umstead (Pittsburgh, 1971), 35–48.

[24] Walter Map, *De Nugis Curialium: Courtiers' Trifles*, ed. and trans.
M. R. James, revised by C. N. L. Brooke and R. A. B. Mynors (Oxford, 1983), 102.

a test of his prowess. Lancelot takes on her household, who appear to be raping her, but just as he gains the upper hand the Lady calls the game off. But yet another ordeal awaits Lancelot. He has promised to sleep with the lady in return for her hospitality. Lancelot, however, can only think of Guinevere and is absolutely mortified. He lies completely still in bed until the maiden realizes he has no interest. She takes her leave and then begins to speak to herself:

'Si vos voel a Deu comander;
si m'an irai . . .'

. . . .

'Des lores que je conui primes
chevalier, un seul n'an conui
que je prisasse, fors cestui,
La tierce part d'un angevin;
car si con ge pans et devin,
il vialt a si grant chose antendre
qu'ainz chevaliers n'osa enprendre
si perilleuse ne si grief;
et Dex doint qu'il an veigne a chief.'   (*Lancelot*, 1260–78)

'I would like to commend you to God, and will be off . . .' 'Since I met my first knight, I have never known one that I would prize at one third of a penny compared with him. For I think and guess that he has undertaken so great an enterprise that no other knight before him undertook one so dangerous and hard; may God give him success.'

Besides the overall correspondences between this scene from *Lancelot* and the temptation scene in *Gawain*, it is in particular the lady's monologue which betrays a direct influence. For at the end of the Lady's first visit to Gawain's bedroom she, too, ponders in herself that:

'Þaȝ I were burde bryȝtest,' þe burde in mynde hade,
'Þe lasse luf in his lode—for lur that he soȝt
    boute hone,
    Þe dunte þat schulde hym deue,
    And nedez hit most be done.'
Þe lady penn spek of leue,
He granted hir ful sone.   (1283–9)[25]

---

[25] I have not followed the edition which places a full stop after line 1283, at the cost of garbled syntax. Unlike Tolkien and Gordon, I take lines 1284 and following to be part of the Lady's internal monologue, as I fail to see why the *Gawain*-poet's suggestion that the Lady knows of Gawain's appointment at the Chapel is 'a serious flaw in the handling of the plot' (110).

The gist of their monologues is the same. Both are spoken just after or before the ladies take their leave. In addition, an echo of the first part of the lady's monologues in Chrétien's *Lancelot* can be found in lines 1268–75 of *Gawain*. But the most important similarities between this scene from *Gawain* and Chrétien's *Lancelot* are to be found in the minute observation of the strategies with which unpleasant situations can be avoided. The Lady does not thrust herself on her guest. When she leaves, Chrétien drops a hint that she normally sleeps naked:

> si est an sa chanbre venue,
> et si se couche tote nue ... (*Lancelot*, 1263–4)

So she went to her room, where she went to bed stark naked.

As she lies down on Lancelot's bed, however, she does not undress entirely but keeps on her 'chemise'.

> et la dameseile s'i couche,
> mes n'oste mie sa chemise. (*Lancelot*, 1202–3)

And the damsel went to his bed, but she did not take off her chemise.

Why not? Because in case Lancelot has no appetite she will not have fully committed herself and will therefore be able to withdraw while allowing some uncertainty on which to construct the face-saving fiction that sex was not what she was after. How does Lancelot cope? He observes that the lady has not undressed entirely and decides that her policy is worth following:

> Et il se couche tot a tret,
> mes sa chemise pas ne tret,
> ne plus qu'ele ot la soe feite. (*Lancelot*, 1213–15)

And he lies down at the far end of the bed, but, like her, he does not take off his shirt.

When Lancelot observes the maximum distance between himself and her, the lady perceives that he is clearly not interested in what she has to offer. She therefore decides to leave, but not without maintaining the semblance that nothing extraordinary has in fact taken place:

> 'S'il ne vos doit peser,
> sire, de ci me partirai.
> En ma chambre couchier m'irai
> et vos an seroiz plus a eise.' (*Lancelot*, 1248–51)

'If you do not object, sir, I will leave you, and sleep in my room, so that you will be more comfortable.'

In the end, as Marie-Luce Chênerie writes, Lancelot's would-be lover 'leaves the room in all her dignity . . . appearances have been saved; she offered nothing and nothing has been refused . . . we will admire the delicacy of this suggestion'.[26] Lancelot is of course not in the least sad to see her go: 'the knight does not mind at all, but freely lets her go' ('au chevaliers mie ne grieve, | einz l'an leisse aler volentiers': 1262–3). In this comic ritual of leave- taking, it is only the author's hint that Lancelot lets her go happily which betrays his relief. I suspect that the same hint is present when Gawain grants the Lady of the Castle leave 'ful sone' (1289).

The lady's display of tact does not stop at this. The next day she accompanies Lancelot on his quest. When Lancelot spots a comb with the Queen's golden hair entangled in it, he nearly collapses. The lady leaps from her palfrey to assist him but at this moment Lancelot is overcome by shame and asks her what she has dis-mounted for. The lady weighs her options and decides against telling him the truth:

> Ne cuidiez pas que le porcoi
> la dameisele l'an conoisse,
> qu'il an eüst honte et angoisse,
> et si li grevast et neüst,
> se le voir l'en reconeüst;
> si s'est de voir dire gueitiee,
> einz dit come bien afeitiee:
> 'Sire, je ving cest peigne querre,
> por ce sui descendue a terre;
> que de l'avoir oi tel espans,
> ja nel cuidai tenir a tans.'   (*Lancelot*, 1446–56)

Do not think that the lady revealed her motives, because it would have caused him shame and embarrassment, and would have hurt his feelings. And so she abandons the idea of telling the truth, and says courteously: 'Sir, I came to fetch this comb, that is why I got down on the ground. I was so eager to have it that I could not stop myself.'

---

[26] '[Elle] quitte la chambre avec toute sa dignité . . . les apparences sont sauvés, elle n'offrait rien et on ne lui a rien refusé . . . on admirera la délicatesse de cette suggestion' (Marie-Luce Chênerie, *Le Chevalier errant dans les romans arthuriens en vers des XIIe et XIIIe siècles* (Geneva, 1986), 575).

Rather than recognizing Lancelot's near-collapse for what it is, by admitting that she has come to help Lancelot, she hides 'le voir' from him, and pretends she has only come to get the comb. Like Gawain, who feigns sleep, she has a highly developed sense of the 'honte' and the 'angoisse' to which an open acknowledgement of the *faux pas* could lead.

But Gawain's ingenuity is to be taxed further. By pretending not to see the Lady of the Castle he had given her the opportunity to save her role as Bertilac's wife. The Lady, however, will not be ignored, and she makes her intentions abundantly clear:

> 'ȝe ar welcum to my cors,
> Yowre awen won to wale;
> Me behouez of fyne force
> Your seruaunt be, and schale.' (1237–40)

Much has already been said about the potential ambiguity of these lines. As Tolkien and Gordon pointed out in their edition, 'cors' need mean no more than 'person'.[27] More speculatively, David Mills has suggested another possible *double-entendre* between 'cor(t)s' (courts) and 'cors' (body), 'won' (delight) and 'won' (dwelling).[28] The ambiguity of a word, however, does not simply manifest itself in the act of enunciation. If we only had the context of the *First Continuation* to go by, in which Gawain responds to the same offer by taking 'cors' in the literal sense, and sleeps with the damsel, we would never have known that the word 'cors' could be equivocal. And likewise, if Gawain had decided to act like the French hero of the *First Continuation*, there would surely have been no reason to consult the *MED* for semantic polyvalence. Meaning would in that case be fixed because speaker and hearer agree on one. Single meaning and ambiguity arise, in other words, out of a process of negotiation. What makes us alive to the multiplicity of meanings in the Lady's words is precisely the fact that these meanings are being contested, that their negotiations do not come to a halt in an agreement between the Lady and Gawain. What the Lady intends as

---

[27] This is how the lady in the *Mule sans frein* intends it when she thanks Gawain for restoring to her a lost bridle with the words: ' "Sire", fait ele, "il est bien droiz | Que je mete tot a devise / Lo mien cors a vostre servise" ' (' "Sir", she says, "it is only right that I put myself entirely in your service" ': 1082–4). For a similar formula see *Cligés*, 2304. See also Burrow, *A Reading*, 80–1.

[28] David Mills, 'An Analysis of the Temptation Scenes in *Sir Gawain and the Green Knight*', *Journal of English and Germanic Philology*, 67 (1968), 612–30.

a come-on, Gawain deliberately misreads as politeness pure and simple. Only by a misprision of the sexual innuendo does he activate the other, innocuous side of the Lady's words. In fact, his response to the Lady of the Castle is no less tactful than his decision not to see the Lady enter the bedroom. The 'speches skere' (1261) with which he replies to her innuendoes are a deliberate misrecognition of her adulterous intentions. By mistaking her in this way, Gawain can dissuade her, without giving open recognition that he is in fact aware of what she is after.

What makes Gawain's polite dissuasions possible is the saving ambiguity of 'luf-talk'. Potentially one of the most pronounced 'face-threatening acts', advances and love-talk are hedged in by hints, metaphors, double-talk, and circumlocutions which allow the speaker to go 'off-record', not to commit himself to one attributable intention, and thereby to avoid being held accountable for any offence or unpleasantness.[29] Love-talk, born of and used in situations where so much self-esteem is at stake, contains for this reason a considerable interpretative leeway. Is it mere dalliance or does it serve an ulterior purpose? When Gawain sits beside the Lady in Bertilac's hall, sharing in the public joy, neither the Lady's glances, nor Gawain's response to them, can escape this potential ambivalence:

> Such semblaunt to þat segge semly ho made,
> Wyth stille stollen countenance, þat stalworth to plese,
> Þat al forwondered watz þe wyȝe, and wroth wyth hymseluen,
> Bot he nolde not for his nurture nurne hir aȝaynes,
> Bot dalt with her al in daynté, how-se-euer þe dede turned
>   towrast.
>
> (1658–63)

Although the Lady 'wyth stille stollen countenance' intimates her love for her neighbour, Gawain responds to her as if all were done 'in daynté'. Unwillingly admitted to the Lady's secret communications, Gawain finds himself placed in a 'collusive relationship'[30] vis-à-vis Bertilac and his retainers, and the only way he can avoid causing offence to the Lady and the crowd who observe the scene is

[29] I draw here on the study by Penelope Brown and Stephen C. Levinson, *Politeness: Some Universals in Language Use* (Cambridge, 1987). For a different linguistic approach to *Gawain* see Kim Sydow Campbell, 'A Lesson in Polite Non-Compliance: Gawain's Conversational Strategies in Fitt 3 of *Sir Gawain and the Green Knight*', *Language Quarterly*, 28 (1990), 53–62.

[30] The term is Goffman's, *Presentation of Self*, 174.

by acting as an interpreter, by translating her advances into an acceptable form of 'nurture'. But just as the Lady's innuendoes can be interpreted as a form of urbane dalliance only, Gawain's gallantry can also be mistaken for a sign of an illicit love-affair. The 'dede' of dalliance can always be turned 'towrast'.

Chrétien similarly draws attention to the language of love. An episode from *Cligés* will serve as an illustration. In the passage below, the lovers Cligés and Fenice say goodbye while the bystanders look on:

> Molt ot fez sopirs et sangloz
> Au partir celez et coverz,
> Que uns n'ot tant les ialz overz,
> Ne tant i regart cleremant
> Qu'au departir certenemant
> De verité savoir peüst
> Qu'au antr'aus deus amor eüst. (*Cligés*, 4284–90)

There were many hidden and concealed sighs and tears at the departure, so that, however hard one had looked, and however clearly one had seen it, it would have been impossible to say or know for certain whether the two who departed were in love.

As Chrétien makes clear, it is not that their behaviour cannot be interpreted as a sign that 'antr'aus deus amor eüst'. But no one can tell positively. By slightly disguising their emotions, passion and polite gallantry become indistinguishable. In point of fact, even for Fenice Cligés's parting words take on the very ambivalence which had benefited the couple earlier on:

> Cligés par quele entancion
> 'Je sui toz vostres' me deïst,
> S'amor dire ne li feïst?
> Mes ce me resmaie de bot
> .   .   .   .   .
> Que c'est une parole usee
> Si repuis bien estre amusee.
> .   .   .   .   .
> Don ne me sai auquel tenir,
> Car ce porroit tost avenir
> Qu'il le dist por moi losangier. (*Cligés*, 4366–97)

With what intention did Cligés say: 'I am all yours', if it was not out of love? . . . But what really worries me is that it is a cliché, and I may be deluded . . . So I do not know how to take it, for it might well be that he said it to flatter me.

Was Cligés's parting word a trite commonplace or a token of his love? Even Fenice herself can no longer be sure.

But the closest analogue to the passage from *Gawain* above is in Chrétien's *Yvain*, where Laudine entertains Arthur's court, which has arrived to participate in the festivities in honour of her and Yvain's wedding:

> et la dame tant les enore
> chascun por soi et toz ansanble,
> que tel foi i a cui il sanble
> que d'amors veignent li atret
> et li sanblent qu'ele lor fet;
> et cez puet an nices clamer
> qui cuident qu'el les voelle amer,
> quant une dame est si cortoise . . . (*Yvain*, 2456–63)

and the lady honours them all so well, collectively and individually, that there were some who thought that her attention was inspired by love; but I would call them fools for thinking that a lady who is courteous to them loves them . . .

Like Gawain, Laudine acts only in 'daynté', but, like the *Gawain*-poet, Chrétien shows that her courtesies can always be mistaken for love. At stake in these moments from *Gawain* and Chrétien is a confusion not so much about the meaning of words or actions but about their *force*,[31] or, in Chrétien's words, the speaker's 'entancion' at the moment of enunciation—a confusion, to be precise, about whether gallantry is intended as a means to an end, as an invitation to reciprocate love, or is merely an urbane manner of speech which seeks to achieve no such perlocutionary effect.

In order to see how Gawain exploits this ambiguity of 'luf-talk' to his advantage, let us look at a dialogue from the first bedroom visit. The passage opens with his response to the Lady's offer of her 'cors':

> 'In god fayth,' quoþ Gawayn, 'gayn hit me þynkkez,
> Þagh I be not now he þat ȝe of speken;
> To reche to such reuerence as ȝe reherce here

---

[31] The term is J. L. Austin's. I quote from his *Philosophical Papers* (1961, repr. Oxford, 1970), 251: 'Besides the question that has been very much studied in the past as to what an utterance *means*, there is a further question distinct from this as to what was the *force* . . . of the utterance. We may be quite clear what "Shut the door" means, but not yet at all clear on the further point as to whether as uttered at a certain time it was an order, an entreaty, or whatnot. What we need besides the old doctrine about meanings is a new doctrine about all the possible forces of utterances . . .'.

I am wyȝe vnworþy, I wot wel myseluen . . .'
.   .   .   .

'In god fayth, Sir Gawayn,' quoþ þe gay lady,
'Þe prys and þe prowes þat plesez al oþer,
If I hit lakked oþer set at lyȝt, hit were littel daynté;
Bot hit ar ladyes innoȝe þat leuer wer nowþe
Haf þe, hende, in hor holde, as I þe habbe here,
To daly with derely your daynté wordez,
Keuer hem comfort and colen her carez,
Þen much of þe garysoun oþer golde þat þay hauen . . .'
.   .   .   .

'Madame,' quoþ þe myry mon, 'Mary yow ȝelde,
For I haf founden, in god fayth, yowre fraunchis nobele,
And oþer ful much of oþer folk fongen bi hor dedez,
Bot þe daynté þat þay delen for my disert nys euen,
Hit is the worchyp of yourself þat noȝt bot wel connez.'
'Bi Mary,' quoþ þe menskful, 'me thynk hit an oþer;
For were I worth al þe wone of wymmen alyue,
And al þe wele of þe worlde were in my honde,
And I schulde chepen and chose to cheue me a lorde
.   .   .   .

Þer schulde no freke vpon folde bifore yow be chosen.'
'Iwysse, worþy,' quoþ þe wyȝe, 'ȝe haf waled wel better;
Bot I am proude of þe prys þat ȝe put on me,
And soberly your seruaunt, my souerayn I holde yow,
And yowre knyȝt I becom, and Kryst yow forȝelde!'
(1241–79)

The Lady's words are again potent with sexual innuendo. She responds to Gawain's modest retort that he is unworthy of the price she sets on him by imagining just how popular he would be with ladies. If they had his company, they would find delightful words, comfort, and relief from their sorrows. The word 'comfort', like its Latin counterpart *solatia*, has the connotative meaning of sexual enjoyment. The word 'carez' too is by no means straightforward. The 'carez' which Gawain would relieve could refer to 'pangs of love'.[32] While the Lady's subordinate clause is hypothetical, she connects the hypothetical fulfilment of the ladies' desire explicitly with her own situation when she reminds Gawain that what for her imagined ladies must remain wishful thinking can in her case become reality: 'as I þe habbe here . . .'. Her whole speech implies

---

[32] See the *MED* s.v. 'cares' 2b and 'comfort' 3a.

that the potential value of Gawain to ladies can now become a reality, if only Gawain would live up to it.

Gawain's clever response to her argument revolves around the interpretative choice Fenice imagines apropos of Cligés's parting words. Apparently unaware that the Lady might have said this out of love for him, he replies to it as if her words were indeed 'une parole usee' and as if she had indeed said it 'por losangier'. Thanking her for her 'fraunchis nobele', from which her 'praise' must have sprung, Gawain then denies the value she has set on him as if that had been the Lady's only intention. When the Lady next suggests—again in a hypothetical clause—that she would list Gawain as her first choice, Gawain responds again by a deliberate misprision of the perlocutionary effect the Lady is trying to achieve. Purporting to take her proposition merely as a supposition for the sake of argument, he commends her on her good choice in reality: 'ȝe haf waled wel better', and gallantly offers his service.

Let us look at one more example of the way Gawain manages to keep the Lady at bay. During her first visit to Gawain's bedroom, the Lady had asked Gawain for a kiss. When she entertains her guest the following morning she reminds him of the instruction in politeness she had given him the day before:

> 'What is þat?' quoþ þe wyghe, 'Iwysse I wot neuer;
> If hit be sothe þat ȝe breue, þe blame is myn awen.'
> 'ȝet I kende yow of kyssyng,' quoþ þe clere þenne,
> 'Quere-so countenance is couþe quikly to clayme;
> þat bicumes vche a knyȝt þat cortaysy vses.'
> 'Do way,' quoþ þat derf mon, 'my dere, þat speche,
> For þat durst I not do, lest I deuayed were;
> If I were werned, I were wrang, iwysse, ȝif I profered.'
> 'Ma fay,' quoþ þe meré wyf, 'ȝe may not be werned,
> ȝe ar stif innoghe to constrayne wyth strenkþe, ȝif yow lykez,
> ȝif any were so vilanous þat yow devaye wolde.'
> 'ȝe, be God,' quoþ Gawayn, 'good is your speche,
> Bot þrete is vnþryuande in þede þer I lende,
> And vche gift þat is geuen not with goud wylle.'
> (1487–1500)

As usual Gawain plays the dummy, pretending not to understand what the Lady is driving at. When she reminds him of yesterday's kiss, his response is again phrased as a hypothetical statement so as to avoid talking about kisses to be given here and now. Moreover,

Gawain suggests that in certain conditions a kiss might be inopportune, in the hope that by investigating the conditions in which a kiss is felicitous, he will be seen to explore possible routes of escape. Of course the route Gawain explores had already been blocked by the Lady when she implied that her 'countenance' is 'couþe'. But the Lady's suggestion that a kiss would be welcome to her is an implication contained in a general maxim—'where favour is plain to see, one should not hesitate to stake one's claim'—which does not explicitly refer to her particular situation. As Gawain implies when he expresses his doubts about having met this condition, he does not count himself so lucky as those who can rely on their ladies' favour. When the Lady then suggests that even if he were refused he could easily take a damsel by force, Gawain is quick to point out an impropriety in her suggestions, for, in Arthur's land, the use of force is frowned on.[33] In this way Gawain succeeds in diverting the Lady's moves on to the safe ground of a debate about the dos and don'ts of love.[34]

Gawain's tactics in the temptation scenes are therefore not to reject the Lady's love-talk, but to participate in a way that will define it as nothing more than playful banter. True, this is not the way the Lady of the Castle sees it, when she expresses disappointment with Gawain's reluctance to show off his skills in love-talk:

> And I haf seten by yourself here sere twyes,
> 3et herde I neuer of your hed helde no wordez
> Þat euer longed to luf, lasse ne more ...   (1522–4)

And her assessment of the situation has been reduplicated by numerous critics who argue that the *Gawain*-poet endowed his hero with an 'English' moral uprightness that precluded his participation in

---

[33] The rule is also rehearsed by Chrétien's Gawain, who in the *Perceval* reminds a knight whom he punished for rape: 'qu'an la terre le roi Artu l sont puceles asseürees' ('In King Arthur's land the safety of maidens is assured': 6876–7).

[34] J. F. Kiteley has rightly seen similarities between the temptation scenes in *Gawain* and Andreas Capellanus' *De Amore*: 'The *De Arte Honeste Amandi* of Andreas Capellanus and the Concept of Courtesy in *Sir Gawain and the Green Knight*', *Anglia*, 79 (1961), 7–16. Not noted by Kiteley is the parallel between Gawain's tactics and those of the noblewoman courted by a man of higher rank (*De Amore*, pp. 136–42). The suitor begs her for the 'reward' (*praemium*) for his service, but the lady pretends not to know what he is driving at. Like Gawain, she plays the dummy. When he, like the Lady of the Castle, must of necessity be more explicit, he is told off for asking her too crudely (*explicito affatu*). In works where love remains for the most part a matter of rhetoric, such similarities are only to be expected and they need not point to direct influence.

the 'French' game of courtly love.[35] But in fact Gawain shows a remarkable adeptness at playing the courtly lover. Moments before the Lady expresses her surprise at not hearing any words 'þat ever longed to luf' from her guest the *Gawain*-poet describes the two busily talking 'Of druryes greme and grace' (1507). When she reprimands Gawain for not indulging in love-talk she is right only in so far as we credit her definition of love-talk as a prelude to action. For words of 'druryes' she has had from Gawain in plenty.

Gawain's knowledge of the corpus of love-literature and his ability to *act* the lover are clearly demonstrated in the opening exchange between the Lady and Gawain:

> 'God moroun, Sir Gawayn', sayde þat gay lady,
> 'Ȝe ar a sleper vnslyȝe, þat mon may slyde hider;
> Now ar ȝe tan as-tyt! Bot true vus may shape,
> I schal bynde yow in your bedde, þat be ȝe trayst':
> Al laȝande þe lady lanced þo bourdez.
> 'Goud moroun, gay,' quoþ Gawayn þe blyþe,
> 'Me schal worþe at your wille, and þat me wel lykez,
> For I ȝelde me ȝederly, and ȝeȝe after grace,
> And þat is þe best, be my dome, for me byhouez nede':
> And þus he bourded aȝayn wiþ mony a blyþe laȝter.
> 'Bot wolde ȝe, lady louely, þen leue me grante,
> And deprece your prysoun, and pray hym to ryse,
> I wolde boȝe of þis bed, and busk me better;
> I schulde keuer þe more comfort to karp yow wyth.'
>
> (1208-21)

The Lady shows herself to be well versed in the conventional metaphors of courtly love. She is the person who wages war on the lover, who captures her powerless lover whom only a truce can save. This is of course the stuff on which the representations of love in both lyrics and romances are based.[36] And Gawain, the magisterial love-talker, answers the Lady in kind. He is the Lady's prisoner, completely dependent on her will. Between the Lady and Gawain,

---

[35] This argument is an old one, but it appears to have lost little of its attraction. See Else von Schaubert, 'Der englische Ursprung von Syr Gawayne and the Grene Knyght', *Englische Studien*, 57 (1923), 331–446; Paul Christopherson, 'The Englishness of *Sir Gawain and the Green Knight*', in *On the Novel*, ed. B. S. Benedikz (London, 1971), 46–56; and Arlyn Diamond, '*Sir Gawain and the Green Knight*: An Alliterative Romance', *Philological Quarterly*, 55 (1976), 10–29.

[36] See John Stevens, *Medieval Romance: Themes and Approaches* (London, 1973), 188–92.

an imaginary play-world interposes itself, whose stylized conventions had been elaborated by numerous texts, such as the following by the *trouvères* Blondel de Nesle and Gace Brulé respectively:

> Et bien set [la dame] que sui en prison.
> S'or ne me met a guarison,
> Nule autre ne m'en puet jeter.

And my lady knows well that I am in prison, and if she does not bail me out, no one else can release me.

> De tantes parz ai esté assailiz
> Que je n'ai mais pooir de moi deffendre,
> Ne je suis si forz ne si hardiz
> Qu'envers Amors osasse plus contendre.[37]

I am assailed from so many sides that I have no power to defend myself, and I am not so strong or bold as to fight Love any longer.

Gawain cannot be faulted for his ignorance of the corpus of love-literature or his inability to enact it.

As a virtuoso performer of the game of courtly love, Gawain has in actual fact much in common with the way Chrétien de Troyes presents the hero in his romances.[38] During the feast in honour of Yvain and Laudine's wedding, we meet Lunete and Gawain engrossed in playful flirtations:

> La dameisele ot non Lunete.
> . . . .
> A mon seignor Gauvain s'acointe
> qui molt la prise, et qui molt l'ainme,
> et por ce s'amie la clainme,
> qu'ele avoit de mort garanti
> son compaignon et son ami;
> si li offre molt son servise.

The damsel's name was Lunete . . . She introduces herself to Gawain, who thinks highly of her, and likes her a lot, and for that reason he calls her his

[37] Quotations are from Roger Dragonetti's exhaustive study *La Technique poétique dans la chanson courtoise* (Bruges, 1960), 107, 110–11. For more examples of the metaphors of battle and imprisonment see his section 'Le Vocabulaire féodal', 61–113.

[38] Derek Brewer misrepresents the character of Gawain in the romances of Chrétien when he describes him as a 'promiscuous knight' whose many 'amorous adventures' are fables of 'sexual valour'. In point of fact, Gawain's only would-be amorous adventure, in Chrétien's *Perceval*, is rudely interrupted by indignant townspeople. I am therefore in disagreement with his view of the temptation scenes as a confrontation between the the 'English' Gawain who 'repudiates the French character': 'Courtesy and the *Gawain*-Poet', in *Patterns of Love and Courtesy: Essays in Memory of C. S. Lewis*, ed. J. Lawlor (London, 1966), 54–85, at 75, 81.

amie, since she had saved his companion and friend [Yvain] from death. He insistently offers her his service.

Lunete then tells Gawain of Yvain's adventures:

> Mes sire Gauvains molt se rit
> de ce qu'ele li conte et dit:
> Ma dameisele, je vos doing
> et a mestier et sanz besoing
> un tel chevalier con je sui.
>
> . . . . .
>
> —Vostre merci, sire, fet ele.   (*Yvain*, 2417–42)

Sir Gawain laughs heartily about her story and says: Damsel, I put myself at your disposal, whenever you need me . . . Thank you, sir, she replies.

There is no reason to assume that Gawain or Lunete regard these offers of love and service as anything more than a pleasant and elegant pastime. The English Gawain, too, simply deems it polite to meet the ladies at Castle Hautdesert and to offer them 'To be her seruaunt soþly' (976). As Chrétien suggests, the rationale behind his character's *plaisanterie* is not passion but his gratitude for Lunete's efforts on his friend Yvain's behalf. To take to heart Chrétien's saying that gallantry must not be misconstrued as love—'cez puet an nices clamer | qui cuident qu'el les voelle amer' (*Yvain*, 2461–2)— we need to distinguish both in *Gawain* and *Yvain* between love in game and love in earnest. Whereas later verse romances about Gawain show him interested primarily in the latter, the romances of Chrétien, with the possible exception of his last romance,[39] resemble *Gawain* in portraying a knight whose penchant for acting the lover is simply part and parcel of social gracefulness.

What the 'play' between Gawain and the Lady of the Castle presupposes is the difference between who they are and what they do, between themselves and the models of love-literature they follow, between fiction and reality. That is why Gawain can safely accept this kind of 'confort', and why, when the Lady's thoughts turn out to be far from 'clene', Gawain must double his efforts to impose his vision of their dalliance as a game. While the Lady attempts to break down the boundary which separates the lovers of fiction from herself and her host, Gawain attempts to keep the Lady

---

[39] Frappier's influential view that the *Perceval* portrays Gawain as a frivolous lady-killer has come under attack. See Guy Vial, *Le Conte du Graal, la Première Continuation* (Geneva, 1987), 12–24.

in the realm of play where actions are 'non- consequential' and 'do not denote what these actions *for which they stand* would denote'.[40] Gawain's misreadings of the Lady's advances as merely playful serve as a hint that she must not confuse their dalliance with the real thing, not simply because of the different meaning it carries in the play-world, but because as play their actions are only a stand-in, representing what Gawain insists to be absent in reality.

The Lady of the Castle, however, chooses not to take the hint and does not avail herself of the opportunity for an honourable retreat. If Gawain pretends to be deaf to her intentions, the Lady can decide not to hear Gawain's. The problem of his tactful approach is that it circumvents the issue; it cannot address it openly. His tact ultimately keeps all options open, including the choice to 'lach þer hir luf'.

In an ingenious way the *Gawain*-poet succeeds in conveying the increasing difficulty of Gawain's tactful deferrals. After the first temptation scene the Lady's only triumph is a goodbye kiss. But she uses the small territorial advantage she has gained to great effect. In the second temptation scene she refers to her previous session with her guest as a lesson on which they should build and, though not without difficulty, she wrests from Gawain the first kiss of the day half-way through her visit to his bedchamber. The third temptation scene involves no preliminaries at all. She opens a window, walks up to his bed, and kisses Gawain even before he has the chance to welcome her. No time is wasted on any preambles:

> Þe lady luflych com laȝande swete,
> Felle ouer his fayre face, and fetly hym kyssed;
> He welcumeȝ hir worþily with a wale chere.
> He seȝ hir so glorious and gayly atyred,
> So fautles of hir fetures and of so fyne hewes,
> Wiȝt wallande joye warmed his hert.
> With smoþe smylyng and smolt þay smeten into merþe,
> Þat al watz blis and bonchef þat breke hem bitwene,
>   and wynne.
>   Þay lanced wordes gode,
>   Much wele þen watz þerinne;
>   Gret perile bitwene hem stod,
>   Nif Maré of hir knyȝt mynne.

$$(1757-69)$$

---

[40] I quote from Gregory Bateson's thoughtful discussion of play in his article 'A Theory of Play and Fantasy', in *Play: Its Role in Evolution and Development*, ed. J. Brunner (London, 1976), 119–29, at 120.

Gawain, struck by the lady's beauty, is at this point on the verge of surrender. The scene recalls Perceval's temptation in the *Queste del saint graal*. Perceval is also about to give in to a lady's temptations, until he sees the cross on the hilt of his sword and returns to his senses:

Et lors resgarde la damoisele qui li est si bele, ce li est avis, que onques n'ot veue sa pareille de biauté. Si li plest tant et embelist, por le grant acesmement qu'il voit en li et por les douces paroles que ele dit; qu'il en eschaufe outre ce que il ne deust. (*Queste del saint graal*, p. 109)

And then he saw the maiden, who seemed to him so beautiful that he had never seen her equal in beauty. She pleased and delighted him, because of the beauty he sees and the sweet words she says to him. They heated him more than they should.

Gawain is equally overwhelmed and inflamed by the sight of the Lady. The personifications of Gawain's feelings—'Wiȝt wallande joye warmed his hert', 'al watz blis and bonchef þat breke hem bitwene'—suggest Gawain is no longer acting, but being acted on. Gawain and the Lady still speak, but the poem no longer lets us listen in on their conversation, as if to suggest it has become too private. Significantly, it is when we next hear Gawain speak that we know he has pulled back from the 'gret perile' of intimacy: 'God shylde', quoþ þe schalk, 'þat schal not befalle!' (1776).

Finding her guest as resistant as ever, the Lady of the Castle decides, in her final opportunity to break through Gawain's defences, to get her message across whatever the cost:

> Quoþ þat burde to þe burne, 'Blame ȝe disserue,
> Ȝif ȝe luf not þat lyf þat ȝe lye next,
> Bifore alle þe wyȝez in þe worlde wounded in hert,
> Bot if ȝe haf a lemman, a leuer, þat yow lykez better,
> And folden fayth to þat fre, festned so harde
> Þat yow lausen ne lyst—and þat I leue nouþe;
> And þat ȝe telle me þat now trwly I pray yow,
> For alle þe lufez vpon lyue layne not þe soþe
>   for gile.'
>   Þe knyȝt sayde, 'Be sayn Jon,'
>   And smeþely con he smyle,
>   'In fayth I welde riȝt non,
>   Ne non wil welde þe quile.'
>
> 'Þat is a worde', quoþ þat wyȝt, 'þat worst is of alle;
> Bot I am swared for soþe, þat sore me þinkkez'.
>   (1779–93)

The sudden directness of the Lady's words is striking. There are no ambiguities here which allow Gawain to extricate himself from overtly acknowledging what the Lady is after. Does he love her or another, she asks, and she insists on a straightforward answer: 'layne not þe soþe for gile.' We cannot understand why Gawain feels he must now refuse her 'lodly' and compromise his courtesy, unless we realize that he can here no longer tactfully misread the Lady's intentions in a way that will save her face. She drops all her cover in an attempt to hit home and thus deprives Gawain of the possibility of maintaining for her benefit the illusion that she was merely playing an urbane game. The Lady speaks her mind and demands the truth. Gawain does his best to soften its impact. There is his gentle smile, an indirect answer which picks up on the question whether he has a lover rather than the question whether he loves her, and a slight qualification at the end in 'þe quile'. But if the purpose of courtesy is to avoid unpleasant situations, then Gawain has indeed fallen short of this ideal. As the Lady's response makes clear, the truth hurts, however much Gawain tries to cushion it. But in so far as the Lady insists on the 'soþe' in a way which allows Gawain no scope for any strategic misreading of her intentions, and offers him, in Goffman's words, 'no excuse for excuse', she leaves him no other choice.[41]

The Art of Make-Believe

The Lady of the Castle, is, as we have seen, an expert reader of medieval romance. As she tells Gawain stories about knights and their lady-loves, Gawain must counter by insisting on the difference between his own situation and the episodes in romance in which knights equip themselves with lovers. The difference is not simply that he is not the 'Gauvain' of many French verse romances, always ready to indulge in a love-affair. For while the Lady of the Castle reduces the difference between the history Gawain is in the process of writing and the histories of previous romances to a deviance in Gawain's character, she directs attention away from her own questionable credentials as a romance-heroine. Maidens, widows, and hosts' daughters may be fair game for the wandering knight, but in

---

[41] Goffman, *Presentation of Self*, 228.

the long history of Gawain's love-life there is not a single affair with the host's wife. Courtly romances underwrite a law of hospitality which anthropologists have observed to be as universal as the prohibition of incest: *any usurpation of the host's role by the guest is taboo.*[42]

A whole series of anecdotal stories about Gawain, written in the thirteenth and fourteenth centuries in Italian and Latin, take this very moral as their subject. In these stories Gawain hears of a castellan who maltreats his guests. Gawain decides to receive hospitality from this castellan to quench his curiosity. But to his surprise he is treated very well. When he takes leave of his host he asks him why he has not been beaten like all the others. The host explains:

Cum milites veniunt ad domum meam, ego nitor eis honorem facere; ipsi vero in contrarium faciunt et dicunt: 'Domine, domine, ego nolo, hoc non faciatis!' et nolunt in domo mea mihi dominari.[43]

When knights come to my house, I go out of my way to honour them; they, however, oppose me and say: 'Lord, lord, I will not do this, don't do that!' They do not allow me to be a lord in my own home.

Because Gawain has respected the fact that the host should be the master in his own house and cannot allow a guest to step into his shoes, he escapes scot-free. Of the many versions of this anecdote, Antonio Pucci's fourteenth-century Italian telling, which includes a temptation by the host's wife,[44] spells out most explicitly the nature of the transgression which sleeping with the host's wife behind his back would involve. To commit this sin would be to assume the place of the host, or, as Gawain puts it, 'to be traytor to þat tolke þat þat telde aȝt' (1775). This is what the Lady wishes Gawain to

[42] Julian Pitt-Rivers, 'The Law of Hospitality', in *The Fate of Shechem* (Cambridge, 1977), 94–112.
[43] Kittredge, *A Study of Sir Gawain*, 96–7. See also his edition of three Latin analogues in the appendix, 272–3.
[44] Antonio Pucci, 'Uno Capitolo d'Antonio Pucci', ed. Alessandro Wesselofski, *Rivista di Filologia Romanza*, 2 (1875), 221–7. The closest Middle English analogue to Pucci's *canzone* is *Sir Gawain and the Carl of Carlisle*, ed. Donald B. Sands, *Middle English Verse Romances* (1966, repr. Exeter, 1981), in which the guest's test of obedience includes an order to kiss the host's wife but to leave the 'prevey far' (466) or rather to preserve it for the host's daughter, whom the host gives to his guest instead. The *Carl* demonstrates the rule of romance that, while the host's wife is taboo, the guest can sleep with the host's daughter, since in doing so he will not arrogate to himself the functions of the host. The Carl's interdiction and the offer of his daughter thus deflect the possibility of what Tony Tanner in *Adultery in the Novel*, 12, has called a 'category-confusion' between guest and host.

forget when she compares Gawain with the heroes of romances who bring 'blysse into boure': that she is not suited for a narrative about knights who acquire lovers. She is not a potential bride but the wife of the paterfamilias, and is in this sense 'mother' rather than 'lover'.

If I invoke here the metaphors of an Oedipal drama it is not because on some mysterious 'latent' or 'underlying' level the Lady is really Gawain's mother, as some critics have argued,[45] but because the law of hospitality which forbids Gawain to usurp the place of the host by sleeping with his wife resembles the Oedipal prohibition at the literal level. Obedience to the Father or the paterfamilias entails a sacrifice, be it the son's desire to be at one with the mother, or the guest's desire for the host's wife or anything which might encroach on the host's privileges. In both cases participation in culture requires that roles are distinguished and distances are kept in play, between father and son, or between host and guest.

The Lady's temptations take as their object of attack the differentiations between Gawain and his literary model, guest and host, the wife of the paterfamilias and a lover of one's own. As I have argued in an earlier section, Gawain knows the importance that attaches to maintaining the distinction between the Lady as lover and as Bertilac's wife, between the amorous ladies and the knights whom they inspire in chivalric romance and his own situation. But in the face of Gawain's awareness that in his own adventure the host's wife functions as a dangerous opponent, the *Gawain*-poet's Lady conjures up a romance-paradigm which hides from Gawain and the reader that she continues to play the role she had played all

---

[45] See Derek Brewer, 'The Interpretations of Dreams, Folktale and Romance with Special Reference to *Sir Gawain and the Green Knight*', NM 77 (1976), 569–81, and his *Symbolic Stories: Traditional Narrative and the Family Drama in English Literature* (Cambridge, 1980), 72–91. See also Christopher Wrigley's '*Sir Gawain and the Green Knight*: The Underlying Myth', in *Studies in Medieval English Romances: Some New Approaches*, ed. Derek Brewer (Cambridge, 1988), 113–28; Anne Wilson, *Traditional Romance and Tale: How Stories Mean* (Cambridge, 1976), 96–108; and Enrico Giaccerini, 'Gawain's Dream of Emancipation', in *Literature in Fourteenth-Century England*, ed. Piero Boitani and Anna Torti (Tübingen, 1983), 49–64. The formulations 'latent', 'underlying', 'at a deeper level', which these studies continually oppose to the 'literal', 'manifest', or 'superficial' level show a tendency to discard the literal level without being fully aware that this is the *only* level which gives access to whatever 'hidden significances' these studies claim to unravel. If readings of this nature are to be fruitful, the question that needs to be asked is how the literal level engages structures or paradigms which psychoanalysts have associated with the Oedipal conflict, and it is only with reference to the letters of a text that such questions can be answered and accounted for.

along: not that of a lady whose love will support the knights she admires, but, like the mother of the family drama, a figure whose love puts obstacles in the way of success.

Her temptations withstood three times, the Lady acknowledges defeat. But as she is about to leave the room she retraces her steps and asks Gawain, as if in a final by-the-way, for a gift to remember him by. When Gawain refuses she eventually offers him the green girdle, and although Gawain first refuses it, he quickly changes his mind when she reveals that the girdle has the power to keep its wearer from harm:

> Þen kest þe knyȝt, and hit come to his hert
> Hit were a juel for þe jopardé þat hym iugged were:
> When he acheued to þe chapel his chek for to fech,
> Myȝt he haf slypped to be vnslayn, þe sleȝt were noble. (1855–8)

After Gawain has spent three mornings belabouring the discrepancy between previous romances and his own situation, it is finally a love-gift with magical properties in which Gawain and the reader suspend their disbelief. After many hours in which Gawain stubbornly refuses to be ruled by the authority of previous romances, he and the reader fall for one of the oldest commonplaces of romance: the talismanic love-token.

The motif may be found, before the birth of Arthurian romance, in Benoît de Sainte-Maure's *Roman de Troie*, in which Medea presents her lover Jason with magical gifts that will assist him in his adventure of the Golden Fleece. In Arthurian romance, Yvain similarly receives a gift with protective qualities from Laudine. Before he leaves her on his round of tournaments, Laudine gives him a magical ring that will protect him from harm:

> Mes or metroiz an vostre doi
> cest mien anel, que je vos prest;
> de la pierre quex ele est
> vos voel dire tot en apert:
> prison ne tient ne sanc ne pert
> nus amanz verais et leax,
> ne avenir ne li puet max;
> mes qui le porte, et chier le tient
> de s'amie li resovient,
> et si devient plus durs que fers . . . (*Yvain*, 2602–11)

Now I will put this ring of mine on your finger, and I lend it to you. And I want to tell you plainly about the nature of its stone: no true and faithful lover will be taken prisoner or will shed blood, and nothing bad can happen to him. But he who wears it, and cherishes it, will remember his beloved. Then he will become tougher than iron.

The ladies of the Vulgate *Lancelot*, too, trust that the gift of a girdle will boost the morale of their champions. When Gawain undertakes a combat for the lady of Roestoc, her servant advises her as follows:

'Et je voes loeroie que vous li donisiés aucune druerie et par aventure cuers li croisteroit, car dames ont aidié a faire maint preudome.' Et ele s'i acorde bien. [The Lady gives her gift to Gawain and says] 'si vous aport de mes drueries et vous pri que vos les portés en ramenbrance de moi. Et sachiés que je suis tout vostre. Or si combatés por vostre amie durement.' Lors li baille le coroie et le fremal, et il le chaint et met le fremal a son col. (LVIa, 31–2)

'It would be praiseworthy if you gave him some love-token. It might increase his courage, for ladies have often helped men in this way.' And she agrees completely. 'I am bringing you a token of my love, and I pray you wear it in remembrance of me. And know that I am wholly yours. So fight for your lady-love as hard as you can.' Then she hands him the belt and the lace, and he ties it around him and puts the lace around his neck.

Like the many chivalric heroes who have gone before him, Gawain in *Sir Gawain and the Green Knight*, who has thus far refused to give in to the Lady's seductions in order to preserve an allegiance to the host, ends up by embracing, as romance-heroes do, a 'luf-lace', which she insists must remain hidden from her husband:

> And [she] biso3t hym, for hir sake, disceuer hit neuer,
> Bot to lelly layne fro hir lorde; þe leude hym acordez
> þat neuer wy3e schulde hit wyt, iwysse, bot þay twayne
> for no3te. (1862–5)

This love-token is a gift which Gawain thinks is known only to himself and the Lady. No longer a threat to Gawain, the Lady becomes Gawain's partner in a 'secret coalition' which, Gawain believes, excludes the host.[46]

The Lady of the Castle seems suddenly to have undergone a structural change which transforms her from Gawain's earlier enemy into an adjuvant, who, like the ladies of romance, hands out a gift so that her loved one may thrive on its beneficial properties. If *Gawain* may retrospectively be analysed as a narrative in which the

---

[46] J. G. A. Marino, 'Games and Romance', doctoral dissertation (University of Pittsburgh, Penn., 1975), 262. See also Geraldine Heng, 'Feminine Knots and the Other in *Sir Gawain and the Green Knight*', PMLA 106 (1991), 500–14, at 504.

Lady of the Castle represents Gawain's 'enmy kene' (2406), the function of the Lady's offer of the girdle is precisely to hide this structure momentarily beneath a familiar romance-paradigm in which the Lady appears as helper rather than opponent. The girdle lures Gawain and the reader into believing they are in a different romance, in which ladies assist their lovers in their quests. True, Gawain knows that she is Bertilac's wife, and that in that capacity she is quite different from the marriageable ladies of romance, but still he believes her love-gift might save his life. And the reader colludes in Gawain's wishful thinking. Rationally, we know perfectly well that girdles are not magical talismans, but fancying ourselves to be in the fantastic world of romance where such magical love-gifts abound, we, like Gawain, overlay our knowledge of the way things are with the belief that we are in a romance where things can be different.

The joke the *Gawain*-poet plays on Gawain and the reader is his obfuscation and subsequent revelation of what we could always have known: that a green girdle is, after all, a green girdle, and that the Lady is Bertilac's wife rather than Gawain's secret admirer. What Gawain learns from the Green Knight when the joke is revealed is not simply that it is foolish to suspend this distinction and the distinctions which inevitably follow—those between mine and thine, between the privileges of guest and host, between self and the knights of romance who can do the impossible when armed with love-tokens. He learns also that to believe one can get away with suspending these distinctions is to believe in magic.

Sir Gawain and the Green Knight is not the only romance that makes its hero and its audience believe in magic when it is not there. There is an important connection here between the *Gawain*-poet and Chrétien de Troyes, who frequently lures us into a world of make-believe, only to explode the fiction in which we had suspended our disbelief. The episode of the magic tower from *Cligés* will illustrate this. Like Gawain, Cligés and Fenice are convinced that the miraculous inventions of Fenice's nurse Thessala and Cligés's servant John will enable them to escape from reality.[47]

[47] The following discussion of Chrétien's *Cligés* owes much to Peter Haidu, *Aesthetic Distance in Chrétien de Troyes: Irony and Comedy in Cligés and Perceval* (Geneva, 1968), 100–3. *Cligés* offers the closest analogue to *Gawain*'s motif of magic which does not work. For other uses of the motif see Helen Cooper's 'Magic that does not Work', *M&H* 7 (1976), 131–46. On magic in Arthurian romance, see also Peter Noble, 'Magic in Late Arthurian Verse Romances', *BBSIA* 44 (1992), 245–54.

Because Fenice is married to Cligés's uncle, she is reluctant to desert her husband for his nephew by eloping to Arthur's kingdom. In this case they would surely be defamed for their infidelity. With the help of Thessala, Fenice feigns death, and John builds a tower with invisible entrances, constructed in such a way that the couple will be able to spend the rest of their lives there without ever being found out. Thus they will be able to enjoy each other without incurring shame. When Fenice gets tired of being locked away in a tower and yearns for fresh air, John agrees to wave his magic wand yet again. He opens an invisible door and reveals to the lovers' eyes the most paradisal garden they have ever seen:

> Lors vet Jehanz ovrir un huis
> Tel que je ne sai, ne ne puis
> La façon dire ne retraire.
> Nus fors Jehan le poïst faire.
> Ne ja nus dire ne seüst
> Que huis ne fenestre i eüst,
> Tant con li huis ne fust overz,
> Si estoit celez et coverz.   (*Cligés*, 6297–304)

Then John opens a door—I do not know what kind of door, and cannot say how he did it. Only John could have done it. And no one could have said there was a door or window in it, for unless the door was open, it was hidden and concealed.

As in *Sir Gawain and the Green Knight*, the marvellous in *Cligés* seems to offer the heroes a final victory over the real. As the green girdle, had it worked, would have allowed Gawain to survive a beheading 'vnslayn', to refuse the Lady's love and yet draw on the power of her 'luf-lace', to withhold what is rightfully the host's without incurring reproach, and to err without consequence, so John's magic seems to create an alternative world in which the couple can have it both ways. Fenice can live with her husband's nephew without being slandered, the couple can hide away in a tower, while enjoying the seasonal changes of nature.

Such is the power of the Lady and John's fictions that despite the knowledge that we cannot eat the cake and have it, Gawain, the couple in *Cligés*, and their readers submit to them. But just as the green girdle turns out to be no more than the piece of cloth which we might have known a girdle to be, the magic of John's construction dissipates before the reader's eyes. While Fenice and Cligés live out their impossible dream of wish-fulfilment, a knight named

Bertrand who happens to be hunting in the neighbourhood sees his hawk disappear in the tower. We have been told that the walls of the tower are so high that no one could possibly scale it:

> Et li vergiers ert clos antor
> de haut mur qui tient a la tor,
> Si que riens nule n'i montast,
> Se par la tor sus n'i entrast.   (*Cligés*, 6333–6)

And the garden is enclosed by a high wall connected to the tower so that no one can get in unless through the entrance in the tower.

But Bertrand does the impossible, and hastens to penetrate the impenetrable hide-out to retrieve his hawk.

> Tantost se vet au mur aerdre
> Et fet tant que oltre s'an passe.
> Soz l'ante vit dormir a masse
> Fenice et Cligés nu a nu.   (*Cligés.*, 6360–3)

Then he begins to scale the wall, until he comes to the top. Beneath the tree he sees Fenice and Cligés sleeping naked in each other's arms.

Like us, the couple have been deceived into believing that they can have their paradise on earth. I use this formulation deliberately, for Chrétien consciously fashioned Jehan's tower after medieval descriptions of heaven, and in particular after Drythelm's vision of heaven in Bede's *Ecclesiastical History*. Like Bertrand in *Cligés*, Drythelm and his guide encounter an apparently unscalable wall, without doors or windows, when, inexplicably, they suddenly find themselves standing on top of it:

Cumque me in luce aperto duceret, vidi ante nos murum permaximum, cuius neque longitudine hinc vel inde neque altitudine ullus esse terminus videretur. Coepi autem mirari quare ad murum accederemus, cum in eo nullam ianuam uel fenestram uel ascensum alicubi conspicerem. Cum ergo pervenissemus ad murum, statim nescio quo ordine fuimus in summitate eius.[48]

When he led me in open light, I saw before us an extremely high wall. There seemed to be no limit to its length and height in every direction. I began to wonder why we were headed towards it, since I did not see a door, a window, or an ascent anywhere in it. But when we had reached the wall, we suddenly stood on its summit—how, I do not know.

---

[48] Bede, *Ecclesiastical History of the English People*, ed. and trans. B. Colgrave and R. A. B. Mynors (Oxford, 1969), 492–3.

When Bertrand similarly leaps over the high wall, Fenice and Cligés's paradise is lost. They have been inhabiting an illusion. And so, as in *Gawain*, the heroes and readers harshly awake to reality and the realization they have been duped by their credulity.

It may well be true that *Cligés* suggests a correspondence between the magicians Thessala and John, and Chrétien de Troyes.[49] Both create the most outrageous fictions, build castles in the air, and yet always find an audience willing to make these their homes. But a more accurate representation of both Chrétien and the *Gawain*-poet must be the Lady of the Castle, a teller of romances which she herself knows to be fictitious, a manipulator of wishful thinking, as unreliable and shifty as the poets who lead their readers up the well-trodden paths of escapism which they mercilessly expose as blind alleys.

Chrétien and the *Gawain*-poet's art is one of deception, and time and again they wrongfoot their audience and fictional characters, until a startling subversion of expectations catches us realizing we have been tricked into believing we were in a different narrative. Consider, for another example, the way Chrétien plays games with the reader in his *Chevalier de la charrete*. Lancelot is on his way to the Sword Bridge, and has to pass through the Stony Passage, which, as Lancelot is warned, is guarded by an army of hostile men:

'Ne vos sera mie randuz
maintenant que vos i vandroiz;
d'espee et de lance i prandroiz
maint cop, et s'an randroiz assez
einz que soiez outre passez.'   (*Lancelot*, 2170–4)

'It will never be surrendered to you on your arrival. You will have to put up with many blows of sword and spear, and will have to deal many, before you get through.'

When Lancelot arrives at the passage, numerous men with axes stand ready to defend it. Lancelot defeats one knight and the men-at-arms leap forward brandishing their axes. Like Lancelot, we brace ourselves for a fight, since this is the way romances usually test their heroes, but what actually happens defeats our expectations:

[49] See Michelle A. Freeman, *The Poetics of 'Translatio Studii' and 'Conjointure': Chrétien de Troyes's Cligés* (Lexington, Ky., 1979), 91–7, 157–61, and Grace M. Armstrong, 'Women of Power: Chrétien de Troyes's Female Clerks', in *Women in French Literature*, ed. M. Guggenheim (Stanford, Calif., 1988), 19–46, at 41–2.

> et li sergent as haches saillent,
> mes a esciant a lui faillent,
> qu'il n'ont talant de feire mal
> ne a lui ne a son cheval.
> (*Lancelot*, 2229–302)

and the soldiers leap forward with their axes, but they miss him on purpose, since they have no wish to hurt him or his horse.

The dangers, as it turns out, have no material reality outside Lancelot's and our minds. Once he has conquered his fear and confronted his opponents, the objects of his fear dissolve.[50]

The *Gawain*-poet springs a similar surprise on us. Not only do we suspend our disbelief in the green girdle, but we are also convinced that Gawain is destined to receive the blows of a demonic Green Knight. Again, our familiarity with romances in which knights are brought face to face with monsters strengthens us in our belief that something awful is about to happen. And indeed, when Gawain arrives at the macabre Green Chapel, and hears the Green Knight whetting a huge axe, the scene seems set for violence. But, like Lancelot's opponents, who strike blows that studiously avoid their target, the Green Knight strikes two blows in the air and a third that does no more than nick Gawain's skin.

As in *Lancelot*, the terrible encounter with the enemy existed only in our imagination. In the romances of Chrétien and the *Gawain*-poet this imagination is at the mercy of poets who play with it at their will, who deliver us from evil and enchantments just as easily as they plant them in our minds.

---

[50] On Chrétien's manipulation of expectations in the *Lancelot* see Evelyn Mullaly, *The Artist at Work: Narrative Technique in Chrétien de Troyes*, Transactions of the American Philosophical Society, 78 (Philadelphia, 1988), 137–41.

4 Honour and Honesty: The Heroic Ideal in Courtly Romance

Introduction

REMEMBERED MAINLY as a story of adulterous love, the *Chevalier de la charrete* has often been seen as a romance with whose values its creator felt ill at ease. In search of symptoms of Chrétien's supposed discomfort with its morality, critics have interpreted his attribution of the 'matiere et san' (26) to his patroness, and his presentation of Lancelot's adventures as non-committal or ironic.[1] Such a view of the *Charrete*, however, leaves out of consideration the work's pervasive and serious interest in the themes of honour and virtue, and, relatedly, in the foundations of heroism.[2] An episode in the *Charrete* which illustrates that interest is the adventure of the Sword Bridge. On his mission to free the Queen from Meleagant's clutches, Lancelot—or, better, the Knight of the Cart, for we know him by this stage only by his ignominious nickname—prepares to cross a bridge that consists of nothing more than a long and sharp sword. On the other side of the bridge the Knight of the Cart and his companions can make out the contours of two roaring lions that look certain to devour the knight in the unlikely event that he should manage to survive the crossing. All warn him of the danger but the Knight of the Cart remains determined to take his chances.

[1] Wendelin Foerster in *Der Karrenritter* (Halle, 1899) first took this line on the *Charrete*, which has since dominated criticism. For an overview of scholarship on the work, see Douglas Kelly, 'The *Charrete* in Modern Scholarship', in his *Sens et Conjointure in the Chevalier de la Charrete* (The Hague, 1966), 1–22.

[2] Three important articles that have shown the *Charrete*'s ethical commitments are J. Mandel, 'Elements in the *Charrete* World: The Father–Son Relationship', *MP* 62 (1964–5), 97–104; Emmanuel J. Mickel, 'The Theme of Honor in Chrétien's *Lancelot*', *Zeitschrift für Romanische Philologie*, 91 (1975), 243–72; and David Hult, 'Lancelot's Shame', *Romance Philology*, 42 (1988), 30–50. Most recently, Jill Mann has pointed to the importance of the *Lancelot* in Chrétien's formulation of a new heroic ideal: *Geoffrey Chaucer* (Hemel Hempstead, 1991), 202–3.

'Seignor, fet il, granz grez aiez
quant por moi si vos esmaiez;
d'amor vos vient et de franchise.
Bien sai que vos an nule guise
ne voldrïez ma mescheance;
mes j'ai tel foi et tel creance
an Deu qu'il me garra par tot:
cest pont ne ceste eve ne dot
ne plus que ceste terre dure,
einz me voel metre en aventure
de passer outre et atorner.
Mialz voel morir que retorner.'
Cil ne li sevent plus que dire,
mes de pité plore et sopire
li uns et li autres molt fort.　　　(*Lancelot*, 3079–93)

'Lords, he says, my thanks go to you for your concern on my account; it is your love and kindness that made you say it. I know well that you would in no way want me to come to grief, but I have such faith and belief in God that he will always protect me. I am no more afraid of this bridge or this river than I am afraid of this solid land. I want to take the adventure, and will get ready to cross. I would rather die than back off.' They do not know what more to say, but all weep and sigh for pity.

Leaving his sorrowful friends behind, the Knight of the Cart ventures the crossing. He makes it to the other side, oblivious to his wounds, and finds to his surprise that the lions had only been a figment of his overwrought imagination:

Lors li remanbre et resovient
des deux lyons qu'il i cuidoit
avoir veüz quant il estoit
de l'autre part; lors s'i esgarde:
n'i avoit nes une leisarde,
ne rien nule que mal li face.　　　(*Lancelot*, 3118–23)

Then he remembers and recalls the two lions which he thought he had seen when he was at the other side of the river. He looks but there was not even a lizard, or any other thing that could harm him.

The hero, and the reader, have been 'deceüz' (3128).

The episode of the Sword Bridge poses a dilemma for the hero with which readers of Chrétien will be thoroughly familiar.[3] Should

---

[3] For other examples, see Erec's determination to undertake the adventure of the Joy of the Court, despite King Evrain's advice (*Erec et Enide*, 5560–5608), or Yvain,

the hero listen to the well-intended and eminently reasonable advice
of his friends, abandon the mission, and stay in full control of his
own destiny, or should he place his trust in God, leap into the
darkness, and hope for the best? Should the knowledge that death
may be waiting round the corner dissuade him from pursuing the
course which he feels is right? Questions such as these are the stuff
of Arthurian romance. Take as another example an episode from
the Vulgate *Lancelot*, in which Lambègues faces the choice of
delivering himself up to his mortal enemy, King Claudas, and
rescuing his besieged city, or saving his own skin. The inhabitants of
the town try to persuade Lambègues to stay, but he will not budge:

Quant il l'oent, si commenchent tuit a plorer et dient que che ne sera ja
souffert, car trop seroit grant damages, se en teil eage rechevoit mort, car
encore puet venir a moult grant honor. (Vulgate *Lancelot*, XVIIa 30)

When they heard this, they all broke down in tears and said this would
never be tolerated, because it would be too great a shame if he should lose
his life at his young age, because he could still achieve great honour.

But Lambègues sets out towards his doom, despite the resistance of
his peers, and despite the 'grant honor' that might have come with
a longer life. He bravely surrenders himself and his arms to Claudas,
who, having intended to behead his enemy, is so impressed with his
courage and selflessness that, as well as ending the siege of the city,
he grants Lambègues his life and offers him his friendship:

Et Claudas l'espee prinse, si se lieve an haut et fait samblant que ferir le
voelle par mi le chief . . . 'Et jehui ne desiroie se ta mort non, mais je ne le
desirai jamais, car nus ne fist onques autreteil valor com tu as faite, qui a la
mort t'abandonoies por sauver les autres gens.' (Vulgate *Lancelot*, XVIIa,
35–7)

And Claudas took the sword and made as if to strike him on his head . . .
'If today I had desired your death, I will never more do so, because no one
ever acted so bravely as you did, when you surrendered yourself to a certain
death to save other people.'

The morality that can be distilled from these key moments in
romance is perhaps not as revolutionary as has sometimes been
believed.[4] The primacy of conscience, or personal persuasions, over

who follows the promptings of his heart and sets out towards the Pesme Aventure
against the resistance of bystanders (*Yvain*, 5157–71).

[4] See Colin Morris, *The Discovery of the Individual, 1050–1200* (New York,
1972), 136–7.

life and honour is commonplace in patristic writing, finding its most influential advocacy in Boethius' *Consolation of Philosophy*.[5] For Boethius, as for Lancelot or Lambègues, happiness depends on the willingness to renounce the gifts of fortune and to disregard the opinions of others for the greater good of inner conviction. There are differences, of course. Unlike Boethius, for whom a clear conscience and worldly recognition are in perennial tension, these heroes end up reaping the benefits of following their hearts without hesitation. Their willingness to put themselves at risk eventually pays off. The conflict between integrity on the one hand, and the love of life, honour, and reward on the other, which Boethius had to accept as a fact of life, turns out in courtly romances to be merely illusory, for doing what one feels to be right is ultimately most advantageous. Following one's conscience is not a renunciation of social recognition, but the way that leads to it.

Chrétien's ethics may in this respect owe more to the Stoic wisdom, transmitted by Cicero's *De Officiis*, that the interests of the *honestum* (the morally right) and the *utile* (the advantageous) are never irreconcilable, but can only *seem* that way. I may seem to be stretching the imagination when I associate Chrétien's romances with Stoic philosophy, but the distance between the two has become progressively smaller as we have come to know more about the social and intellectual roots of court culture. These roots lie in the symbiosis of clerics and knights at court, reflected in a clerical literature that could appeal to laymen, a literature of compromise, which insisted on moral and religious obligations without altogether denouncing the ways of the world.[6] It is this compromise which explains why the court-cleric's literature departed from patristic asceticism, and why it frequently resorted to classical writings on virtues and vices.[7]

Among these, Cicero's *De Officiis* held a crucial place. It had always been available in the Middle Ages, and from the twelfth

[5] For a brief discussion of the themes of *conscientia* and *fama* in medieval theology and their ramifications for the ideal of the hero in the period see Morton W. Bloomfield, 'The Problem of the Hero in the Later Medieval Period', in *Concepts of the Hero in the Middle Ages and the Renaissance*, ed. Norman T. Burns and Christopher Reagan (London, 1975), 27–48.

[6] See Joachim Bumke, *Höfische Kultur: Literatur und Gesellschaft im hohen Mittelalter*, 2 vols. (Munich, 1986), ii. 430, and Josef Fleckenstein, '*Miles* und *Clericus* am Könings-und Fürsterhof', in *Curialitas: Studien zu Grundfragen der höfisch-ritterlichen Kultur*, ed. J. Fleckenstein (Göttingen, 1990), 302–25.

[7] Pierre Riché, *De l'éducation antique à l'éducation chevaleresque* (Paris, 1968), 71.

century onwards the work became staple reading in cathedral schools and universities, in the original, in excerpts, or in contemporary adaptations.[8] Significantly, these adaptations were composed for the same audiences that read or listened to romance. The hugely popular *Moralium dogma philosophorum*, attributed to William of Conches, was written for Henry II.[9] Vernacular adaptations and translations of this work quickly appeared for the benefit of noblemen. Frequently, versions of the *Moralium dogma* are found in medieval manuscripts alongside romances such as the *Roman de sept sages*, Chrétien's *Perceval* and the continuations, the *Queste del saint graal*, and Chrétien's *Erec* and *Cligés*.[10] There remains of course a wide gulf between argumentative moral treatises and texts that tell stories, but medieval writers could, and did, bridge it. In the twelfth century Otto of Freising points the Ciceronian moral of the complementarity of the honest and the expedient in the flow of his history,[11] while Walter of Châtillon seems to invoke it in his *Alexandreis*.[12] Indeed, Cicero himself relies on stories to make his point, and we will be in a better position to see the connections between

[8] See Michael Lapidge, 'The Stoic Inheritance', in *A History of Twelfth-Century Philosophy*, ed. Peter Dronke (Cambridge, 1988), 81–112, at 91–3, and N. E. Nelson, 'Cicero's *De Officiis* in Christian Thought: 300–1300', *University of Michigan Publications: Language and Literature*, 10 (1933), 59–160. Maurice Testard's introduction to his edition of the first book of St Ambrose's *De Officiis* lists the many medieval adaptations of Cicero's work: *Les Devoirs* (New York, 1968), 52–87. The popularity of Cicero's *De Officiis* is also documented by Theodore Silverstein, 'Sir Gawain in a Dilemma, or Keeping Faith with Marcus Tullius Cicero', *MP* 75 (1977), 1–17, at 2–4. On medieval interpretations of Cicero see also Hans Baron, 'Cicero and the Civic Spirit in the Middle Ages and the Early Renaissance', *Bulletin of the John Rylands Library*, 22 (1938), 72–94. For the revival of Stoic philosophy and the renewed interest in the *De Officiis* see Philippe Delhaye, *Enseignement et morale au XIIe siècle* (Fribourg, 1988), 65. The possible influence of Stoic philosophy on vernacular romances, first proposed by Ehrismann, has been hotly debated in the field of Germanic studies. The major contributions to the debate have been collected by Günter Eifler, *Das ritterliche Tugendsystem* (Darmstadt, 1970). Taking stock of the debate, Bumke restates many of Ehrismann's observations', *Höfische Kultur*, 416–22.
[9] Philippe Delhaye, 'Une adaptation du *De Officiis* au XIIe siècle: Le *Moralium dogma philosophorum*', *Recherches de théologie ancienne et médiévale*, 16 (1949), 227–58, at 256–7.
[10] Jean Charles Payen, 'Le Livre de philosophie et de moralité d'Alain de Cambrai', *Romania*, 87 (1966), 145–74, at 151–2, and *Das Moralium dogma philosophorum des Guillaume de Conches: Lateinisch, Altfranzösisch und Mittelniederfränkisch*, ed. John Holmberg (Uppsala, 1929), 42–4.
[11] Nelson, 'Cicero's *De Officiis*', 100–1.
[12] Walter of Châtillon, *Alexandreis* (V. 326–7), ed. Marvin L. Colker (Padua, 1978).

his moral philosophy and courtly romance if we compare the episode of the Sword Bridge with one of these illustrative stories.

Two friends have been imprisoned by the tyrant Dionysius, who has sentenced one of them to death. The tyrant allows the victim a temporary respite from imprisonment to make arrangements for his family, while his friend stands surety for his return. Reunited with his family he has to choose between keeping his promise to return to prison or preserving his life by staying home. Should he follow his conscience and go back to face what he believes to be a certain death, or should he take the route of expedience? Like the heroes of Chrétien, the friend obeys the dictates of his conscience. I quote the story's conclusion from an Old French translation of the *Moralium dogma*:

Cil s'en ala et reuint au iour et quant li tyranz vit ce, si ot d'eus pitié et si lor pria que il le receüssent en amor et en compaignie et si les quita . . . Ja soit ce que li comencemenz samblast perilleus, la fins en fu bone. Ausi poez vous veoir que honeste chose, quex qu'ele soit au comencement, touz iors est profitable en la fin et chose deshoneste ne au comencement ne a la fin ne portera ia porfit. (pp. 172–4)

Thus he went back and arrived on the set day, and when the tyrant saw this, he took pity on them, begged them to include him in their friendship and company, and acquitted them . . . Even though the beginning seemed dangerous, the end was good. Thus you may see that an honest thing, however it appears in the beginning, is always profitable in the end and that a dishonest thing will never be profitable either in the beginning or the end.

Honesty is the best policy even where it seems to bring harm. Any conflict between the morally right and the expedient is in the final analysis only chimerical. So it is in Chrétien's *Lancelot* and the Vulgate *Lancelot*. As the death penalty is waived on the prisoner's return in Cicero, and as Lambègues's virtue brings about a change of heart in his mortal enemy, so the lions at the other end of the Sword Bridge evaporate once the Bridge is crossed. That, I take it, is the point of Chrétien's revelation that the lions existed only in Lancelot's fearful imagination. To believe that the path of the *honestum* leads only to death is always to fall victim to a *trompe-l'œil*.

Like Chrétien's adventure of the Sword Bridge, Gawain's rendezvous at the Green Chapel illustrates the principle that 'honeste chose, quex qu'ele soit au comencement, touz iors est profitable en la fin'.[13] Like Lancelot, Gawain is warned not to keep his appointment, for the only good that can come from his truthfulness is death. But Gawain declines the opportunity to retreat. Like Lancelot, he thanks the guide for his philanthropic concern, and, placing his trust in God, takes the adventure:

'Graunt merci', quoþ Gawayn, and gruchyng he sayde:
'Wel worth þe, wyȝe, that woldez my gode,
And þat lelly me layne I leue wel þou woldez.
Bot helde þou it neuer so holde, and I here passed,
Founded for ferde for to fle, in fourme þat þou tellez,
I were a knyȝt kowarde, I myȝt not be excused.
Bot I wyl to þe chapel, for chaunce þat may falle,
And talk wyth þat ilk tulk þe tale þat me lyste,
Worþe hit wel oþer wo, as þe wyrde lykez
        hit hafe.
    Þaȝe he be a sturn knape
    To stiȝtel, and stad with staue,
    Ful wel con Dryȝten schape
    His seruauntez for to saue.'   (2126–2139)

In *Gawain*, too, we seem to have arrived at a crossroads in the plot where the paths of the *honestum* and that of the *utile* diverge. Indeed, the way of honesty has even less to recommend itself than in Lancelot's case. There is no Queen to be set free, only a game to be finished. Fear of losing face is no incentive to persist, since the guide has promised not to divulge his retreat. There is only the prospect of decapitation as the expected outcome of Gawain's loyalty.

And yet, after his decision to be as good as his word, the beheading stroke turns out to have been no more real than the fierce lions guarding the Sword Bridge. As the threat of the lions is dispelled, the monstrous Green Knight becomes the genial host Bertilac. I have in

---

[13] An excellent case for the *Gawain*-poet's familiarity with Cicero's *De Officiis* or its medieval adaptations has been made by Silverstein, 'Sir Gawain', who analyses the fifth set of virtues symbolized by the pentangle, 'fraunchyse', felaȝchyp', 'clannes', 'cortaysye', and 'pité', in terms of the virtues that make up Cicero's ideal of justice, namely *liberalitas, amicitia, innocentia, mansuetudo,* and *pietas.* In addition to emphasizing the overriding importance of *fides* in both *Gawain* and the *De Officiis*, he notes a parallel to Gawain's exclamation—'Corsed worth cowarddyse and couetyse boþe! I In yow is vylany and vyse þat vertue disstryez' (2374–5)—in the Ciceronian notion that fear and covetousness impede the exercise of virtue: 'le cui mestier dui talent destorbent, c'est paors et couoitise' (*Moralium dogma*, p. 96). Where Silverstein is mainly concerned with the Ciceronian concepts that lie behind the *Gawain*-poet's vocabulary, the emphasis in this chapter is on the way the *Gawain*-poet translates these at the level of the plot.

the previous chapter discussed the way these surprising twists in the romances of Chrétien and the *Gawain*-poet catch us in the realization that we have been tricked into expecting a different conclusion to the narrative. But their practical jokes need not be without serious import. If they confront us with our credulity, they also reveal that we were wrong in thinking that righteousness might end in death. Chrétien and the *Gawain*-poet manipulate our perceptions to create a situation where 'one course is likely to appear expedient, and another morally right', only to concur with Cicero that 'the appearance is deceptive'.[14]

The ethic which we have seen at work, which emphasizes the knight's absolute duty to go where his conscience leads him, has important implications for the heroic ideal in the romances of Chrétien and *Gawain*. Moreover, it provides a framework which will allow us to understand why and how the heroes of Chrétien and the *Gawain*-poet fail. The following two sections will be concerned with their conceptions of the heroic ideal and the shortcomings of their knights.

The Ideal of the Hero

If there is one quality which epitomizes the mentality of the hero in epic literature, it is his unquenchable thirst for honour. In the chivalric literature of the later Middle Ages, the hero who, like Beowulf, is 'lofgeornost' (3182) had a continuing appeal. Historians leave us in no doubt that honour was as central to the mental universe of the nobility of the later Middle Ages as it had been for the warrior societies that had preceded it.[15] We are as well informed about the correlation between honour and violent competitiveness.[16]

[14] 'Atque in talibus rebus aliud utile interdum, aliud honestum videri solet. Falso . . .' (*De Officiis*, III. xviii), ed. G. P. Goold, LCL (London, 1968). The denouement of the *Franklin's Tale* points a similar moral. For the influence of a Christianized Stoic ethos in the works of Chaucer and his contemporaries, see J. D. Burnley, *Chaucer's Language and the Philosophers' Tradition* (Cambridge, 1979), 17, and Denise N. Baker, 'Chaucer and Moral Philosophy', *MAE* 60 (1991), 241–56.
[15] Maurice Keen, *Chivalry* (New Haven, Conn., 1984), 252. See also Sidney Painter, *French Chivalry* (1940, repr. Ithaca, NY, 1962), 34–7, and Malcolm Vale, *War and Chivalry* (London, 1981), 1–32.
[16] See Mervyn James, *English Politics and the Concept of Honour, 1485–1642*, Past and Present Supplement 3 (Cambridge, 1978), 2–6, for a discussion of the correlation and for further references.

Cultures where heroic stature is measured in terms of honour, in terms of the esteem with which one is held in the opinions of others, are characterized by aggressive assertiveness for the simple reason that esteem is ultimately as vital to one man of honour as to another, and therefore the object of intense rivalry. One wins honour only at the expense of others. The man in pursuit of honour cannot avoid confrontations which typically involve brute force. As Huizinga put it, 'where blood flows, honour is satisfied'.[17]

The heroism of honour, in which might is right, is inevitably at odds with an emphasis on moral rectitude. Cicero's *De Officiis* announces the inevitable fall from grace of the epic hero, who, in his quest for honour, puts the *utile* before the *honestum*. His truly great man does not regard his standing in the eyes of others, or outward fortunes, but has eyes only for moral honesty:

cum persuasum est nihil hominem, nisi quod honestum decorumque sit, aut admirari aut optare aut expetere oportere nullique neque homini neque perturbationi animi nec fortunae succumbere. (*De Officiis*, I. xx)

because he is persuaded that nothing should be admired or desired or sought after unless it is honest and proper, and that no man should be subject to any man, to passions, or to fortune.

The centrality of virtue moralizes heroism, displacing its foundations from the illustrious deed that catches the eye to the underlying morality of a course of action. Accordingly, deeds of prowess make way for inner strength:

Omnino illud honestum, quod ex animo excelso magnificoque quaerimus, animi efficitur, non corporis viribus. (*De Officiis*, I. xxiii)

The honesty which we seek in a lofty and magnanimous soul is brought about only by strength of the mind, not of the body.

Cicero's hero displays not necessarily physical but moral strength.[18]

[17] Johan Huizinga, *Homo Ludens: A Study of the Play-Element in Culture* (Boston, Mass., 1950), 116.

[18] The impact of Cicero's idea of greatness as springing from honesty rather than reputation appears from the semantic change of the word 'honour', which, under the influence of the Stoic *honestum*, slowly acquires the meaning of inner virtue as opposed to the esteem bestowed by others. See Bumke, *Höfische Kultur*, 428; George Fenwick Jones, ' "Lov'd I not Honor More": The Durability of a Literary Motif', *Comparative Literature*, 11 (1959), 131–43, at 140; and, by the same author, *Honor in German Literature* (Chapel Hill, NC, 1959), 46. The revaluation of honour from domination of others to domination of self which Alcuin Blamires and Jill Mann have

It is precisely this new mode of heroism which we find in Chrétien's *Lancelot* and *Sir Gawain and the Green Knight*. It is not that considerations of honour and shame have been eliminated from their Arthurian world. Nor have they disappeared from ours. Honour and shame exist in any society in which identity is founded on an interplay between private and public. The difference between their Arthurian world and the epic world lies rather in what it takes to be the source of honour. In the romances of Chrétien and the *Gawain*-poet this source is not the extortion of submission by force, but personal integrity.

This explains why Lancelot's performance in the tournament where Guinevere commands him to do his worst does not detract from his heroic stature even though it earns him the contempt of all onlookers, with the exception of the Queen. On the contrary, it enhances his heroism, for it shows the strength of character that lies behind his unwavering loyalty in the face of collective reproach. For Lancelot the dictates of his inner voice carry more authority than the trumpet of popular acclaim.

Unlike the traditional hero, Lancelot acts according to inner convictions, tolerating the scorn of those who judge by appearances rather than intentions. Attaching less importance to externals than to his heart, Lancelot's heroism is not solely dependent on making an impression. Indeed, many of Lancelot's greatest achievements seem to go completely unnoticed. After Lancelot has rescued the Queen, the populace is convinced that Gawain has accomplished the feat and they acclaim the wrong man as the Queen's saviour (*Lancelot*, 5312–19). Is Chrétien here showing up the vanity of honour? I believe so, for the case of the false attribution of praise is also one of Boethius' arguments against striving for honour, and probably Chrétien had the *Consolation of Philosophy* in mind when he describes Gawain's shame on hearing his name exalted without cause. Boethius' 'Nam qui falso praedicantur, suis ipsi necesse est laudibus erubescant' ('Those who are proclaimed without reason must needs feel ashamed for their praise') accurately predicts Gawain's embarrassment.[19]

traced in Chaucer suggests a similar shift from epic 'honour' to *honestum*. See Blamires, 'Chaucer's Revaluation of Chivalric Honor', *Mediaevalia*, 5 (1979), 245–69, and Mann, *Geoffrey Chaucer*, 165–85.

[19] Boethius, *Consolatio Philosophiae*, ed. Karl Büchner (Heidelberg, 1960), III, pr. 6.

'Seignor, de neant m'alosez;
del dire hui mes vos reposez
qu'a moi nule chose n'an monte.
Ceste enors me fet une honte . . .'   (*Lancelot*, 5321–4)

'Lords, you praise me for nothing; Stop talking about me at once, because
it has nothing to do with me. This honour shames me . . .'

Honour and merit are equally at odds when the hostess at the castle
of the Flaming Lance refuses to allow the Knight of the Cart to sleep
on the Perilous Bed on account of his bad reputation. Taking the
stories of her guest's ride in the cart as sufficient evidence of his
depravity, she warns him he will pay dearly if he goes anywhere near
it. One is not surprised that Lancelot persists, or that he manages to
survive the adventure of the Flaming Lance, but it seems bizarre that
after he has carelessly thrown away the lance and put out the fire in
his bed he turns over and drops off to sleep again, without anyone
in the castle noticing a thing.

Neither that night, nor the following day, does the adventure
make any impression on anyone in the household, not even on
Gawain, who has slept in the hall with Lancelot. In fact, no one but
Lancelot, in a brief moment of wakefulness, registers the adventure
at all. Critics have in various ways wished this anomaly away,[20] but
the absence of applause or astonishment at Lancelot's feat fits the
Charrete's emphasis on virtue as opposed to honour or recognition
perfectly. Lancelot's heroism does not need the validation of the
limelight.

This is why Lancelot's heroic gestures are so often self-effacing
and passive rather than the aggressive acts of assertion which are the
traditional hero's indispensable weapons in the competition for
esteem. The adventures of the Perilous Bed, of the Cart, or Lancelot's 'recreantise' at the tournament figure a hero who is wholly
divested of the epic urge to dominate and who instead patiently
endures humiliation and suffering. Lancelot's adventure at the
Sword Bridge is no exception. It calls for an approach that signals a
striking departure from convention:

Et cil de trespasser le gort
au mialz que il set s'aparoille,

[20] Douglas Kelly has defended Chrétien against the deprecatory comments of
Foerster and Weston, but the best he has to say of Chrétien's 'weakness' is that it 'is
not particularly noticeable', *Sens et Conjointure*, 111–12.

> et fet molt estrange mervoille,
> que ses piez desarme et ses mains . . . (*Lancelot*, 3094–7)

And he prepares himself as best as he can to cross the abyss, and he does something strange and marvellous: he disarms his feet and his hands . . .

His armour removed, Lancelot treads on the sword, willingly sacrificing the blood that pours from his hands and feet. The parallel with Christ's wounds is unmistakable, though it would be wrong to reduce it to a parodic element in the romance.[21] It makes the entirely serious point that heroism does not lie in self-aggrandizement but in self-immolation.

An ethics which predicates honour on virtue is bound to inaugurate a different kind of heroism, just as it is bound to expose the man who seeks honour irrespective of honesty as a *poseur*, whose relentless efforts to make himself heard or seen reveal a despicable dependence on others and a blindness to the vital issues of right and wrong. This exposure is Meleagant's fate in Chrétien's *Lancelot*. It will not do to put his belligerent one-upmanship and his double-dealing down to flaws of character, unless we realize that they are, in Chrétien's vision, the tragic consequences of a way of thinking espoused not just by Meleagant but by the chivalric community of medieval Europe.[22]

Unlike Lancelot, who puts private imperatives before his reputation and can therefore bear popular rejection or neglect, Meleagant is not driven by a conscience, for he has none, but by a desire to command respect. Put in a different way, while Lancelot's actions are motivated by an internalized sense of obligation, Meleagant's logic is that of honour and shame.[23] Meleagant's ostentatious challenge at King Arthur's court, his blatant kidnapping of Guinevere, his refusal to give in to the wishes of Lancelot and Bademagu, the

[21] D. W. Robertson, *A Preface to Chaucer* (Princeton, NJ, 1962), 451.

[22] In a study of honour in *Yvain*, René Girard presents Chrétien as a 'satirist unraveling what he regards as the logic of devouring ambition in the feudal aristocracy of his time': 'Love and Hate in *Yvain*', in *Modernité au Moyen Age: Le Défi du passé*, ed. Brigitte Cazelles and Charles Méla (Geneva, 1990), 249–62. In the *Lancelot*, Chrétien likewise satirizes this logic, principally through the person of Meleagant.

[23] I draw here on the anthropological distinction between shame and guilt cultures which has had considerable currency in criticism of medieval literature. For some applications of these anthropological concepts see Derek Brewer's introduction to *The Morte Arthur: Parts Seven and Eight* (London, 1968), 23–35, and Mark Lambert's *Style and Vision in Le Morte Darthur* (New Haven, Conn., 1975), 176–94.

care he takes to ensure that the confrontation will come to a head in a duel in the presence of Arthur's court, all these are designed to elicit, or rather to exact, awe and admiration.

His thirst for publicity is brought across vividly when, after secretly imprisoning Lancelot, he makes himself conspicuous at King Arthur's court, and reminds all the onlookers of the joust he has arranged with Lancelot:

> Et quant il vint *devant le roi,*
> molt plains d'orguel et de desroi
> a comanciee sa reison:
> 'Rois, *devant toi an ta meison*
> ai une bataille arramie;
> mes de Lancelot *n'i voi mie,*
> qui l'a enprise ancontre moi.
> Et neporquant, si con je doi,
> ma bataille, *oiant toz,* presant,
> *ces que ceanz voi an presant.*
> .   .   .   .   .   .
> je *voi* chevaliers ceanz,
> *qui furent a noz covenanz,*
> et bien dire le vos savroient,
> se voir reconuistre an voloient.
> mes se il le me vialt noier,
> ja n'i loierai soldoier,
> einz le *mosterrai* vers son cors.' (*Lancelot,* 6151–73; italics mine)

And when he came before the king, full of arrogance and pride, he began to pontificate: 'King, before you, and in your hall, I have arranged a combat. But Lancelot, who has undertaken this combat against me, is nowhere to be seen. But nevertheless, as I should, I offer this battle, in the hearing of all, to those whom I see present . . . I see knights sitting here, who witnessed our agreement, and they can underwrite this, if they wanted to reveal the truth. But if someone would deny it, I will not hire a champion, but prove it on his body personally.'

There is not a moment when Meleagant forgets he is being watched by a crowd and no opportunity he misses to point out he was seen, is being seen, and is willing to show. The reason for Meleagant's obsession with publicity is his deluded notion that high ratings demonstrate superiority. Hence Meleagant cannot help drawing attention to the fact that Lancelot is out of the picture. According to the viewing figures which Meleagant has furtively manipulated by imprisoning his rival, no one watches Lancelot and all watch Meleagant. *Ergo*, Meleagant is best. Such must indeed be the conclusion of an evaluation which takes a knight's place in the public eye as its only criterion for judgement.

Bademagu's chastisement of his son sums up Chrétien's refutation of Meleagant's code of honour and brings it face to face with the heroism of virtue with which Chrétien supplants it. Returning from Arthur's court, Meleagant holds forth on the indelible impressions he has made on the members of the Round Table. Of course, his trained eye quickly spots the presence of an audience, whom he treats to a particularly fine example of the logic of honour:

> Et si vos dirai or androit,
> ou Meleaganz est venuz,
> qui, *oiant toz gros et menuz*,
> dist a son pere *molt en haut*:
> 'Pere, fet il, se Dex vos saut,
> se vos plest, or me dites voir
> se cil ne doit grant joie avoir
> et se molt n'est de grant vertu
> qui a la cort le roi Artu
> par ses armes se fet doter.'
> Li peres, *sanz plus escoter*,
> a sa demande li respont:
> 'Filz, fet il, tuit cil qui boen sont
> doivent enorer et servir
> celui qui ce puet desservir,
> et maintenir sa conpaignie.'
> (*Lancelot*, 6252–67; italics mine)

And now I will tell you of the arrival of Meleagant, who says loudly to his father, in the hearing of all, small and great: 'Father, as God may save you, and if you please, tell me in truth, is he not worthy who makes himself feared at King Arthur's court with feats of arms?' The father, without listening further, replies to his question: 'Son, he says, the good should honour and serve those who deserve it, and keep their company.'

We need not dwell long on Meleagant's thought processes, for we have seen them at work before. He confuses merit with recognition, which he cannot conceive of obtaining by any other means than force, since for men of honour 'the ultimate vindication of honour is violence'.[24] To be honoured is therefore to be feared. Unfortunate-

[24] Julian Pitt-Rivers, 'Honour and Social Status', in *Honour and Shame: The Values of Mediterranean Society*, ed. J. G. Peristiany (London, 1965), 19–77, at 29.

ly for Meleagant, his father is not impressed. Bademagu refuses to give his son the attention and approval to which Meleagant's every word and action is geared. He does not hear him out, and rather than endorsing his son's words he puts forward an alternative ethics in which honour is not the outcome of fierce rivalry but is freely awarded to deserving individuals. 'Cil qui boen sont' are not necessarily the victors in a violent competition for esteem; they can be those who selflessly bestow honour where honour is due.[25] Freely honouring someone who is worthy, which Meleagant sees as a diminution of one's own esteem and hence as an admission of defeat, is in this analysis a crowning virtue.

The virtue of *reverentia* is only one of the many forms of humility which Bademagu recommends to his son:

> 'voirs est que boens cuer s'umilie,
> mes li fos et li descuidiez
> n'iert ja de folie vuidiez.
> Filz, por toi le di, que tes teches
> par sont si dures et si seches
> qu'il n'i a dolçor n'amitié;
> li tuens cuers est trop sanz pitié:
> trop es de la folie espris.
> C'est por coi ge te mespris;
> c'est de qui molt t'abeissera.
> Se tu es preuz, assez sera
> qui le bien an tesmoignera
> a l'ore qui besoignera;
> n'estuet pas prodome loer
> son cuer por son fet loer
> que li fez meïsmes se loe;
> neïs la monte d'une aloe
> ne t'aïde a monter an pris
> tes los, mes assez mains t'en pris.' (*Lancelot*, 6308–26)

'It is true that a noble heart humbles itself, but the foolish and the arrogant will never abandon folly. Son, and I say this for your benefit, your manners are so harsh and abrasive that there is neither kindness nor humanity in them. You are too full of folly. This is what I disdain in you, and what will bring you low. If you are wise, there will be enough people who will testify to it when it matters. A gentleman should not praise his own

---

[25] In the adaptation of the *De Officiis*, the *Moralium dogma*, this quality goes by the name of *reverentia* or 'honorabletez': 'Reverentia est virtus personis gravibus vel aliqua prelatione sublimatis debite honorificationis cultum exhibens' (pp. 26, 128). Cf. Cicero, *De Officiis*, I. xxviii.

bravery to advertise his deed, for the deed speaks its own praise. Your boastfulness does not increase its value a bit, and will not help you rise in esteem; on the contrary, I esteem you less for it.'

One does not achieve renown by successful self-advertising, but by practising virtuous and humble deeds which will testify to one's nobility when it matters. Again we find Cicero anticipating Bademagu's reprimands:

Vera autem et sapiens animi magnitudo honestum illud, quod maxime natura sequitur, in factis positum, non in gloria iudicat principemque se esse mavult quam videri; etenim qui ex errore imperitae multitudinis pendet, hic in magnis viris non est habendus. (*De Officiis*, I. xix)

True and wise greatness of spirit takes honesty, which nature seeks above all, to be located in deeds, not in fame, and prefers to be the first rather than to be considered as such; after all, someone who is dependent on the erroneous opinions of the ignorant masses cannot be ranked among great men.

And, as in the *Charrete*, this ethic entails modes of heroism that can dispense with ostentation and self-glorification and allow for humility and gentleness:

Nec vero audiendi qui graviter inimicis irascendum putabunt idque magnanimi et fortis viri esse censebunt; nihil enim laudabilius nihil magno et praeclaro viro dignius placabilitate atque clementia. (*De Officiis*, I. xxv)

We should not listen to those who think that one should fall violently on one's enemies and who think that such is the nature of a great man. For nothing is more praiseworthy in a great and eminent man than kindness and pity.

Both in Chrétien's *Lancelot* and in the *De Officiis* the ethic of virtue dooms the epic hero. Moral qualities such as 'dolçor' or 'placabilitas', 'pité' or 'clementia', oust aggression and assertiveness as admired ideals, while the 'man of honour' stands exposed as a callous loudmouth.

King Arthur's court in the opening of *Sir Gawain and the Green Knight* clearly resembles the aristocratic community of honour in whose image the earliest Arthurian writings had created the Fellowship of the Round Table. Throughout the twelfth-century chronicles of Arthur, the members of the Round Table are driven by the desire to enhance and to uphold their honour against rivalling communities and against each other. The story of the founding of the

Round Table clearly pictures the rivalry among the Arthurian knights, who are always ready to vindicate their honour with the sword. According to Wace, the Round Table has its origin in a quarrel that breaks out over the relative merits of its members.[26] When the table arrangements force the Arthurian community to make its pecking-order explicit, no knight is willing to concede the place of honour to another. Laȝamon has an evocative description of the erupting violence:

> Æle hafode an heorte leches heȝe
> and lette þat he weore betere þan his iuere
> Þat folc wes of feole londe; þer was muchel onde
> for þe an hine talde haeh, þe oþer muche herre.
> . . . .
> Þa duȝede wærþ iwraþþed, duntes þer weoren riue;
> ærest þa laues heo weorpen, þa while þa heo ilæsten,
> and þa bollen seoluerne mid wine iuulled,
> and seoþþen þa uustes uusden to sweoren.
>   (Laȝamon's *Brut*, 11353–70)

Each had proud feelings in his heart and thought that he was better than his fellows. Those men were from many lands; there was fierce rivalry because the one accounted himself great, the other considered himself much greater . . . The courtiers grew angry, blows were frequent there; first they threw the loaves, as long as they lasted, and the silver bowls filled with wine, and next fists flew at necks.[27]

The barons do not shy away from confrontation when their honour is at stake. Arthur's ingenious solution to their hawkishness is a Round Table, where no knight can sit above another. It needs the implementation of a social structure which suspends considerations of precedence while the knights are at court to defuse the tensions among the barons for whom intransigence implies honour and compromise shame.[28] Clearly this is a fellowship in which contemporary noblemen would have recognized themselves. For them, too, honour 'could only be safeguarded by constant vigilance, by readiness to retaliate against anything that could be remotely construed as a public insult'.[29] A thin line separates the Round Table and its

[26] Wace, *Brut*, ll. 9747–52.
[27] *Laȝamon's Arthur: The Arthurian Section of Laȝamon's Brut*, ed. and trans. W. R. J. Barron and S. C. Weinberg (London, 1989).
[28] On the history of the Round Table, see Beate Schmolke-Hasselmann, 'The Round Table: Ideal, Fiction, and Reality', *AL* 2 (1982), 41–75.
[29] Blamires, 'Chaucer's Revaluation', 248–9.

intended audience, described by the author of *Jacob's Well* as always 'desyring worshyp aforn othere', 'lokynge after reuerence, to sytten above, to spekyn first, to have the woordys out of anothere mannys mouth, to takyn worscip of the world, passing alle othere'.[30]

Typically, the honour of the Round Table is won at the expense of other communities. Again and again, honour leads them to the battlefield, and even feasts are moves in a contest of honour. Arthur organizes them not in the first place to celebrate past achievements but:

> Pur ses richeises demustrer
> Et pur faire de sei parler.
> (Wace's *Brut*, 10199–200)

To demonstrate his riches and to make himself talked about.

War and conspicuous consumption express Arthur's concern to command the world's respect. Without constantly making his superiority manifest, Arthur stands to lose honour, to relinquish his hold on the imagination of others on whose esteem honour depends. Hence the restlessness and impatience which forever spur Arthur on in his conquests. As Peter of Langtoft put it: 'Arthur does not wait, he does not want to rest' ('Arthur ne demort, ne volt reposer').[31] The disastrous consequences of slackening the urge to be the focus of attention are sketched in the *Perlesvaus*. The romance opens with Arthur, who at the height of his fame loses his former passion for bravado. The resulting inaction prompts all honourable knights to seek their fortune elsewhere. Arthur himself realizes that the decline of his reputation is due to his inertia:

—Certes, dame, dist li rois, ge n'é volenté de fere largesce ne chose qui tort a honeur; ainz m'est mes talenz muëz en floibece de cuer, e par ce sé ge bien que je pert mes chevaliers e l'amor de mes amis. (*Perlesvaus*, p. 26)[32]

—Truly, lady, says the king, I have not had the will to be liberal or undertake something honourable. Thus my resolve has made way for feeble-heartedness, and I know well that it is costing me my knights and the love of my friends.

---

[30] Quoted in G. R. Owst's *Literature and Pulpit in Medieval England* (Oxford, 1966), 309.

[31] *The Chronicle of Pierre de Langtoft*, ed. T. Wright, 2 vols., RS (London, 1866, repr. 1964), i. 160.

[32] The episode is probably borrowed from the *First Continuation*, I. 3247–52.

The *Perlesvaus* clearly points to the constant need to keep a high profile, and to provide opportunities where knights can prove their mettle, for shame immediately rears its head when such opportunities are missed.

There could not be a greater contrast between the feeble Arthur of the *Perlesvaus* and the enthusiastic king of *Sir Gawain and the Green Knight*. In the best tradition of the restless leader of a community of honour, the *Gawain*-poet describes Arthur as someone who:

> louied þe lasse
> Auþer to longe lye or to longe sitte ... (87–8)

This Arthur is not plagued by a lack of resolve, but has well absorbed the proverbial saying that 'Rest and fame do not go well together' ('Ne s'acordent pas bien ansanble | Repos et los ...': *Cligés*, 155–6). Unlike the Arthur of the *Perlesvaus*, he does not fail in his duty to create opportunities for the demonstration of prowess. He upholds the custom not to eat before he has either heard of an adventure, 'Oþer sum segg hym bisoȝt of sum siker knyȝt | To joyne wyth hym in iustyng ...' (96–7).[33] Here, as in the *Lancelot*, we see the correlation between the traditional concept of honour and prowess. The Green Knight's challenge to Arthur's court makes that link explicit:

> 'What, is þis Arþures hous', quoþ þe haþel þenne,
> Þat al þe rous rennes of þurȝ ryalmes so mony?
> Where is now your sourquydrye and your conquestes,
> Your gryndellayk and your greme, and your grete wordes? (309–12)

---

[33] This custom is an Arthurian commonplace. The motif was first introduced in Chrétien's *Perceval*, and was then taken over by the poet of the *First Continuation* (I. 3322–31), from which the *Gawain*-poet probably borrowed it:

> 'Ne place Dieu que la m'aveigne
> Qu'a haute fest que cort teigne
> . . . .
> Qu'eve soit pris ne donee
> Devant que estrange novele
> Ou alcune aventure bele
> I soit, voiant toz, avenue.
> La costume ai ensi tenue
> Toute ma vie dusque chi.'

It is not impossible that the *Gawain*-poet found the motif in another source, for it was so conventional that it led to parody—witness the hilarious opening of *Jaufré*, in which Arthur's hoped-for adventure takes hours to arrive.

The honour of 'Arþures hous' is grounded on aggression or boast-fulness. Arthur's first response to the Green Knight is entirely consistent with these assumptions. After the Green Knight has brought up the matter of Arthur's reputation and that of his knights, Arthur promptly concludes that he must be looking for a fight:

> Arthour con onsware,
> And sayde, 'Sir cortays kny3t,
> If þou craue batayl bare,
> Here faylez þou not to fy3t.'   (275–8)

However inappropriate Arthur's response may seem to today's readers, it is induced by a mentality that would have not have raised many eyebrows among its contemporary audience. What other response might one expect when a stranger asks for evidence of the 'los' of Arthur's Round Table? Must not any proof of honour boil down to some form of 'batayl bare'?

But the Green Knight confounds the Round Table with a proposition that is not easily digested by its members. He does not challenge them to take part in a contest of strength, as Arthur had anticipated. He does not in fact create a field of epic honour at all. If honour is to be won on the battlefield or in the lists, as the code of chivalry insists,[34] this is because there is an opponent who puts up a defence. Honour demands a demonstration of 'manhod' and prowess, which in turn requires a competitor's resistance. As much as resistance may seem to work against physical force, it is as true to say that it enables a show of strength to be staged in the first place. The players of the beheading game, however, have to strike or suffer blows without defence. Depriving the aggressors of resistance, the *Gawain*-poet presents the Round Table with a test which renders the demonstration of prowess completely pointless, and from which honour, in the prevalent sense of the glory derived from feats of arms, cannot therefore accrue.

---

[34] Note, for instance, the speech of Sir Enguerrant in Antoine de la Salle's *Petit Jehan de Saintré*, ed. Jean Misrahi and Charles A. Knudson, TLF (Geneva, 1965), p. 103: 'Seigneurs, car les tres nobles previleiges de honneur mondains requierent aux nobles cuers que par le tresnoble mestier d'armes chascun de bien en mieulz a son pouoir se employe de acquerir la tresnoble grace d'honneur soit en armes d'emprinses ou soit en guerres guerroiables et en tout autres honestes façons' ('Sirs, the noble privileges of worldly honour require from all noble hearts that, in the noble vocation of warfare, each should do his utmost to acquire the noble grace of honour, in duels, in war, or in other honourable ways'). For further examples see Lee Patterson, *Chaucer and the Subject of History* (Madison, Wis., 1991), 171–9.

The analogues of the beheading game state this explicitly. In the *Perlesvaus*, Lancelot hesitates to behead his compliant opponent for fear that it will harm his reputation (p. 137). Two versions of the *First Continuation* specify that the reluctance of Arthur and his barons to accept the challenge is due to their awareness that the beheading game can bring them no honour:

> Ainz dïent tuit li chevalier
> Molt seroit fols cil qui ferroit,
> Qu'en auenture se metrait,
> Si n'i aroit pris ne honneur.
> (*First Continuation*, I. 3368–71)

All the knights say that the one to strike the blow would be foolish, because he would put himself at risk, without getting renown or honour from it.

> Li rois pansive chier a faite.
> Esbaïs sont grant et menor
> An leur cuer pansent quelle honor
> Pueent avoir de lui ferir.
> (*First Continuation*, II. 7148–87)

The king looks pensive. Small and great are abashed, pondering in their hearts what honour might be had from striking him.

The point, which all discussions of the theme of honour in *Gawain* have overlooked, could not be more evident.[35] From the few things the player of the beheading game might hope to achieve, honour, as it was traditionally understood, is excluded.

In the face of an imminent catastrophe after the Green Knight's survival of his decapitation, the gratuitousness of Gawain's undertaking has become painfully obvious. Gawain is bound to seek out the Green Chapel and must suffer his opponent's blow defencelessly, and all this for the sake of a game. Like Chrétien's Lancelot, he must assume postures which tradition would brand as unheroic, or condemn as dishonourable or foolish. Lancelot takes beating after beating in the tournament, or disarms in order to cross the Sword

---

[35] Articles on the theme of honour in *Gawain* have tended to assume that the *Gawain*-poet largely takes honour and shame for granted. See Lorette Wasserman, 'Honor and Shame in *Sir Gawain and the Green Knight*', in *Chivalric Literature*, ed. Larry D. Benson and John Leyerle (Kalamazoo, Mich., 1980), 77–90, and John Burrow, 'Honour and Shame in *Sir Gawain and the Green Knight*', in his *Essays on Medieval Literature* (Oxford, 1984), 117–31. It seems to me that the *Gawain*-poet is more sceptical about honour and shame than Burrow or Wasserman believe. I am in general agreement with Robert L. Kindrick's 'Gawain's Ethics: Shame and Guilt in *Sir Gawain and the Green Knight*', *Annuale Medievale*, 20 (1981), 5–32.

Bridge. Gawain must willingly yield his neck to the Green Knight. As Jill Mann has written about the romance hero, 'the narrative images that express his heroism . . . are not images of aggressive action, but of passive suffering, the courage to abandon the self to danger without resistance or evasion'.[36]

Moreover, unlike the epic hero, whose fights against monstrous and evil opponents endow his enterprises with a moral urgency, Gawain's confrontation with the Green Knight seems utterly pointless. What has society to gain from the beheading game other than Gawain's survival, which is precisely what Gawain endangered by volunteering for the game in the first place? As the *Gawain*-poet's terminology insists, Gawain has decided to play a game, and, as the player of a game can only win by freely entering into a world where he stands to lose, Gawain can do no more than hope for the restoration of happiness which he voluntarily put at stake. In the world of the epic events are loaded, even overburdened, with momentous significance. But Gawain's adventure, like so many adventures in the romances of Chrétien, seems devoid of profit or purpose. Knights who wish to go in pursuit of adventures must put questions about their sense in abeyance, for adventures do not yield their meaning until after they have been tried. They lend themselves only to a retrospective reading.[37] Before taking the leap of faith which *aventure* requires, its significance must remain a mystery. One must pursue adventure *despite* considerations of honour, profit, and common sense.

The barons make the point well when they contrast Gawain's task with more suitable career prospects:

> 'Bi Kryst, hit is scaþe
> Þat þou, leude, schal be lost, þat art of lyf noble!
> To fynde hys fere vpon folde, in fayth, is not eþe.
> Warloker to haf wroȝt had more wyt bene,
> And haf dyȝt ȝonder dere a duk to haue worþed:
> A lowande leder of ledez in londe hym wel semez,

---

[36] Mann, *Geoffrey Chaucer*, 178.

[37] See Sarah Kay's observations about *Erec* in 'Commemoration, Memory, and the Role of the Past in Chrétien de Troyes: Retrospection and Meaning in *Erec et Enide, Yvain* and *Perceval*', *Reading Medieval Studies*, 17 (1991), 31–50, at 36–7. In a perceptive comparative study of *Erec et Enide* and *Sir Gawain and the Green Knight*, T. A. Shippey has shown that the pursuit of seemingly pointless adventures creates joy out of nothing, meaning out of randomness: 'The Uses of Chivalry: *Erec* and *Gawain*', *MLR* 66 (1971), 241–50.

And so had better haf ben þen britned to noȝt,
Hadet wyth an aluisch mon, for angardez pryde.
Who knew euer any kyng such counsel to take
As knyȝtez in cauelaciounz on Crystmasse gomnez!' (674–83)

Would it not have been wiser, they say with the benefit of hindsight, to have prevented Gawain from pursuing this silly adventure by giving him a dukedom? Weighing the pros and cons, the loss and the profit, the barons cannot but conclude that Gawain has embarked on a senseless mission of self-destruction. As a safe short-cut to esteem, a dukedom might have prevented Gawain from taking the tortuous and hazardous route to honour which now seems to have turned towards disaster. As it is, Gawain seems destined never to achieve the distinction that a man of his calibre would have deserved. With their eyes firmly fixed on the *utile*, the barons cannot of course see eye to eye with what honesty now demands of Gawain. Being men of honour, they prefer epic to romance, would have preferred to see Gawain in the role of a 'lowande leder of ledez', and regret that he should ever have been released into a realm of adventure which condemns the knight to submit passively and pointlessly to the strokes of an 'aluisch mon' and to die in oblivion.

In contrast, Gawain's heroism consists in maintaining an unconditional allegiance to private imperatives, however shameful and unpromising the consequences. His patience and indifference to considerations of honour are further put to the test in the temptation scenes, when Gawain endures the censure of the Lady of the Castle, who cleverly presents herself as the spokeswoman for the *communis opinio*. When Gawain shows himself reluctant to act on her wishes, she expresses not just her own disappointment but accuses Gawain of shame, of having failed to live up to the norms of society at large.

'For schame!
I com hider sengel, and sitte
To lerne at yow sum game;
Dos, techez me of your wytte,
Whil my lorde is fro hame.' (1530–4)

The choice of sleeping with the lady or desisting has been rephrased as a choice between honour and shame. The concept of honour we encounter here will be familiar. Not unlike the battlefield, the bedroom is a field of honour for the warrior, where glory depends on taking trophies. It is won at the expense of others, and where male opponents may be shamed in combat, women are conquered when they surrender their sexual purity.[38] With an opportunity to gain honour, should not a man be quick to respond?

Time and again the Lady of the Castle's version of honour is echoed in medieval literature. In the Vulgate *Lancelot*, a maiden who is trying to seduce Lancelot accuses him of shame when Lancelot will not sleep with her:

Et quant ele voit un bel lieu plaisant, si li mostre et dit: 'Veez, sire chevaliers, dont ne serait il bien honnis qui tel lieu passeroit avec bele dame ne avec bele dameisele sans fere plus?' (Vulgate *Lancelot*, XXVI. 11)

And when she saw a pleasant spot, she showed it to him and said: 'Look, sir knight, would not a knight be shamed if he passed such a place with a beautiful lady or damsel without doing anything?'

In *Troilus and Criseyde*, Pandarus mocks Troilus' indecision in his courtship of Criseyde as follows:

'Frend, syn thow hast swych distresse,
And syn the list myn argumentz to blame,
Why nylt thiselven helpen don redresse
And with thy manhod letten al this grame?
Go ravysshe here! Ne kanstow nat, for schame!'
(*Troilus and Criseyde*, IV. 526–30)

Like the Lady of the Castle, Pandarus equates honour with an assertion of 'manhod', and 'schame' with scruples or hesitation. And, like Pandarus, whose view of honour is but a step away from a licence to rape,[39] the Lady of the Castle appeals to Gawain's 'manhod' when she reminds him he is 'stif innoghe to constrayne wyth strenkþe' (1497), and could therefore take her by force. In the end, honour reduces not only relations between men, but also those between men and women, to simple questions of superior physical strength.[40]

It is symptomatic of the *Gawain*-poet's scepticism about this mentality that he puts his hero in a situation where an adherence to conventional notions of honour and shame would have paved the

---

[38] G. F. Jones, *Honor*, 29.
[39] Cf. Mann, *Geoffrey Chaucer*, 167.
[40] Consider also the scene in the *Chevalier à l'épée*, ll. 581–9, in which Gawain defies the threats of an enchanted sword that protects the chastity of the host's daughter, who shares Gawain's bed, for fear that his honour will be impugned should the word get out that he let this opportunity go by.

way to perdition.[41] Instead of proving his 'manhood' Gawain must draw strength from his temperance and self-control, even if that means that he must cut a sorry figure beside the Lady of the Castle's heroic exemplars. A similar contrast between sexual aggression and restraint appears in the episode of the amorous hostess from *Lancelot*. After a meal Lancelot's hostess leaves him to divert himself, but Lancelot soon hears cries of help. On entering her bedroom he witnesses an attempted rape which his hostess has stage-managed.

> A tant d'une autre chanbre voit
> l'uis overt, et vient cele part,
> et voit tot en mi son esgart
> c'uns chevaliers l'ot anversee,
> si la tenoit antraversee
> sor le lit, tote descoverte . . .   (*Lancelot*, 1062–7)

He immediately sees the door open in the other room, and he goes towards it and comes face to face with a knight who had thrown her on her back and held her spread on the bed, completely undressed . . .

After he has freed the Lady from her assailants, the Lady reminds Lancelot that it now falls to him to lie with her. As Chrétien writes, most people would not have thought twice about the offer (946–9), but Lancelot's heart remains with Guinevere and he cannot bring himself to comply. Instead he lies still on his bed, as far away from her as possible, sweating with anxiety. One would be hard put to imagine a greater discrepancy than that between the earlier sexual assault on the Lady and Lancelot's timidity, between the rapists' ruthlessness and the hero's anguished paralysis. But if a society in which honour is the vindication of manhood might deem Lancelot's or Gawain's passivity unusual or shameful, then shame is something the heroes must learn to put up with. Rather than pandering to the expectations of a culture for which honour typically had a 'biological base',[42] the heroes must resist the pressures of orthodoxy. This resistance involves a disregard for their names, which is totally uncharacteristic of their age. While a 'good name' appears in hosts of chronicles and chivalric handbooks as the knight's most prized

---

[41] The *Gawain*-poet's scepticism about an ethic that holds might for right also surfaces in *Cleanness*, in which he describes the immoral behaviour of the antediluvian giants as follows: 'He watȝ famed for fre þat feȝt loued best, | and ay þe biggest in bale þe best watȝ halden' (275–6).

[42] The expression is from Derek Brewer's 'Honour in Chaucer', *Essays and Studies*, 26 (1973), 1–19, at 6.

possession,[43] it is precisely their names, the pre-condition for any social recognition, which Gawain and Lancelot are willing to sacrifice. Like so many other knights of Chrétien, Lancelot embraces anonymity and even tolerates the unflattering appellation of the Knight of the Cart, while Gawain listens patiently as the Lady of the Castle calls his name into question. As we have seen in the previous chapter, the Lady tempts Gawain with the attractions of a literary reputation, with the *name* which so many twelfth- and thirteenth-century romances have made for him. The situation calls to mind the famous scene in which 'Geffrey' declines the invitation to declare his name, and to win his place in the House of Fame:

> 'Frend, what is thy name?
> Artow come hider to han fame?'
> 'Nay for sothe frend,' quod y;
> 'I cam noght hyder, graunt mercy,
> For no such cause, by my hed!
> Sufficeth me, as I were ded,
> That no wight have my name in honde.'
> (*House of Fame*, 1871–6)

For the *Gawain*-poet and for Chaucer self-awareness matters more than name and fame. The *Gawain*-poet's hero must in the temptation scenes be strong enough to answer the Lady's narrative fashioning by saying with Chaucer: 'I wot myself best how y stonde . . .' (1877). Unfortunately for Gawain, we will see that his *conscientia* briefly lapses.

The Failure of Conscience

We are so accustomed to chivalric success stories that we cannot fail to be struck by the fact that the protagonists of Chrétien and the *Gawain*-poet fail. Moreover, the failures of their heroes do not usually involve their reputation in the chivalric community at large but their private integrity. Consider Yvain and Perceval. Their reputation soars in the estimation of their peers. I quote Chrétien's

---

[43] Note the representative example from Richard of Devizes's chronicle which records Richard the Lionheart encouraging his knights as follows: 'I, your lord and your king, love you. I am solicitous for your good name. I tell you that if by chance you go away from here without revenge, the base repute of this flight will go ahead of you': *Cronicon Richardi Divisensis de tempore regis Richardi primi*, ed. and trans. John T. Appleby (London, 1963), 20. Cf. Kindrick, 'Gawain's Ethics', 20.

description of the glory which they have achieved in their many tournaments and one-to-one combats:

> Et furent la voille devant
> revenu del tornoiemant
> ou mes sire Yvains ot esté;
> s'an ont tot le pris aporté,
> ce dit li contes, ce me sanble ...   (*Yvain*, 2683–7)

The evening before, they had returned from a tournament which Yvain had attended. They had won the prize; at least, that is what the story seems to say.

> Ensi les .v. anz demora,
> et por ce ne lessa il mie
> a requerre chevalerie;
> et les estranges avantures,
> les felenesses et les dures
> ala querant, si les trova
> tant que mout bien s'i esprova
> n'onques n'anprist chose si grief
> dom il ne venist bien a chief.
> .l. chevaliers de pris
> a la cort le roi Artus pris
> dedanz les .v. anz anvea.   (*Perceval*, 6016–27)

And so he lived for five years, and during that time he never stopped looking for chivalric exploits. He pursued strange adventures, terrible and demanding ones, and proved himself accomplished in all, and he never undertook anything, however tough, which he did not bring to a successful end. In five years he dispatched fifty famous knights as prisoners to Arthur's court.

And yet, at precisely the point that their standing in the eyes of the world has reached an all-time high, Chrétien reveals the brittleness of fame. Their apparent success in fact masks an inner fault. Yvain has broken a promise to Laudine, Perceval has forgotten God. Seeking sufficiency in preconceived ideals of honour and heroism, they have wandered from themselves. They have won renown at the expense of their conscience, and must pay the price for their culpability.

Lancelot's failure will seem a joke in comparison to Yvain's or Perceval's. His moment of weakness occurs when the Cart, the pillory of the land of Gorre, crosses his path. The dwarf who drives the Cart promises to bring Lancelot to the Queen. For a brief moment Lancelot hesitates between getting in or avoiding the ride and the shame of appearing a criminal:

> mar le fist et mar en ot honte
> que maintenant sus ne sailli,
> qu'il s'an tendra por mal bailli;
> mes Reisons, qui d'Amors se part,
> li dit que del monter se gart,
> si le chastie et si l'anseigne
> que rien ne face ne anpreigne
> dom il ait honte ne reproche.   (*Lancelot*, 362–9)

It would bring him disgrace and shame that he did not jump on the cart promptly, because it will give him cause for regret. But Reason, who is in conflict with Love, tells him to guard himself from getting on, and upbraids and instructs him not to do or undertake anything which might earn him shame and reproach.

Like the crises in *Yvain* and *Perceval*, Lancelot's dilemma revolves around a choice between private imperatives or worldly esteem. And while Lancelot in the end makes the right choice, preferring the slurs of 'la boche' to a violation of the 'cuer' (370), Queen Guinevere, who has in her mysterious way learnt of Lancelot's brief pause, takes amiss his initial reluctance to obey his heart. Even a moment's hesitation in the choice between the right and the advantageous offends Guinevere. A *jeu d'esprit* on the part of Chrétien, no doubt, but perhaps not one without philosophical weight, for a slight hesitation in the choice between the two is enough to earn Cicero's disapproval:

Etenim non modo pluris putare, quod utile videatur, quam quod honestum sit, set etiam haec inter se comparare et in his addubitare turpissimum est. (*De Officiis*, III. iv)[44]

It is not only most immoral to prefer what seems expedient to that which is honest; it is immoral even to weigh the two options and waver between them.

The gravest transgressions in the *Lancelot* are, however, those of Meleagant. He is the outstanding example of a knight who does not stop to consult his conscience but lives in ruthless pursuit of per-

---

[44] Cf. the *De Officiis*, III. ix, where Cicero condemns those who momentarily hesitate between the *honestum* and the *utile*: 'A moment's hesitation is wicked, even if the wrong choice is never made' ('in ipsa enim dubitatione facinus inest, etiamsi ad id non pervenerint').

sonal gain. Concerned only with honour and with impressing audiences around him, he does not look within for absolute standards of right and wrong. That is why Meleagant does not think twice when he has the chance to lock up Lancelot *when no one is looking*. Confusing good and bad with honour and reproach, he has no scruples about crimes perpetrated in secrecy. After all, for the man of honour, deception or lies can only spell shame if they are detected. As Julian Pitt-Rivers writes, 'an action may be potentially dishonourable, but it is only when this action is publicly condemned that it dishonours'.[45]

An ethics of guilt strikes at the heart of the amorality of the logic of honour. As Cicero's *De Officiis* insists, right and wrong must not be confused with the question of whether one is found out or not, for the honest man stands accused not by someone else but by his own conscience. Using the hypothetical instance of a ring that could make one invisible, and which would enable an unscrupulous person to commit offences without punishment, Cicero argues that the good man should put the *honestum* first, and remove from his speculations any hope that his actions can escape notice (*De Officiis*, III. viii). I quote the adaptation of the *Moralium dogma*:

Atque etiam ex omni deliberatione celandi spes remouenda est. Satis enim nobis persuasum debet esse, etiam si deos omnes celare possimus, nihil tamen auare, nihil iniuste, nihil libidinose, nihil inconuenienter esse faciendum . . . Et si vir sapiens anulum habeat huius efficacie, quod eum inuisibilem reddat, non tamen sibi plus licere putet peccare, quam si non haberet. Honesta enim bonis viris, non occulta queruntur. (*Moralium dogma*, p. 71)

Moreover, the hope of concealment must be removed from any deliberation. We should content ourselves with the conviction that, even if we could hide from all the gods, we should do nothing unjust, lustful, or improper . . . And if a wise man had a ring that might make him invisible, he should not think it gives him more licence to sin than if he did not possess it. For good men seek what is honest, not what is secret.

Cicero's wise man remains honest with himself even when he fears no detection. It is not the sanctions of society which keep him on the right track but the automatic pilot of his conscience.

One of the *Gawain*-poet's departures from his source for the beheading game is to make his hero move into situations where sanctions cannot apparently reach him should he want to sin and

---

[45] Pitt-Rivers, 'Honour', 37.

where he, too, must resist the temptation solely on the strength of his super-ego. His main source for the beheading game was a metrical version of the *First Continuation*,[46] but in this version the second beheading takes place at Arthur's court, in the presence of Caradoc's peer-group. Instead of following his source, the *Gawain*-poet took inspiration from Chrétien's description of Erec and Enide's dolorous departure from Arthur's court. Like Chrétien, he first gives a long description of the arming of the heroes as they prepare for their quests. The motif of arming has a very long literary tradition,[47] but Chrétien and the *Gawain*-poet are alone in specifying that the heroes are armed by a squire who deposits their equipment on a carpet:

> Et Erec un autre apela,
> si li comande a aporter
> ses armes por son cors armer.
> Puis s'an monte en unes loiges,
> et fist un tapiz de Limoiges
> devant lui a la terre estandre;
> et cil corrut les armes prandre
> cui il l'ot comandé et dit,
> ses aporta sor le tapit.
> Erec s'asist de l'autre part . . .   (*Erec*, 2620–9)

And Erec called another squire and ordered him to bring the arms to arm himself. Then he went upstairs to a gallery, and a carpet from Limoges was spread before him on the ground. The squire ran to fetch his arms as he had been commanded and told, and put them on the carpet. Erec sits down at the other end.

> He dowellez þer al þat day, and dressez on þe morn,
> Askez erly hys armez, and alle were þay broȝt.

---

[46] The closest analogue is a lost metrical version that can now only be reconstructed on the basis of a prose redaction, *Le Tresplaisante et Recreative Hystoire du Perceval le galloys* (Paris, 1530). Relevant passages from it have been edited by Benson, *Art and Tradition in Sir Gawain and the Green Knight* (New York, 1965), 249–57.

[47] The conventionality of the motif in *Gawain* has been well discussed by Derek Brewer, 'The Arming of the Warrior in European Literature and Chaucer', in *Chaucerian Problems and Perspectives: Essays Presented to Paul E. Beichner CSC*, ed. Edward Vasta and Zacharias P. Thundy (Notre Dame, Ind., 1979), 221–43, repr. in Brewer's *Tradition and Innovation in Chaucer* (London, 1982), 142–60. However conventional the motif may be in epic literature, I do not think Brewer is right in taking it as evidence for the *Gawain*-poet's deep traditionalism. Gawain's mission, after all, precludes the use of arms.

Fyrst a tulé tapit ty3t ouer þer þe flet,
And miche watz þe gyld gere þat glent þeralofte;
Þe stif mon steppez þeron . . .   (566–70)[48]

Armed to the teeth, the heroes take leave of their friends:

—Sire, ne puet estre autremant.
Je m'an vois, a Deu vos comant.
. . . .

Del plorir tenir ne se puet
li rois, quant de son fil depart;
les genz replorent d'autre part;
dames et chevalier ploroient,
por lui molt grant duel demenoient.
. . . .

Et il lor dist por renconfort:
'Seignor, por coi plorez si fort?
je ne sui pris ne mahaigniez;
an cest duel rien ne gahaigniez.
Se je m'an vois, je revenrai
quant Deu pleira et je porrai.'   (*Erec*, 2733–54)

—Sir, it cannot be otherwise. I must go, and I commend you to God . . . The
king could not stop crying when he said goodbye to his son. His men, too,
wept. Ladies and knights were crying and were very sorry for him . . . And
he says to them consolingly, 'My lords, why do you weep so much? I am
neither captured nor injured. This sorrow leads you nowhere. I may be
leaving, but if God wills it and I have the power, I shall return.'

Þer watz much derue doel driuen in þe sale
Þat so worthé as Wawan schulde wende on þat ernde,
To dry3e a delful dynt, and dele no more
        wyth bronde.
    Þe knyght mad ay god chere,
    And sayde, 'Quat schuld I wonde?
    Of destinés derf and dere
    What may mon do bot fonde?'   (558–65)

Wel much watz þe warme water þat waltered of y3en,
When þat semly syre so3t fro þo wonez
        þad daye.   (684–6)

[48] The similarities between the two descriptions have been noted by D. D. R.
Owen, 'Parallel Readings with *Sir Gawain and the Green Knight*', in *Two Old
French Gauvain Romances*, ed. D. D. R. Owen and R. C. Johnston (Edinburgh,
1972), 159–208, at 178.

The point of these departures is, I think, to isolate the hero from the community of honour. And Gawain departs not only from spectators on whose presence honour and esteem always depend, but also from the only witnesses to the promise he made to the Green Knight. Out of their sight, what obliges Gawain to keep his promise? The answer is nothing, except for an internalized sense of right and wrong.

The *Gawain*-poet's skill in manœuvring his hero into situations where Gawain has no reasons for going to the Chapel, other than the demands of integrity, finds its clearest expression in the guide's offer to conceal Gawain's retreat. I quote the relevant lines of the guide's proposition:

> 'Cayrez bi sum oþer kyth, þer Kryst mot yow spede,
> And I schal hyȝ me hom aȝayn, and hete yow fyrre
> Þat I schal swere bi God and alle his gode halȝes,
> As help me God and þe halydam, and oþez innoghe,
> Þat I schal lelly yow layne, and lance neuer tale
> Þat euer ȝe fondet to fle for freke þat I wyst.'   (2120–5)

The *Gawain*-poet's source for the offer of secrecy is a scene in the Vulgate *Lancelot*, in which the guide who accompanies Duke Clarence to the Valley without Return tries to persuade Clarence to go home.[49] As far as the guide is concerned, nobody will ever know:

'Ha sire, dist li vaslés, je vos jurrai orendroit sor les sains de ce ceste chapel que ja por moi nel sarra ne home ne feme.' (Vulgate *Lancelot*, XXI. 16–7).

Sir, says the squire, I will swear to you on the saints of this chapel that no man or woman will hear about it from me.

The option to abandon honesty for practicality is made more attractive still by the offer of concealment. The guides leave Gawain or Clarence the option of abandoning their quests without incurring shame. But where the man of honour can retreat without consequence, the virtuous man must continue. Moved not by the fear of censure but by an unconditional commitment to the *honestum*, good men, as Cicero put it, seek the right, not secrecy. And so Gawain descends to the Chapel to keep his appointment.

For all the *Gawain*-poet's use of Old French romances, of the Vulgate *Lancelot* for the guide's offer to retreat, and possibly of

---

[49] Marjory Rigby, '*Sir Gawain and the Green Knight* and the Vulgate *Lancelot*', *MLR* 78 (1983), 257–66.

the episode of the Sword Bridge for Gawain's polite and pious refusal to retreat, the passage bears all the hallmarks of his genius, for woven into it is an unmistakable echo of an earlier scene in *Gawain*. The guide's suggestion to 'lelly layn' Gawain's dishonesty clearly recalls the lady's promise to 'lelly layn' the love-gift from her husband (1863). Gawain is under an obligation to return the gift to his host, but what if the host does not know? His ignorance enables Gawain to hang on to what he believes is a life-saver. Like the guide, the Lady of the Castle's assurance of secrecy means that Gawain can save his life without his honour being implicated.

Again the *Gawain*-poet confronts his hero with an impossible dilemma. Should Gawain keep his promise to a host in a seemingly trivial game of exchanges or should he break a promise and save his life by deceiving a host who will never know the difference? This time Gawain is too overwhelmed by the benefits of the girdle to give much thought to moral rectitude:

> Þen kest þe knyȝt, and hit come to his hert
> Hit were a juel for þe jopardé þat hym iugged were:
> When he acheued to þe chapel his chek for to fech,
> Myȝt he haf slypped to be vnslayn, þe sleȝt were noble. (1855–8)

Like the protagonists of Chrétien de Troyes, our hero makes an error of judgement when he banishes the imperatives of honesty from his thoughts. To Gawain the possession of the girdle seems expedient *despite* his moral obligation to return it to his host. As honesty and expediency appear to pull in opposite directions, Gawain does not recognize that what is morally wrong can never be advantageous. Cicero accurately describes where Gawain goes wrong:

Cum igitur aliqua species utilitatis obiecta est, commoveri necesse est; sed si, dum animum attenderis, turpitudinem videas adiunctam ei rei, quae speciem utilitatis attulerit, tum non utilitas relinquenda est, sed intellegendum, ubi turpitudo sit, ibi utilitatem esse non posse. (*De Officiis*, III. viii)

When we are confronted with something that seems advantageous, it cannot but affect us. But if, when you think about it, there seems to be something immoral about it, then you are not to dismiss the expedient, but should understand that there can be no expedience where there is wickedness.

Failing to realize that any conflict between the *honestum* and the *utile* must in the end be specious, Gawain takes the *apparent* efficacy of the green girdle at face value. He must wait for Bertilac's revelation that the utility of the green girdle has been deceptive before he, too, understands the inescapable truth of Cicero's saying that 'ubi turpitudo sit, ibi utilitatem esse non posse'.

Like Chrétien's heroes, Gawain fails because of a temporary blindness to his sense of moral right. There is no better indication of Gawain's failure of conscience than his confession at the chapel of Castle Hautdesert:

> Þere he schrof hym schyrly and schewed his mysdedez,
> Of þe more and þe mynne, and merci besechez,
> And of absolucioun he on þe segge calles;
> And he asoyled hym surely and sette hym so clene
> As domezday schulde haf ben di3t on þe morn.　(1880–4)

Why is there no mention of the green girdle here? The question has led to much speculation. Is Gawain wittingly holding back on the priest, and in that case, why does the *Gawain*-poet assure us he has confessed all his sins? Is his intended retention of the girdle not worth confessing and, if so, why all the fuss about it at the Green Chapel? Or does he not include the fact of the girdle in his confession because he fails to recognize it as a sin?[50] The last possibility, suggested by Spearing, is certainly the simplest, but I do not think we can go as far as to say that Gawain does not somewhere deep down know it is a sin, as Spearing seems to imply when he claims that for Gawain 'as for many chivalric heroes, the criteria of conduct are not fully internalized'.[51] Gawain is no man of honour like Meleagant, for whom wrong only exists when it is witnessed. After all, Bertilac does not have to teach Gawain that the girdle should have been returned. He needs only to remind Gawain of it. Gawain has, in other words, allowed himself to forget, and is not the point of the description of Gawain's confession to make us all forget? The fact of Gawain's dishonesty has not only been suppressed by Gawain; it has been suppressed by the *text*, which states without reservations that Gawain has confessed everything and received due absolution. It is thus not just Gawain but the text that turns a blind eye to the girdle, tricking the reader into sharing Gawain's delusion that we might be in a narrative in which the girdle

[50] For a discussion of the various views on the confession see A. C. Spearing, *The Gawain-Poet: A Critical Study* (Cambridge, 1970), 224–5.
[51] Ibid. 226.

figures not as stolen property but as a talisman that might just do the trick.

The disowning of guilt is only one of many symptoms of a temporary blindness which sets in when Gawain accepts the girdle. At the same time we forget that green girdles are pieces of cloth rather than magical objects, and forget the distinction between Gawain's situation and the alternative endings of romance in which ladies bestow love-tokens on the heroes to secure success. We identify with Gawain, who in turn identifies with the heroes of the Lady's escapist fictions. And if these heroes happily cherish their love-gifts without thinking of restoring them or needing to list them in confession, then why should Gawain be expected to? It is entirely consistent with the economy of the plot that an internalized sense of guilt disappears the moment Gawain loses himself in the Lady's romance paradigms in which heroes gratefully accept love-gifts without having to think about restoring them. Guilt presupposes the ability to differentiate one's own self from the image presented to one by others,[52] and it is precisely this personal autonomy which Gawain compromises by becoming the Lady's 'champion'.

But guilt returns when the Green Knight turns out to be none other than Bertilac, who explodes the fiction of a secret love-gift. Immediately Gawain feels the shame he did not feel before, for exposure makes the potentially dishonourable fact shameful. But Gawain's shame also triggers a realization of guilt, which comes across particularly strongly in Gawain's desire to make a full confession at the Green Chapel, to engage in the painstaking self-analysis which he had omitted in the chapel of Castle Hautdesert. Gawain's penance thus matches the nature of his failure. The acknowledgement and indeed the proclamation of his sinfulness substitute for its earlier disavowal and concealment. Honesty has taken the place that secrecy had usurped.

Gawain's pangs of conscience clearly show that he has absorbed the moral of his adventure. He has learnt that however daunting the path of honesty may seem, one must stick to it, even if one can cut corners without being seen. There is nothing confused about the fact

[52] Pierre Bourdieu, 'The Sentiment of Honour in Kabyle Society', in *Honour and Shame: The Values of Mediterranean Society*, ed. J. G. Peristiany (London, 1965), 191–241, at 211: 'The point of honour is the basis of the moral code of an individual who sees himself always through the eyes of others, who has need of others for his existence, because the image he has of himself is indistinguishable from that presented to him by other people.'

184 HONOUR AND HONESTY

that this moral should be pointed by the disclosure of a spectator, Bertilac, who has witnessed all. For guilt, too, assumes an audience, a metaphysical audience, always present even when one believes oneself to be alone. From a Christian perspective that audience is God;[53] in William of Conches's adaptation of Cicero's ethics it is the *vir bonus*:

Eligendus est autem nobis vir bonus et semper ante oculos habendus, ut sic *tamquam illo spectante* uiuamus et omnia *tamquam illo uidente* faciamus. (*Moralium dogma*, pp. 26–7)

We should always have a good man before our eyes, living as if he were watching, and acting as if he were seeing all.

The idea of being judged, even when nobody appears to be watching, is precisely what the spectacular climax at the Green Chapel has in store for us. It actualizes the imaginary onlooker in the shape of Bertilac. Gawain formulates the implications of a ubiquitous audience when he exclaims on his return to Arthur's court that:

'For mon may hyden his harme, bot vnhap ne may hit,
For þer hit onez is tachched twynne wil hit neuer.' (2511–12)

The reality of an inner fault is there, no matter how good we are at hiding it. As Cicero puts it, wrong can never be made right, however successfully it may be covered up:

enim, quod turpe est, id quamvis occultetur, tamen honestum fieri nullo modo potest. (*De Officiis*, III. ix)

for that which is immoral can never be made honest, even when we conceal it.

The motto may not be as grand as the parting speeches of the epic hero but the *Gawain*-poet thought it important enough to make it Gawain's final words in the romance.

Conscience for the Layman

The preceding sections have shown that Chrétien's romances, in particular his *Lancelot*, and *Sir Gawain and the Green Knight*

<hr />

[53] One of the most powerful expressions of this idea is Bernard of Clairvaux's chapter on confession in his *Liber ad milites templi de laude novae militiae*. Attacking prevalent notions of honour and shame, Bernard contrasts the improper shame

privilege matters of conscience, the 'heart' or 'trouþe'. I have suggested that this emphasis entails a shift in the heroic ideal, from the epic hero engaged in competitive and aggressive pursuits of power and glory, to a hero whose greatest achievement lies in staying totally committed to a cause that requires passivity and humiliation, without apparently holding out any hope of reward or significance. Against the backdrop of this ideal we see the resemblances behind the failures of the knights of Chrétien and the *Gawain*-poet. Lancelot hesitates between private directives and his public reputation. Yvain and Perceval enjoy the success of a glorious chivalric career but forget personal obligations to a wife and to God. Gawain furtively keeps a girdle, preferring life without shame to virtue and death. At some crucial point in the plot, the path of virtue and advantage seems to bifurcate, and at the crossroads the heroes hesitate or take the wrong turning, in the mistaken belief that they can dissociate the expedient from the honest. But all heroes come to rue their error of judgement, their distorted sense of priorities.

The evidence asks us to rethink some of the age-old preconceptions about the solidarity of courtly romances with the chivalric community of honour, which much scholarship has uncritically accepted. Can we really say that:

it is clear from the large body of courtly romances written from the twelfth century onwards, which portrays an idealized society living in accordance with the chivalric code, that honour was an integral part of that code and that the Church had not succeeded in persuading the nobility of the merits of humility.[54]

Definitely not if we take seriously Bademagu's dictum that 'boens cuer s'umilie', or look at the symbolism of Gawain's pentangle and the adventures of the Sword Bridge or the Green Chapel. There are certainly men of honour in their romances for whom a heroism of humility is unappetizing or downright unacceptable. The *Gawain*-poet's Round Table are completely taken aback by a beheading game where blows are suffered without resistance—confounded in their belief that the romance to be generated will bring 'justyng' or

---

that leads to concealment with the 'bonus pudor' which his 'new knight' should feel regardless of any human spectators ('et omnis licet humanus arbiter forte absit'): *Sancti Bernardi Opera*, ed. J. Leclerq and H. M. Rochais, 8 vols. (Rome, 1963), iii. 205–39, at 237.

[54] Bernard Hamilton, *Religion in the Medieval West* (London, 1986), 134.

'batayl bare'. Chrétien's Meleagant will have nothing of forbear-
ance and gentleness either. When Bademagu asks him to let Guinevere go without a fight he retorts disdainfully:

> je ne sui mie si hermites
> si prodon ne si charitables,
> ne tant ne voel estre enorables
> que la rien que plus aim li doigne. (*Lancelot*, 3276–9)

I am not such a hermit, so gentlemanly and charitable, and I do not want to
be so honourable as to give him the person I love most.

For Chrétien's caricature of a man of honour, compliance or compromise stains honour. Meleagant's language clearly issues from a
cult of manhood which relegates any qualms of conscience to the
hermitage. Yet the more we hear Meleagant on the subject of
'manliness', the more Chrétien convinces us that the values which
Meleagant banishes to the realm of the cleric would grace Meleagant as they grace Lancelot. In contrast to modern criticism,
Meleagant's rhetoric aligns the heroism for which Lancelot stands
with the Church rather than in opposition to it, and I think for good
reasons. For where better to look for the development and the
dissemination of an internalized sense of right and wrong than
among clerics? Heirs to a long tradition of theological writings that
opposed the virtue of *conscientia* to the vanity of *fama*, they not
only sought to pass on the heritage of conscience to other clerics but
also to laymen, principally or at least most successfully by imple-
menting scrupulous self-analysis in the confessional.[55]

One of the surest indications of the receptiveness of Chrétien de
Troyes and the *Gawain*-poet to this development is the importance
which the motif of confession plays in their romances.[56] For Chrétien's romances the frequency of the motif is the more remarkable
since they precede the canon of the Lateran Council of 1215 which
made one annual auricular confession compulsory for laymen. But

---

[55] See Aron Jakovlecic Gurevich, *Medieval Popular Culture* (Cambridge, 1988),
101–2, and Jacques Le Goff, *The Birth of Purgatory*, trans. Arthur Goldhammer
(London, 1984), 215–16.

[56] Jean Charles Payen has investigated the link between the history of penance and
Old French literature extensively in *Le Motif du repentir dans la littérature française
médiévale* (Geneva, 1968). See pp. 365–403 for a discussion of the romances of
Chrétien, who, according to Payen, employs the motif frequently. John Burrow's
Ricardian Poetry (London, 1971), 106–11, has highlighted the importance of confession in Chaucer, Gower, Langland, and the *Gawain*-poet, and has suggested their
indebtedness to twelfth-century French poets.

Chrétien's knights are ahead of their time. One may think of Lance-lot, who acknowledges his 'mesfet' to Guinevere and receives her absolution, or of Yvain, who bares his soul to Laudine at the end of the *Chevalier au lion*. The regret and self-recrimination of Perceval at his uncle's hermitage, or that of Gawain at the Green Chapel, are the most conspicuous instances of the correlation between confession and a *prise de conscience* in their romances. The scenes provide telling evidence for the overlap between the innovations of courtly romance and the endeavours of churchmen to make inroads on the thought processes of laymen which were largely conditioned by considerations of honour and shame.

The motif of confession adds a dimension to the romances of Chrétien and the *Gawain*-poet which may seem alien to Cicero's *De Officiis*, which is interested in interpersonal relations, not in the relationship between the sinner and God. However, courtly ro-mancers seem to have appreciated that Christianity could accom-modate and be enriched by Cicero's pragmatic and social conception of conscience as the regard due to fellow men. Like Cicero, their works are primarily concerned with reciprocal agree-ments and transactions between people. Hence the significant fact that knights in courtly romance often confess not to God or his priestly intermediary, but to a lay person: to Laudine, to Guinevere, to Bertilac.

Much ink has been spilt on the question whether Gawain's confes-sion to his host Bertilac can be valid, given that Bertilac is not a priest, but there is no sign that the *Gawain*-poet felt that Gawain's confession to his host was out of place. The *Gawain*-poet and Chrétien de Troyes give conscience and confession social applica-tions; they regulate and restore horizontal bonds between people, and no longer only man's relationship with God. Classical moral philosophy was especially relevant to them—and to the later Middle Ages in general—because it provided a means of laicizing con-science, of reconciling the strictest observance of moral rectitude with the hope or expectations for a rewarding public life on earth.[57]

[57] For the formulation of this compromise, see G. F. Jones, *Honor*, 109–10, and Bumke, *Höfische Kultur*, 419, 428–30.

5 The Social Function of Courtly Romance

❧

Chrétien de Troyes and the Gawain-Poet in their Historical Context

IN MY previous chapter I have taken issue with interpretations of courtly romance as an idealized portrayal of an entrenched nobility. Such interpretations form part of a more general trend to view chivalry in its various manifestations as a flight away from an unbearable history. Summarizing scholarship on chivalry to date, Michel Stanesco writes: 'The commonplaces on the chivalric culture of the High Middle Ages are tenacious and at times ineradicable. Most widespread is the one of the knight as a useless survivor of the past, incapable of grasping the direction of history.'[1] Stanesco's book shows how, from Huizinga's classic *The Waning of the Middle Ages* onwards, scholars have regarded chivalry, including chivalric romance, as 'an anachronism, a "vain show", a "phantasm of the past", an illusory compensation for the disarray of the present'.[2]

The reasons for this 'disarray' have typically been sought in the momentous changes which started around the twelfth century, changes which brought about the gradual marginalization of feudal knighthood. Two of these changes must be singled out: the rise of stronger forms of government, which much of the criticism on romance mistakenly equates with the rise of centralized monarchies; and the revival of commercial exchanges and the concomitant ascendancy of tradesmen and artisans. While efficient government affected the relative independence in which the feudal lords had previously lived, money provided an access to power other than

---

[1] 'Les lieux communs sur la culture chevaleresque du Moyen Age flamboyant sont tenaces et parfois inexpugnables. Le plus répandu est celui du chevalier considéré comme une inutile survivance du passé, incapable de saisir "le sens de l'histoire" ' (*Jeux d'errance du chevalier médiéval* (Leiden, 1988), 233).

[2] '. . . un anachronisme, une "vaine parade", un "fantasme du passé", une compensation illusoire aux désarrois du présent' (ibid. 233–4).

landed property and military strength on which the dominance of the medieval knight traditionally depended.[3]

The aim of this chapter is not to question the impact which these changes must have had on a feudal nobility which had for so long enjoyed almost unchallenged power, but rather to question the assumption that Arthurian romance displays a resentment and resistance to such changes, whether it be by banning them from its fictions, or by heaping scorn on their exponents. Generations of critics, of English and French romances alike, have seen chivalric romance as a conservative expression of medieval knighthood, as a genre whose innovative ideals reflect in the final analysis only the inventiveness with which its composers managed to circumvent historical reality.[4] But neither the social circumstances of writers like Chrétien de Troyes or the *Gawain*-poet, nor a close examination of their romances, lends much support to their supposed commitment to conservative feudal values, hostile both to efficient government and to the increasing importance of merchants and skilled workmen who had begun to reap the profits of the late medieval revival of trade and money.

In the case of Chrétien de Troyes, clues about his social position may be gleaned from the dedications of *Lancelot* and *Perceval* to Marie de Champagne and Count Philip of Flanders. The vital role which the counties of Champagne and Flanders played in the rebirth of trade has been well documented by historians. The fairs of Champagne, one of which was at Troyes, and the fair of Ypres in Flanders were among the international centres of commerce during Chrétien's lifetime.[5] The dedicatees of Chrétien's romances by no means looked upon the flourishing commercial activities in their

---

[3] See Georges Duby, *The Three Orders: Feudal Society Imagined*, trans. Arthur Goldhammer (Chicago, 1980), 295. On the rise of commercial activity and the process of state formation in this period see also Fredric L. Cheyette, 'The Invention of the State', in *Essays on Medieval Civilization*, ed. B. K. Lackner and K. R. Philips (Austin, Tex., 1978), 143–78, and Lester K. Little, *Religious Poverty and the Profit Economy in Medieval Europe* (London, 1978), 3–18.

[4] For two recent examples see Marie-Louise Ollier, 'Utopie et Roman Arthurien', CCM 27 (1984), 223–32, and, on English romance, Stephen Knight, 'The Social Function of Middle English Romances', in *Medieval Literature: Criticism, Ideology, and History*, ed. David Aers (Brighton, 1986), 99–122. It should be noted that although Knight considers romance as a whole as a 'cultural concealment of a disturbing reality' (107), he considers *Gawain* as an exception to the rule.

[5] Jacques Bernard, 'Trade and Finance in the Middle Ages', in *The Middle Ages*, ed. Carlo M. Cipolla, Fontana Economic History of Europe (London, 1972), 274–338, at 308.

counties with disdain. On the contrary, they were quick to jump on the economic bandwagon, demonstrating that 'the institution and development of fairs could yield notable accretions of revenue . . . [their] patronage evidently played its part in the expansion of the medieval economy'.[6]

Moreover, the fact that both were subjects of the King of France, whom Erich Köhler holds responsible for undermining feudal independence,[7] should not blind us to the fact that they were themselves powerful heads of state. The Count of Champagne, Henry the Liberal, for example, ruled over about 2,000 vassals.[8] Historians believe that they were at this time in charge of a more efficient machinery of government than the Capetian kings.[9] Ensuring a continued influx of literate administrators to their courts, and maintaining an alliance with the bourgeoisie, they managed to 'establish administrative centres for the exercise of their authority, to expand their own dominial resources and to raise up a political counterweight to the overmighty nobility'.[10] To find the earliest evidence of state formation in the twelfth century we must look not merely at Louis VII or the young Philip Augustus, but to the territorial states of Champagne and Flanders. As Theodore Evergates writes in conclusion to his detailed study of the county of Champagne, the 'traditional concentration on a royal perspective, even when royal authority and power were only theoretical in most of the kingdom, and the view that the princes and barons were divisive forces in medieval society are simply not pertinent at the regional or local level . . . It was the territorial princes, not the king, who provided the crucial leadership in medieval society and in the development of state organization before the thirteenth century.'[11] Chrétien's patrons should therefore not be confused with the noblemen increasingly threatened by the rise of the state and money. They were

---

[6] Edward Miller, 'Government Economic Policies and Public Finance', in *The Middle Ages*, ed. Cipolla, 339–70, at 356–7.

[7] Köhler, *Ideal und Wirklichkeit in der höfischen Epik* (Tübingen, 1956), 18.

[8] Michel Bur, 'Les Principautés', in *La France médiévale*, ed. J. Favier (Vitry-sur-Seine, 1983), 239–64, at 251.

[9] On the County of Flanders see John W. Baldwin, *The Government of Philip Augustus: Foundations of French Royal Power* (Berkeley, Calif., 1986), 7, and Jean Longnon, 'La Champagne', in *Histoire des institutions françaises au Moyen Age*, 5 vols., ed. F. Lot and R. Fawtier (Paris, 1957), i. 123–36, at 135–6.

[10] Miller, 'Government Economic Policies', 357, and Bur, 'Les Principautés', 251.

[11] Evergates, *Feudal Society in the Baillage of Troyes under the Counts of Champagne, 1152–1284* (Baltimore, 1975), 151.

in fact those from whom this threat emanated. Nominal as royal power was in Chrétien's days, it does not seem to have worried the Counts of Flanders or Champagne overmuch. In fact, they had close familial and economic links with the Capetian house, which 'in the second half of the twelfth century transformed [their] long-standing hostility into close friendship'.[12]

It is striking that the *Gawain*-poet, too, has long been seen as a poet from a small baronial household, hostile to King Richard II's absolutist tendencies and his francophile court.[13] But while the *Gawain*-poet's dialect is north-west Midlands in origin, he is anything but provincial. The close of the fourteenth century saw a busy traffic between the north-west Midlands and the capital in which the *Gawain*-poet may well have participated.[14] Michael J. Bennett's research in particular has drawn attention to the lack of opportunities for patronage in the north-west Midlands on the one hand, and to the large group of Cheshiremen with which Richard II surrounded himself at the end of his reign on the other.[15] His suggestion that the *Gawain*-poet may well have been attracted by the prospects of patronage by the king, or by the pre-eminent Cheshire courtiers established at his household, deserves serious consideration. The manuscript in which *Gawain* has come down to us may not at first suggest distinguished patronage, but Cotton Nero A. x is the first collection of English texts to contain a large number of illuminations, and it is likely that the codex and the illuminations were copies made from a precious *de luxe* manuscript, fit for presentation to a wealthy patron.[16]

Internal evidence from the works of the *Gawain*-poet has lent support to Bennett's hypothesis of a London base. In her study of the commercial background to *Gawain*, Jill Mann has pointed to

[12] Baldwin, *Government*, 9. See also S. Hofer, *Chrétien de Troyes: Leben und Werke* (Graz, 1954), 11, and John F. Benton, 'The Court of Champagne as a Literary Center', *Speculum*, 36 (1961), 551–91, at 554.

[13] See James R. Hulbert, 'A Hypothesis Concerning the Alliterative Revival', *MP* 28 (1931), 405–22.

[14] Elizabeth Salter, 'The Alliterative Revival', *MP* 64 (1966–7), 146–50, 233–7.

[15] Bennett, '*Sir Gawain and the Green Knight* and the Literary Achievement of the North-West Midlands: The Historical Background', *Journal of Medieval History*, 5 (1979), 63–88, and his *Community, Class and Careerism: Cheshire and Lancashire Society in the Age of Sir Gawain and the Green Knight* (Cambridge, 1983). See also R. R. Davies, 'Richard II and the Principality of Chester', in *The Reign of Richard II: Essays in Honour of May McKisack*, ed. F. R. H. du Boulay and C. M. Barron (London, 1971), 256–79.

[16] Gervase Mathew, *The Court of Richard II* (London, 1968), 117.

the fusion of mercantile and chivalric values which might have appealed to 'an audience of sophisticated and wealthy merchants and knights', most easily found in London.[17] We must postulate precisely such a community if the *Gawain*-poet was indeed familiar with any of the texts by Italian authors that have been proposed as sources for his (possible) other works: Dante's *Divina Commedia* and Boccaccio's *Olympia* for the *Pearl*,[18] and Jacopo della Lana's commentary on the *Divina Commedia* for *St Erkenwald*, sometimes attributed to the *Gawain*-poet.[19] For it is only in London, with its flourishing community of Italian bankers and merchants, that the most recent Italian literature seems to have been readily accessible.[20]

A London connection is likewise suggested by a probable reference to the work of which recent research no longer seems cognizant. In the inventory of books of Sir John Paston II, there is a mention of a work called 'the Greene Knight'. This could of course be the early sixteenth-century ballad version of *Sir Gawain*, which we know from the Percy Folio, if we are willing to allow the hypothetical possibility, proposed long ago by Frederic Madden, that a written version of the ballad already existed 'in some intermediate shape' before 1479 when Paston's inventory was drawn up at the latest.[21] But a far simpler explanation is that John Paston owned *Sir Gawain and the Green Knight*. Bound in Paston's 'blak

[17] Jill Mann, 'Price and Value in *Sir Gawain and the Green Knight*', *Essays in Criticism*, 36 (1986), 298–318.

[18] On the *Gawain*-poet and Dante see A. C. Spearing, *The Gawain-Poet: A Critical Study* (Cambridge, 1970), 15–18. The first to propose *Olympia* as a source was William H. Schofield, 'The Nature and Fabric of the *Pearl*', *PMLA* 19 (1904), 154–215. Recently, debate on the matter has been rekindled. John Finlayson has argued for a direct relationship in his '*Pearl*, Petrarch's *Trionfo della Morte* and Boccaccio's *Olympia*', *English Studies in Canada*, 9 (1983), 1–13. David Carlson, while listing a significant number of similarities, follows Gollancz in regarding these as one of the 'strange coincidences' of literary history, because he believes it unlikely that the 'linguistically marginal English poet' from the remote Midlands, 'far from the new literary currents', could be in touch with the latest Italian literary fashions. See his 'The *Pearl*-Poet's *Olympia*', *Manuscripta*, 31 (1987), 181–9, and Sir Israel Gollancz, *Pearl: An English Poem of the XIVth Century* (London, 1921), which gives a text and translation of Boccaccio's *Olympia*.

[19] Gordon Whatley, 'Heathens and Saints: *St Erkenwald* in its Legendary Context', *Speculum*, 61 (1986), 330–63.

[20] Ibid. 336.

[21] Frederic Madden, *Syr Gawayne: A Collection of Ancient Romance Poems* (London, 1839), 352. The mention of '⟨l. . .⟩ the Green Knight' in Paston's inventory and Madden's uneconomical hypothesis about it seem to have attracted no attention in later research on the poem.

bok' with such refined works as Chaucer's *Legend of Good Women*, his *Parliament of Fowls*, Lydgate's *Temple of Glass*, and Chartier's *La Belle Dame sans mercy*, *Gawain* makes a more plausible manuscript companion than the crude ballad version, if by this time it indeed existed.[22]

Moreover, while the *Gawain*-poet's dialect seems marginal to us today, we must not forget that this impression is the product of the rise of a standard English language, based on the London dialect, in the fifteenth century.[23] On the evidence of manuscripts before 1425, the degree of linguistic tolerance in the cultural centre of England was high. Alliterative works, such as the *Parliament of Three Ages*, the alliterative *Morte*, the *Pistill of Susan*, *William of Palerne*, or *Mum and the Sothsegger*, are as likely to have been appreciated in London as in the north, as they are frequently combined in manuscripts with works in southern dialects.[24] Certainly, Richard II would have had no difficulty in understanding the *Gawain*-poet's dialect. As medieval chroniclers make clear, his Cheshire bodyguard spoke to him in their regional brogue. And the problem, as they saw it, was not that they failed to communicate, but that they understood each other far too well.[25]

Many alliterative poems may in fact have been written in London. *Piers Plowman* and *Winner and Waster* are a case in point.[26] Another example is *St Erkenwald*, often attributed to the *Gawain*-poet, which evokes a vivid picture of late fourteenth-century London, celebrated by the poet as 'þe metropol & þe mayster

---

[22] *Paston Letters and Papers of the Fifteenth Century*, ed. Norman Davis, 2 vols. (Oxford, 1976), i. 516–18. The third item in the fragmentary list reads: 'Item, a blak bok wyth the Legende off Lad⟨. . .⟩ saunce Mercye, þe Parlement off Byr⟨. . .⟩ Glasse, Palatyse and Scitacus, The Med⟨. . .⟩ the Greene Knyght, valet⟨. . .⟩'.

[23] John H. Fisher, 'Chancery and the Emergence of Standard Written English in the Fifteenth Century', *Speculum*, 52 (1977), 870–99.

[24] Elizabeth Salter, *Fourteenth-Century English Poetry: Contexts and Readings* (Oxford, 1983), 77–8. Cf. David A. Lawton's recent assessment: 'At least before 1425, there is no reason to assume an audience for Middle English alliterative poems distinct from that of other literary works': 'The Diversity of Middle English Alliterative Poetry', *Leeds English Studies*, 20 (1989), 143–72, at 149.

[25] See Michael J. Bennett, 'The Court of Richard II and the Promotion of Literature', in *Chaucer's England: Literature in Historical Context*, ed. Barbara Hanawalt (Minneapolis, 1992), 3–20, at 11, and Chris Given-Wilson (ed. and trans.), *Chronicles of the Revolution*, Manchester Medieval Sources (Manchester, 1993), 57, 73–4, 77.

[26] A convincing case for relating *Winner and Waster* to the court of Edward III has been made by Juliet Vale, *Edward III and Chivalry: Chivalric Society and its Contexts 1270–1350* (Exeter, 1982), 73–6.

toun' (5).[27] I have no further evidence that would support the identification of the *Gawain*-poet as 'Huchown of the Awle Ryale' (mentioned in Wyntoun's *Chronicle* as the author of several English alliterative poems) or as 'Maistir Massy' (mentioned in Hoccleve's *Regiment of Princes*).[28] But if these men were indeed poets of alliterative verse, Hoccleve and Wyntoun suggest that London was their home: Westminster, or the 'Awle Ryale', the royal court.

We may safely conclude that the *Gawain*-poet's dialect would not have debarred him from the milieu of a city like London. This milieu might explain the *Gawain*-poet's amalgamation of different social discourses in his chivalric romance. As I argued in my previous chapter, one of these discourses is clerical. Gawain's confession to Bertilac, in a language drawn from penitential handbooks and manuals for confessors, suggests the importance which the *Gawain*-poet attaches to self-examination. But, as we have seen, the *Gawain*-poet laicizes conscience and confession, so that they find a new relevance, beyond the vertical relations between people and God, in the relations between two lay knights: Gawain and his host. The ethical orientation of *Gawain*, then, is neither exclusively clerical nor exclusively chivalric. Insisting on personal integrity but interested in wordly transactions between people, it combines the two perspectives in a way that makes it impossible to separate the one from the other.

This perfect fusion of the two explains the difficulty of determining the *Gawain*-poet's social position on the basis of the narratorial voice projected by this romance or, for that matter, by his other works such as *Pearl* or *Patience*. Research into the sources of his poems would suggest a clerical background. His reading shows his knowledge of Latin, for it includes Marbod of Rennes's *Naufragium Jonae prophetae* and perhaps Boccaccio's *Olympia*.[29] His acquaintance with theories of value in Aristotle and his commentators, and his grounding in legal thought, suggest an education and training

[27] For a survey of scholarship on the question of the attribution of the work to the *Gawain*-poet see Ruth Morse's edition of *St Erkenwald* (Cambridge, 1975), 45–8. Paul Nigel Hartle makes a strong case for the *Gawain*-poet's authorship of *St Erkenwald* on lexical grounds: 'Middle English Alliterative Verse and the Formulaic Theory', doctoral dissertation (University of Cambridge, 1981), 102–13.
[28] See Erik Kooper, 'The Case of the Encoded Author: John Massey in *Sir Gawain and the Green Knight*', NM 83 (1982), 158–68, and Bennett, 'Court of Richard II', 7.
[29] Finlayson, '*Pearl*', and Attila Fáy, 'Marbodean and Patristic Reminiscences in *Patience*', *Revue de littérature comparée*, 49 (1975), 284–90.

that would have been exceptional for a layman.[30] Yet the *Gawain*-poet does not address his audience *as* a cleric. In his prologue to *Patience* he represents himself as listening to a sermon, in the epilogue to *Pearl* as a man about to receive communion, and in *Gawain* as a sympathetic and knowledgeable observer of aristocratic life. His brand of piety is not such as would have divided an audience into clerical and lay camps. Religious sentiments and matters of conscience figure in *Gawain* only in so far as they were the common ground that clerics and knights shared—or should share.

The *Gawain*-poet's ethics of conscientious worldliness impinges on a third order: that of the merchant. It is a historical fact that treatments of honesty, the application of conscience to reciprocal agreements, usually also touch on commerce. Honesty may be defined as the self-imposed adherence to contracts, and Cicero's *De Officiis* shows how easily an exploration of this virtue shades into a discussion of fair trading. A thirteenth-century definition of 'honest works and virtues' as 'merchandise of quality' illustrates the relevance of honesty to the experience of the medieval merchant.[31] And as *Gawain*-criticism has shown, this relevance was not lost on the *Gawain*-poet, who consistently describes the agreements and exchanges to which Gawain is bound as if they were commercial transactions that require the punctiliousness of an honest tradesman.[32]

[30] See Mann, 'Price and Value'; Howard H. Schless, '*Pearl*'s "Princes Paye" and the Law', *ChauR* 24 (1989), 183–5; Robert J. Blanch and Julian N. Wasserman, 'Medieval Contracts and Covenants: The Legal Coloring of *Sir Gawain and the Green Knight*', *Neophilologus*, 68 (1984), 598–610; and their ' "To Ouertake your Wylle": Volition and Obligation in *Sir Gawain and the Green Knight*', *Neophilologus*, 70 (1986), 119–29. Henry Lyttleton Savage's suggestion in *The Gawain-Poet: Studies in his Personality and Background* (Chapel Hill, NC, 1956), 206–8, that the Green Knight's assurance that he has not come 'in fere of feȝtyng wyse' (267) is a translation of the Anglo-Norman legal term 'a fuer de guerre', 'with violent intent', deserves more attention. It makes more sense than Tolkien and Gordon's gloss 'in a company of fighting men'. As Dominica Legge has shown, the phrase 'a fuer de guerre' is typical of Chancery documents and could thus provide a clue to the *Gawain*-poet's social position: 'A Fuer de Guerre', *MAE* 5 (1936), 121–2.
[31] The Anonimo Genovese, quoted in Aldo Scaglione, *Knights at Court: Courtliness, Chivalry, and Courtesy from Ottonian Germany to the Italian Renaissance* (Berkeley, Calif., 1991), 183.
[32] R. A. Shoaf, *The Poem as Green Girdle: Commercium in Sir Gawain and the Green Knight* (Gainesville, Fla., 1984); Mann, 'Price and Value'; and Stephanie Trigg, 'The Romance of Exchange: *Sir Gawain and the Green Knight*', *Viator*, 22 (1991), 251–66.

Clerics, knights, and merchants: *Sir Gawain and the Green Knight* speaks for the interests of all three orders, and for none of these exclusively. *Gawain* resembles, in this respect, the 'public poetry' of the Ricardian period, for, as Anne Middleton has shown, this poetry 'envisions a society composed of members whose different stations, functions, and ways of life yield different perspectives on the common world, which it is the aim of the speaker to respect, to bring to mutual awareness, and to resolve into common understanding'.[33] If the *Gawain*-poet's amalgamation of mercantile, clerical, and chivalric discourses is comparable to Langland, Chaucer, and Gower's 'public poetry', we might again speculate about the poet's connections with London, the city where people from different backgrounds—mercantile, legal, clerical, and aristocratic—interacted and had begun to form a textual community whose heterogeneity might explain the broad social appeal which *Gawain* shares with some of his contemporaries.

Judging by *Sir Gawain and the Green Knight*, Arthurian romance was not inherently obsolete, but a form which a sophisticated poet could adapt to the historical circumstances of his own day and age. It might still be argued that the *Gawain*-poet's admixture of *chevalerie*, *clergie*, and *bourgeoisie* is exceptional among Arthurian romances, that it implies a radical break from a tradition that eulogized a troubled feudal nobility averse to social change. The problem with this argument is that even the earliest Arthurian romances, by Chrétien de Troyes, were written for patrons committed both to reviving commerce and to consolidating their power at the nobility's expense. The success of their monopolization of power may be measured by the growing importance of their courts, where Chrétien probably found his employment.[34]

Rather than seeing Chrétien's romances as archaic, we might consider the possibility that his romances reflected, or even promoted, historical change, and that they offer precedents for the *Gawain*-poet's fusion of different social perspectives in his chivalric romance. In the following three sections, I shall argue that the *Gawain*-poet's unison of clerical, chivalric, and mercantile ideals may be understood as the outcome of a literary and historical tradition of Arthurian romances which attempted to bring chivalry

[33] Middleton, 'The Idea of Public Poetry in the Reign of Richard II', *Speculum*, 53 (1978), 94–114, at 98.
[34] Duby, *Three Orders*, 323.

up to date. To do so is not to deny that *Gawain* is a child of its time—its links with contemporary Ricardian poetry are unmistakable. But children also have parents, and it is to the family history of Arthurian romance that the following sections are devoted.

Clergie *and* Chevalerie

A serious defect in the argument that Arthurian romances are an idealized and reactionary self-representation by the feudal nobility is that they were not written by knights but by clerics.[35] As we have seen, the *Gawain*-poet probably was a cleric, and we can be certain that Chrétien was. Wolfram von Eschenbach calls him 'master', which marks him out as a cleric.[36] Chrétien knew Latin, had studied the arts of the quadrivium and the trivium, and seems to have been familiar with the philosophy of the intellectual centres of Chartres and Paris.[37]

The full implications of a clerical authorship for Arthurian romances still need to be thought through. Can it still be argued that courtly romances identify with a feudal nobility under threat if their authors were for the most part clerics in secular service? For, as Alexander Murray and R. I. Moore have shown, the cleric at court frequently found himself competing with the knight for the prince's favour, offering him the power not of the sword but of reason.[38] The cleric cannot in this light be regarded as merely the knight's mouthpiece. The two inhabit a space of potential ideological

[35] See the list in C. Stephen Jaeger's *The Origins of Courtliness: Civilizing Trends and the Formation of Courtly Ideals 939–1210* (Philadelphia, 1985), 233, and Joachim Bumke, *Höfische Kultur: Literatur und Gesellschaft im hohen Mittelalter* (Munich, 1986), 685. Where romances represent the act of recording romances, the writer is always a cleric. Note, for instance, the Vulgate *Lancelot*, LXXIa. 48: 'Chelui jor furent assis li .III. chevaliers en la Table Ronde et furent mandé li clerc qui metoient en escript les proeches des compaignons de la maison le roy Artu.' Cf. the Non-Cyclic *Lancelot*, p. 571.

[36] Jean Frappier, *Chrétien de Troyes: L'Homme et l'œuvre* (Paris, 1957), 15.

[37] See Thomas Elwood Hart, 'Chrestien, Macrobius, and Chartrean Science: The Allegorical Robe as a Symbol of Textual Design in the Old French *Erec*', *MS* 43 (1981), 250–96. On Chrétien and Alan of Lille see C. Lutrell, 'The Figure of Nature in Chrétien de Troyes', *Nottingham Medieval Studies*, 17 (1973), 3–16. Tony Hunt, *Chrétien de Troyes: Yvain* (London, 1986), 80–93, deals with the links between Abelard and Chrétien.

[38] Alexander Murray, *Reason and Society in the Middle Ages* (Oxford, 1978), 212–37, and R. I. Moore, *The Creation of a Persecuting Society: Power and Deviance in Western Europe* (Chicago, 1980), 135–45.

conflict. In Peter Haidu's words: 'The values of the two groups are fundamentally different: we are dealing with the opposition between peace, submission, and rational self-control on the one hand, and war, anarchic turmoil, and conspicuous consumption on the other.'[39]

This way of conceiving the tensions between the knight and the cleric is by no means anachronistic. It can be no coincidence that the dawn of the golden age for clerical careerism at secular courts also sees the development of debates about their relative superiority.[40] In these debates the *clerus* and the *miles* are distinguished by a similar set of binary oppositions, so striking that the genre finds its way into the examples of Matthew of Vendôme's *Ars Versificatoria* as an illustration of the rhetorical figure of antithesis (p. 174). The knight in these debates arouses admiration for his bravery, the clerics for their wisdom. The knight is bad-mannered and foul-mouthed, while the cleric is courteous and discreet. Usually, the victors in these debates are, not surprisingly, the clerics who wrote them. Thus, in the *Council of Remiremont*,[41] Eve, the judge, urges her listeners to love clerics:

Precor vos summopere clericos diligere
Quorum sapientia disponuntur omnia;
Totum quicquid agimus vel cum nos desipimus,
Causas nostras agere student, atque regere . . .   (186–9)

I pray you to love clerics with all your heart, for in their wisdom all things are ordered. Even when we go wrong they take pains to run and direct our affairs . . .

---

[39] 'Les valeurs de ces deux groupes sont foncièrement différentes: il s'agit de l'opposition de la paix, la soumission, le contrôle rationel de soi, à la guerre, au tourbillonnement anarchique, à la dépense sans mesure' (Haidu, 'Le Sens historique du phénomène stylistique: La Sémiose dissociative chez Chrétien de Troyes', *Europe* (Oct. 1982), 36–47, at 46).

[40] For a discussion and edition of these debates see Charles Oulmont, *Les Débats du clerc et du chevalier dans la littérature poétique du moyen-âge* (Paris, 1911), and H. Walther, *Das Streitgedicht in der lateinischen Literatur des Mittelalters* (Munich, 1920), 145–53. For some brief and general remarks on the way the debates reflect the different mentalities of the cleric and the knight see Giuseppe Tavani's 'Il dibattito sul chierico e il cavaliere nella tradizione mediolatina e vulgare', *Romanisches Jahrbuch*, 15 (1964), 51–84. To Tavani's most complete list of debates between clerics and knights may be added the short altercation about whether the cleric or the layman is the better lover in Andreas Capellanus' *De Amore*, 184–6. A detailed study which looks at the debates and the socio-historical relations between knights and clerics at court is Fleckenstein's '*Miles* und *Clericus*'.

[41] Ed. Oulmont, *Les Débats*.

That these debates had not lost their relevance in fourteenth-century England is indicated by *Winner and Waster*. In this debate, composed some time after 1352, the men of arms, who constitute the army of Waster, are also placed in opposition to Winner's army, which comprises clerics, lawyers, and merchants, men who 'lordes cane lere thurgh ledyng of witt' (223).[42] The latter present a case which contrasts their shrewd saving with Waster's reckless consumption, while Waster juxtaposes his *largesse* with Winner's meanness. The fact that Edward III finds a place for both views in his household testifies to the importance which matters of finance and administration had acquired in the England of the *Gawain*-poet's day.[43]

With its emphasis on spending and saving, the debate between Winner and Waster dramatizes the conflict between knights and clerics somewhat differently than the conventional debates between the *miles* and the *clerus*. Nevertheless, this opposition between winning and wasting follows logically from the polarizations of the conventional debate, which contrasts the knight's recklessness with clerical discretion. And debates of this conventional nature continued to be read in England. Additions by an English fifteenth-century hand to one such debate, in a manuscript in Cambridge University Library, Dd XI. 78, show their continuing appeal.[44] The writer of these marginalia still knew so much about the genre that he could add some lines of a late twelfth-century debate, the *Altercatio Phyllidis et Florae*, to create what he believed would make a more satisfactory ending.

This debate in the Cambridge manuscript, which I shall henceforth refer to as the Cambridge debate, illustrates the way a cleric might have seen the differences between the knight and himself:

> Miles eques Martis et clericus est eques artis,
> Practicus hic, speculator ibi, natura prioris,
> Postremi racio . . .   (51–3)

The knight is a soldier of Mars, and the cleric a soldier in art, the first is practical, the other speculative; the first cares for nature, the second for reason.

[42] Ed. Stephanie Trigg, EETS OS 297 (Oxford, 1990).
[43] Juliet Vale, *Edward III and Chivalry: Chivalric Society and its Contexts 1270–1350* (Bury St Edmunds, 1982), 73–5.
[44] Ed. Walther, *Das Streitgedicht*, 248–53.

Here we encounter again the oppositions between the power of reason and the power of brute force, which, along with the related opposition between self-control and impulsive behaviour, mark out the area of conflict between the learned administrator and the warrior.

These oppositions between clerical and chivalric perspectives do not surface in *Sir Gawain and the Green Knight.* The knights in this romance are simply not like the turbulent 'soldiers of Mars'. Whether knights were as civilized in actuality is another question. In the *Gawain*-poet's England, the chivalric lack of restraint was 'clearly perceived as a pressing social problem', aggravated by the expansion of aristocratic households to which contracts by indenture gave rise.[45] But in *Gawain*'s Arthurian world clerics live harmoniously with knights. Indeed, they are suspiciously like one another: pious, well-mannered, and scrupulous. Both are, above all, courtiers. This harmony is an aspect of a larger ideal which the *Gawain*-poet sets before our eyes, and which remained powerfully attractive in the later Middle Ages and beyond: the union of *chevalerie* and *clergie*. As Caxton wrote in his *Mirrour of the World*, the two are, or, rather, ought to be, interdependent: 'ffor cheualerye sieweth alway clergye where she goth'.[46] The ideal had been long in the making and we can trace back its history through the thirteenth-century *Image du Monde*, which Caxton adapted into English, to Chrétien de Troyes, who in his prologue to *Cligés* praised France as epitomizing the communion of *chevalerie* and *clergie*.

The particular institution that united *chevalerie* and *clergie* in Chrétien's France was the court. Here clerics and knights were brought together and merged, for the first time in the twelfth

---

[45] Maurice Keen, *English Society in the Later Middle Ages 1348–1500* (Harmondsworth, 1990), 191. Both the numbers of the bastard feudal band and their relatively loose connections with their lord could make for explosions of violence. Confronted with the growth of bastard feudal bands, Richard II sought to maintain effective royal government by building up a band of armed retainers larger than that of any of his retainers, by becoming the 'biggest bastard feudal lord of all': David Starkey, 'The Age of the Household', in *The Later Middle Ages*, ed. Stephen Medcalf (London, 1981), 225–90, at 264. Richard II's recruitment of Cheshire retainers reflects this policy: James L. Gillespie, 'Richard II's Cheshire Archers', *Transactions of the Historic Society of Cheshire and Lancashire*, 125 (1975), 1–40. Their reputation for unruly and 'beast-like' behaviour must have brought the need for refinement and restraint close to the *Gawain*-poet's home. See Bennett, '*Sir Gawain and the Green Knight*', 79, and Adam of Usk's *Chronicle*, ed. and trans. E. M. Thompson (1904, repr. Lampeter, 1990), 39–40.

[46] *Caxton's Mirrour of the World*, ed. Oliver Prior, EETS ES 60 (London, 1913), 30.

century, under the common denominator of *curiales* (courtiers).[47] The term, I emphasize, did not just refer to knights, but also to clerics. In past scholarship courts, courtiers, and courtliness have mostly been regarded as purely secular and aristocratic manifestations, but they owe at least as much to the input of clerics.

To the medieval mind, the importance of clerics in the dissemination of ideals of courtesy was obvious. As a debate between the cleric and the knight puts it:

> Tuis cil monde sevent bien
> Que chevalier ne sevent rien
> Ne de deduit ne de franchise,
> Se il ne l'ont de clerc aprise. (*Jugement d'Amours*, 289–92)[48]

The whole world knows well that knights do not know anything about charm and gentleness, unless they have learnt it from the cleric.

The same point emerges from an anecdote, related by the thirteenth-century Dominican Etienne de Bourbon, about some knights who interrupted Alan of Lille's lectures in Montpellier in order to ask this cleric for a definition of *courtoisie*.[49] Gerald of Wales was equally convinced that the knight William of Barri, who had been committed to his care, owed his manners and eloquence to the 'polite words' (*dicta faceta*) and the courtly anecdotes (*narraciones curialitati accommodas*) uttered by himself and the clerics of the archbishop of Canterbury.[50]

These anecdotes bear out the role of clerics in formulating and promoting *courtoisie*. The relevance of a clerical investment in courtliness for Arthurian romance will become apparent when we examine the qualities that make up its hero: the courtly knight, who, as we shall see, bears an uncanny resemblance to the cleric.

---

[47] Fleckenstein, '*Miles* und *Clericus*', 314.

[48] Oulmont, *Les Débats*, 136. Cf. the debate *Melior et Ydoine*, ll. 331–4: 'Trestout le sen de nostre vie, I Queintise e curtoisie, I Valour e amur e druerie, I C'est escrit de clergie': ibid. 194. For other examples and a brief discussion see David F. Hult, *Self-Fulfilling Prophecies: Readership and Authority in the First Roman de la Rose* (Cambridge, 1986), 198–200.

[49] *Anecdotes historiques*, ed. A. Lecoy de la Marche (Paris, 1877), 245–6. The anecdote also occurs in the *Mirror for Princes* by the Pseudo-Thomas: Thomas Zotz, '*Urbanitas*: zur Bedeutung und Funktion einer antiken Wertvorstellung innerhalb der höfischen Kultur des hohen Mittelalters', in *Curialitas: Studien zu Grundfragen der höfisch- ritterlichen Kultur*, ed. J. Fleckenstein (Göttingen, 1990), 392–451, at 433–4.

[50] Gerald of Wales, *Speculum duorum*, ed. and trans. Yves Lefèvre, R. B. C. Huygens, and Brian Dawson (Cardiff, 1974), 152. On which, see M. T. Clanchy, *From Memory to Written Record* (1979, 2nd edn. Oxford, 1993), 251.

The Clerical Knight in Romance

No literary figure, with the possible exception of Tristan, illustrates the amalgamation of clerical ideals of reason and *courtoisie* with boldness in battle better than Gawain. In *Sir Gawain and the Green Knight* and the romances of Chrétien, his reputation for courtesy is such that it occupies not only the poets themselves, but even the characters in their romances. The gracious manners of Gawain are the talk of the court. In Chrétien's *Cligés*, Fenice picks on his politeness to strike up a conversation with her lover:

> Fenice a parole l'en mist
> De Bretaigne premieremant;
> Del san et de l'afeitement
> Mon seignor Gauvain li anquiert . . .   (*Cligés*, 5106–9)

Fenice first engages him in a conversation about Britain, and asks him about Sir Gawain's wisdom and manners . . .

Apparently, Gawain's good manners are such common knowledge that they can safely be used as a conversational gambit. In *Sir Gawain and the Green Knight*, the hero's revelation of his identity causes a stir in Bertilac's dining-hall, and his hosts relish the thought of what 'þat fyne fader of nurture' (919) can teach them about the 'sleȝtez of þewez | And þe teccheles termes of talkyng noble' (916–17). Chrétien and the *Gawain*-poet's romances thus turn a rule of romance—that Gawain must be *courtois*—into an expectation busily debated within the world of romance itself.

Apart from being renowned for courtesy, the Arthurian Gawain also has a considerable reputation for learning. Geoffrey of Monmouth mentions briefly that he grew up with Pope Sulpicius in Rome. Geoffrey is silent on the reasons for Gawain's stay in Rome, but Wace's *Brut* specifies that he had gone to Rome to receive proper schooling. He also makes much of the deliberation to which Gawain subjects his words and his deeds:

> De saint Soplice, l'apostoire,
> La ki aume ait repos en gloire,
> Ert Walwein nuvelment venuz.
>
> . . . .
>
> Pruz fu et de mult grant mesure,
> D'orguil ne de surfait n'out cure;
> Plus volt faire que il ne dist
> E plus duner qu'il ne pramist.   (*Brut*, 9849–60)

Gawain had just returned from pope saint Sulpicius; may his soul rest in heaven . . . He was worthy and very sensible. He did not care for arrogance or excess. His deeds exceeded his words, and his gifts exceeded his promises.

When Arthur chooses Gawain to accompany the messengers to the emperor, Wace makes clear Arthur does so because of the schooling Gawain has received in Rome. He sends Gawain along,

> Qui a Rome out lunges esté.
> Pur ço qu'il erent bien preisied,
> Bien cuneü, bien einseinnied
> A li rois cez ansanble pris . . .   (*Brut*, 11654–7)

Who had been in Rome for a long time. The king chose them because they were renowned, well-known, and well-educated.

From Wace onwards, Gawain's reputation for *clergie* spreads to later works, both English and French. In *Hunbaut*, Arthur decides to send Gawain as a messenger to the only remaining rebel in his realm. His motives are similar to the ones given by Wace's Arthur:

> Gauvains mes niés est de grant pris
> Et conneüs de mainte gent,
> Et si est preus et biaus et gent,
> Bien parlans et cortois et sage,
> De lui vel faire mon message.   (*Hunbaut*, 110–14)

Gawain, my nephew, is famous, and known by many people, and he is so worthy and beautiful, handsome and charming, well-spoken, courtly, and wise, that I will make him my messenger.

Peter of Langtoft, too, emphasizes Gawain's eloquence, and in particular his knowledge of Latin:

> Li messagers sont venuz devaunt cel emperer,
> Wawayn parla primes, kar il fu latymer.   (*Chronicle*, I. 194)

The messengers came before the emperor; Gawain was the first to talk, for he knew how to interpret their language.

In his early fourteenth-century chronicle, Robert Mannyng of Brunne continues the tradition of the clerkly Gawain:

> Lothes sone, sire Wawayn
> Hade bene at Rome to lere Romayn
> Wyþ Supplice þe Apostoille to wone,
> Honur to lerne, langage to kone;
> & þere was he dubbed knyght.   (*Chronicle*, 10667–71)

In order to see how this ideal of the knight who has successfully assimilated clerical values contrasts with the ideal of the warrior-knight we must return to a crucial passage in Wace, in which Gawain responds to Cador's bellicose resentment of a life of peace. In the argument between Gawain and Cador we find echoes of the conflicting outlooks of the knight and the court-cleric found in the debates between the *miles* and the *clerus* of the same period:

> 'En grante crieme ai, dist il, esté,
> E mainte feiz en ai pensé,
> Que par oisdives et par pais
> Devenissent Bretun malveis.
> Kar oisdive atrait malvastied
> E mainte hume ad aperecied.
> Uisdive met home en peresce,
> Uisdive amenuse prüesce,
> Uisdive esmuet les lecheries,
> Uisdive esprent lé drueries.
> Par lunc repos e par uisdive
> Est juvente tost ententive
> A gas, a deduit e a tables.
> . . . . . .
> Ja lunge pais nen amerai
> Ne unques lunge pais n'amai.'
> 'Sire cuens, dist Walwein, par fei,
> De neient estes en effrei.
> Bone est la pais emprés la guerre,
> Plus bele e mieldre en est la terre;
> Mult sunt bones les gaberies
> E bones sunt les drueries.
> Pur amisté e pur amies
> Funt chevaliers chevaleries.'   (*Brut*, 10737–72)

'I think it is a great shame, and I have often thought about it, that the Britons have become weak through idleness and peace. For idleness goes hand in hand with weakness, and many a man has been laid low because of it. Idleness makes men luxurious, diminishes their prowess, encourages wantonness and chambering. Rest and idleness cause the young to be preoccupied with pleasure, with pastimes and dice . . . I have never liked long peace, and never shall.' 'Lord earl', said Gawain, 'do not be afraid. Peace is welcome after war. It makes the country more beautiful and richer. Merriment and flirtations are delectable. Thanks to friendship and lady-loves, knights become chivalrous.'

Like these debates, this passage opposes bravery and courtesy, the requirements of war and those of peace. The transformation of the warrior into the courtier, which occurs when clerical ideals of courtesy and *mesure* gain a foothold within the court, is perceived by Wace as a conflict between generations. That Wace was here projecting his own times back on to an Arthurian past is suggested both by the similarities between Cador's speech and the objections to courtliness put forward by some of Wace's contemporaries, and the fact that Gawain's reply is Wace's own invention and a departure from his source, the *Historia Regum Britanniae*.[51] The lines are thus a fascinating reflection by a medieval writer on what he seems to have regarded as a turning-point in history, the ousting of the inveterate warrior by a new generation to whom these clerical ideals appealed. Cador's objections to a pacified order of knights, indeed, his objections to the institution of a court, where a knight must renounce his warlike impulses and be confined to indoor amusements, is suggestive of the antagonism with which the soldier of Wace's own day may have met social ideals or structures which would undermine his personal interests. One may compare Cador's response to that of an actual knight, Sir John Hawkwood, who, greeted by two friars who wish him peace, rejoined: 'May the Lord take away your alms . . . do you not know that I live by war and that peace would be my undoing?' Cador and John Hawkwood reveal the personal stake which the soldier has in maintaining a continual state of war.[52]

But if Sir John Hawkwood would have chosen Cador's side, Gawain's advocacy of peace must have earned the sympathy of the two friars, and presumably of a third cleric, Wace himself, who departed from his source to allow Gawain a challenging final word to Cador's belligerence. Particularly revealing is the way Wace's Gawain links, as I have done earlier, the notion of *courtoisie* with peace and stability within the state. Peace holds out the alluring promise of a land of plenty. Diametrically opposed to the 'terre gaste', the wasteland, which in Arthurian romance typically represents a countryside destroyed by aristocratic violence,[53] the beautiful and fruitful lands which Gawain conjures up suitably reward the soldier who becomes a courtier and sublimates his violent impulses.

---

[51] Jaeger, *Origins of Courtliness*, 178–80.

[52] The anecdote is recounted and discussed by Maurice Keen, 'Chivalry, Nobility, and the Man of Arms', in *War, Literature, and Politics*, ed. Christopher Thomas Allmand (London, 1976), 32–45.

[53] See R. Howard Bloch, 'Wasteland and Round Table', *NLH* 11 (1980), 255–76.

A very similar confrontation between the warrior and the 'clerical' knight occurs in the famous episode of the drops of blood in Chrétien's *Perceval*. While Perceval intently gazes on three drops of blood on the snow,[54] three attempts to escort him back are made by Arthur's court, who are camping in the vicinity. Sagremor, suitably nicknamed 'the Impetuous' (4199), and Kay quickly lose their patience when Perceval, absorbed in deep thoughts, fails to respond to their orders. Both resort to force but are defeated and return despondent. Arthur then orders Gawain to meet Perceval in full armour. Unlike Sagremor or Kay, Gawain approaches Perceval in as friendly a way as possible, and makes some polite conversation. Perceval then reveals to him the reasons for his reverie, while Gawain applauds him for the delicacy of his thoughts:

> devant moi on ice leu
> avoit .iii. gotes de frés sanc
> qui anluminoient le blanc.
> An l'esgarder m'estoit avis
> que la fresche color del vis
> m'amie la bele i veïsse,
> ja mez ialz partir n'an queïsse.
> —Certes, fet mes sire Gauvains,
> cil pansers n'estoit pas vilains,
> ençois estoit cortois et dolz,
> et cil estoit fos et estolz
> qui vostre cuer an remuoit.   (*Perceval*, 4426–37)

Before me on this spot were three drops of fresh blood, which shone on the white snow. Looking at them I thought I saw the fresh complexion of my beautiful girlfriend, and I never wished to take my eyes away from it.— Certainly, said Sir Gawain, that is not a churlish thought, but it is courteous and kind, and he who wanted to tear your heart away from it was foolish and proud.

Gawain evinces here a quality which is an essential ingredient of *courtoisie*: to see reality not in terms of conflict, resistance, or confrontation, but to see it through the eyes of another, to empathize with another by surrendering for a moment the primacy of one's own concerns.[55] When next the two exchange names, they

---

[54] The startling picture of the blood on the snow recurs in *Sir Gawain*: 'when the burne seye the blod blenk on the snowe' (2315). Although the situation is different— Gawain sees his own blood and realizes he has survived—the *Gawain*-poet's use of this vivid image may well be indebted to Chrétien.

[55] Henri Dupin, *La Courtoisie au Moyen Age* (Paris, 1931), 51.

have established a firm friendship, based on an instinctive recognition of the refinement of spirit which they share. Having disarmed each other, in both senses of the word, the two return to Arthur's court:

> Lor cort li uns l'autre anbracier,
> il comancent a deslacier
> andui lor hiaumes et vantailles
> et traient contremont les mailles.
> Ensi s'an vont joie menant ...   (*Perceval*, 4477–81)

So they run to embrace each other, and begin to take off each other's helmets and visors, and they undo each other's armour. Thus they go, in joy ...

Gawain thus accomplishes his mission not by use of arms—helms, ventails, and coats of mail are cast aside—but by exercising courtesy and diplomacy.

One other faculty comes to Gawain's aid on his venture, namely his capacity to grasp the linguistic transformations which inform Perceval's reading of blood and snow as metaphors for Blanche-fleur's face. Both Perceval and Gawain have mastered a highly troped discourse which leaves the interpreter to trace a considerable trajectory between the material sign and its ultimate referent, the imagined face of the lady. The practice and understanding of such a troped language is, as rhetorical handbooks and romances illustrate, a sign of social status and an indication of refinement.[56] The fact that Perceval the 'nice', who before this adventure could only take signs literally, for the first time in this romance transcends the material aspects of what he sees and hears thus marks an important stage in his career. Denyse Delcourt has well described what is at stake in this episode:

The progress of Perceval means that he must detach himself gradually from the signifier (the concrete object) and learn to make adequate use of his reason. William of Saint Thierry would say that he must pass from an 'animal state'—characterized by a 'way of thinking enslaved to the body'— to a rational state in which the work of the mind consists precisely in liberating the essence from corporeal images ...[57]

[56] On the equation of troped language and social status in rhetorical handbooks and in *Aucassin and Nicolette*, see R. Howard Bloch, 'Money, Metaphor, and the Mediation of Social Difference', in *Symposium*, 30 (1981), 18–33.

[57] 'Le progrès du "nice" suppose, de cette façon, qu'il se détache graduellement du signifiant (de la chose concrète) et qu'il apprenne à se servir adéquatement de sa raison. Guillaume de Saint-Thierry ... dirait que le jeune homme doit passer d'un

The extent of his enculturation into the courtly milieu is suggested by the fact that he has internalized the rules of the court-poet's rhetorical *descriptio* of the lady, in which the mingling of the colours of white and red, and the image of the snow landscape, are common motifs. Compare, for example, the remarkably similar descriptions of Sagremor and the Lady of the Castle:

> Jusqu'au fermail d'antroverture,
> Vi del piz nu sanz coverture
> Plus blanc que n'est la nois negiee. (*Cligés*, 835–7)

Up to the neckband of her dress, I saw her flesh, naked and uncovered, whiter than freshly fallen snow.

> Riche red on þat on rayled ayquere
>
> . . . , ...
>
> Hir brest and hir bryȝt þrote bare displayed,
> Schon schyrer þen snawe þat schedez on hillez . . . (952–6)

Where the 'animal' mind sees only blood and snow, the court-cleric, and his creations, Perceval and Gawain, who immediately identifies with Perceval's absorption, have the capacity to elevate these objects into poetic images for female beauty.

Kay, however, who is well aware of Gawain's reputation for courtesy, heaps scorn on the use of diplomacy and discretion:

> Bien savez paroles antandre,
> qui sont et beles et polies.
>
> . . . . . .
>
> Certes an un bliaut de soie
> poez ceste bataille fere.
> Ja ne vos an convondra trere
> espee ne lance brisier. (*Perceval*, 4360–9)

You have a way with beautiful and polished words . . . You could have fought this combat dressed in silk. Not once did you need to use your sword or spear.

When, as a means of solving problems, the use and understanding of courtly rhetoric—'paroles antandre' can mean both to understand and to select words—replace 'bataille', Kay is up in arms. As in Wace, we see here a conflict between the warrior and the courtly knight. That the figure of the courtly knight also speaks for clerical

"état animal"—caractérisé par une "manière de penser asservie au sens du corps"—à un état rationnel dans lequel le travail de l'esprit vient justement libérer l'être des images corporelles . . .' (Denyse Delcourt, *L'Éthique du changement dans le roman français du douzième siècle* (Geneva, 1990), 129–30).

interests is unmistakable. It is not only that Gawain exemplifies the supremacy of verbal diplomacy over armed combat, but also that his insight into the workings of semantic conversion, his awareness of the metaphorical potential of snow and blood, which to Kay and Sagremor remained just material things, place him in a literate culture.[58]

The Cambridge debate actually makes clear that this ability to go beyond *materia* distinguishes the cleric from the knight:

> Mars sensu militat, alter [the cleric]
> Est intellectu carpens iter; hic resolutas
> Res a materia, reliquus, res materiales
> Inspicit, hic uerum, reliquus, quid gloria rerum,
> Hic infinitum, reliquus, quo fine politum;
> Fulminat in rebus Mars et materiebus,
> Veri perspector est in racionibus Hector. (53–9)

Mars battles with his senses, the other takes the road of the intellect. The first examines material things, the other examines concepts separated from their material form. The one studies the truth of the matter, the other vainglorious things; the first studies infinity, the other the ends of beauty. Mars fulminates in things and in matter, Hector is a purveyor of truth in matters of reason.

Gawain and Perceval thus resemble the cleric not only because they use restraint rather than brute force as a way of resolving situations, but also because they are masters in the art of transcending the concrete object. The two capacities of bodily restraint and sophisticated interpretation may be seen as related. As courtesy involves the sublimation of violent instincts into acceptable forms of social interaction, the courtly interpreter resists a 'bestial' interpretation, which takes the sign at face value, in favour of a more refined one. This is perhaps why the knight of Mars's fixation on the material level constitutes, in the words of the passage above, an act of aggression, of 'fulmination'.

In the episodes from Wace's *Brut* and Chrétien's *Perceval*, we can observe how far the courtly knight, epitomized by Gawain, has departed from an earlier conception of the *miles* as a mounted warrior, and has taken on the characteristics of the cleric. If, as recent research has suggested, the cleric played an important role in the dissemination of ideals of *mesure* and refinement, then the social

[58] Brian Stock, *The Implications of Literacy* (Princeton, NJ, 1983), 525.

function of romance can be seen as the propagation of these ideals to an audience of fighting men. The figure of the courtly knight, half-knight, half-cleric, may have helped to make such a programme of instruction and correction palatable and desirable.[59]

This project of instruction, essential to the Arthurian *roman courtois*, explains the common ground between courtesy books and courtly romances which we have explored in the chapter on the convention of hospitality. I argued there that both courtly romance and courtesy books attempt to perpetuate a protocol of polite behaviour for guests and hosts. Among the accomplishments of *courtoisie* we find not just injunctions about hospitality, but also advice about the art of delicate speech. I quote again Philippe de Navarre's summary of the duties incumbent on the clerics of secular households:

Li maitre as fils de riche homme se doivent mout traveillir d'apanre a eus cortoisie et biau parler, et honorer la gent, et cortoisement recoillir, et eux apanre les estoires et les livres des autors . . . (*Quatre Ages*, p. 13)

The masters to the sons of a rich man should do their best to teach them courtesy and eloquence, how to honour people and receive them politely, and they should teach them the stories and books of the great authors . . .

We have previously looked at the shared etiquette of 'cortoisement recoillir' in Arthurian romance and courtesy books. To document the civilizing impulse of courtly romances further let us turn to the other aspect of *courtoisie* which Philippe mentions: the intricacies of 'biau parler'.[60]

One of the most frequent lessons which courtesy books impart to the young gentleman is to avoid talking too much:

Pauca loquaris; qui garrit, ineptus habetur;
qui tacet, is placet, et pro sapiente tenetur. (*Facetus*, 172)

Speak little. He who talks too much appears stupid. But he who is silent pleases, and is considered wise.

In Chrétien de Troyes's *Perceval*, Gornemant teaches the hero a similar lesson:

[59] Jaeger, *Origins of Courtliness*, 234, and Bumke, *Höfische Kultur*, 446–51.
[60] For the importance of the art of conversation in twelfth-century romance and in the education of noblemen see E. H. Ruck, *Index of Themes and Motifs in Twelfth-Century French Arthurian Poetry* (Cambridge, 1991), 114–18, and Bumke, *Höfische Kultur*, 437.

> Et gardez que vos ne soiez
> trop parlanz ne trop noveliers. (*Perceval*, 1646–7)

And make sure you are not too talkative or too inquisitive.

As a consequence of this rule Perceval does not ask the question at the Grail Castle, and astonishes Blanchefleur's vassals when he keeps silent as Blanchefleur waits for him to open the conversation. The vassals, on the other hand, make 'grant parole' (1874) of this, and comment:

> Dex, fet chascun, mout me mervoil
> se cil chevaliers est mulax. (*Perceval*, 1860–1)

My God, says everyone, I really wonder whether this knight is mute.

The unfortunate consequences to which keeping silence at the wrong moments can lead are also described in an English adaptation of *Facetus* material:

> Go not forth as a dombe freke
> Syn God hase laft the tonge to speke
> Lest men say be sibbe or couthe,
> 'Yond is a man with-outen mowthe'.
> (*Boke of Curtaysye*, 256–9)[61]

There is thus a time for silence and a time for speech. As Chrétien later says in his *Perceval*:

> j'ai oï sovant retraire
> que ausi se puet an trop taire
> com trop parler, a la foiee. (3237–9).[62]

I have often heard it said that it is possible to be too silent, as well as too talkative.

Or, as the *Facetus moribus et vita* puts it:

> Pauca loqui debet qui vult urbanus haberi;
> Nec prorsus taceat, sed meditata ferat. (15–16)[63]

Anyone wishing to considered well-behaved, should not talk too much, nor be utterly silent, but take the middle way.

In fact, Perceval's mother had earlier encouraged this middle way. She advises him to engage 'prodomes' in conversation (*Perceval*, 561) and to put questions to strangers:

---

[61] Ed. F. J. Furnivall, in *Book of Nurture &c.*, EETS OS 32 (London, 1868).
[62] Cf. Ecclesiastes 3: 7.
[63] Ed. and trans. A. G. Elliot, 'The *Facetus*', *Allegorica* 2/2 (1977), 27–57.

> ja en chemin ne an ostel
> n'aiez longuement conpaignon
> que vos ne demandiez son non . . . (*Perceval*, 556–8)

Never travel with, or host, someone for long, without asking him his
name . . .

Courtesy books teach the same rule:

> S'avec aucun sur chemin vas
> Que tu mie ne cognoistras,
> Demande son nom et son estre,
> Quel part il va, et donc doit estre.
> (*Cy ensuyt facet*, 301–4)[64]

If anyone travels with you, whom you do not know, ask him his name and
his identity, where he is headed and where he has to be.

While Gawain in *Sir Gawain and the Green Knight* does not ask his
host's name, leaving his identity shrouded in mystery, Bertilac and
his household put this question to him after supper:

> Þenne watz spyed and spured vpon spare wyse
> Bi preué poyntez of þat prynce, put to hymseluen,
> Þat he beknew cortaysly of þe court þat he were . . . (901–3)

The name must be asked tactfully, 'bi preué poyntez', for, as Chrétien's *Lancelot* suggests, it is not done to ask the guest's name
directly:

> Premieremant li vavasors
> comança son oste a enquerre
> qui il estoit, et de quel terre,
> mes son non ne li anquist pas. (*Lancelot*, 2076–9)

First the vavasour asks his guest who he is, and from what land, but he does
not enquire after his name.

In both cases, the hosts are also aware that the time for satisfying
their curiosity is at the end of the meal.[65] I take my example of this
point of etiquette from the Anglo-Norman *Petit Traitise de Nurture*:

> Estrange ne devez aresoner
> Au comencement del manger,
> Ne trop de noveles lui demandez
> K'il ne ert de manger desturbez.

---

[64] Ed. Jozef Morawski, *Le Facet en français* (Poznan, 1923).
[65] Jonathan Nicholls, *The Matter of Courtesy: Medieval Courtesy Books and the
Gawain-Poet* (Bury St Edmunds, 1985), 128.

> Aprés manger, si vous volez,
> Aventure et noveles demandez. (*Petit Traitise*, 133–8)[66]

Among strangers, you ought not to reason too much at the beginning of the meal. Do not ask him too many questions, so that you do not keep him from his dinner. After dinner, if you like, you can ask about what has happened and what is new.

Chrétien, too, demonstrates an awareness of this rule in his romances. Only Perceval at the Grail Castle postpones the appropriate time for asking questions—after supper—until the next morning: 'So he has put the thing off', and concentrates on his drink and food' ('Ensi la chose est respitiee | s'antent a boivre et a mengier': 3289–9). This departure from normality becomes particularly apparent if we compare it with a scene from *Erec et Enide*, in which Erec, puzzled by the unorthodox reception he receives from King Evrain's subjects, enquires after the adventure of the Joy of the Court:

> Molt furent servi lieemant,
> tant qu'Erec estrosseemant
> leissa le mangier et le boivre,
> et comança a ramantoivre
> ce que au cuer plus li tenoit:
> de la Joie li sovenoit,
> s'an a la parole esmeüe ... (*Erec et Enide*, 5543–9)

They were well served, until Erec suddenly left his drink and his food, and began to talk about what was closest to his heart. He remembered the Joy and broached the subject ...

While Perceval 's'antent a boivre et a mangier', Erec stops eating and drinking ('leissa le mangier et le boivre'), and asks his question at exactly the right time, in the final stages of, or just after, dinner. As Perceval later learns from the Loathly Lady, the moment was too fine an opportunity to miss:

> Mout est maleüreus qui voit
> si bel tans que plus ne covaigne,
> si atant tant que plus biax vaigne.
> Ce es tu, li maleüreus,
> qui veïs qu'il fu tans et leus
> de parler, et si te taüs! (*Perceval*, 4638–43)

[66] Ed. H. Rosamund Parsons, 'Anglo-Norman Books of Courtesy and Nurture', *PMLA* 44 (1929), 383–455.

Unhappy he who sees the most convenient moment, and waits for a better one to come. You are this unhappy one, who saw that it was the time and the place to speak, and kept silent!

Warned by Gornemant to restrain his garrulity, Perceval deviates from the proper timetable, imagining he can afford to put the question off until next morning, only to find that by then the Fisher King and his attendants have all vanished. When Perceval's return to the Grail castle in Manessier's *Third Continuation* offers him another chance he does not make the same mistake again:

> Quant il dou manger lever durent,
> Par devant les tables roiaux
> Passa la lance et li Graaux.
> . . . .
> Percevaux, qui bien s'an prant garde,
> Soupire et puis lou roi esgarde
> Et li a dit de maintenant . . .
> (Manessier's *Continuation*, 32616–29)

When they were about to get up from their dinner, the lance and the grail passed before the king's dais . . . Perceval, who watched it closely, sighed and looked at the king, and spoke to him instantly . . .

The timing of speech thus turns out to be a decisive factor in the knight's quest.

And so, of course, is the content of speech, which, as courtesy books stipulate, must always be modest:

> Si tu es hom de grant valeur
> Ne t'en vante pas, c'est foleur. (*Cy ensuyt facet*, 333–4)

If you are a valorous man, do not boast of it, for that is foolish.

The characters in the romances of the *Gawain*-poet and of Chrétien de Troyes consistently put this advice into practice. At the end of the combat between Yvain and Gawain in *Yvain*, the two heroes courteously declare themselves vanquished. Neither wishes to be regarded as the victor:

> Tant sont andui franc et gentil
> que la victoire et la querone
> li uns a l'autre otroie et done;
> ne cist ne cil ne la vialt prendre . . . (*Yvain*, 6352–5)

They are so kind and gracious to each other that they both grant and give the victory and the crown to the other. Neither of the two wants to accept this.

In this vein the show of modesty continues until King Arthur puts an end to it. A similar contest in courtesy occurs in *Sir Gawain and the Green Knight*, when both Gawain and his host insist that the other deserves most thanks for the marvellous time they have been having (1031–41).

In Chrétien's *Perceval*, Gawain's affected modesty draws admiration from the Queen of the Castle of Maidens. She asks him whether he belongs to the famous knights of the Round Table, and Gawain answers:

> —Dame, fet il, ge n'oseroi
> dire que des plus prisiez soie.
> Ne me faz mie des meillors
> ne ne cuit estre des peiors.
> E ele li respont: 'Biau sire,
> grant corteisie vos oi dire,
> que ne vos ametez le pris
> del mialz, ne del blasme le pis.' (*Perceval*, 7875–82)

Lady, he says, I would not dare say that I am among the most renowned. I do not count myself among the best, and not among the worst either. And she responds: 'Dear sir, I have heard you say a very courteous thing, since you do not impute to yourself the glory of the best, or the blame of the worst.'

Gawain keeps the display of humility within reasonable boundaries. He follows in this the advice set out by the *Facetus*:

> Sis humilis mediante modo, nimium fugiatur;
> qui nimis est humilis, hic vacuus esse putatur. (*Facetus*, 14)

Be humble in good measure; excess is to be avoided. He who is too humble may seem silly.

The lady who compliments Gawain on his behaviour obviously recognizes his reply as a sign of good breeding when she commends it as 'grant cortoisie'. Because of this awareness of the rules of etiquette shown by characters within the romance world, such demonstrations of modesty inevitably become tainted with self-display. Indeed, the ultimate effect that Gawain achieves by effacing himself is to raise himself on the ladder of sophistication.

In *Sir Gawain* the characters are equally skilled in dramatizing modesty topoi. Gawain's speech to Arthur's court is a masterpiece of professed modesty by which he nevertheless succeeds in putting himself forward as the best candidate and in further enhancing his reputation for courtesy. In Castle Hautdesert such polite self-depreciations continue. After preparing a delicious meal for their guest, the hosts proclaim the poorness of their *haute cuisine*:

> 'Þis penaunce now ȝe take
> And eft hit schal amende.' (896–7)

Gawain, too, plays down his worth. In the temptation scenes, he maintains that the Lady puts too high a price on him:

> 'To reche to such reuerence as ȝe reherce here
> I am wyȝe vnworþy, I wot wel myseluen.' (1243–4)

Similar declamations of worthlessness are made by the Lady of the Castle, when she offers Gawain the green girdle:

> And þat ho bede to þe burne, and blyþely bisoȝt,
> Þaȝ hit vnworþi were, þat he hit take wolde. (1834–5)

But she knows full well that this 'unworthy' gift has an enormous value from which her self-conscious depreciations detract nothing.

A similar form of courtliness lies in lavishing praise on fellow knights and ladies. Again, these expressions of gratitude or thanks can easily become theatrical. A French courtesy book, for example, recommends that the recipient of a gift must take pains to laud the donor:

> Et s'aucuns par sa courtoisie
> Te fait don, forment l'en mercye.
> Le don et le donneur loer
> Dois plainement de ton pouuoir.
> (*Ci commence facet*, 485–8)[67]

If someone courteously gives you a gift, thank him often. You should openly praise the giver and the gift with all your might.

Such, too, is Christine de Pisan's advice to the lady when she receives a trinket:

She will . . . receive their trinkets with pleasure. She will make much of even a trifle and say that there is nothing else so good nor so fine. She will thank them warmly . . . (*Treasure of the City of Ladies*, I. xxii)[68]

The effort which the text urges should go into showing one's gratitude illustrates the principle of 'noblesse oblige'. In Chrétien de

---

[67] Ed. Morawski, *Le Facet*.

[68] Christine de Pisan, *The Treasure of the City of Ladies or the Book of the Three Virtues*, trans. Sarah Lawson (Harmondsworth, 1985), 84.

Troyes the fulfilment of these obligations of politeness abounds. When *Erec* receives a palfrey as a goodbye gift he praises it profusely:

> Quant Erec le palefroi vit,
> ne le loa mie petit . . .   (*Erec et Enide*, 1397–8)

When Erec saw the palfrey, he praised it not a little.

The litotes (ne . . . mie petit) conveys the trouble Erec takes to show his gratitude. Authenticity bows before Erec's realization that certain occasions demand a public display of gratitude. As the *Moralium dogma philosophorum* puts it:

caue ne clam gratias referas. Ingratus est qui nemotis arbitris agit. (19)[69]

Make sure you do not thank people in secret. He who thanks without witnesses is ungrateful.

Another polite accolade occurs when Erec and his company visit King Evrain's castle. In full hearing of Evrain, who leads Enide by the hand, they join in to express their admiration for the tastefulness of his interior design:

> a l'antrer anz tuit loé
> le biau sanblant au roi Evrain. (5517–18)

On entering they all complimented king Evrain on the nice decorations.

In *Sir Gawain and the Green Knight*, we likewise encounter praise of this nature. Gawain voices it during his first meal in Castle Hautdesert:

> Þe freke calde hit a fest ful frely and ofte
> Ful hendely . . .   (894–5)

Like Erec, Gawain puts a conscious effort into his tributes. The *Gawain*-poet's delightful qualification 'ful . . . ofte' makes that clear. But neither in *Erec* nor in *Gawain* does such a public show of thankfulness carry pejorative connotations. On the contrary, they are sure signs of 'hendelayk'. In their romances, where, as in courtesy books, self-depreciation and acclamations of others are polite gestures and are recognized as such, they ultimately redound, to paraphrase the *Gawain*-poet, to the 'worship' (1267) of those who voice them.

[69] William of Conches, *Moralium dogma philosophorum*, ed. John Holmberg (Uppsala, 1929).

The commendations of refined behaviour bear out the didactic element in the romances of the *Gawain*-poet and Chrétien de Troyes. In effecting the gradual transition from warrior to courtier, their romances and the early courtesy books may have given valuable lessons in politeness and discretion. This also provides some confirmation about their clerical background. Not only would their project of *correctio* fall well within the tasks and duties of the cleric, but the courtesy books, whose advice their romance-heroes put into action, remained until the fifteenth century largely a clerical product.[70] The first books of instruction in good manners are Latin texts, while English, Anglo-Norman, and French courtesy books still depend directly on these Latin originals. The Latin texts were both used for instruction in manners and as Latin school-texts. When Cotgrave defined the word 'facetus' in his dictionary of 1611, he still referred to the work as a school-text for the gentleman: 'Facet, A primmer, Or grammar, for a young scholler.'[71] With the learning of a language, the 'young scholler' learns manners—an effective pedagogical method apparently well known to medieval teachers. And since the 'clergy and the literate clerks who staffed the chapels and administrations of the aristocracy' were responsible for lessons in Latin,[72] it is likely that we must look to the same group for the instruction in good manners. As Chaucer's lines from the *Monk's Tale* suggest—'In yowthe a maister hadde this emperour | To teche hym lettrure and curteisye' (2495–6)—the clerics, the teachers of 'lettrure', were also the teachers of courtesy.

I have so far examined the way the courtly knight, epitomized by Gawain, embodies clerical ideals. The opposition of knights like Cador in the *Brut* or Kay in *Perceval* to these ideals is suggestive of the hostility with which courtly knights may have been viewed by knights reluctant to trade in the military vocation of the knight at war for self-restraint at a court in peace.[73] However, Gawain's

[70] Bumke, *Höfische Kultur*, 448–9.

[71] Quoted in F. Brentano, *Relationship of the Latin Facetus Literature to the Medieval English Courtesy Poems*, Bulletin of the University of Kansas, Humanistic Studies 5/2 (Lawrence, Kan., 1936), 62.

[72] Nicholas Orme, *From Childhood to Chivalry: The Education of English Kings: 1066–1530* (London, 1984), 124. See also Orme's remarks on the role which imaginative literature may have played in education, 81–6.

[73] A letter to the learned Henry the Liberal, husband of Chrétien's patroness Marie de Champagne, shows that the suspicion of knights for the 'clerical knight' was very real. In it Nicolas de Montieramey praises Henry for being able to follow the ways of clerics, without arousing the jealousy or anger of his knights. The relevant passage

response to Cador in the *Brut*, and his successful attempt to retrieve
Perceval, at which Kay failed so miserably, suggest the appreciation
of courtly romance for the knight who has mastered the self-
restraint and verbal diplomacy which form the basis of the court-
cleric's way of life. The heroism of feeling and intellect prove
superior to brute force. This is, of course, a point frequently made
in support of the cleric in the debates between the *miles* and the
clerus. The 'commendatio clerici et clericatus'[74] in the Cambridge
debate represents the cleric's superior kind of heroism as follows:

> Clericus arte uigens non est pedes, in racione
> Militat artis eques, nec querit res, sed earum
> Causas inquirit, naturas inuenit, actus
> Qualificat.
> . . . .
> Hic, hic, est miles, cui semper mens animatur.
> Spiritualis eques in pugna materialem
> Non ascendit equum; pedes est eques hic in agone.
> Hic scutum fidei portat, gladii uice uerbum,
> Loricam fert iusticie galeamque salutis.
> Sic armatur eques, sic militat omnis in arte,
> Celesti superans quecumque pericula marte.   (21–40)[75]

The cleric who excels in the arts is no foot-soldier. As a knight of the arts he
battles in the field of reason, seeking not things but their causes, discovering
their dispositions, and charting their motions . . . This, this, is the true
knight, whose mind is always alert. The spiritual knight does not mount a
material horse in a struggle: this knight is a foot-soldier in combat. He
carries the sword of faith, his words are his sword. He carries the plates of
justice and the helmet of salvation. Thus this knight is armed, thus he fights
all in the field of the arts, overcoming every danger in his divine combat.

If we admit the similarities between the knight of this debate and
Kay or Cador on the one hand, and the cleric and Gawain on the
other, we must conclude that Chrétien's or Wace's advocacy of
Gawain's viewpoint has much in common with a 'commendatio
clerici et clericatus'.

The 'commendatio' has a bearing on courtly romance far beyond
these individual passages from the *Brut* or *Perceval*. It encapsulates

---

of this letter is printed in R. Bezzola's *Les Origines et la formation de la littérature
courtoise en occident (500–1200)*, 3 vols. (Paris, 1944–63), ii. 373–4.

[74] These are the words of the rubric introducing the passage quoted below.

[75] Cf. Ephesians, 6: 13–17.

in miniature both one of the morals in the romances of Chrétien and *Gawain*, and the poetic technique they adopt to point this moral. In the same way as courtly romance, the 'commendatio' attempts to redefine the true goals of knighthood in terms other than those of martial combat. The true knight, says the 'commendatio', finds his vocation in the realm of reason, words, faith or faithfulness, justice, and peace. While others undertake quests for things, he tries to gain a deeper understanding of their nature and purpose. That, according to the cleric, is the battle which the 'real' knight engages in.

The romances of Chrétien and the *Gawain*-poet attempt a very similar redefinition of true knighthood, which stands in contrast to the tautological definition given by Calogrenant, who in *Yvain* introduces himself to the Giant Herdsman with the words: 'Je sui . . . uns chevaliers' in search of 'avanture, por esprover | ma proesce et mon hardemant' (*Yvain*, 358–63). The inadequacy of Calogrenant's conception of his vocation is revealed by the shame he incurs during the adventures from which he confesses he returns not as a proven knight but as a proven fool. Calogrenant acts without thinking. He does not possess the introspection which would allow him to examine his motives and his conscience.

That medieval authors interpreted Calogrenant's self-definition in this way is indicated by the writers who picked up on this passage. Perceval in Manessier's *Continuation* echoes Calogrenant's words:

> Uns chevaliers sui, sire.
>
> . . . . . .
>
> Et vois errant aval la terre
> Por pris et por honor conquerre.
>
> . . . . . .
>
> A maint chevalier me combat,
> Maint an ocis, maint en abat
> Et maint an ai retenu pris;
> Einsis vois acroissant mon pris.

I am a knight sir . . . and I go roaming about the lands to conquer glory and honour . . . I fight many knights, and have killed and defeated many, and made many prisoners. Thus I live, furthering my reputation . . .

To which the hermit replies:

> S'a vos sauver volez antendre,
> Ces alees et ces venues
> Qu'avez si longuemant tenues

> Vos covient guerpir et laissier,
> Et vostre orgoilleux cuer plessier ... (37780–810)

If you have any interest in your salvation, you should leave and abandon the ways and manners to which you have held for so long, and soften your proud heart ...

The *Roman des Eles*, a short didactic work by Raoul de Houdenc, written, like Manessier's *Continuation*, in the first quarter of the thirteenth century, is just as critical as the hermit of those who:

> Mes ne sevent qu'a lor non monte,
> Quar tel por chevalier se tient
> Que ne set qu'au non apartient,
> For seul que tant 'Chevalier sui'.
> (*Roman des Eles*, 46–9)[76]

They do not know what their title demands of them. They think themselves chivalrous without knowing what this name means, other than saying 'I am a knight'.

What these writers demand from the knight is that he internalize some of the violence he directs on to his surroundings in the form of critical self-scrutiny; that his action should be matched by reflection.

Yvain, who goes out to revenge Calogrenant, lacks, like his cousin, the self-awareness without which no triumph can last in the long run. He leaves Laudine with a promise to return in a year's time in order to enhance his glory in tournaments, but despite his assurances he forgets his pledge. At this point in the story, Yvain departs from the company of knights, no longer caring for their ways, and loses his wits. He regains Laudine with the help of Lunete's cunning, but only after a series of adventures in which he comes to the rescue of others and returns services rendered to him. Yvain's madness reflects not only his own misery upon realizing that he has failed in his obligations towards others. It also functions as an outward reflection of the foolishness of a knight who undertakes deeds of chivalry without consulting his conscience. As Yvain later explains, it was his 'nonsavoir' (6772) which led him into trouble. Yvain has come to understand that the knight needs this 'savoir'. As Joan Tasker Grimbert has put it recently: 'Il doit ... saisir le sens profond de la lutte. Il doit réfléchir.'[77]

---

[76] Ed. Keith Busby (Amsterdam, 1983).
[77] *Yvain dans le miroir: Une poétique de la réflexion dans le Chevalier au Lion de Chrétien de Troyes* (Amsterdam, 1988), 141.

As Yvain accomplishes miracles of chivalry at tournaments when he is reminded of a broken promise, Gawain has pulled out of his dreaded encounter with the Green Knight alive and well when his opponent blames him for having clung to a green girdle which should have been returned. Too fixated on the appointment at the Green Chapel and on dealing successfully with his opponent, Gawain does not fully realize that any material attributes, be it a green girdle or his heavy armour with which he arrives at the Green Chapel, are poor substitutes for the 'scutum fidei'. Assuming that the real ordeal will be at the Green Chapel, he does not recognize the nature of the challenge life poses, a challenge which requires not only prowess or valour but personal integrity.

In Yvain's round of tournaments, or at the perilous Chapel, the criterion of personal integrity may appear inconsequential to these knights. Under this misapprehension, Yvain and Gawain fail to keep faith with Laudine and Bertilac. But when it turns out that precisely under these circumstances Laudine and Bertilac are measuring them with the yardstick of loyalty and find them lacking, they learn a very similar lesson to the one dispensed by the cleric in the Latin debate: that the knight who in battle ascends only a 'material horse' will find he can accomplish little more than a foot-soldier. That Yvain and Gawain take this lesson to heart is shown by the way the knights now turn inwards to reflect on their past deeds, recognizing them as 'nonsavoir' or as 'fauty . . . fare' (2386).

The correspondences between their knights and the clerics of the debates suggest that Chrétien de Troyes and the *Gawain*-poet are introducing clerical ideals in their romances. In the methods they use, the Cambridge debate provides a final illuminating parallel. When in this debate the cleric argues against the knight, he represents himself as a knight engaged in a nobler form of battle, refracting the conflict between the *clerus* and the *miles* as one between one sort of knight and another. Although the final question of the debate, whether the knight or the cleric is the better knight, is left open,[78] it exemplifies the success with which the cleric has managed to redefine knighthood in the course of the debate. He has dislocated it from its traditional meaning to such an extent that it has

---

[78] The final two lines run: 'Let my lady's judgement decide whether the knight is more splendid and knightly, or the cleric' ('Discuciat racio domine, quis clarior et quis I Equior, an clarus clerus an equus eques').

become possible to argue that a cleric makes a better knight than the knight himself.

I do not propose that we read this question as one which might seriously have occupied the medieval mind. However, about the rhetorical strategies which clerics might—and did—adopt to advocate their vision, the clerical 'commendationes' reveal a great deal. Their strategy is not to dislodge the language of chivalry, but rather to appropriate it for their own ends. They do not elaborate a discourse which can compete with that of knights, armour, battles, and quests, but they use them in a different sense, by turning them into metaphors. Accordingly, we find Abelard presenting his clerical career as a form of warfare, preferring, like the poet of the Cambridge debate, the conflicts of debate above those of battle:

> et quoniam dialecticarum rationum armaturam omnibus philosophie documentis pretuli, his armis alias commutavi et tropheis bellorum conflictus pretuli disputationum.[79]

and because I preferred the armour of dialectical reason to all other branches of philosophy, I decided to change other arms for these and to favour the combat of disputations above the trophies of war.

In his *Summa de Arte Praedicatoria*, Alan of Lille suggests a similar rhetorical technique to the cleric when addressing an audience of knights. Adapting the standard doctrine of the two swords, one wielded by the knight against injustice, the other by the cleric in defence of faith, Alan proposes that the ideal knight should wield both swords, clerical and knightly. His illustrative sermon turns the knight's activity into a *figura*:

> Militia enim exterior figura est interioris militiae, et sine interiori, exterior est inanis et vacua. Sicut autem sunt duo hominis partes, corporalis et spiritualis, ita sunt duo gladii pertinentes ad propulsandos diversos insultus hominum; materialis, quae repelluntur injuriae; et spiritualis, quo repelluntur molestiae mentis.[80]

Chivalry is after all the exterior figure for an inner chivalry, and without this inner chivalry, the external is empty and vain. Just as there are two sides to a man, the corporeal and the spiritual, so there are two swords designed to

---

[79] *Historia Calamitatum*, ed. J. Monfrin (Paris, 1959), 63–4. See also the relevant analysis of this passage by R. W. Hanning, 'Love and Power in the Twelfth Century, with Special Reference to Chrétien de Troyes and Marie de France', in *The Olde Daunce: Love, Friendship, Sex, and Marriage in the Medieval World*, ed. Robert R. Edwards and Stephen Spender (New York, 1991), 87–103, at 88–9.

[80] PL 210, cols. 109–98, at col. 186.

chase away human abuses: the material, with which injustices are banished, and the spiritual, which banishes the things that trouble the mind.

Unlike the Cambridge debate, which posits the clerical and the chivalric spheres as mutually exclusive opposites, Alan fuses the two in his outline of what the knight should aim for. By making chivalry figurative, he succeeds in redefining its direction: away from the battlefield alone, and towards the mind where the knight will equally find 'molestiae' to combat. The shift, which we have likewise observed in the fictions of Chrétien and the *Gawain*-poet, is towards internalization, towards the discovery of metaphorical enemies within.

As Geoffrey de Vinsauf's *Poetria Nova* says, using metaphors makes it possible to graft one's own meaning on to the words of others. It can therefore offer the poet a means of recognizing himself in an alien discourse:

> Talis transsumptio verbis
> Est tibi pro speculo: quia te specularis in illo
> Et proprias cognoscis oves in rure alieno.
> (*Poetria Nova*, 802–4)[81]

This verbal transfiguration serves you as a mirror: in it you may see yourself reflected, and see your own cattle in a a stranger's pasture.

This is what Alan of Lille and Abelard do: they use chivalric discourse for their own purposes, and lead their own sheep to graze in the knight's pasture.

The tendency towards a '*semiotization* of chivalry'—'the tendency . . . to make the arms and gestures of the knight into signs of something else' and thus to 'subvert the *proprietas* of chivalric war by making it figurative'—also characterizes the romances of Chrétien de Troyes.[82] Gawain's substitutions of force of arms by force of words in the *Perceval* is an example of a metaphorical transposition,

[81] Alexandre Leupin has recognized that Geoffrey is particularly concerned in his discussions of the figure of *transsumptio* with the way it allows the writer to rejuvenate the antiquated: 'Si vetus est verbum, sis physicus et veteranum | Redde novum . . .' (762–3): 'Absolute Reflexivity: Geoffrey de Vinsauf's *Poetria Nova*', in his *Barbarolexis: Medieval Writing and Sexuality*, trans. Kate M. Cooper (Cambridge, Mass., 1989), 17–38. It is precisely in terms of this kind of *transsumptio*, a reinterpretation of an obsolete ideology so as to bring it in line with the modern times, that the figurative uses of chivalry in Alan of Lille's *Summa*, or the romances of Chrétien and the *Gawain*-poet, may be interpreted.

[82] Eugene Vance, 'Chrétien's *Yvain* and the Ideologies of Change and Exchange', *Yale French Studies*, 70 (1986), 42–62, at 47.

and it is with a keen awareness of these processes of conversion that Kay airs his grievances on Gawain's safe return:

> Mout fu or la bataille griés
> et perilleuse sainnemant,
> que tot ausi heiteemant
> s'en retorne com il i mut,
> c'onques d'autrui cop ne reçut
> n'autres de lui cop ne santi
> n'onques de rien ne desmanti. (*Perceval*, 4496–502)

The battle has been fierce and dangerous without risk, for he returns as cheerfully as when he left, and no one dealt a blow or received one, without a blow being struck.

Kay protests against what in his mind is the inappropriateness of the new semantic domains of courtesy and verbal diplomacy which are being brought to bear on the battle-hardened knight. To Kay, the two can never seriously be reconciled in the word 'bataille'. Whatever we make of Kay's rancour, to the reality of these processes of semiotization in Chrétien's romances he is a perceptive witness.

For some further examples we may turn to Chrétien's *Yvain*. After the hero of this romance has spent most of his early career in pursuit of vengeance, the language of warfare is suddenly evoked figuratively to describe Yvain's despair after Laudine's messenger has exposed him as a traitor to her lady:

> Ne het tant rien con lui meïsme,
> ne ne set a cui se confort
> de lui qui soi meïsme a mort.
> Mes ainz voldroit le san changier
> que il ne se poïst vengier
> de lui qui joie s'a tolue.   (*Yvain*, 2792–7)

He hates nothing as much as himself, and he does not know to whom to turn for comfort, since he has killed himself. But he would sooner go mad than not being able to take revenge on the person who has taken away his happiness.

From this point onwards, Yvain seeks vengeance, not on opponents, but on his former self, which did not live up to the word given to Laudine. The final result of this conquest will be the restoration of his relationship with Laudine. To describe the development of this relationship Chrétien again uses the language of warfare. On seeing her for the first time she holds him 'prisoner' (1514, 1940–4). He surrenders to her but Lunete arranges a 'truce' (2031–9). However, by overstaying Yvain breaks the truce, and opens hostilities by dealing Laudine a dreadful blow: 'Mes sire Yvains la dame a morte . . .' (2744). Only at the very end of the romance does Yvain finally make a 'lasting peace' with Laudine (6801).

In a similar vein, the *Gawain*-poet displaces the language of combat to describe Gawain's dealings with the Lady of the Castle. She takes him prisoner. He surrenders himself and asks for mercy (1210–16). Gawain 'defends' himself well (1283, 1551), while the Lady tries to 'subjugate' him (1770). These metaphors are more than conventions. Inasmuch as both Chrétien and the *Gawain*-poet do not restrict the relevant habitat of the knight to the battlefield but transport their heroes into the domain of human relationships with pitfalls and conflicts of its own, the metaphors of warfare enable them to stake out an area in their romances for unarmed confrontations, while underlining its claim to the knight's fullest attention. The fact that both Yvain and Gawain are too preoccupied with tournaments or the threat of a battle-stroke to give an unblemished performance in this domain has unpleasant consequences for both of them. By slighting these metaphors as mere conventions, the reader can only repeat the mistake of the heroes, who are not alive to their appositeness in suggesting the profound dangers which underlie social interaction.

Surely, this is the point of the most spectacular example of the semiotization of a combat, Gawain's encounter with the Green Knight. In an adventure which retells Gawain's adventures at Castle Hautdesert—the three strokes of the axe representing Gawain's performance during the three temptation scenes—the expected confrontation with a hostile opponent in fact merely recalls Gawain's past, thus relocating the danger Gawain thought he would face on the battleground from which no one has allegedly returned alive, to the apparently safe surroundings of Bertilac's castle. In both *Gawain* and Chrétien's *Yvain*, the most dangerous challenges are those of unarmed conflict.

A sure sign of the modernity of these ideas is the outcry against them by conservative clerics. Denunciations of the courtly knight, who, instead of fighting, devotes his time to pursuing the new-fangled ways of the court, abound in the later Middle Ages. As Georges Duby has shown, the stream of accusations against 'clerical' or effeminate knights, by clerics who were not willing to abandon the doctrine of the three orders as a working hypothesis, was a fruitless attempt to maintain an antiquated ideology.[83] In the late twelfth century Nigel Whiteacre voices his abomination of half-knights, half-clerics, as follows:

Sic igitur sunt in ecclesia clerici sine scientia litterarum, sicut plerique milites sine usu et exercitio armorum, qui etiam nomen habentes ex re vocantur ab aliis Sanctae Mariae.[84]

There are thus many clerics in the Church without a knowledge of letters, just as there are many knights without practice and exercise in arms, who are therefore appropriately nicknamed by others as 'Knights of Saint Mary'.

These outbursts against this new creature, the courtly knight, continued into the fifteenth century. They were perhaps at their loudest during the reign of Richard II, who made fashion, elegance, and refined manners a hallmark of his court.[85] Thomas of Walsingham, for example, had this to say about the huge numbers of clerics and chamber-knights with which Richard II had surrounded himself:

These were more knights of Venus than knights of Bellona, more valiant in the bedchamber than on the field, armed with words rather than weapons, prompt in speaking but slow in performing acts of war. These fellows, who are in close association with the King, care nothing for what a knight ought to know.[86]

The indignation about knights who talk rather than fight in this period still echoes the protests by Cador and Kay in Wace's *Brut* and Chrétien's *Perceval*.[87] But, despite the alarm of conservative

[83] *Three Orders*, 54–5.
[84] *Tractatus contra curiales et officiales clericos*, ed. A. Boutemy (Paris, 1959), 222.
[85] Patricia J. Eberle, 'The Politics of Courtly Style at the Court of Richard II', in *The Spirit of the Court*, ed. G. S. Burgess and Robert A. Taylor (Woodbridge, 1985), 168–78, and Lee Patterson, 'Court Politics and the Invention of Literature: The Case of Sir John Clanvowe', in *Culture and History 1350–1600: Essays on English Communities, Identities and Writing*, ed. David Aers (New York, 1992), 7–41.
[86] *Historia Anglicana*, quoted in Eberle, 'The Politics of Courtly Style', 176. On the suspicions aroused by the chamber knights and court-clerics at Richard's court see also Chris Given-Wilson, *The Royal Household and the King's Affinity: Service, Politics and Finance in England 1360–1413* (New Haven, Conn., 1986), 153, 182.
[87] A difference is perhaps the greater awareness in the fourteenth century that self-restraint and *courtoisie* have political implications. As Eberle has shown, the alarm among English writers about Richard's 'courtly style' bears out an awareness of the connections between *courtoisie*, subjection, and dependence on the ruler. That at a time when courtliness was being busily attacked or defended as a political issue the *Gawain*-poet should place so much emphasis on this value perhaps suggests his sympathies for, or involvement with, the royal court.

clerics, the knights of Chrétien talk more than, or at least as much as, they fight. As we have seen in the previous chapter, theirs is not the cult of 'manliness' espoused by contemporaries. Indeed, the hero of *Gawain* is a clear example of a knight who is demonstrably 'feminized'. Judging from some of the sources and analogues which I have indicated for *Gawain*—the Maiden's Quest in *Yvain* for Gawain's lament in the Wild Forest, the discreet damsels in *Yvain* and *Lancelot* for his tactful way of dealing with the Lady of the Castle—the knight's behaviour seems to have been modelled on that of women. And while Nigel Whiteacre says knights look on half-knights, half-clerics with disdain and scornfully refer to them as 'Knights of Saint Mary', the hero of courtly romance adopts the title with pride. Gawain carries her image on his shield, and without a hint of mockery the *Gawain*-poet calls him 'Mary's Knight' (1796). The fusion of *chevalerie* and *clergie* is welcomed rather than criticized by Wace, Chrétien, and the *Gawain*-poet.

The amalgamation of clerical and chivalric ideals in the figure of the courtly knight, the knight's dramatization of courtly etiquette, and the semiotization of martial language: all bear witness to the way in which Chrétien and the *Gawain*-poet were reshaping an ideology which up to the twelfth century still equated the *miles* with a warrior. The changes in their romances mark not so much an escape from reality, but rather a positive response to the changes which the later Middle Ages witnessed when princes, with the help of alliances with the bourgeoisie and a clerical bureaucracy, were able to institute more efficient governments. They managed to minimize internal warfare, and to clamp down on the relative independence of their vassals. As a result we witness in this period a growth of the institution of the court around which gravitated an increasing number of clerics and noblemen thrown into dependence on the ruler's favour.[88] The *translatio* of the traditional *bellator* and his way of life into an ideal of the courtly knight who is pacified, well-mannered, and diplomatic is perhaps best regarded as an effort—in which clerics such as Chrétien and the *Gawain*-poet played their part—to adapt a chivalric ideology to the demands of a changing society, and to make these adaptations attractive.[89]

[88] Duby, *Three Orders*, 324.

[89] Cf. Jean Frappier, 'Vues sur les conceptions courtoises dans les littératures d'oc et de oïl au douzième siècle', *CCM* 2 (1959), 135–56, at 149, and Eugene Vance, 'Signs of the City: Medieval Poetry as Detour', *NLH* 4 (1973), 557–74, at 571.

The later Middle Ages witnessed continual reinterpretations of chivalry that attempted to bring it up to date with the emergence of relatively pacific states. Historians have focused on the transformation of the tournament, formerly a practice for war, into a spectacle and a game,[90] the transformation of the chivalric duel as a means of settling private disputes into a 'regularized, ritualized, beautified' form of judgement supervised by the king,[91] or the metamorphosis of the order of knighthood, traditionally a military alliance which cut across national boundaries, into ways of cementing political allegiances which would strengthen the ruler's position.[92] Within this context, the romances of Chrétien and the *Gawain*-poet appear not to escape from history or to work against its tides, but to be riding on its waves.

Mercantilism in Romance

One of the orders of knighthood, instituted to strengthen the monarch's hold on power, was the Order of the Garter, founded by Edward III, who had gathered around his court substantial numbers of clerical administrators, merchants, and money-lenders. Edward III and, after him, Richard II were responsible for the social advancement of merchants. Indeed, they went so far as to confer knighthood on a number of them.[93] Since knights in their turn became engaged in mercantile activities, it becomes impossible to maintain 'merchant' and 'knight' as completely distinct social categories.[94]

[90] Jacques Heers, *Fêtes, jeux et joutes dans les sociétés d'Occident à la fin du Moyen-Âge* (Montreal, 1971), 79. As Larry D. Benson has shown, the direction of the tournament's change from a practice for war to a festival seems to have been dictated by Chrétien's romances: 'The Tournament in the Romances of Chrétien de Troyes and *L'Histoire de Guillaume de Maréchal*', in *Chivalric Literature: Essays on Relations between Literature and Life in the Later Middle Ages*, ed. Larry D. Benson and John Leyerle (Kalamazoo, Mich., 1980), 1–24.
[91] Victoria L. Weiss, 'Knightly Conventions in *Sir Gawain and the Green Knight*', doctoral dissertation (Lehigh University, Penn, 1977), 111.
[92] Malcolm Vale, *War and Chivalry* (London, 1981), 35–8.
[93] The presence of merchants and money-lenders becomes a particularly salient characteristic of the English royal court at the end of Edward III's reign. The English kings of the fourteenth century themselves became members of guilds. See Sylvia Thrupp, *The Merchant Class of Medieval London* (Chicago, 1948), 31, and Given-Wilson, *The Royal Household*, 153.
[94] J. Vale, *Edward III*, 63, 75.

In twelfth-century France the line which separated the two classes was already beginning to blur. Like the Kings of England, the Counts of Flanders and Champagne conferred considerable privileges on merchants and urban communities from whom they derived handsome revenues. It was partly because they recognized the profitability of a prosperous economic climate that they were able to consolidate their authority within their principalities. Moreover, even as early as the twelfth century we have evidence that knights themselves turned to trade. Others were related to the third estate by descent or marriage.[95] Does courtly romance reflect this gradual breakdown of social barriers between the knight and the merchant? On the debatable assumption that courtly romance shudders at social developments which were undermining the position of the feudal nobility, this question has generally been answered negatively. With some notable exceptions,[96] critics who have asked themselves the question have argued that commerce and economics are either excluded or vilified in romance.[97]

For many courtly romances, this view does not stand up to scrutiny. In *Floris and Blanchefleur* or the Tristan legends, the knights often disguise themselves as merchants. In part, the reason for this lies in the anonymity and mobility of the merchant and his reputation as a clever rhetorician. But, as Madeleine Cosman has pointed out, the merchant disguises are also sure signs of the respectability which the merchant had gained.[98] In Gottfried's *Tristan*, the 'Koufman' belongs to the group of 'edelez herzen' whom Gottfried addresses. Thomas D'Angleterre interrupts his story about Caerdin, whom Tristan sends to England as a merchant in disguise to contact Ysolt, to acclaim the flourishing commercial centre of England:

[95] Evergates, *Feudal Society*, 117, 125–6.
[96] Vance, 'Chrétien's *Yvain*', and Mann, 'Price and Value'. A monograph which tends to view commerce in *Gawain* negatively, but contains a useful appendix of words in *Gawain* drawn from the commercial sphere is Shoaf's *The Poem as Green Girdle*. Judith Kellogg believes that Chrétien's romances promote mercantile values despite the author's intentions: *Medieval Artistry and Exchange: Economic Institutions, Society, and Literary Form in Old French Narrative* (New York, 1989), 73–112. I acknowledge a major debt to these studies.
[97] See, for example, Köhler, *Ideal and Wirklichkeit*, 18, and David Aers, ' "In Arthurus Day": Community, Virtue and Individual Identity in *Sir Gawain and the Green Knight*', in his *Community, Gender and Individual Identity: English Writing 1360–1430* (London, 1988), 153–78.
[98] Madeleine Pelner Cosman, *The Education of the Hero in Arthurian Romance* (Chapel Hill, NC, 1966), 30.

Lundres est mult riche cité.

. . . .

Le recovrer est de Engleterre:
Avant d'iloc ne l'estuet querre.
Al pé del mur li curt Tamise;
Par la vent la marchandise
De tutes les teres qui sunt
U marcheant cristien vunt.
Li hume i sunt de grant engin.   (*Tristan*, 1379–91)

London is a very rich city . . . It is the treasury of England, there is no need to seek further than it. At the foot of its walls runs the Thames. It conveys the merchandise from all countries where Christian merchants go. The people there are very wise.

Certainly we find nothing in this romance, in all likelihood written by a cleric at the court of Henry II, which suggests any hostility to the 'marcheant'. The fact that, on a diplomatic mission to France, Edward III likewise opted for the disguise of a merchant,[99] perhaps in imitation of the heroes of the Tristan romances, only goes to show that the esteem in which merchants were held by Thomas D'Angleterre was not short-lived.

This esteem was by no means universal. John W. Baldwin's research has shown how clerics of this period harboured and perpetuated the traditional ecclesiastical suspicions about the merchant's pursuit of gain.[100] The Church Fathers take considerable glee in imagining the horrors of the merchant at sea, powerless against the onslaught of the winds and the waves:

Mercatores a negotiationibus periculosa transfretatione maris lucella quaerentes. Sollicita vita hominum, inquieta conversatio, et quodam semper in turbine, ventis ipsis mobilior quibus volvitur, et huc atque illuc saepe jactatur. Utique accusatis crebra naufragia, quis vos navigare compellit? (Ambrose, *De Elia et Jejunio*, cap. 19)[101]

You merchants, seeking profit from your trading in the dangerous crossing of the sea! How worrying is the life of these men, how restless their walk of life, always in turmoil, more changeable than the winds that shake them and that cast them hither and thither. Of course, you complain about the many shipwrecks, but who compels you to sail?

[99] May McKisack, *The Fourteenth Century*, Oxford History of England (Oxford, 1959), 111–12. See Froissart's *Méliador*, ed. A. Longnon (Paris, 1895–9), ll. 11817–12616, for another late occurrence of the motif of the merchant disguise.

[100] John W. Baldwin, *Masters, Princes and Servants: The Social Views of Peter the Chanter and his Circle*, 2 vols. (Princeton, NJ, 1970), i. 261–3.

[101] PL 14, col. 722.

St Augustine never tires of repeating similar representations of the merchant at sea, adding some detail about the merchant's fruitless exclamations:

exclamas in mari exagitatibus tempestate, Deus libera me! Non audis respondentem, Quare? Misi te? Avaritia tibi iussit ut acquireres quod non habebas . . . (Augustine, serm. 164, cap. iv)[102]

you exclaim in the upheavals of a storm at sea: 'God save me'. You do not hear his response. Why? Did I send you there? Avarice commanded you to acquire what you did not yet have . . .

Similar diatribes were repeated by clerics like Peter the Chanter in the later Middle Ages, and even became a fit subject for elegant poetry.[103]

With this background in mind I wish to turn to *Guillaume d'Angleterre* by an author who introduces himself as 'Crestiens', and who may be Chrétien de Troyes.[104] The story tells of the separation and the final reunion of Guillaume, his wife, and their two sons. On God's command Guillaume leaves his kingdom and after many misfortunes he finds employment in the service of a rich burgher who entrusts him with some money so that Guillaume can carry on his trade independently. On one venture, Guillaume and his fellows are surprised by a sudden storm at open sea. Tossed about by the high waves, they call on God for help:

> Vers Dieu merci nous amplaidiez,
> Qu'il ait de nous misericorde
> Et mete antre ces vans acorde,
> Qui por noiant nous contralient,
> Aus guerroient et nous ocient.
> An ceste mer ont grant pooir
> Cis vant, bien le peut an savoir,
> Seignor an sont, bien i apert;
> Qui que leur outrage compert,

---

[102] This and some other tirades against merchants, drawn mainly from Augustine's sermons, have been brought together by Sister Marie Madeleine Getty, *The Life of the North Africans as Revealed in the Sermons of St Augustine* (Washington, DC, 1931), 12–17.

[103] See Marbod of Rennes's poem 'Dissuasio navigationis ob lucrum', PL 171, col. 1723, and Baldwin, *Masters*, 262.

[104] Critical opinion remains divided on the question whether this 'Crestiens' is to be identified as Chrétien de Troyes. The recent editor of *Guillaume* regards the question as undecidable: A. J. Holden, *Chrétien: Guillaume d'Angleterre*, TLF (Geneva, 1988), 35.

Il n'i avront ja nul domaige;
Nous mar veïsmes lor outraige,
De ce dom il font lor deduit
Seromes nous mort et destruit.
Aussi font or li vant lor guerre
Com font li baron de la terre,
Qui de ce dom il se deduient
Ardent la terre et la destruient;
Aus barons puet an comparer
Les vans et la terre a la mer,
Que par aus est troublez li mondes,
Si com cil vans troublent cez ondes.
(Guillaume, 2292–312)

Let us turn towards God for mercy, so that he may take pity on us and calm these winds which harmfully fight and battle against us, and are killing us. Over this sea the winds hold great power—that is easy to see—they clearly are its lords. He who incurs their wrath will never be released from it. To our misfortune we see their outrages; while they make merry, death and destruction fall on us. And the winds make war like the barons of the land, who for their amusement set fire to the country and destroy it. The barons may be compared to the winds and the country to the sea, for due to them the world is in turmoil, just as the sea is in turmoil because of the winds.

There are clear parallels between this passage and the representations of the avaricious merchant endlessly reiterated by the Church Fathers: the merchant harassed by wind and water, calling on God for mercy. Moreover, having outlined this initial situation, Crestien, like Ambrose, proceeds to allegorize the winds, but this time in a way which seems to turn a long anti-mercantile tradition on its head. The waves symbolize not the merchant's restless existence and insatiable desires, but are likened to the barons of the land, who, by continually fighting among each other, destroy the people and lay waste the realm. The author's sympathies in this passage clearly do not lie with the feudal lords. Crestien puts down all the troubles of this world to them. He instead sides whole-heartedly with the merchants whose welfare is undermined by baronial hawkishness.

On whichever side of the common authorship question one comes down, it is notable that Chrétien de Troyes, too, abstains from airing the traditional hostility against merchants. His romances actually display a vivid interest in matters of finance.[105] Prices in his

---

[105] See the section on commerce and trade, and metaphors of commerce, in Ruck, *Index*, 17–18, 69.

romances are calculated in a variety of currencies: the silver mark (*Erec*, 2808), the Angevin penny (*Lancelot*, 1273), while the thirty bushels of money on display at Erec's coronation are in sterling (*Erec*, 6629–32). Living, as Chrétien probably did, in Troyes, whose fairs attracted merchants from all over Europe, these currencies may well have passed through his hands personally. In trying to convey the affluence of a town, Chrétien draws on his experience of these fairs to describe the cornucopia of goods:

> Bien poïst an et dire et croire
> qu'an la vile eüst toz jorz foire,
> qui de tant d'avoir estoit plainne,
> de cire, de poivre et de grainne
> et de panes veires et grises
> et de totes marcheandises. (*Perceval*, 5711–16)[106]

One might plausibly say and believe that the town had its fair every day, so well stocked was it, with wax, pepper, scarlet cloths, with vair and grey furs, and all kinds of merchandise.

Only in one episode in Chrétien's *Perceval* do merchants come under attack, not from Chrétien, but from Meliant and his supporters, who have set up a tournament. When Gawain refuses to join in, they accuse him of being a merchant in chivalric disguise, who is trying to evade taxes, and to sell his arms for gain (*Perceval*, 4846). But, as Paule le Rider has rightly pointed out, their taunts at the merchant can hardly be taken at face value.[107] The tournament, organized by Meliant *cum suis* to bring about Thibaut's destruction—'ils les volsist toz destruire' (4865)—gives those who sneer at what they believe to be a merchant the opportunity to plunder the corpses on the battlefield for 'gaaing' (5104). This word reverberates throughout the passage to remind the reader of the rapacious greed of Meliant and his fellows-in-arms. Thanks to Gawain, who joins in the tournament the next day, Thibaut defeats his opponents. The episode is thus designed not only to demonstrate the inappropriateness of their aspersions on Gawain or merchants, but also to bring home their applicability to those who cast them.

In the same romance, merchants actually prove their use when they rescue Blanchefleur's besieged castle from starvation by deliver-

---

[106] Cf. *Lancelot*, 1480–5.
[107] Paule le Rider, 'L'Auteur et son personnage', in *Le Chevalier dans le Conte du Graal* (Paris, 1978), 243–5.

ing an abundance of goods. Due to aristocratic contentiousness, the town is reduced to dire straits. Fortunately a group of merchants, who, like Guillaume and his companions in *Guillaume d'Angleterre*, have survived the 'patristic' storm at sea, arrive with an enormous cargo of provisions (2522–5). They are jubilantly welcomed by the inhabitants, and well paid for their merchandise:

> Or ont bien fet lor besoigne
> cel qui achatent et qui vandent. (*Perceval*, 2554–5)

Now they who buy and sell have done their business well.

Chrétien gives the standard medieval definition of merchants as those who sell what they buy, in distinction to artisans, who only sell what they buy after improving the product. In the absence of such obvious labour, clerics condemned merchants for selling not labour but time, which belongs to God.[108] As Baldwin's research shows, it was only from the twelfth century onwards that a moral justification of the merchant's occupation was undertaken, most lucidly by Thomas of Chobham.[109] According to Thomas, the supply of goods from places of abundance to places of scarcity provided the merchant with a rightful claim to profit and respectability. I quote from his *Summa*, where, after distinguishing the merchant from the artisan, he explains why trade should be considered a viable option for laymen:

Hoc [commercium] autem bene licet laicis, etiam si nullam emendationem apponant rebus quas prius emerunt et postea vendunt. Aliter enim multus defectus esset in multibus regionibus, quia mercatores de eo quod abundat in uno loco usque in alium locum in quo eiusdem rei est egestas deferunt. (Thomas of Chobham, *Summa*)[110]

This form of commerce is therefore allowed to laymen, even if they do not improve the things that they first bought and then sell. Otherwise there would be great scarcity in some regions, because merchants bring goods that abound in one place to another place where these goods are scarce.

We cannot know for sure whether Chrétien was aware of these apologies for merchants which started to appear in his lifetime. At

[108] Jacques Le Goff, 'Temps de l'église et temps du marchand', in his *Pour un autre Moyen-Age* (Paris, 1977), 46–65.

[109] See also Hugh of St Victor, *Didascalicon*, trans. Jerome Taylor (New York, 1961), 76–7, and Baldwin, *Masters*, 265.

[110] Ed. F. Broomfield (Louvain, 1968), 301. Thomas of Chobham's defence of merchants soon became commonplace. It was incorporated in Peraldus' *Summa vitiorum*, and hence into Chaucer's *Parson's Tale* (777–9).

any rate, his conception of the value of merchants is very similar. They supply Blanchefleur's castle with the food that rescues its inhabitants from starvation, thus adding another proud victory in the merchant's war against shortages.

The implicit admiration for merchants in the episode from the *Perceval* was not lost on Chrétien's continuators. In the *Second Continuation*, Perceval returns to Castle Beaurepaire, which has by this stage become a thriving city. Among the inhabitants, there is a community of merchants to which the poet devotes particular attention:

> Dedanz les murs grant ville avoit,
> Qui noblement pueplee estoit
> De chevaliers et de sergenz,
> De borjois et de marcheanz,
> Larges, cortois et bien apris,
> Qui vandoient et vair et gris
> . . . .
> Espices de maintes manieres,
> Qui precïeuses sont et chieres.
> De tot ce i ot tel planté
> Qu'ainz an chastel ne an cité
> N'oï l'an d'autelle parler.
> (*Second Continuation*, 22583–99)

Within the walls there was a great town, nobly populated by knights, sergeants, artisans, and merchants, liberal, courtly, and well-educated, who sold vair and grey fur . . . and spices of many kinds that were precious and dear. There was such abundance in the town that I have never heard of a castle or city to match it.

Having ensured that Beaurepaire survives Chrétien's fiction, the merchants have here brought the city to prosperity, an achievement with which the narrator is clearly impressed. Perhaps the most significant word with which he qualifies the merchants is 'cortois'. Traditionally used exclusively to refer to clerics or knights, the word in the *Second Continuation* has a wider application, including the 'borjois' and 'marcheanz'.[111] The next time Perceval returns to

---

[111] The extension of the word 'courtois' to include the third order is a widespread thirteenth-century development that also affects its Latin and English counterparts. On the Latin word *curialis*, see Zotz, '*Urbanitas*', 436–7. The change in the English 'curtais' is well illustrated by *Floris and Blauncheflur* (*c.*1250), which consistently rhymes 'curtais' with 'burgais' in ll. 133–4, 183–4, 319–20, 659–60 of MS Cambridge UL, Gg. iv. 27.2 (the C version), ed. F. C. de Vries (Groningen, 1966).

Blanchefleur's Castle, in Gerbert de Montreuil's *Continuation* of about 1230, the town is as flourishing a commercial centre as ever:

> Ce samble uns paradis terrestres;
> Par terre getent le tapis,
> Ne lor chaut s'il en valent pis;
> Chevalier et clerc et borjois
> Se perent de pales d'orfrois.
> Cil fil a ces borjois bohordent,
> Cointement s'acesment et hordent . . .
>
> (*Fourth Continuation*, 6314-20)

It seems a terrestrial paradise. They put carpets on the ground, not caring if this diminished their value. Knights, clerics, and burghers were decked out in gold-embroidered clothes. The sons of the burghers jousted, and acquitted themselves well and fought with dexterity.

As we follow the history of Beaurepaire through *Perceval* and its later continuations, the tradesmen, already instrumental for the town's well-being in Chrétien's romance, seem to rise progressively in the poets' esteem. They are joyously welcomed in *Perceval*. In the *Second Continuation* the 'marcheanz cortois' have settled at Beaurepaire and have turned the town into a horn of plenty. In the final continuation their sons show off their skills in 'bohordes', which makes them among the first to have infiltrated an activity previously reserved for the professional warrior.[112]

But, like *Sir Gawain*, the romances of Chrétien de Troyes engage with mercantilism not by turning chivalric romances into romances about merchants but by bringing commercial values into play at the heart of the knight's activities. In order to show how they do this, I wish to examine Chrétien's *Yvain* in conjunction with *Gawain*. One of the most striking ingredients in these romances is the continual exchange of services, gifts, pledges, and battle-strokes. In Chrétien's *Yvain*, Lunete, grateful for the honour Yvain has once shown her, in turn protects Yvain when an angry mob attempts to find their lord's murderer. As Chrétien emphasizes, Lunete stands out for her willingness to reciprocate services done to her or to initiate such exchanges. She is 'de grant foi et de grant aïe' (2413). Thus we find her paying back her debt to Yvain by doing all she can to serve him.

[112] The 'bohordes' were loosely organized tournaments. See N. Denholm Young, 'The Tournament in the Thirteenth Century', in *Studies in Medieval History Presented to F. M. Powicke* (Oxford, 1948), 240-68, at 249.

> Quan qu'ele puet vers lui *s'aquite*
> de l'enor qu'il li avoit feite.
> (*Yvain*, 1284–5; italics mine)[113]

When she can, she pays him back the honour that he has done her.

In this episode, where Yvain is in hiding, the commercial vocabulary which will henceforth permeate the romance begins to take shape. When she procures the first reconciliation between Laudine and him, Chrétien writes:

> La dameisele qui fu brete,
> fu de lui servir an espans,
> si le fist *creance* et *despans*
> de tot quan que il li covint.
> (*Yvain*, 1584–7; italics mine)[114]

The thoughtful damsel was eager to serve him, and to give him everything on credit and at her expense, whenever he needed it.

Lunete expends her efforts on Yvain on credit. Having repaid the debt outstanding to her, she now obliges Yvain in the expectation of eventual repayment. In this way Chrétien enmeshes his characters from the outset in a nexus of economic exchange which leaves one party indebted to another.

The first beheading game in *Sir Gawain and the Green Knight* also puts in motion a dynamics of debt and repayment. The contract, the 'couenaunt', of the beheading game stipulates that he who strikes a blow must receive one a year later. As critics of the romance have pointed out, the *Gawain*-poet exploits the commercial implications of an exchange of blows to the full.[115] The first stroke, for example, is envisaged as a service on credit, whose debt will be settled a year later:

> 'I may be funde vpon folde, and foch þe such *wages*
> As þou deles me to-day bifore þis douþe ryche.'   (396–7)

Chrétien de Troyes frequently describes the blows of opponents as a commercial exchange as well. Note the 'exchanges' in *Cligés*:

> Molt sont andui li vasal *large*
> De cos *doner* a grant planté,
> S'a chascun boene volanté
> De tost *randre* ce qu'il *acroit*,
> Ne cil ne cist ne s'an recroit,

---

[113] Cf. T-L s.v. 'acquiter', col. 487.
[114] Cf. T-L s.v. 'creance', col. 1019, and s.v. 'despens', cols. 1686–7.
[115] Shoaf, *The Poem as Green Girdle*, 50.

Que tot sanz *conte* et sanz mesure
Ne *rande chetel* et *ousure*
Li uns a l'autre sanz respit.
(*Cligés*, 4034–41; italics mine)

The vassals are very generous in giving each other things in great plenty, and each is willing to return immediately what he has received. Neither the one nor the other refuses to return promptly the goods plus interest without counting or measuring.

But although these commercial metaphors amply display the poet's mastery of artful conceits, they do not give the reader any particular insight into the similarities between the experiences of the merchant and the knight. Whereas for the merchant the settlement of a debt may be painful, and the fulfilment of his part of the contract in 'boene volanté' admirable, the question of 'boene volanté' is not really at issue in Cligés's combat. Repayment here takes the form of returning the blows of one's opponent. In settling this kind of debt the warrior does not face the moral dilemma of the merchant who must act against his immediate interest when he has to repay a loan with interest. In fact, the warrior does not face a dilemma of 'volanté' at all. In hitting back he merely acts on his instincts.[116] As Eugene Vance has written, the ethics of the *bellator* is one of coercive or compulsive exchange, rather than an 'ethics founded on freedom of consent'.[117]

Gawain, too, must fulfil his part of the bargain, but not by dealing out payment in the form of a blow but by receiving it. The mercantile metaphors in *Gawain* are therefore not merely fanciful. Like the merchant who owes a debt that may cost him dearly, Gawain is bound by a contractual obligation to which he has freely consented, but which requires him to act against his impulses. Moreover, in the absence of any compulsion by physical force, the basis for Gawain's or the merchant's compliance is not self-preservation but a personal respect for the contracts they have sealed.

Contractual obligations of this kind continue to occupy Gawain and Yvain. When, in the opening of *Yvain*, Lunete lends her service on credit, Yvain must reciprocate by repaying her this debt. He frees Lunete from the stake, and when next Lunete does Yvain a good

[116] Note Perceval's automatic response when Gornemant asks him what he would do if someone struck him: 'Amis, se vos ancontrïez | uns chevaliers, que ferïez | si'l vos feroit?—Jel referroie' ('Friend, if you were to meet a knight, and he would hit you, what would you do?—I would hit him back': *Perceval*, 1507–9).
[117] 'Chrétien's *Yvain*', 49.

turn by reconciling him for the second time with Laudine, the two
meditate on the question who owes whom after these dealings:

> 'Certes, ma dolce amie,
> ce ne vos porroie je mie
> *guerredoner*, en nule guise . . .'
> —Sire, fet ele, or ne vos chaille;
> ne ja n'en soiez an espans
> qu'assez avroiz pooir et tans
> a feire bien moi et autrui.
> Se je ai fet ce que je *dui*,
> si m'an doit an tel gré savoir
> con celi qui autrui avoir
> *anprunte*, et puis si le *repaie*.   (*Yvain*, 6685–91)

'Certainly, my sweet friend, I can never repay you in any way . . .'—Sir, she
says, not to worry. Do not be anxious about it, for you will have plenty of
possibilities and opportunities to return the favour to me or someone else.
If I have done what I owe you, then you are no more indebted to me than
to someone who borrows from a person and then pays him back.

To adopt Lunete's metaphors, the relationship between Yvain and
Laudine hinges on a series of business transactions in which the two
borrow, and repay their dues. In his continual quest to offer his
services and to repay those of others Yvain must prove his trust-
worthiness so as to restore the credit he has lost in an earlier breach
of contract with Laudine. Like a tradesman, he becomes aware in
the course of the romance of the importance of delivering his goods
in time. As various characters in the romance invest their trust in the
Knight of the Lion, Yvain hastens from adventure to adventure to
live up to these investments. As he explains to Gawain's relatives:

> sachiez bien certainnement
> que volentiers et boenemant,
> se trop n'eüsse grant besoing
> et mes afeires ne fust loing,
> demorasse encor une piece.   (*Yvain*, 4033–7)

you should know that I would willingly and gladly stay a bit longer, if it was
not for the fact that I have some very important business to do and my
affairs take me far from here.

The potential commercial overtones of the words 'besoing' and
'afeires' underline the affinity of Yvain and the merchant.[118]

---

[118] Cf. T-L s.v. 'afaire', col. 168 and s.v. 'besoigne', col. 945.

In *Sir Gawain*, this affinity between the hero and the merchant is even more explicit. In a second contract between Gawain and his host, the two arrange to exchange their winnings on three consecutive days. On each occasion the exchange is discussed as a commercial transaction. I quote the host and Gawain's words on the third day of business:

> 'Bi Kryst', quoþ þat oþer knyȝt, 'ȝe cach much sele
> In cheuisaunce of þis chaffer, ȝif ȝe hade goud chepez.'
> 'ȝe, of þe chepe no charg,' quoþ chefly þat oþer,
> 'As is pertly payed þe chepez þat I aȝte.'   (1938–41)

In describing relations of interdependence, such as those between Yvain and Lunete, or Gawain and his host, in which voluntary adherence to the agreed rules replaces compliance wrested by force, it is natural, perhaps inevitable, that mercantile language is brought to bear on the knight. Like the merchant, the knight must under these circumstances honestly abide by the contract; he must keep a good bargain.

Laudine, too, involves the hero in a contractual agreement. She allows Yvain to leave her for one year in pursuit of feats of arms, but he must give his word to return. In response to his question about whether the terms of the contract take account of any delays brought about by *force majeure* such as physical injury, Laudine lends him a ring which will protect him from any harm:

> Mes or metroiz an vostre doi
> cest mien anel, que je vos *prest*;
> et de la pierre quex ele est
> vos voel dire tot en apert:
> prison ne tient ne sanc ne pert
> nus amanz verais et leax,
> ne avenir ne li puet max . . .
>   (*Yvain*, 2602–8; italics mine)

Now put this ring on your finger. It is mine, and I will lend it to you. Let me tell you about the stone in it. No true and loyal lover can be taken prisoner or shed blood, and nothing bad can happen to him . . .

Some intriguing similarities exist between Yvain's situation and that of Gawain, who accepts from the Lady a love-gift which also has the power to preserve the bearer from harm:

> 'For quat gome so is gorde with þis grene lace,
> While he hit hade hemely halched aboute,

> Þer is no haþel vnder heuen tohewe hym þat myȝt,
> For he myȝt not be slayn for slyȝt vpon erþe.' (1851–4)

The crucial correspondence lies not in the talismans, but in the fact that neither Gawain nor Yvain may keep these gifts. Gawain owes his winnings to the host. Yvain must return the gift in a year's time to Laudine, for it is not a keepsake, but a loan.

When he overstays and fails to hand the ring back, Laudine's messenger points out to Yvain that he has violated the contract. The terms of her accusation make it absolutely clear that Chrétien wishes us to consider Yvain's failure to return to Laudine as an illegal withdrawal from an economy of loans and restitutions. While Laudine has invested her heart in him, Yvain has failed to return to pay up. Unlike the loyal lover who takes care of his lady's heart, and then gives it back—'et si le raporte' (2743)—Yvain has kept it in illegal possession, and thus proved himself a hypocritical thief—a 'larron ipocrite' (2739). It remains for the messenger to demand the restitution of the ring, the symbol of the heart Yvain has had on loan but has omitted to return.

> 'Par moi que ci an presant voiz
> [Laudine] te mande que tu li envoiz:
> rant li, qu'a randre le t'estuet.' (*Yvain*, 2773–5)

'Through me, whom you see present here, Laudine asks you to return it. Hand it back, for do so you must.'

Note the legal tone which Chrétien strikes as he has the maiden explain the legal technicality that in Laudine's absence she acts as her representative.

Gawain, too, is found guilty of failing to return to his host a gift which was not his to keep. At the Chapel, the Green Knight, alias Bertilac, points out to Gawain that the article of clothing he is wearing belongs to him by right:

> For hit is my wede þat þou weres, þat ilke wouen girdel . . . (2358)

Belatedly, Gawain now offers to part from the girdle, accusing himself, as the messenger accuses Yvain, of 'trecherye and vntrawþe' (2384).

Both *Yvain* and *Gawain* may deal exclusively with knights, but they impress on their readers and their heroes a moral which would have meant as much to the merchant as to the knight:

'Trwe mon trwe restore,
Þenne þar mon drede no waþe.' (2354–5)

Given this interplay and overlap between commercial and chivalric discourses in the romances of Chrétien and the *Gawain*-poet, it
may be time to abandon the tenacious supposition that their romances sought to transport a threatened class of feudal knights into a
realm of fairy, secure from the corrosive influences of efficient
government and the growth of a profit-economy. As far as the
historical evidence goes, the fact that Chrétien and the *Gawain*-poet
were probably clerics at the court of kings and counts who were
actively promoting these developments, such a claim seems highly
unlikely. On the evidence of their romances, the importance these
poets attach to the cleric's pacific virtues of introspection, refinement, and self-restraint seems rather to point towards the private
governance of the individual which increasingly centralized states
were demanding of their subjects. In the process of grafting these
virtues on to the *miles pugnans*, their substitution of an ethic which
extorts obedience by force by an ethic of exchange based on a
self-imposed adherence to contracts follows as a logical consequence. I see, for these reasons, no wistful escapism in the romances of Chrétien or the *Gawain* poet, but a rigorous redefinition
of knighthood which enabled them to adjust the fictional knight,
and hence the knights who would have listened to their romances,
to the changing times.

Conclusion

Sir Gawain and the Green Knight is a conventional romance, deeply rooted in the tradition of the Old French *roman courtois*, which, thanks to the literary tastes of contemporary noblemen and merchants, had been kept alive and well in fourteenth-century England. The *Gawain*-poet's assertion that 'Mony aunterez here-biforn | Haf fallen suche er þis' (2527–8) is as near as we get to the author's own assessment of the relation between his own romance and those of his predecessors, but it suggests a consciousness of the sum of past 'aunterez' of which he believed his own romance to form a part. It has been notoriously difficult for modern readers to understand the *Gawain*-poet's comfortable sense of belonging, and I cannot see how we ever will if we do not familiarize ourselves with its sources and analogues, compare their themes and motifs, their narrative technique, their morality, and their design on the world outside the text.

This is what I have tried to do in the previous chapters, which have followed Gawain as he travels reluctantly through the wilderness, arrives at the castle where he is courteously received, is tested and tempted in the bedroom, as he faces the dilemmas posed by the Lady and the guide, until, at the Green Chapel, he awakens to the realization of failure and the awareness of guilt. At each stage I have documented the *Gawain*-poet's indebtedness to the Old French courtly romances, in particular to those by Chrétien de Troyes. What unites their representations of their fictional characters and the world in which they move is the interest they take in cultural progress and civilized interaction. We have seen the aesthetic glory of the castles they describe, the elaborate etiquette of hospitality and the art of conversation, and the delicate feel for tact exhibited by Gawain or the damsels of Chrétien's *Yvain* and *Lancelot* as they attempt to save the Lady of the Castle or the chivalric heroes from embarrassment. And as there is civilization in their romances, we find in them rudeness and chaos, be it in the Wild Forest, the court's inverted mirror image where lawlessness and hardships reign supreme, or in the person of the Challenger, who refuses to take the slightest notice of the rules of hospitality that might protect guest and host from the ambivalent and potentially explosive situation of strangers obtruding on strangers.

There is no denying that, in representing politeness and rudeness, the *Gawain*-poet was following conventions that can be found in many courtly romances, as well as in the courtesy books with which they share a significant but underexplored common ground. This conventionality, as I have emphasized, must not simply be seen in opposition to self-consciousness, psychological depth, suspense, and historical specificity. If the romances we have looked at are representative, conventional poets seem in fact all the more aware of rules and precedents, and of the imaginative distance that separates author and artefact.[1] Take, for example, the figure of Gawain. As early as the romances of Chrétien a well-defined type of knight is crystallizing. We become aware of his characteristics, fixed or accumulated in an ongoing literary history, but no more so than the romances themselves. His courtesy becomes a fashionable topic for discussion or a conversational gambit in *Gawain* and the romances of Chrétien. His reputation as a lover is as well known to the ladies of the Continuations of the *Perceval* or the Lady of the Castle as to the reader. We have also seen how Chrétien invokes previous hospitality episodes when he describes Calogrenant's uneventful sojourn with his host in *Yvain* in order to raise and defeat the expectations of his protagonist and his audience that hospitality will be the springboard for adventures of love or prowess. The *Gawain*-poet, too, manipulates his readers by means of previous romance paradigms; so successfully that we quickly forget the dubious status of the green girdle and the strings attached to it, and believe that it might indeed be a talismanic love-gift which Gawain can cling to in good faith and which might save him from his apparently gruesome enemy. As these instances show, the very plausibility of conventions gives them the power to deceive and to mislead.

Nowhere is this potential more evident than in the conventions of politeness with which the characters of courtly romances are all too familiar. When they praise their hosts, make light of their own

---

[1] Cf. Paul Alpers's observations on the subject of pastoral poetry in his 'Convening and Convention in Pastoral Poetry', *NLH* 14 (1983), 277–304.

merits, or put a brave face on their inner turmoil, we frequently see the pains they take to keep up appearances, and to play the roles that high society expects. But lip-service to the standard rules of comportment also allows for more disquieting forms of deceit. In *Sir Gawain*, and in many romances, the gestures of hospitality are a perfect false front for a lethal trap. Poems about the supremacy of control and reflection over instinct, form over matter, verbal diplomacy over physical force, the courtly romances show at times a privileged insight into the discontents of civilization. For conflicts in the *roman courtois* are never less fraught, less dangerous, or less consequential for being unarmed. The Lady of the Castle's seductive arguments and their sources and analogues indicate that pacified transactions present only different kinds of confrontations, in which the heroes of courtly romance prove in effect far more vulnerable than in combat. Where the blows of an opponent usually fail to make them collapse, the false appearances of others, and their own duplicity, usually succeed. Under the pressure of social decorum conflict and dangers do not disappear but go underground or are internalized. Thus, rather than creating characters who are two-dimensional, conventionality, the awareness of how things should be, psychologizes them. Conformity to expected procedures and patterns of behaviour allows the heroes of romance, and their creator, to hide behind appearances. And the possibility that there might be more to them than meets the eye is precisely what makes them come alive.

The insistence in the romances of Chrétien and the *Gawain*-poet on conscience as opposed to fame, on honesty as opposed to honour, adds to the psychological depth of the heroes. Unlike the epic man of honour, whose behaviour is motivated externally by the approval or sanctions of others, Chrétien's heroes and Gawain supervise themselves. Lancelot bears public humiliation but remains determined to follow his heart. Gawain stays committed to a hopeless and senseless mission, ultimately for no other reason than to be honest with himself. The need for continuous self-evaluation comes across forcefully in the motif of confession, which restores the heroes to self-awareness, when their conscience has failed them and they have been plunged into the consequent crisis.

To the modern reader, the themes of self-awareness, confession, and conscience, and the conventions of polite behaviour, discretion, and rudeness may not seem revolutionary. They have since taken hold of literature and life to such an extent that their presence is often regarded as self-explanatory, as it is difficult to imagine them as anything other than traditional elements. Yet they are clearly implicated in historical developments. The ideal of the courtly knight, endowed with a super-ego that translates his impulses into social decorum, and that speaks to him in a voice louder than that of the community of honour, is largely a newcomer to twelfth-century literature. The concern for restraint and *politesse* is likewise a novelty, at least among laymen, as is the concomitant invention of rudeness, implicit in the fantasies of Wild Men or Wild Forests.

Norbert Elias plausibly suggested that for the cultivation of this new sensibility we must look to the court, which gradually transformed once incalcitrant warriors into well-behaved and self-disciplined courtiers. Here instincts had to be sublimated, which left the knight at court with an intimation of the complex relations between face and feelings that led him to psychologize himself and others. Elias's strength was to have seen that courtliness, and, we might add, the figure of the courtly knight, were not just idealistic aspirations but were anchored in social and political realities. Elias focused especially on the gradual domestication of the feudal warrior in the wake of the emergence of centralized and internally pacified states. In the context of his findings, it need not surprise us that the earliest courtly romances, those by Chrétien, were products of and for a court-culture. Over this culture presided the Counts of Champagne and Flanders, whose government and control was surprisingly efficient and tight, and who seem to have appreciated that, in the increasingly complex web of interdependency at their courts, rules of etiquette and deference could help to oil the wheels, and to safeguard their own pre-eminence.[2] I have argued that for the *Gawain*-poet we may envisage a similar milieu. Possibly, he was one of the many Cheshiremen who had flocked to the household of Richard II, whose cult of courtliness drew criticism from many of the *Gawain*-poet's contemporaries.[3] Among these was William Langland, who describes Meed's reception at the court of Westminster in a self-conscious and questioning evocation of the courtly

[2] Georges Duby, *The Three Orders: Feudal Society Imagined*, trans. Arthur Goldhammer (Chicago, 1980), 301–2.

[3] See Patricia J. Eberle, 'The Politics of Courtly Style at the Court of Richard II', in *The Spirit of the Court*, ed. G. S. Burgess and Robert A. Taylor (Woodbridge, 1985), 168–78, and Louise Fradenburg, 'The Manciple's Servant Tongue: Politics and Poetry in the *Canterbury Tales*', *ELH* 82 (1985), 85–118.

atmosphere and elegant alliterative style that is so typical of
Gawain.[4]

> Curteisly the clerk thanne, as the Kyng highte,
> Took Mede bi the myddel and mente hire into chambre.
> Ac ther was murthe and mynstralcie Mede to plese;
> That wonyeth at Westmynstre worshipeth hire alle.
> Gentilliche with joye the justices somme
> Busked hem to the bour ther the burde dwellede,
> Conforted hyre kyndely by Clergies leve . . .
>
> (*Piers Plowman*, III. 9–15)

If we set any store by Langland's gift for discerning the institutional
attachments of literary styles—an issue recently discussed by James
Simpson[5]—then the passage gives us some confirmation of Michael
Bennett's thesis about the intimate link between courtly alliterative
poetry, including *Gawain*, and the royal court.

The court's social structure, however, cannot adequately explain
the emergence of ideas of politeness and self-discipline alone, as
Elias thought. For they seem to have had their origin not at court but
in the monastic ideals of *disciplina* and deliberative comportment.[6]
And, as the passage from *Piers* seems to suggest, in accounting for
their spread beyond the walls of the monastery to secular courts we
have to reckon with the role of the curial 'clerk'. Research continues
to show that, from the twelfth to the sixteenth century, the transmission of courtliness and civility depended on the mediation of
clerics.[7] As debates between the *miles* and the *clericus* insist, refinement and *politesse* flowed from the cleric, the educator at court, to
the layman. In school-texts, such as the *Facetus* or the *Urbanus*,
soon available in vernacular translations, clerics were beginning to
codify polite behaviour, also for the benefit of laymen. The common
ground between courtesy books and the *roman courtois* bears witness to a very similar didactic strain in the works of Chrétien and his

---

[4] James Simpson, *Piers Plowman: An Introduction to the B-Text* (London, 1990),
10–12. In the quotation from *Piers* below, I have adopted Simpson's emendation of
l. 10.

[5] Ibid. 14–15.

[6] Jonathan Nicholls, *The Matter of Courtesy: Medieval Courtesy Books and the
Gawain-Poet* (Bury St Edmunds, 1985), 22–44, and D. Knox, '*Disciplina*: The
Monastic and Clerical Origins of European Civility', in *Renaissance Society and
Culture*, ed. J. Monfasani and R. G. Musto (New York, 1991), 107–35.

[7] Aldo Scaglione, *Knights at Court: Courtliness, Chivalry, and Courtesy from
Ottonian Germany to the Italian Renaissance* (Berkeley, Calif., 1991), 47–86.

continuators, and the *Gawain*-poet. Their fictional ideal of the courtly knight, who, as I have shown, unites chivalric and clerical ideals, adumbrates and advertises the fusion of *chevalerie* and *clergie* to which later medieval court-clerics were aspiring. Ideas of comportment thus 'followed the dominant cultural development' of the Middle Ages, namely 'the transition from a culture and religion sustained predominantly by clerics and religious institutions to one more secular in organization, transmission and content',[8] and in this transition the cleric in secular service was the crucial hinge.

Courtliness, discretion, and self-restraint were not the only ideals which clerics sought to inculcate in the knights who read or listened to their romances. They also handed down to laymen an ethic of introspection and moral deliberation. I refer here not primarily to the Christian penchant for scrupulous self-examination, whose impact on the heroes of romance may appear from the frequent confessions in romance. For despite the frequent mentions of religious observances, the poets of courtly romances are more interested in social relations between people than in vertical relations between individuals and God. Ethical considerations do not for that reason disappear from the text. On the contrary, the heroes of Chrétien, and, to a greater extent, the *Gawain*-poet's hero, are caught in a network of moral imperatives, mutual obligations, promises, and debts that demand an absolute commitment even if they conflict with their own interests or with common sense. Here we see most closely the courtly romancers' affinity with the ethics of Cicero's *De Officiis* and the *Moralium dogma*. The social applications of conscience in the moral philosophy of these works laid the basis for a compromise between contemplative introspection and participation in the affairs of the world, which became immensely fruitful when the balance between communications between God and man, and communications between people, began to tilt in favour of the latter. Moreover, as Cicero's reflections on reciprocal agreements and the obligations they entail frequently shade into a discussion of fair trading, the ethic of courtly romance leads the knight into the world of the merchant. His first steps into this world are, as we have seen, visible in the romances of Chrétien. His footprints in *Gawain* are firmer and more numerous.

[8] Knox, '*Disciplina*', 117. It should be noted that Knox takes the thirteenth century to be the beginning of this development, whereas I believe it was well on the way in the twelfth century, if not even earlier: Scaglione, *Knights at Court*, 86.

These, I believe, were the shared characteristics between the *Gawain*-poet and the poets of the *roman courtois*. They drew from a common inventory of literary themes and motifs, exploited conventionality to manipulate expectations, and to create suspense and psychological depth; historically, they participated in a long and concerted effort to discipline and refine chivalric behaviour, by laicizing clerical ideals of courtliness and *conscientia*. The conclusions have, I hope, contributed to clarifying the relation between the *Gawain*-poet and Old French courtly romance, which was not simply one of a poet standing on the shoulders of his precursors, but one of a poet determined to look in the same direction.

Bibliography

❧

PRIMARY SOURCES

ABELARD, *Historia Calamitatum*, ed. J. Monfrin (Paris, 1959).

ADAM OF USK, *Chronicle*, ed. and trans. E. M. Thompson (1904, repr. Lampeter, 1990).

ALAN OF LILLE, *Distinctiones dictionum theologicalium*, PL 210, cols. 685–1012.

—— *Summa de Arte Praedicatoria*, PL 210, cols. 109–98.

AMBROSE, *De Elia et Jejunio*, PL 14, cols. 696–730.

ANDREAS CAPELLANUS, *De Amore*, ed. P. G. Walsh (London, 1982).

ANTOINE DE LA SALLE, *Petit Jehan de Saintré*, ed. Jean Misrahi and Charles A. Knudson, TLF (Geneva, 1965).

L'Atre périlleux, ed. Brian Woledge, CFMA (Paris, 1936).

AUGUSTINE, *Enarrationes in psalmos*, CCSL 38–40.

BARTHOLOMAEUS ANGLICUS, *On the Properties of Things*, trans. John Trevisa, ed. M. C. Seymour *et al.*, 2 vols. (Oxford, 1975).

BEDE, *Ecclesiastical History of the English People*, ed. and trans. B. Colgrave and R. A. B. Mynors (Oxford, 1969).

BERNARD OF CLAIRVAUX, *Liber ad milites templi de laude novae militiae*, ed. J. Leclerq and H. M. Rochais, *Sancti Bernardi Opera*, 8 vols. (Rome, 1963), iii. 205–39.

BERNARDUS SILVESTRIS, *Cosmographia*, trans. Winthrop Wetherbee (New York, 1973).

—— *The Commentary on the First Six Books of the Aeneid of Vergil Commonly Attributed to Bernardus Silvestris*, ed. Julian Ward Jones and Elizabeth Francis Jones (Lincoln, Nebr., 1977).

—— *Cosmographia*, ed. Peter Dronke (Leiden, 1978).

BEROUL, *The Romance of Tristan*, ed. Norris J. Lacy (New York, 1989).

Bliocadran, ed. L. D. Wolfgang (Tübingen, 1976).

BOCCACCIO, GIOVANNI, *Decameron*, ed. C. Segre (Milan, 1966, repr. 1984).

BOETHIUS, *Consolatio Philosophiae*, ed. Karl Büchner (Heidelberg, 1960).

Boke of Curtaysye, ed. F. J. Furnivall, *Book of Nurture &c*, EETS OS 32 (London, 1868).

BREWER, ELISABETH (ed.), *Sir Gawain and the Green Knight: Sources and Analogues* (1973, repr. Woodbridge, 1992).

BRYANT, SIR FRANCIS, *Dispraise of the Life of a Courtier* (London, 1548).

'The Cambridge Debate': see Walther (ed.), *Das Streitgedicht.*

Caxton's Book of Courtesy, ed. F. J. Furnivall, EETS ES 3 (London, 1868).

Caxton's Mirror of the World, ed. Oliver Prior, EETS ES 60 (London, 1913).

CHAUCER, GEOFFREY, *The Riverside Chaucer*, 3rd edition, ed. Larry D. Benson *et al.* (Boston, Mass., 1986).

—— *The Romaunt of the Rose and Le Roman de la Rose: A Parallel-Text Edition*, ed. R. Sutherland (Oxford, 1967).

Le Chevalier à l'épée, ed. D. D. R. Owen and R. C. Johnston, *Two Old French Gauvain Romances* (Edinburgh, 1972).

CHRÉTIEN DE TROYES, *Le Chevalier de la charrete (Lancelot)*, ed. Mario Roques, CFMA (Paris, 1983).

—— *Le Chevalier au lion (Yvain)*, ed. Mario Roques, CFMA (Paris, 1982).

—— *Cligés*, ed. Alexandre Micha, CFMA (Paris, 1982).

—— *Le Conte du Graal (Perceval)*, ed. Félix Lecoy, 2 vols., CFMA (Paris, 1984).

—— *Erec et Enide*, ed. Mario Roques, CFMA (Paris, 1981).

—— *Arthurian Romances*, trans. D. D. R. Owen (London, 1978).

CHRISTINE DE PISAN, *The Treasure of the City of Ladies or the Book of the Three Virtues*, trans. Sarah Lawson (Harmondsworth, 1985).

CICERO, *De Inventione*, ed. T. E. Page, LCL (London, 1959).

—— *De Officiis*, ed. G. P. Goold, LCL (London, 1968).

—— *De Oratore*, ed. E. H. Warmington, LCL (London, 1967).

Cleanness, ed. J. J. Anderson (Manchester, 1977).

Continuations of the Old French Perceval of Chrétien de Troyes, ed. William Roach, 5 vols. (Philadelphia, 1949–83):

    I. *The First Continuation: Redaction of MSS TVD*, ed. William Roach (1949).

    II. *The First Continuation: Redaction of MSS EMQU*, ed. William Roach and Robert H. Ivey (1950).

    III. *The First Continuation: Redaction of MSS ALPRS, with Glossary*, ed. William Roach and Lucien Foulet (1952–5).

    IV. *The Second Continuation*, ed. William Roach (1971).

    V. *The Third Continuation (by Manessier)*, ed. William Roach (1983).

The Council of Remiremont: see Oulmont (ed.), *Les Débats.*

DANIEL OF BECCLES, *Urbanus Magnus*, ed. J. Gilbart Smyly (Dublin, 1939).

DANTE ALIGHIERI, *De vulgari eloquentia*, ed. Vincenzo Mengaldo (Padua, 1967).

The Didot-Perceval, ed. William Roach (Philadelphia, 1941).

ETIENNE DE BOURBON, *Anecdotes historiques*, ed. A. Lecoy de la Marche (Paris, 1877).

Facetus cum nihil utilius, ed. Carl Schroeder, *Der deutsche Facetus* (Berlin, 1911).

Facetus moribus et vita (Aurigena's *Facetus*), ed. and trans. A. G. Elliot, 'The *Facetus*', *Allegorica*, 2/2 (1977), 27–57.

FITZ NIGEL, RICHARD, *Dialogus de Scaccario*, ed. and trans. Charles Johnson (London, 1950).

Floris and Blanchefleur, ed. F. C. de Vries (Groningen, 1966).

The Fourth Continuation (by Gerbert de Montreuil), 3 vols., ed. Mary Williams and Marguerite Oswald, CFMA (Paris, 1922–75).

FROISSART, JEAN, *Méliador*, ed. A. Longnon, SATF (Paris, 1895–9).

GARIN LE BRUN, *L'Enseignement*, ed. Carl Appel, 'L'Enseignement de Garin le Brun', *Revue des langues romanes*, 33 (1889), 403–??.

GEOFFREY OF MONMOUTH, *Vita Merlini*, ed. E. Faral, *La Légende arthurienne: Études et documents*, 3 vols. (1929, repr. Paris, 1969), vol. iii.

—— *Historia Regum Britanniae*, trans. L. Thorpe, *History of the Kings of Britain* (Baltimore, 1968).

GEOFFREY DE VINSAUF, *Poetria Nova*, ed. and trans. Ernest Gallo, *The Poetria Nova and its Sources in Early Rhetorical Doctrine* (The Hague, 1971).

GERALD OF WALES, *Giraldus Cambrensis, Opera*, 8 vols., RS (London, 1861–91), vol. v: *Topographia Hibernica*, ed. James F. Dimmock (London, 1867).

—— *Speculum duorum*, ed. and trans. Yves Lefèvre, R. B. C. Huygens, and Brian Dawson (Cardiff, 1974).

GERBERT DE MONTREUIL, *La Continuation de Perceval*, ed. Mary Williams and Marguerite Oswald, 3 vols., CFMA (Paris, 1922–75).

GETTY, SISTER MARIE MADELEINE (ed.), *The Life of the North Africans as Revealed in the Sermons of St Augustine* (Washington, DC, 1931).

GIVEN-WILSON, CHRIS (ed. and trans.), *Chronicles of the Revolution*, Manchester Medieval Sources (Manchester, 1993).

The Grene Knight, ed. Frederic Madden, in *Syr Gawayne: A Collection of Ancient Romance Poems* (London, 1839).

GUILLAUME D'ANGLETERRE, *Chrétien: Guillaume d'Angleterre*, ed. A. J. Holden, TLF (Geneva, 1988).

GUILLAUME LE CLERC, *The Romance of Fergus*, ed. Wilson Frescoln (Philadelphia, 1983).

GUILLAUME DE LORRIS and JEAN DE MEUN, *Le Roman de la Rose*, ed. F. Lecoy, 3 vols., CFMA (Paris, 1976–82).

—— *The Romaunt of the Rose and Le Roman de la Rose: A Parallel-Text Edition*, ed. R. Sutherland (Oxford, 1967).

HARTMANN VON AUE, *Erec*, ed. Albert Leitzmann (Tübingen, 1985).

HARTMANN VON AUE *Erec*, trans. J. W. Thomas (Lincoln, Nebr., 1982).
HENRI D'ANDELI, *Bataille des vii ars*, ed. L. J. Paetow (Berkeley, Calif., 1914).
HENRYSON, ROBERT, *The Poems of Henryson*, ed. Denton Fox (Oxford, 1981).
HUGH OF ST VICTOR, *Didascalicon*, trans. Jerome Taylor (New York, 1961).
Hunbaut, ed. Margaret Winters, *The Romance of Hunbaut: An Arthurian Romance of the Thirteenth Century* (Leiden, 1984).
Jaufré, ed. and trans. R. Lavaud and R. Nelli, *Les Troubadours* (Paris, 1960).
Lancelot: Roman en prose du XIIIe siècle, ed. A. Micha, 9 vols., TLF (Geneva, 1978–82).
Lancelot do Lac: The Non Cyclic Old French Prose Lancelot, ed. Elspeth Kennedy, 2 vols. (Oxford, 1980).
LANGLAND, WILLIAM, *The Vision of Piers Plowman: A Complete Edition of the B-Text*, ed. A. V. C. Schmidt (London, 1978).
LA3AMON, *La3amon's Arthur: The Arthurian Section of La3amon's Brut*, ed. and trans. W. R. J. Barron and S. C. Weinberg (London, 1989).
LOMBARD, PETER, *Commentarium in psalmos*, PL 191, cols. 1–1296.
MANESSIER, *The Third Continuation*, ed. William Roach (Philadelphia, 1983).
MANNYNG OF BRUNNE, ROBERT, *Chronicle*, ed. F. J. Furnivall, 2 vols., RS (London, 1887).
MAP, WALTER, *De Nugis Curialium: Courtiers' Trifles*, ed. and trans. M. R. James, revised by C. N. L. Brooke and R. A. B. Mynors (Oxford, 1983).
MARBOD OF RENNES, 'Dissuasio navigationis ob lucrum', PL 171, col. 1723.
MATTHEW OF VENDÔME, *Ars Versificatoria*, ed. E. Faral, *Les Arts poétiques du XIIe et du XIIIe siècle* (1924, repr. Paris, 1958), 106–93.
MEDER, THEO (ed. and trans.), *Hoofsheid is een ernstig spel* (Amsterdam, 1988).
MORALIUM DOGMA: see William of Conches.
MORAWSKI, JOZEF (ed.), *Le Facet en français* (Poznan, 1923).
La Mule sans frein, ed. D. D. R. Owen and R. C. Johnston, *Two Old French Gauvain Romances* (Edinburgh, 1972).
NIGEL WHITEACRE (NIGELLUS WIREKER), *Tractatus contra curiales et officiales clericos*, ed. A. Boutemy (Paris, 1959).
OULMONT, CHARLES (ed.), *Les Débats du clerc et du chevalier dans la littérature poétique du moyen-âge* (Paris, 1911).
PARSONS, H. ROSAMUND (ed.), 'Anglo-Norman Books of Courtesy and Nurture', *PMLA* 44 (1929), 383–455.

Partenopeu de Blois, ed. Joseph Gildea, 2 vols. (Villanova, Penn., 1967).

Paston Letters and Papers of the Fifteenth Century, ed. Norman Davis, 2 vols. (Oxford, 1976).

Pearl: An English Poem of the XIVth Century, ed. Sir Israel Gollancz (London, 1921).

Perlesvaus, ed. William A. Nitze and T. Atkinson Jenkins, *Le Haut Livre du Graal: Perlesvaus*, 2 vols. (Chicago, 1932–7).

PETER OF LANGTOFT, *The Chronicle of Pierre de Langtoft*, ed. T. Wright, 2 vols., RS (1866, repr. London, 1964).

PETRARCH, FRANCESCO, *Petrarch's Lyric Poems*, ed. Robert M. Durling (Cambridge, Mass., 1976).

PETRUS ALFONSUS, *Disciplina Clericalis*, ed. A. Hilka and W. Söderhjelm (Helsinki, 1911).

PHILIPPE DE NAVARRE, *Les Quatre Ages de l'homme*, ed. M. de Fréville, SATF (Paris, 1888).

PUCCI, ANTONIO, 'Uno Capitolo d'Antonio Pucci', ed. Alessandro Wesselofski, *Rivista di Filologia Romanza*, 2 (1875), 221–7.

Queste del saint graal, ed. Albert Pauphilet, CFMA (Paris, 1984).

RAOUL DE HOUDENC, *Roman des Eles*, ed. Keith Busby, *Le Roman des Eles: The Anonymous Ordene de Chevalerie* (Amsterdam, 1983).

—— *Vengeance Raguidel*, ed. M. Friedwagner, 2 vols. (Halle, 1897).

RENAUT DE BEAUJEU, *Le Bel Inconnu*, ed. G. Perrie Williams, CFMA (Paris, 1929).

RICHARD OF DEVIZES, *Cronicon Richardi Divisensis de tempore regis Richardi primi*, ed. and trans. John T. Appleby (London, 1963).

Rigomer, ed. W. Foerster, *Les Merveilles de Rigomer de Jehan*, 2 vols. (Dresden, 1908–15).

ROBERT DE BLOIS, *Beaudous*, ed. Jacob Ulrich, *Robert de Blois: Sämtliche Werke*, 3 vols. (Berlin, 1889–95), vol. i.

Ruodlieb: The Earliest Courtly Novel, ed. H. Zeydel (Chapel Hill, NC, 1959).

St Erkenwald, ed. Ruth Morse (Cambridge, 1975).

Sir Amadace, ed. M. Mills, *Six Middle English Romances*, Everyman Library (London, 1973).

Sir Gawain and the Carl of Carlisle, ed. Donald B. Sands, *Middle English Verse Romances* (1966, repr. Exeter, 1981).

Sir Gawain and the Green Knight, ed. J. R. R. Tolkien and E. V. Gordon, revised by Norman Davis (Oxford, 1967).

Sir Perceval of Galles, ed. J. Campion and F. Holthausen, Alt- und Mittelenglische Texte 5 (Heidelberg, 1913).

THOMAS D'ANGLETERRE, *Les Fragments du roman de Tristan*, ed. Bartina H. Wind, TLF (Geneva, 1960).

THOMAS OF CHESTRE, *Libeaus Desconus*, ed. M. Mills, EETS OS 261 (London, 1969).

THOMAS OF CHOBHAM, *Summa*, ed. F. Broomfield (Louvain, 1968).

Le Tresplaisante et Recreative Hystoire du Perceval le galloys (Paris, 1530), ed. Larry D. Benson, *Art and Tradition in Sir Gawain and the Green Knight* (New York, 1965), 249–57.

Vulgate *Lancelot*: see *Lancelot: Roman en prose*.

WACE, *Brut*, ed. Ivor Arnold, *Le Roman de Brut de Wace*, 2 vols., SATF (Paris, 1938–40).

—— *Roman de Rou*, ed. A. J. Holden, 3 vols. (Paris, 1970–3).

WALTER OF CHÂTILLON, *Alexandreis*, ed. Marvin L. Colker (Padua, 1978).

WALTHER, H. (ed.), *Das Streitgedicht in der lateinischen Literatur des Mittelalters* (Munich, 1920), 248–53.

WILLIAM OF CONCHES, *Das Moralium dogma philosophorum des Guillaume de Conches: Lateinisch, Altfranzösisch und Mittelniederfränkisch*, ed. John Holmberg (Uppsala, 1929).

Winner and Waster, ed. Stephanie Trigg, EETS OS 297 (Oxford, 1990).

Yder, ed. and trans. Alison Adams, *The Romance of Yder* (Cambridge, 1983).

Ywain and Gawain, ed. Albert B. Friedman and Norman T. Harrington, EETS OS 254 (London, 1964).

ZATZIKHOVEN, ULRICH VON, *Lanzelet*, ed. K. A. Hahn (Berlin, 1845, repr. 1965).

—— *Lanzelet*, trans. K. G. Webster, revised by R. S. Loomis (New York, 1951).

SECONDARY SOURCES

ACKERMAN, R. W., 'Castle Hautdesert in *Sir Gawain and the Green Knight*', in *Mélanges Jean Frappier*, 2 vols. (Geneva, 1970), i. 1–7.

AERS, DAVID, ' "In Arthurus Day": Community, Virtue and Individual Identity in *Sir Gawain and the Green Knight*', in *Community, Gender and Individual Identity: English Writing 1360–1430* (London, 1988), 153–78.

AJAM, LAURENT, 'La Forêt dans l'œuvre de Chrétien de Troyes', *Europe* (Oct. 1982), 120–5.

ALPERS, PAUL, 'Convening and Convention in Pastoral Poetry', *NLH* 14 (1983), 277–304.

ARMSTRONG, GRACE M., 'Women of Power: Chrétien de Troyes's Female Clerks', in *Women in French Literature*, ed. M. Guggenheim (Stanford, Calif., 1988), 19–46.

AUERBACH, ERICH, *Mimesis: Dargestellte Wirklichkeit in der abendländischen Literatur* (Berne, 1946).

AUSTIN, J. L., *Philosophical Papers* (1961, repr. Oxford, 1970).

BAKER, DENISE N., 'Chaucer and Moral Philosophy', *MAE* 60 (1991), 241–56.

BALDWIN, JOHN W., *The Government of Philip Augustus: Foundations of French Royal Power* (Berkeley, Calif., 1986).

—— *Masters, Princes and Servants: The Social Views of Peter the Chanter and his Circle*, 2 vols. (Princeton, NJ, 1970).

BARON, HANS, 'Cicero and the Civic Spirit in the Middle Ages and the Early Renaissance', *Bulletin of the John Rylands Library*, 22 (1938), 72–94.

BARRON, W. R. J., *English Medieval Romance* (London, 1985).

—— 'Chrétien de Troyes and the *Gawain*-Poet: Master and Pupil or Twin Temperaments?', in *The Legacy of Chrétien de Troyes*, 2 vols., ed. Norris J. Lacy, Douglas Kelly, and Keith Busby (Amsterdam, 1988), ii. 255–84.

BARTLETT, ROBERT, *The Making of Europe: Conquest, Colonization and Cultural Change 950–1350* (London, 1993).

BATESON, GREGORY, 'A Theory of Play and Fantasy', in *Play: Its Role in Evolution and Development*, ed. J. Brunner (London, 1976), 119–29.

BAYRAV, S., 'Le Thème de la joie dans la littérature chevaleresque', *Dialogues*, 3 (1953), 3–19.

BECHMANN, ROLAND, *Trees and Man: The Forest in the Middle Ages* (New York, 1990).

BENNETT, MICHAEL J., '*Sir Gawain and the Green Knight* and the Literary Achievement of the North-West Midlands: The Historical Background', *Journal of Medieval History*, 5 (1979), 63–88.

—— 'Courtly Literature and North-West England in the Later Middle Ages', in *Court and Poet*, ed. G. S. Burgess (Liverpool, 1981), 69–78.

—— *Community, Class, and Careerism: Cheshire and Lancashire Society in the Age of Sir Gawain and the Green Knight* (Cambridge, 1983).

—— 'The Court of Richard II and the Promotion of Literature', in *Chaucer's England: Literature in Historical Context*, ed. Barbara Hanawalt (Minneapolis, 1992), 3–20.

BENSON, LARRY D., *Art and Tradition in Sir Gawain and the Green Knight* (New York, 1965).

—— 'The Tournament in the Romances of Chrétien de Troyes and *L'Histoire de Guillaume de Maréchal*', in *Chivalric Literature: Essays on Relations between Literature and Life in the Later Middle Ages*, ed. Larry D. Benson and John Leyerle (Kalamazoo, Mich., 1980), 1–24.

BENTON, JOHN F., 'The Court of Champagne as a Literary Center', *Speculum*, 36 (1961), 551–91.

BERCOVITCH, S., 'Romance and Anti-Romance in *Sir Gawain and the Green Knight*', *Philological Quarterly*, 44 (1965), 30–7.

BERGNER, HEINZ, 'Gawein und seine literarischen Realisationen in der englischen Literatur des Spätmittelalters', in *Artusrittertum im späten*

Mittelalter: Ethos und Ideologie, ed. Friedrich Wolfzettel (Giessen, 1984), 3–15.

BERNARD, JACQUES, 'Trade and Finance in the Middle Ages', in *The Middle Ages*, ed. Carlo M. Cipolla, Fontana Economic History of Europe (London, 1972), 274–338.

BERNHEIMER, R., *Wild Men in the Middle Ages* (Cambridge, Mass., 1952).

BERRY, FRANCIS, '*Sir Gawayne and the Grene Knight*', in *The Age of Chaucer*, ed. Boris Ford, Pelican Guide to English Literature (Harmondsworth, 1954), 148–58.

BEZZOLA, R., *Les Origines et la formation de la littérature courtoise en occident (500–1200)*, 3 vols. (Paris, 1944–63).

BLAMIRES, ALCUIN, 'Chaucer's Revaluation of Chivalric Honor', *Mediaevalia*, 5 (1979), 245–69.

BLANCH, ROBERT J., and WASSERMAN, JULIAN N., 'Medieval Contracts and Covenants: The Legal Coloring of *Sir Gawain and the Green Knight*', *Neophilologus*, 68 (1984), 598–610.

—— ' "To Ouertake your Wylle": Volition and Obligation in *Sir Gawain and the Green Knight*', *Neophilologus*, 70 (1986), 119–29.

BLOCH, R. HOWARD, *Medieval French Literature and Law* (Berkeley, Calif., 1977).

—— 'Wasteland and Round Table', *NLH* 11 (1980), 255–76.

—— 'Money, Metaphor, and the Mediation of Social Difference', *Symposium*, 30 (1981), 18–33.

BLOOMFIELD, MORTON W., '*Sir Gawain and the Green Knight*: An Appraisal', in *Essays and Explorations* (Cambridge, Mass., 1970), 131–57.

—— 'The Problem of the Hero in the Later Medieval Period', in *Concepts of the Hero in the Middle Ages and the Renaissance*, ed. Norman T. Burns and Christopher Reagan (London, 1975), 27–48.

BOARDMAN, PHILIP C., 'Middle English Arthurian Romance: The Repetition and Reputation of Gawain', in *The Vitality of the Arthurian Legend*, ed. M. Pors (Odense, 1988), 71–90.

BOGDANOW, FANNI, 'The Character of Gawain in the Thirteenth-Century Prose Romances', *MAE* 27 (1958), 154–61.

BORNSTEIN, DIANE, *Mirrors of Courtesy* (Hamden, Conn., 1975).

BORROFF, MARIE, *Sir Gawain and the Green Knight: A Stylistic and Metrical Study* (New Haven, Conn., 1962).

BOURDIEU, PIERRE, 'The Sentiment of Honour in Kabyle Society', in *Honour and Shame: The Values of Mediterranean Society*, ed. J. G. Peristiany (London, 1965), 191–241.

—— 'Codification', in *In Other Words: Essays Towards a Reflexive Sociology*, trans. Matthew Adamson (Cambridge, 1990), 76–86.

BOWERS, R. H., '*Gawain and the Green Knight* as Entertainment', *MLQ* 24 (1963), 333–41.

BRENTANO, F., *Relationship of the Latin Facetus Literature to the Medieval English Courtesy Poems*, Bulletin of the University of Kansas, Humanistic Studies 5/2 (Lawrence, Kan., 1936).

BREWER, DEREK S., 'Courtesy and the *Gawain*-Poet', in *Patterns of Love and Courtesy: Essays in Memory of C. S. Lewis*, ed. J. Lawlor (London, 1966), 54–85.

—— *The Morte Arthur: Parts Seven and Eight* (London, 1968).

—— 'Honour in Chaucer', *Essays and Studies*, 26 (1973), 1–19.

—— 'Chaucer and Chrétien and Arthurian Romance', in *Middle English Studies in Honor of Rossell Hope Robbins*, ed. B. Rowland (London, 1974), 255–9.

—— 'The Interpretations of Dreams, Folktale and Romance with Special Reference to *Sir Gawain and the Green Knight*', NM 77 (1976), 569–81.

—— 'The Arming of the Warrior in European Literature and Chaucer', in *Chaucerian Problems and Perspectives: Essays Presented to Paul E. Beichner CSC*, ed. Edward Vasta and Zacharias P. Thundy (Notre Dame, Ind., 1979), 221–43; repr. in Brewer, *Tradition and Innovation in Chaucer* (London, 1982), 142–60.

——*Symbolic Stories: Traditional Narrative and the Family Drama in English Literature* (Cambridge 1980)

BROWN, PENELOPE, and LEVINSON, STEPHEN C., *Politeness: Some Universals in Language Use* (Cambridge, 1987).

BRUCE, J. D., *The Evolution of Arthurian Romance* (Göttingen, 1928).

BRUCKNER, MATILDA TOMARYN, *Narrative Invention in Twelfth-Century French Romance: The Convention of Hospitality 1160–1200* (Lexington, Ky., 1980).

BRUNNER, KARL, 'Middle English Metrical Romances and their Audience', in *Studies in Medieval Literature in Honor of Professor Albert Croll Baugh*, ed. M. Leach (Philadelphia, 1961), 219–27.

BULLOCK-DAVIS, CONSTANCE, 'Chrétien de Troyes and England', AL 1 (1981), 1–61.

BUMKE, JOACHIM, *Höfische Kultur: Literatur und Gesellschaft im hohen Mittelalter*, 2 vols. (Munich, 1986).

BUR, MICHEL, 'Les Principautés', in *La France médiévale*, ed. J. Favier (Vitry-sur-Seine, 1983), 239–64.

BURKE, JOHN, *Life in the Castle of Medieval England* (London, 1978).

BURNLEY, J. D., *Chaucer's Language and the Philosophers' Tradition* (Cambridge, 1979).

BURROW, JOHN A., *A Reading of Sir Gawain and the Green Knight* (London, 1965).

—— *Ricardian Poetry* (London, 1971).

—— 'Honour and Shame in *Sir Gawain and the Green Knight*', in *Essays on Medieval Literature* (Oxford, 1984), 117–31.

BURROW, JOHN A., *The Ages of Man* (Oxford, 1986).

BUSBY, KEITH, '*Sir Perceval of Galles, Le Conte du Graal*, and *La Continu-ation-Gauvain*: The Methods of an English Adapter', *Études Anglaises*, 2 (1978), 198–202.

—— *Gauvain in Old French Literature* (Amsterdam, 1980).

CAMPBELL, KIM SYDOW, 'A Lesson in Polite Non-Compliance: Gawain's Conversational Strategies in Fitt 3 of *Sir Gawain and the Green Knight*', *Language Quarterly*, 28 (1990), 53–62.

CARLSON, DAVID, 'The *Pearl*-Poet's *Olympia*', *Manuscripta*, 31 (1987), 181–9.

CHAMBERS, ROSS, *Story and Situation: Narrative Seduction and the Power of Fiction* (Minneapolis, 1984).

CHÊNERIE, MARIE-LUCE, *Le Chevalier errant dans les romans arthuriens en vers des XIIe et XIIIe siècles* (Geneva, 1986).

CHENU, MARIE-DOMINIQUE, *Nature, Man, and Society in the Twelfth Century*, trans. J. Taylor and L. K. Little (Chicago, 1968).

CHEYETTE, FREDRIC L., 'The Invention of the State', in *Essays on Medieval Civilization*, ed. B. K. Lackner and K. R. Philips (Austin, Tex., 1978), 143–78.

CHRISTOPHERSON, PAUL, 'The Englishness of *Sir Gawain and the Green Knight*', in *On the Novel*, ed. B. S. Benedikz (London, 1971), 46–56.

CLANCHY, M. T., *From Memory to Written Record* (1979, 2nd edn. Oxford, 1993).

COLDSTREAM, NICOLA, 'Art and Architecture in the Late Middle Ages', in *The Later Middle Ages*, ed. Stephen Medcalf (London, 1981), 172–224.

COOPER, HELEN, 'Magic that does not Work', *M&H* 7 (1976), 131–46.

COSMAN, MADELEINE PELNER, *The Education of the Hero in Arthurian Romance* (Chapel Hill, NC, 1966).

CRANE, SUSAN, *Insular Romance: Politics, Faith, and Culture in Anglo-Norman and Middle-English Literature* (Berkeley, Calif., 1986).

CURTIUS, ERNST ROBERT, *European Literature and the Latin Middle Ages*, trans. Willard R. Trask (New York, 1953).

DAVIES, R. R., 'Richard II and the Principality of Chester', in *The Reign of Richard II: Essays in Honour of May McKisack*, ed. F. R. H. Du Boulay and C. M. Barron (London, 1971), 256–79.

DEAN, CHRISTOPHER, *Arthur of England: English Attitudes to King Arthur and the Knights of the Round Table in the Middle Ages and the Renaissance* (Toronto, 1987).

DELCOURT, DENYSE, *L'Éthique du changement dans le roman français du douzième siècle* (Geneva, 1990).

DELHAYE, PHILIPPE, 'Une adaptation du *De Officiis* au XIIe siècle: Le *Moralium dogma philosophorum*', *Recherches de théologie ancienne et médiévale*, 16 (1949), 227–58.

—— *Enseignement et morale au XIIe siècle* (Fribourg, 1988).

DIAMOND, ARLYN, 'Sir Gawain and the Green Knight: An Alliterative Romance', *Philological Quarterly*, 55 (1976), 10–29.

DODGSON, JOHN MCNEAL, 'Sir Gawain's Arrival in Wirral', in *Early English and Norse Studies Presented to Hugh Smith*, ed. Arthur Browne and Peter Foote (London, 1963), 19–25.

DONNER, MORTON, 'Tact as a Criterion of Reality in *Sir Gawain and the Green Knight*', *PELL* 1 (1965), 306–15.

DOOB, PENELOPE, *Nebuchadnezzar's Children: Conventions of Madness in the Middle Ages* (New Haven, Conn., 1974).

DOUGLAS, MARY, *Purity and Danger: An Analysis of the Concepts of Pollution and Taboo* (1966, repr. London, 1989).

DRAGONETTI, ROGER, *La Technique poétique dans la chanson courtoise* (Bruges, 1960).

DRONKE, PETER, '*Ruodlieb*: Les Premières Traces du roman courtois', *CCM* 12 (1969), 365–82.

—— 'Pseudo-Ovid, *Facetus*, and the Arts of Love', *Mittellateinisches Jahrbuch*, 11 (1976), 126–31.

—— and MANN, JILL, 'Chaucer and the Medieval Latin Poets', in *Geoffrey Chaucer*, ed. D. S. Brewer (London, 1974), 154–83.

DUBY, GEORGES, *L'Économie rurale et la vie des campagnes dans l'occident médiévale* (Paris, 1962).

—— *Guerriers et paysans* (Paris, 1973).

—— *The Three Orders: Feudal Society Imagined*, trans. Arthur Goldhammer (Chicago, 1980).

DUPIN, HENRI, *La Courtoisie au Moyen Age* (Paris, 1931).

EBERLE, PATRICIA J., 'The Politics of Courtly Style at the Court of Richard II', in *The Spirit of the Court*, ed. G. S. Burgess and Robert A. Taylor (Woodbridge, 1985), 168–78.

EIFLER, GÜNTER, *Das ritterliche Tugendsystem* (Darmstadt, 1970).

ELIAS, NORBERT, *The Civilizing Process*, trans. E. Jephcott, 2 vols. (New York, 1982).

EVERGATES, THEODORE, *Feudal Society in the Baillage of Troyes under the Counts of Champagne, 1152–1284* (Baltimore, 1975).

FÁY, ATTILA, 'Marbodean and Patristic Reminiscences in *Patience*', *Revue de littérature comparée*, 49 (1975), 284–90.

FIELD, P. J. C., 'Malory and Chrétien de Troyes', *Reading Medieval Studies*, 17 (1991), 19–30.

—— 'Malory and the *Perlesvaus*', *MAE* 62 (1993), 259–69.

FINEMAN, JOEL, 'The Structure of Allegorical Desire', in *Allegory and Representation*, ed. Stephen J. Greenblatt (Baltimore, 1981), 26–60.

FINLAYSON, JOHN, 'The Expectations of Romance in *Sir Gawain and the Green Knight*', *Genre*, 12 (1979), 1–24.

FINLAYSON, JOHN, 'Definitions of Middle English Romance', *ChauR* 15 (1980), 44–62, 168–81.

—— '*Pearl*, Petrarch's *Trionfo della Morte* and Boccaccio's *Olympia*', *English Studies in Canada*, 9 (1983), 1–13.

FISHER, JOHN H., 'Chancery and the Emergence of Standard Written English in the Fifteenth Century', *Speculum*, 52 (1977), 870–99.

FLECKENSTEIN, JOSEF, '*Miles* und *Clericus* am Könings- und Fürsterhof', in *Curialitas: Studien zu Grundfragen der höfisch-ritterlichen Kultur*, ed. J. Fleckenstein (Göttingen, 1990), 302–25.

FOERSTER, WENDELIN, *Der Karrenritter* (Halle, 1899).

FOULON, CHARLES, 'Les Quatre Repas de Perceval', in *Mélanges J. Wathelet-Willems* (Liège, 1978), 147–87.

FOURNIER, GABRIEL, *Le Château dans la France médiévale: Essai de sociologie monumentale* (Paris, 1978).

FOWLER, DAVID, '*Le Conte du Graal* and *Sir Perceval of Galles*', *Comparative Literature Studies*, 13 (1975), 5–20.

FRADENBURG, LOUISE O., 'The Manciple's Servant Tongue: Politics and Poetry in the *Canterbury Tales*', *ELH* 82 (1985), 85–118.

FRANKIS, P. J., 'Chaucer's "Vavasour" and Chrétien de Troyes', *N&Q* 15 (1968), 46–7.

FRAPPIER, JEAN, 'Le Personnage de Gauvain dans la *Première Continuation* du *Conte du Graal*', *Romance Philology*, 11 (1957), 331–44.

—— *Chrétien de Troyes: L'Homme et l'œuvre* (Paris, 1957).

—— 'Vues sur les conceptions courtoises dans les littératures d'oc et de oïl au douzième siècle', *CCM* 2 (1959), 135–56.

FREEMAN, MICHELLE A., *The Poetics of 'Translatio Studii' and 'Conjointure': Chrétien de Troyes's Cligés* (Lexington, Ky., 1979).

FRYE, NORTHROP, 'Allegory', in *Encyclopedia of Poetry and Poetics*, ed. A. Preminger (Princeton, NJ, 1965), 12–15.

GALLAIS, PIERRE, 'Gauvain et la Pucelle de Lis', im *Mélanges offerts à Maurice Delbouille*, 2 vols. (Gembloux, 1964), ii. 207–29.

—— *Perceval et l'initiation* (Paris, 1972).

GANZEMÜLLER, WILHELM, *Das Naturgefühl im Mittelalter* (Leipzig, 1914).

GAUTIER, LÉON, *Chivalry*, ed. Jacques Levron, trans. D. C. Dunning (London, 1965).

GIACCERINI, ENRICO, 'Gawain's Dream of Emancipation', in *Literature in Fourteenth-Century England*, ed. Piero Boitani and Anna Torti (Tübingen, 1983), 49–64.

GIEBEN, SERVUS, 'Robert Grosseteste and Medieval Courtesy-Books', *Vivarium*, 5 (1967), 47–74.

GILLESPIE, JAMES L., 'Richard II's Cheshire Archers', *Transactions of the Historic Society of Cheshire and Lancashire*, 125 (1975), 1–40.

GIRARD, RENÉ, *Mensonge romantique et verité romanesque* (Paris, 1961).
—— 'From the *Divine Comedy* to the Sociology of the Novel', in *Sociology of Literature and Drama*, ed. Elisabeth and Tom Burns (Harmondsworth, 1973), 101–8.
—— 'Love and Hate in *Yvain*', in *Modernité au Moyen Age: Le Défi du passé*, ed. Brigitte Cazelles and Charles Méla (Geneva, 1990), 249–62.
GIVEN-WILSON, CHRIS, *The Royal Household and the King's Affinity: Service, Politics and Finance in England 1360–1413* (New Haven, Conn., 1986).
GLASSCOCK, R. E., 'England *circa* 1334', in *A New Historical Geography of England*, ed. H. C. Darby (Cambridge, 1973), 136–85.
GOFFMAN, ERVING, *The Presentation of Self in Everyday Life* (Harmondsworth, 1959, repr. 1975).
GREENBLATT, STEPHEN J., 'The Improvisation of Power', in *Literature and Society: Selected Papers from the English Institute: 1978*, ed. Edward W. Said (Baltimore, 1980), 57–99; repr. Greenblatt, *Renaissance Self-Fashioning* (Chicago, 1984), 222–54.
GRIMBERT, JOAN TASKER, *Yvain dans le miroir: Une poétique de la réflexion dans le Chevalier au Lion de Chrétien de Troyes* (Amsterdam, 1988).
GSTEIGER, MANFRED, *Die Landschaftschilderungen in den Romanen Chrestiens de Troyes: Literarische Tradition und künstleriche Gestaltung* (Berlin, 1958).
GUREVICH, ARON JAKOVLECIC, *Medieval Popular Culture* (Cambridge, 1988).
GUTHRIE, JERI S., 'The *JE(U)* in *Le Bel Inconnu*', *Romanic Review*, 75 (1984), 147–61.
HAIDU, PETER, *Aesthetic Distance in Chrétien de Troyes: Irony and Comedy in Cligés and Perceval* (Geneva, 1968).
—— 'Le Sens historique du phénomène stylistique: La Sémiose dissociative chez Chrétien de Troyes', *Europe* (Oct. 1982), 36–47.
—— 'Romance: Idealistic Genre or Historical Text?', in *The Craft of Fiction: Essays in Medieval Poetics*, ed. Leigh A. Arrathoon (Rochester, Mich., 1984), 1–47.
HALASZ, K., *Structures narratives chez Chrétien de Troyes* (Debrecen, 1980).
HAMEL, MARY, 'The *Franklin's Tale* and Chrétien de Troyes', *ChauR* 17 (1983), 316–31.
HAMILTON, BERNARD, *Religion in the Medieval West* (London, 1986).
HANNING, ROBERT W., *The Individual in Twelfth-Century Romance* (New Haven, Conn., 1974).
—— ' "I Shal Finde It in a Maner Glose": Versions of Textual Harassment in Medieval Literature', in *Medieval Texts and Contemporary*

Readers, ed. Laurie A. Finke and Martin B. Shichtman (Ithaca, NY, 1987), 27–51.

—— 'Love and Power in the Twelfth Century', with Special Reference to Chrétien de Troyes and Marie de France', in *The Olde Daunce: Love, Friendship, Sex, and Marriage in the Medieval World*, ed. Robert R. Edwards and Stephen Spender (New York, 1991), 87–103.

HART, THOMAS ELWOOD, 'Chrestien, Macrobius, and Chartrean Science: The Allegorical Robe as a Symbol of Textual Design in the Old French *Erec*', *MS* 43 (1981), 250–96.

HARTLE, PAUL NIGEL, 'Middle English Alliterative Verse and the Formulaic Theory', doctoral dissertation (University of Cambridge, 1981).

HASKINS, CHARLES HOMER, *The Renaissance of the Twelfth Century* (Cambridge, Mass., 1927).

HEAL, FELICITY, *Hospitality in Early Modern Europe* (Oxford, 1990).

HEERS, JACQUES, *Fêtes, jeux et joutes dans les sociétés d'Occident à la fin du Moyen-Age* (Montreal, 1971).

HENG, GERALDINE, 'Feminine Knots and the Other in *Sir Gawain and the Green Knight*', *PMLA* 106 (1991), 500–14.

—— 'A Woman Wants: The Lady, *Gawain*, and the Forms of Seduction', *Yale Journal of Criticism*, 5 (1992), 101–35.

HEYWORTH, P. L., 'Sir Gawain's Crossing of Dee', *MAE* 41 (1972), 124–7.

HOEPFFNER, E., 'Chrétien de Troyes et Thomas D'Angleterre', *Romania*, 55 (1929), 1–16.

HOFER, STEFAN, *Chrétien de Troyes: Leben und Werke* (Graz, 1954).

HOLMES, URBAN T., Jr., and KLENKE, SISTER M. AMELIE, *Chrétien, Troyes and the Grail* (Chapel Hill, NC, 1959).

HOPKINS, ANDREA, *The Sinful Knights: A Study of Middle English Penitential Romance* (Oxford, 1990).

HOSKINS, W. G., *The Making of the English Landscape* (Harmondsworth, 1955).

HUIZINGA, JOHAN, *Homo Ludens: A Study of the Play-Element in Culture* (Boston, Mass., 1950).

HULBERT, JAMES R., 'A Hypothesis Concerning the Alliterative Revival', *MP* 28 (1931), 405–22.

HULT, DAVID F., *Self-Fulfilling Prophecies: Readership and Authority in the First Roman de la Rose* (Cambridge, 1986).

—— 'Lancelot's Shame', *Romance Philology*, 42 (1988), 30–50.

HUNT, TONY, 'Irony and Ambiguity in *Sir Gawain and the Green Knight*', *FMLS* 12 (1976), 1–16.

—— *Chrétien de Troyes: Yvain* (London, 1986).

HUSSEY, S. S., '*Sir Gawain and the Green Knight* and Romance Writing', *SN* 40 (1968), 161–74.

JAEGER, C. STEPHEN, *The Origins of Courtliness: Civilizing Trends and the Formation of Courtly Ideals 939–1210* (Philadelphia, 1985).

JAMES, MERVYN, *English Politics and the Concept of Honour, 1485–1642*, Past and Present Supplement 3 (Cambridge, 1978).

JONES, EDWARD T., 'The Sound of Laughter in *Sir Gawain and the Green Knight*', MS 31 (1969), 343–5.

JONES, GEORGE FENWICK, ' "Lov'd I not Honor More": The Durability of a Literary Motif', *Comparative Literature*, 11 (1959), 131–43.

—— *Honor in German Literature* (Chapel Hill, NC, 1959).

KAY, SARAH, 'Commemoration, Memory, and the Role of the Past in Chrétien de Troyes: Retrospection and Meaning in *Erec et Enide, Yvain and Perceval*', *Reading Medieval Studies*, 17 (1991), 31–50.

KEEN, MAURICE, 'Chivalry, Nobility, and the Man of Arms', in *War, Literature, and Politics*, ed. Christopher Thomas Allmand (London, 1976), 32–45.

—— *Chivalry* (New Haven, Conn., 1984).

—— *English Society in the Later Middle Ages 1348–1500* (Harmondsworth, 1990).

KELLOGG, ALFRED L., 'The Localisation of the Green Chapel in *Sir Gawain and the Green Knight*', in *Chaucer, Langland, Arthur: Essays in Middle English Literature* (New Brunswick, NJ, 1972), 6–10.

KELLOGG, JUDITH, *Medieval Artistry and Exchange: Economic Institutions, Society, and Literary Form in Old French Narrative* (New York, 1989).

KELLY, DOUGLAS, *Sens et Conjointure in the Chevalier de la Charrete* (The Hague, 1966).

—— 'Gawain and *Fin Amors* in the Poems of Chrétien de Troyes', *Studies in Philology*, 67 (1970), 453–60.

KELLY, ROBERT L., 'Allusions to the Vulgate Cycle in *Sir Gawain and the Green Knight*', in *Literary and Historical Perspectives of the Middle Ages*, ed. D. W. Cummins *et al.* (Morgantown, W.Va., 1982), 183–99.

KELLY, THOMAS E., *Le Haut Livre du Graal: A Structural Study* (Geneva, 1974).

—— 'Love in the *Perlesvaus*: Sinful Passion or Redemptive Force?', *Romanic Review*, 66 (1975), 1–12.

KINDRICK, ROBERT L., 'Gawain's Ethics: Shame and Guilt in *Sir Gawain and the Green Knight*', *Annuale Medievale*, 20 (1981), 5–32.

KITELEY, J. F., 'The *De Arte Honeste Amandi* of Andreas Capellanus and the Concept of Courtesy in *Sir Gawain and the Green Knight*', *Anglia*, 79 (1961), 7–16.

KITTREDGE, GEORGE L., *A Study of Sir Gawain and the Green Knight* (Cambridge, Mass., 1916).

KNIGHT, STEPHEN, 'The Social Function of Middle English Romances', in *Medieval Literature: Criticism, Ideology, and History*, ed. David Aers (Brighton, 1986), 99–122.

KNOX, D., '*Disciplina*: The Monastic and Clerical Origins of European Civility', in *Renaissance Society and Culture*, ed. J. Monfasani and R. G. Musto (New York, 1991), 107–35.

KÖHLER, ERICH, *Ideal und Wirklichkeit in der höfischen Epik* (Tübingen, 1956).

KOLVE, V. A., *Chaucer and the Imagery of Narrative: The First Five Canterbury Tales* (London, 1984).

KOOPER, ERIK, 'The Case of the Encoded Author: John Massey in *Sir Gawain and the Green Knight*', NM 83 (1982), 158–68.

KRUEGER, ROBERTA L., 'Constructing Sexual Identity in the High Middle Ages: The Didactic Poetry of Robert de Blois', *Paragraph*, 13 (1990), 105–31.

LACY, NORRIS J. (ed.), *Arthurian Encyclopedia* (Cambridge, 1986).

LAMBERT, MARK, *Style and Vision in Le Morte Darthur* (New Haven, Conn., 1975).

LAPIDGE, MICHAEL, 'The Stoic Inheritance', in *A History of Twelfth-Century Philosophy*, ed. Peter Dronke (Cambridge, 1988), 81–112.

LAWTON, DAVID A., 'The Diversity of Middle English Alliterative Poetry', *Leeds English Studies*, 20 (1989), 143–72.

LE GOFF, JACQUES, 'The Town as an Agent of Civilisation', in *The Middle Ages*, ed. Carlo M. Cipolla, Fontana Economic History of Europe (London, 1972), 71–106.

—— 'Temps de l'église et temps du marchand', in *Pour un autre Moyen-Age* (Paris, 1977), 46–65.

—— *The Birth of Purgatory*, trans. Arthur Goldhammer (London, 1984).

—— *Medieval Civilisation*, trans. Julia Barrow (Oxford, 1988).

—— 'The Wilderness in the Medieval West', in *The Medieval Imagination*, trans. A. Goldhammer (Chicago, 1988), 47–59.

LE RIDER, PAULE, *Le Chevalier dans le Conte du Graal* (Paris, 1978).

LEGGE, DOMINICA, 'A fuer de guerre', MAE 5 (1936), 121–2.

LEJEUNE, RITA, 'Rôle littéraire d'Aliénor d'Aquitaine et de sa famille', *Cultura Neolatina*, 14 (1954), 5–57.

LEUPIN, ALEXANDRE, 'Absolute Reflexivity: Geoffrey de Vinsauf's *Poetria Nova*', in *Barbarolexis: Medieval Writing and Sexuality*, trans. Kate M. Cooper (Cambridge, Mass., 1989), 17–38.

LITTLE, LESTER K., *Religious Poverty and the Profit Economy in Medieval Europe* (London, 1978).

LONGNON, JEAN, 'La Champagne', in *Histoire des institutions françaises au Moyen Age*, 5 vols., ed. F. Lot and R. Fawtier (Paris, 1957), i. 123–36.

LOOMIS, ROGER SHERMAN, 'Edward I, Arthurian Enthusiast', *Speculum*, 33 (1958), 242–55.

—— 'Arthurian Influence on Sport and Spectacle', in *Arthurian Literature in the Middle Ages*, ed. Roger Sherman Loomis (Oxford, 1959), 553–9.

—— *Arthurian Tradition and Chrétien de Troyes* (New York, 1961).

LOOZE, LAURENCE DE, 'Generic Clash, Reader Response, and the Poetics of the Non-Ending in *Le Bel Inconnu*', in *Courtly Literature: Culture and Context*, ed. K. Busby and E. Kooper (Amsterdam, 1990), 113–23.

LUTRELL, C., 'The Figure of Nature in Chrétien de Troyes', *Nottingham Medieval Studies*, 17 (1973), 3–16.

MCKISACK, MAY, *The Fourteenth Century*, Oxford History of England (Oxford, 1959).

MADDEN, FREDERIC, *Syr Gawayne: A Collection of Ancient Romance-Poems* (London, 1839).

MANDEL, J., 'Elements in the *Charrete* World: The Father–Son Relationship', *MP* 62 (1964–5), 97–104.

—— 'Proper Behaviour in Chrétien's *Charrete*: The Guest–Host Relationship', *French Review*, 48 (1974–5), 683–9.

MANN, JILL, 'Price and Value in *Sir Gawain and the Green Knight*', *Essays in Criticism*, 36 (1986), 298–318.

—— *Geoffrey Chaucer* (Hemel Hempstead, 1991).

MARINO, JAMES GERARD AMERICUS, 'Games and Romance', doctoral dissertation (University of Pittsburgh, Penn., 1975).

MARKUS, MANFRED, *Moderne Erzählperspektive in den Werken des Gawain-Autors* (Regensburg, 1971).

MATHEW, GERVASE, *The Court of Richard II* (London, 1968).

MICKEL, EMMANUEL J., 'The Theme of Honor in Chrétien's *Lancelot*', *Zeitschrift für Romanische Philologie*, 91 (1975), 243–72.

MIDDLETON, ANNE, 'The Idea of Public Poetry in the Reign of Richard II', *Speculum*, 53 (1978), 94–114.

MILLER, EDWARD, 'Government Economic Policies and Public Finance', in *The Middle Ages*, ed. Carlo M. Cipolla, Fontana Economic History of Europe (London, 1972), 339–70.

MILLS, DAVID, 'An Analysis of the Temptation Scenes in *Sir Gawain and the Green Knight*', *Journal of English and Germanic Philology*, 67 (1968), 612–30.

MILLS, M., 'The Huntsman and the Dwarf in *Erec* and *Libeaus Desconus*', *Romania*, 87 (1966), 33–58.

MOORE, R. I., *The Creation of a Persecuting Society: Power and Deviance in Western Europe* (Chicago, 1980).

MORRIS, COLIN, *The Discovery of the Individual, 1050–1200* (New York, 1972).

MORRIS, ROSEMARY, 'Time and Place in French Arthurian Verse Romances', *French Studies*, 42 (1988), 257–77.

MULLALY, EVELYN, *The Artist at Work: Narrative Technique in Chrétien de Troyes*, Transactions of the American Philosophical Society, 78 (Philadelphia, 1988).

MURPHY, MARGUERITE S., 'The Allegory of "Joie" in Chrétien's *Erec et Enide*', in *Allegory, Myth, and Symbol*, ed. Morton W. Bloomfield (Cambridge, Mass., 1981), 109–28.

MURRAY, ALEXANDER, *Reason and Society in the Middle Ages* (Oxford, 1978).

NELSON, N. E., 'Cicero's *De Officiis* in Christian Thought: 300–1300', *University of Michigan Publications: Language and Literature*, 10 (1933), 59–160.

NICHOLLS, JONATHAN, *The Matter of Courtesy: Medieval Courtesy Books and the Gawain-Poet* (Bury St Edmunds, 1985).

NITZE, W. A., 'Is the Green Knight Story Really a Vegetation Myth?', *MP* 33 (1936), 351–66.

—— 'Gauvain in the Romances of Chrétien de Troyes', *MP* 50 (1952–3), 219–25.

NOBLE, PETER, 'Magic in Late Arthurian Verse Romances', *BBSIA* 44 (1992), 245–54.

NYKROG, PER, 'Trajectory of the Hero: Gauvain, Paragon of Chivalry 1130–1230', in *Medieval Narrative: A Symposium*, ed. H. Bekker-Nielsen *et al.* (Odense, 1979), 82–93.

OLLIER, MARIE-LOUISE, 'Utopie et Roman Arthurien', *CCM* 27 (1984), 223–32.

—— *Lexique et concordance de Chrétien de Troyes* (Montreal, 1986).

ORME, NICHOLAS, *From Childhood to Chivalry: The Education of English Kings: 1066–1530* (London, 1984).

OSCHINSKY, HUGO, *Der Ritter unterwegs und die Pflege der Gastfreundschaft*, published dissertation (Halle, 1900).

OWEN, D. D. R., 'Parallel Readings with *Sir Gawain and the Green Knight*', in *Two Old French Gauvain Romances*, ed. D. D. R. Owen and R. C. Johnston (Edinburgh, 1972), 159–208.

OWST, G. R., *Literature and Pulpit in Medieval England* (Oxford, 1966).

PAINTER, SIDNEY, *French Chivalry* (1940, repr. Ithaca, NY, 1962).

PATTERSON, LEE, *Chaucer and the Subject of History* (Madison, Wis., 1991).

—— 'Court Politics and the Invention of Literature: The Case of Sir John Clanvowe', in *Culture and History 1350–1600: Essays on English Communities, Identities and Writing*, ed. David Aers (New York, 1992), 7–41.

PAYEN, JEAN CHARLES, '*Le Livre de philosophie et de moralité* d'Alain de Cambrai', *Romania*, 87 (1966), 145–74.

—— *Le Motif du repentir dans la littérature française médiévale* (Geneva, 1968).

PEARCY, J., 'Chaucer's Franklin and the Literary Vavasour', *ChauR* 8 (1973), 33–59.

PEARSALL, DEREK, 'Rhetorical *Descriptio* in *Sir Gawain and the Green Knight*', *MLR* 50 (1955), 129–34.

—— 'Middle English Romance and its Audiences', in *Historical and Editorial Studies in Medieval and Early Modern English for Johan Gerritsen*, ed. Hanneke Wirtjes and Hans Jansen (Groningen, 1985), 37–47.

—— and SALTER, ELIZABETH, *Landscapes and Seasons of the Medieval World* (London, 1973).

PEPIN, RONALD, *Literature of Satire in the Twelfth Century: A Neglected Medieval Genre* (Lampeter, 1988).

PETIT-DUTAILLIS, C., 'The Forest', trans. W. T. Waugh, in *Studies and Notes Supplementary to Stubbs's Constitutional History*, 3 vols. (Manchester, 1914), i. 147–251.

PIEHLER, PAUL, *The Visionary Landscape: A Study in Medieval Allegory* (London, 1971).

PITT-RIVERS, JULIAN, 'Honour and Social Status', in *Honour and Shame: The Values of Mediterranean Society*, ed. J. G. Peristiany (London, 1965), 19–77.

—— 'The Law of Hospitality', in *The Fate of Shechem* (Cambridge, 1977), 94–112.

POLLMAN, LEO, *Chrétien de Troyes und der Conte du Graal* (Tübingen, 1965).

POSTAN, M. M., *The Agrarian Life of the Middle Ages*, Cambridge Economic History of Europe (Cambridge, 1966).

PUTTER, AD, 'Narrative Technique and Chivalric Ethos in *Sir Gawain and the Green Knight* and the Old French *Roman Courtois*', doctoral dissertation (University of Cambridge, 1992).

RACKHAM, OLIVER, *Trees and Woodland in the British Landscape* (London, 1976, repr. 1981).

RENOIR, ALAIN, '*Gawain* and *Parzival*', *SN* 31 (1958), 155–8.

RICHÉ, PIERRE, *De l'éducation antique à l'éducation chevaleresque* (Paris, 1968).

RIGBY, MARJORY, '*Sir Gawain and the Green Knight* and the Vulgate *Lancelot*', *MLR* 78 (1983), 257–66.

ROBERTSON, D. W., *A Preface to Chaucer* (Princeton, NJ, 1962).

RUBERG, UWE, *Raum und Zeit im Prosa-Lancelot* (Munich, 1965).

RUCK, E. H., *An Index of Themes and Motifs in Twelfth-Century French Arthurian Poetry* (Cambridge, 1991).

SALTER, ELIZABETH, 'The Alliterative Revival', *MP* 64 (1966–7), 146–50, 233–7.

SALTER, ELIZABETH, *Fourteenth-Century English Poetry: Contexts and Readings* (Oxford, 1983).

SARGENT, B. N., ' "L'Autre" chez Chrétien de Troyes', *CCM* 10 (1967), 199–205.

—— 'Old and New in the Character-Drawing of Chrétien de Troyes', in *Innovation in Medieval Literature: Essays for Alan Markman*, ed. D. Radcliff-Umstead (Pittsburgh, 1971), 35–48.

SAUNDERS, CORINNE, *The Forest of Medieval Romance* (Woodbridge, 1993).

SAVAGE, HENRY LYTTLETON, *The Gawain-Poet: Studies in his Personality and Background* (Chapel Hill, NC, 1956).

SCAGLIONE, ALDO, *Knights at Court: Courtliness, Chivalry, and Courtesy from Ottonian Germany to the Italian Renaissance* (Berkeley, Calif., 1991).

SCATTERGOOD, V. J., 'Literary Culture at the Court of Richard II', in *English Court Culture in the Later Middle Ages*, ed. V. J. Scattergood and J. W. Sherborne (London, 1983), 29–43.

SCHAUBERT, ELSE VON, 'Der englische Ursprung von *Syr Gawayne and the Grene Knyght*', *Englische Studien*, 57 (1923), 331–446.

SCHLESS, HOWARD H., '*Pearl's* "Princes Paye" and the Law', *ChauR* 24 (1989), 183–5.

SCHMITT, JEAN-CLAUDE, *La Raison des gestes dans l'Occident médiévale* (Paris, 1990).

SCHMOLKE-HASSELMANN, BEATE, 'King Arthur as Villain in the Thirteenth-Century Romance *Yder*', *Reading Medieval Studies*, 6 (1980), 31–43.

—— *Der Arthurische Versroman von Chrestien bis Froissart* (Tübingen, 1980).

—— 'The Round Table: Ideal, Fiction, and Reality', *AL* 2 (1982), 41–75.

SCHNYDER, HANS, *Sir Gawain and the Green Knight: An Essay in Interpretation* (Berne, 1961).

SCHOFIELD, WILLIAM H., 'The Nature and Fabric of the *Pearl*', *PMLA* 19 (1904), 154–215.

SCHOPF, ALFRED, 'Die Gestalt Gawains bei Chrétien, Wolfram von Eschenbach, und in *Sir Gawain and the Green Knight*', in *Spätmittelalterliche Artusliteratur*, ed. Karl Heinz Göller (Paderborn, 1984), 85–104.

SCHREINER, KLAUS, ' "Hof" (*curia*) und "höfische Lebensführung" (*vita curialis*) als Herausforderung an die Christliche Theologie und Frömmigkeit', in *Höfische Literatur, Hofgesellschaft, höfische Lebensformen um 1200*, ed. Gert Kaiser and Jan-Dirk Müller (Düsseldorf, 1986), 67–138.

SHICHTMAN, MARTIN B., 'Gawain in Wace and Laȝamon: A Case of Metahistorical Evolution', in *Medieval Texts and Contemporary*

Readers, ed. Laurie A. Finke and Martin B. Shichtman (Ithaca, NY, 1987), 103–19.

SHIPPEY, T. A., 'The Uses of Chivalry: *Erec* and *Gawain*', *MLR* 66 (1971), 241–50.

SHIRT, DAVID J., 'Chrétien de Troyes et une coutume anglaise', *Romania*, 94 (1973), 178–95.

SHOAF, R. A., *The Poem as Green Girdle: Commercium in Sir Gawain and the Green Knight* (Gainesville, Fla., 1984).

SILVERSTEIN, THEODORE, 'Sir Gawain in a Dilemma, or Keeping Faith with Marcus Tullius Cicero', *MP* 75 (1977), 1–17.

SIMPSON, JAMES, *Piers Plowman: An Introduction to the B-Text* (London, 1990).

SMITHERS, G. J., 'What *Sir Gawain and the Green Knight* is About', *MAE* 32 (1963), 171–89.

SOUTHERN, R. W., *Western Society and the Church in the Middle Ages* (Harmondsworth, 1970).

SPEARING, A. C., '*Sir Gawain and the Green Knight*', in *Criticism and Medieval Poetry* (1962, 2nd edn. London, 1972), 28–50.

—— *The Gawain-Poet: A Critical Study* (Cambridge, 1970).

—— 'Public and Private Spaces in *Sir Gawain and the Green Knight*' (unpublished paper).

STANESCO, MICHEL, *Jeux d'errance du chevalier médiéval* (Leiden, 1988).

STARKEY, DAVID, 'The Age of the Household', in *The Later Middle Ages*, ed. Stephen Medcalf (London, 1981), 225–90.

STAUFFER, MARIANNE, *Der Wald: Zur Darstellung und Deutung der Natur im Mittelalter* (Berne, 1959).

STEINBACH, PAUL, *Der Einfluss des Chrestien de Troyes auf die Altenglische Literatur*, published dissertation (Leipzig, 1886).

STEVENS, JOHN, *Medieval Romance: Themes and Approaches* (London, 1973).

STEVENS, MARTIN, 'Laughter and Game in *Sir Gawain and the Green Knight*', *Speculum*, 47 (1972), 65–78.

STOCK, BRIAN, *Myth and Science in the Twelfth Century: A Study of Bernardus Silvestris* (Princeton, NJ, 1972).

—— *The Implications of Literacy* (Princeton, NJ, 1983).

STROHM, PAUL, 'The Social and Literary Scene in England', in *The Cambridge Chaucer Companion*, ed. Piero Boitani and Jill Mann (Cambridge, 1986), 1–18.

TANNER, TONY, *Adultery in the Novel: Contract and Transgression* (Baltimore, 1979).

TAVANI, GIUSEPPE, 'Il dibattito sul chierico e il cavaliere nella tradizione mediolatina e vulgare', *Romanisches Jahrbuch*, 15 (1964), 51–84.

TESTARD, MAURICE (ed. and trans.), *Les Devoirs (St Ambrose)* (New York, 1968).

THOMAS, MARTHA CAREY, *Sir Gawayne and the Green Knight: A Comparison with the French Perceval*, published dissertation (Zurich, 1883).

THOMPSON, JOHN J., *Robert Thornton and the London Thornton Manuscript* (Woodbridge, 1987).

THOMPSON, M. W., 'The Green Knight's Castle', in *Studies in Medieval History Presented to Allen Brown*, ed. C. Harper-Bill *et al.* (Woodbridge, 1989), 317–25.

THRUPP, SYLVIA, *The Merchant Class of Medieval London* (Chicago, 1948).

TRIGG, STEPHANIE, 'The Romance of Exchange: *Sir Gawain and the Green Knight*', *Viator*, 22 (1991), 251–66.

VALE, JULIET, *Edward III and Chivalry: Chivalric Society and its Contexts 1270–1350* (Bury St Edmunds, 1982).

VALE, MALCOLM, *War and Chivalry* (London, 1981).

VANCE, EUGENE, 'Le Combat érotique chez Chrétien de Troyes', *Poétique*, 12 (1972), 544–71.

—— 'Signs of the City: Medieval Poetry as Detour', *NLH* 4 (1973), 557–74.

—— 'Chrétien's *Yvain* and the Ideologies of Change and Exchange', *Yale French Studies*, 70 (1986), 42–62.

—— *From Topic to Tale: Logic and Narrativity in the Middle Ages* (Minneapolis, 1987).

VIAL, GUY, *Le Conte du Graal, la Première Continuation* (Geneva, 1987).

WALTERS, LORI, 'Le Rôle du scribe dans l'organisation des manuscrits de Chrétien de Troyes', *Romania*, 106 (1985), 303–25.

WALTHER, H., *Das Streitgedicht in der lateinischen Literatur des Mittelalters* (Munich, 1920).

WASSERMAN, LORETTE, 'Honor and Shame in *Sir Gawain and the Green Knight*', in *Chivalric Literature: Essays on Relations between Literature and Life in the Later Middle Ages*, ed. Larry D. Benson and John Leyerle (Kalamazoo, Mich., 1980), 77–90.

WEISS, VICTORIA L., 'Knightly Conventions in *Sir Gawain and the Green Knight*', doctoral dissertation (Lehigh University, Penn., 1977).

WETHERBEE, WINTHROP, *Platonism and Poetry in the Twelfth Century* (Princeton, NJ, 1972).

WHATLEY, GORDON, 'Heathens and Saints: *St Erkenwald* in its Legendary Context', *Speculum*, 61 (1986), 330–63.

WHITAKER, MURIEL, *The Legends of King Arthur in Art* (Cambridge, 1990).

WHITING, BARTLETT J., 'Gawain: His Reputation, His Courtesy, and His Appearance in Chaucer's *Squire's Tale*', *MS* 9 (1947), 189–234.

WILSON, ANNE, *Traditional Romance and Tale: How Stories Mean* (Cambridge, 1976).

WILSON, R. H., 'Malory and the *Perlesvaus*', *MP* 30 (1932), 13–21.

WIRTJES, HANNEKE, 'Bertilak de Hautdesert and the Literary Vavasour', *English Studies*, 64 (1984), 291–301.

WRIGHT, THOMAS L., 'Luf-Talkyng in *Sir Gawain and the Green Knight*', in *Approaches to Teaching Sir Gawain and the Green Knight*, ed. M. Y. Miller and J. Chance (New York, 1986), 77–86.

WRIGLEY, CHRISTOPHER, '*Sir Gawain and the Green Knight*: The Underlying Myth', in *Studies in Medieval English Romances: Some New Approaches*, ed. Derek Brewer (Cambridge, 1988), 113–28.

YOUNG, CHARLES R., *The Royal Forests of Medieval England* (Leicester, 1979).

YOUNG, N. DENHOLM, 'The Tournament in the Thirteenth Century', in *Studies in Medieval History Presented to F. M. Powicke* (Oxford, 1948), 240–68.

ZOTZ, THOMAS, '*Urbanitas*: zur Bedeutung und Funktion einer antiken Wertvorstellung innerhalb der höfischen Kultur des hohen Mittelalters', in *Curialitas: Studien zu Grundfragen der höfisch-ritterlichen Kultur*, ed. J. Fleckenstein (Göttingen, 1990), 392–451.

ZUMTHOR, PAUL, 'Le Roman courtois: Essai de définition', *Études littéraires*, 4 (1971), 75–90.

Index

This index contains the names of medieval authors and medieval texts, as well as a small number of references to the central topics and themes covered in the book. Only those modern scholars discussed or quoted in the text, or referred to on points of importance, have been included in the index.